Road Traffic Accident Claims

For
Catherine, Hannah and Benjamin

Road Traffic Accident Claims

Mark Whalan
Barrister
2 Gray's Inn Square Chambers

CLT Professional Publishing Ltd
A CLT Group Company

© Mark Whalan 2000

Published by
CLT Professional Publishing
A division of Central Law Training Ltd
Stonehills House
Howardsgate
Welwyn Garden City
AL8 6PU

ISBN 1 85811 247 8

Typeset by Saxon Graphics Ltd, Derby
Printed in Great Britain by Antony Rowe

Contents

Table of Cases   vii
Table of Statutes   xxv
Table of Regulations   xxx
Preface   xxxi

PART I: LIABILITY

1.   General Principles of Liability   3
2.   The Driver   13
3.   The Emergency Services   35
4.   Passengers (1): Private Motor Vehicles   47
5.   Passengers (2): Public Service Vehicles   53
6.   Pedestrians   65
7.   The Highway   79
8.   Lights   111
9.   Animals on the Highway   119
10.   Defective Vehicles   129

PART II: DEFENCES AND CONDITIONS OF
           NO LIABILITY

11.   Defences   143
12.   Conditions of no Liability   155

PART III: THE VEHICLE

13.   Repairs, Hire of Replacement Vehicle,
        Credit Hire and Loss of Use   165

PART IV: RECOVERY

14.	Motor Insurance	185
15.	The Motor Insurers' Bureau	195
16.	Recovery of Charges for NHS Treatment in Road Traffic Claims	209
17.	Compensation for Criminal Injuries	213

PART V: PRACTICE AND PROCEDURE

18.	Pre-Action Procedure	221
19.	Pleadings	237
20.	Trial	243
21.	RTA Actions and the Small Claims Track	247

APPENDICES		257
1.	Tables	259
2.	AA Motoring Costs	261
3.	Loss of Use: Case Summaries	264
4.	Motor Insurers' Bureau Agreements	271
5.	Witness Questionnaire	305
6.	Pre-Action Protocol for RTAs	308
7.	Codes of Best Practice on Rehabilitation, Early Intervention and Medical Treatment in PI Claims	336
8.	Letters of Claim	342
9.	Pleadings	348

INDEX	391

Table of Cases

Adams v Dunne [1988] RTR 281, ...189
Adamson v Roberts (1951) DC 681, ...68
Admiralty Commissioner v Chekiang (Owners) [1926] AC 627, 176
Afzal v Ford Motor Co. Ltd [1994] 4 All ER 720, ...255
Ajibade v Leech [1994] CLY 1505, ...181
A.L.Motorworks (Willesden) Ltd v Alwahdi [1977] RTR 276, ..169
Albert v Motor Insures' Bureau [1972] AC 301, ...208
Aldridge   v   Metropolitan   Police   Commissioner   [1998],
unreported, ...42
Alzarrad v Wyatt (1994) CLY 1482, ...267
Amos v Glamorgan County Council (1967) 66 LGR 166, ...46
Ancell v McDermott [1993] 4 All ER 385, ...44,45,46
Anderson v Belfast Co [1943] NI 34, ...54
Andrews v Watts [1971] RTR 484, ...120
Another v Pobert [1968] Crim.L.R. 564, ...30
Appleby v White [1989] CLY 1630, ...178
Ara Services v Hewitt (T/a Hewitt Haulage) (1994) CLY 1518, ...269
Armstrong v Cottrell [1993] PIQR 109, at 112, ...16
Armstrong-James v Radcliffe-Smith (1997)CLY 593, ...255
Artingstoll v Hewen's Garages Limited [1973] RTR 197, ...135
Aspin v J. Bretherton & Son (1947), unreported, ...135
Azzupardi v State Transport Authority [1982] 30 SASR 434, ...56

B (A Minor) v Knight [1981] RTR 136, ...186
Bacon v Cooper (Metals) Ltd [1982] 1 All ER 397, ...168
Baker v E Longhurst & Sons Limited [1933] 2 KB 461, ...111,113
Baker v Francis [1997] PIQR 155, ...207
Baker v Market Harborough Co-operative Society Ltd [1953] 1 WLR
1472, ...10,27
Baker v Willoughby [1970] AC 467, ...5,16,65
Barber v British Road Services (1964) Times, 18 November,
....115,116,117
Barkway v South Wales Transport Co. Ltd [1950] AC 185,
.... 6,50.130
Barker v Herbert [1991] 2 KB 633, ...108
Barna v Hudes Merchandising Corpn. (1962) 106 Sol.Jo 124, ...14

Barrand v British Cellophane (1995) Times, February 16, ...150
Barrett v Western [1994] CLY 1496, ...180
Barry v MacDonald (1966) 110 Sol.Jo. 56, ...70
Barry v Phoenix [1998] CLY 1464, ...170
Bartlett v Sydney Marcus Ltd [1965] 1 WLR 1013, ...138
Bateman v Goodman (1998) Lawtel C8400125, ...67
Bater v Newbold (1991) LEXIS July 30, ...151
Bativala v West [1970] 1 QB 716, ...120
Begum v Ullah (1998) CLY 590, ...198
Behrens v Betram Mills Circus Ltd [1957] 2 QB 1, ...122
Bernstein v Pamson Motors (Golders Green) Limited [1987] 2 All ER
220, ...136
Berrill v Road Haulage Executive [1952] 2 Lloyds' Rep 490, ...4
Biesheuvel v Birrell (1999) Lawtel C8400282, ...144
Bihlen v Perdue [1956] 1 WWR 364, ...61
Bird v Pearce and Somerset County Council [1978] RTR 290, ...96
Birmingham Corporation v Sowsbery [1970] RTR 84, ...176,180
Blades v Peake [1994] CLY 1500, ...181
Bolton v Stone [1951] AC 850, ...110
Boomer v Penn (1965) 52 DLR 673, ...157
Boss v Litton (1832) 5 C&P 407, ...65
Bourhill v Young [1943] AC 92, ...3
Bracegirdle v Oxley [1947] 1 All ER 126, ...14
Bramwell v Shaw [1971] RTR 167, ...86,94
Brandon v Osborne, Garrett & Co [1924] 1 KB 548, ...1 58
Bray v Palmer [1953] 1 WLR 1455, ...27
Bright v Attorney-General [1971] 2 Lloyds Rep 68, ...86
British Road Services Ltd v Slater [1964] 1 All ER 816, ...105
British School of Motoring Ltd v Simms [1971] 1 All ER 317, ...5
Brown v Harrison [1947] WN 191, ...105
Brown & Lynn v Western SMT Co Ltd 1945 S.C. 31, ...17
Brown v Roberts [1982] 2 All ER 263, ...50,186
Browne v De Luxe Care Services [1941] 1 KB 549, ...28
Buck v English Electric Co Lts [1978] 1 All ER 271, ...150,151
Buckingham v D'Souza (1978) unreported, but see Bingham's Motor
Claims Cases, ...147
Bugge v Taylor [1941] 1 KB 198, ...196
Burgess v Heard [1965] Guardian, 25 March, ...111
Burns v Bidder [1967] 2 QB 227, ...74
Burnside v Emerson [1968] 1 WLR 1490, ...81,87,89
Business Appliances Specialists Ltd v Nationwide Credit Corpn, Ltd
[1988] RTR 332, ...137,138

Butland v Coxhead (1968) 112 Sol.Jo. 465, ...116
Butler v Norton [1997] CLY 1804, ...171
Butta v Rai[1997] CLY 1813, ...180
Butters v J.A.Fenner &Co. Ltd (1967) 117 MLJ 213, ...22
Bygraves v Dicker [1923] 2 KB 585, ...63

Caderbank v Burton (1997) CLY 594, .254
Calkin v McFie & Sons Limited [1989] 3 All ER 613, ...146
Campbell v Beck (1994) CLY 1504, ...265
Cambridge v Callaghan (1997) Times, March 21, ...199
Caminer v Northern and London Investment Trust Ltd [1951] AC 88,
. . . . 105
Cane v Jayakody (1995) CLY 1634, ...268
Capps v Miller [1989] 1 WLR 839, ...146
Carroll v Fearon [1932] AC 562, ...139
Carter v Sheath [1990] RTR 12, ...76
Castle v St. Augustin's Links (1921) 28 TLR 615, ...110
Caxton Publishing Co v Sutherland Publishing Co [1939] AC 178,
. 176
Ceylon Motor Ins. Association Ltd v Thambughla [1953] AC 584,
. 192
Challoner v Williams & Ironby [1975] RTR 425, ...24
Chaplin v Hawes (1828) 3 C&P 554, ...8
Chapman v Post Office [1982] RTR 165, ...11,70
Chief Constable of Avon and Somerset v Fleming [1987] 1 All ER 318,
. 196
Chisman v Electromotion (Export) Ltd (1969) 113 Sol.Jo. 246, .117
Chop Seng Heng v The Vannasan son of Sinnapan [1976] RTR 193,
. 99
Clark v Brazier [1997] CL, September 18, ...253
Clark v Wakelin (1965) 109 Sol.Jo. 295, ...19
Clarke v Kato [1998] 4 All ER 417, ...196
Clarke v National Insurance & Guarantee Corpn. Ltd [1964] 1 QB
199, ... 49
Clarke v Vedel [1979] RTR 26, ...208
Clarke v Winchurch [1966] 1 WLR 69, ...19,20,113,114
Clifford v Drymond [1976] RTR 134, .72
Clift v Howes & Ors.(1998) New Law Digest, 11 December QBD,
. . . . 159
Clough v Bussan (West Yorkshire Police Authority) [1990] 1 All ER
430, ...44,45,46
Clunes v Camden and Islington Health Authority [1998] 2 WLR 902,
. . . . 160

Cobb v Williams [1973] RTR 113, ...186
Cockburn v Davies and Provident Insurance plc [1997] CLY 1805,
....171
Cohen v British Gas Corp [1978] CLR 2053, ...98
Cole v De Trafford (No2) [1918] 2 KB 523, ...10
Condon v Condon [1978] RTR 483, ...145
Coote v Stone [1970] 1 WLR 279, ...6
Cox v Dixon (1994) 134 NLJ 236, ...39,43
Coyne v Cawley [1995] CLY 164, ...170
Craig v Glasgow Corporation (1919) 35 TLR 214, ...65
Crank v Brooks [1980] RTR 441, ...74
Crickmore v Bennett Baggs [1995] CLY 1633, ...179
Cross v Kirklees MBC [1997] Times, July 9, ...89,90,91,94
Croston v Vaughan [1938] 1 KB 540, ...6,31
Crowther v Shannon Motor Co. [1975] 1 All ER 139, ...138
Cunliffe v Banks [1945] 1 All ER 459, ...105
Curtis v Betts [1990] 1 WLR 459, ...122,123,126
Cusints v Nottingham Corporation [1970] RTR 365, ...29
Cutter v Eagle Star Insurance Co Ltd [1998] 4 All ER 417, ...196

Daborn v Bath Tramways Motor Co. Limited and Smithey [1946] 2
All ER 333, ...30
Daily Office Cleaning Contractors Ltd v Shefford [1977] RTR
361, ...169
Dale v British Coal Copr (No.2) (1992) 136 Sol Jo LB 199, ...150
Daley v Hargreaves [1961] 1 All ER 552, ...197
Daly v Liverpool Corp. [1939] 2 All ER 142, ...16
Darbishire v Warran [1963] 3 All ER 310, ...166
Davidson v Leggett [1969] 113 Sol. Jo. 409, ...27
Davies v Davies (1994) CLY 103, ...264
Davies v Liverpool Corp [1949] 2 All ER 175, ...54,55
Davies v Swan Motor Co. [1949] 2 KB 291, ...144
Davies v Tate [1993] CLY 1458, ...179
Davis v Burn (1936) 56 CLR 246, ...10
Davis v Hassan (1967) Times, January 13, ...25
Davison v Leggett (1969) 133 JP 552, ...10
Day v Smith (1983) 133 NLJ 726, ...27
D'Costa v Ryan [1994] CLY 1495, ...179
Deen v Davies [1935] 2 KB 282, ...119
De Souza v Waterlow [1999] RTR 71, ...192
Dibor v Kentish Bus & Coach Co. Ltd (1998) CLY 488, ...254
Dickinson v Dell Solar [1930] 1 KB 376, ...153

Dimond v Lovell [1999] 3 WLR 561, ...172,173
Dix v Richard (1996) CLY 2146, ...266
Dolby v Milner (1996) CLY 4430, ...23
Donoghue v Stevenson [1932] AC 562, ...3,135,139
Donohoe v Blundel (1986) CLT 2254, ...147
Donovan v Gwentoys Limited [1990] 1 All ER 1018, ...151
Doonan v SMT Co 1950 SC 136, ...59
Dorricot v Villiers (1997) CLY 1781, ...269
Doughty v North Staffordshire Health Authority (1992) 3 Med LR 81, ...150
Dowling v Dargue (1997) CLY 3769, ...21
Draper v Hodder [1972] 2 QB 556, ...126
Drew v Western Scottish Motor Traction Co (1947) SC 222, ...115
Drury v Camden LBC [1972] RTR 391, ...102
Dunthorpe v Bentley [1996] Times, March 11, ...186
Durbin v Lewis [1997] CLY 17892, ...177,264
Dyer v Bannell (1965) 109 Sol.Jo. 216, ...39
Dymond v Pearce [1972] 1 QB 496, ...100,101,116

Eames v Cunningham & Capps (1948) 92 Sol.Jo. 314, ...70
Eastman v South West Thames Regional Health Authority [1991] RTR 389, ...48
Elipidoforus Shipping Corporation v Furniss Withay (Australia) Ltd (1986) Times, 28 November, ...181
Elizabeth v Motor Insurer's Bureau [1981] RTR 405, ...18
Elliott v Grey [1960] 1 QB 367, ...186
Ellor v Selfridge & Co Ltd (1930) 46 TLR 236, ...11,70
Empson v Smith [1966] 1 QB 426, ...153
Evans v Motor Insurers' Bureau (1997) Times, November 10, ..206
Farnworth Finance Facilities v Attryde [1970] 1 WLR 1053, ...137
Feary v Buckingham [1999] CL July 208, ...174
Fiberton v Goodall and Motor Insurer's Bureau [1997] 451, ...198
Fire Auto and Marine Insurance Co Ltd v Greene [1964] 2 QB 687, ...207
Fitzgerald v ED & AD Cooke Bourne (Farms) Ltd [1964] 1 QB, 120
Fitzgerald v Lane [1988] 2 All ER 961, ...67,69,76
Flack v Withers (1960) Times, March 22, ...31
Fletcher v United Counties Omnibus Co. Limited [1998] PIQR P154, ...56
Ford v Liverpool Corporation (1972) 117 Sol. Jo. 167, ...84,85
Foskitt v Mistry [1974] RTR 1, ...7
Fotheringham v Prudence (1962) Times, 16 May, ...115

Fox v Green (1995) CLY 1618, ...266

Franklin v Landown [1971] 3 All ER 662, ...77

Friend v Facey (1963) Times, March 19, ...120

Froom v Butcher [1976] QB 286, ...48,144,145

Gambino v De Leo [1971] 7 DLR 167, ...20

Gardner v Moore [1984] AC 548, ...215

Gardner v United Counties Omnbus Co. Limited [1996] CLY 4477,
. 56

Garston Warehousing Co.Ltd v O.F.Smart (Liverpool) Ltd [1973]
RTR 377, ...20,21

Gates v Bill [1902] 2 KB 38, ...63

Gaynor v Allen [1959] 2 QB 403, ...5,35,36,39,43

Geeves v London General Omnibus Co. (1901) 17 TLR 249,
. 56

General Accident & Liability Ins Co v Morison [1942] 2 KB 53,   193

GH Myers & Co v Brent Cross Service Co [1934] 1 KB 46, ...133

Gibbons v Priestley [1979] RTR 2, ...4,47,48,51

Gibson v Chief Constable of Strathclyde Police (1999), Times, May
. . . . 11, 45

Gidman v Pure [1994] CLY 1511, ...179

Giles v Thompson [1994] 1 AC 142, ...172

Gilmour's Curator Bonis v Wynn (1995) Times, September . .18, 71

Gilson v Kidman (1938) unreported, but see Bingham's Motor Claims
Cases, ...158

Glasgow Corp v Sutherland [1951] 95 Sol.Jo. 204, ...58

Godfrey v Smith [1955] 2 All ER 520, .206

Godsmark v Knight Brothers (Brighton) Ltd (1960) Times, May 12,
. 25,26

Goke v Willett [1973] RTR 422, ...19,30,31

Gomberg v Smith [1963] 1 QB 25, ...119,126

Goodes v East Sussex County Council (1999) Times, January 7,
. 91,92

Gordon v Proctor (1996) CLY 2154, ...267

Gough v Thorne [1961] 2 All ER 398, .146

Gowen v Owens Radio & TV [1995] CLY 1631, ...170

Greener v DPP [1996] Times, February 15, ...127

Greenock Corpn. v Caledonian Railway Company [1917] AC 556,
. 155

Griffin v Mersey Regional Ambulance [1998] PIQR 34, ...42,43

Griffin & Co v De-La-Haye [1968] 2 Lloyds Rep. 253, ...179

Griffiths v Liverpool Corporation [1967] 1 QB 374, ...83

Guilfoyle v Port of London Authority [1932] 1 KB 336, ...34

Guinnear v London Passenger Transport Board (1948) 92 Sol.Jo. 350, ...53
Gurtner v Circuit [1968] 1 QB 587, ...207,208
Gussman v Grattan-Storey (1968) 112 Sol.Jo. 884, ...31,128

Hale v Hants & Dorset Motor Services Limited [1947] 2 All ER 628, ...60,106
Halford v Brooks [1991] 3 All ER 559, ...150
Hall v London Tramways (1896) RTLR 611, ...54
Hall & Co Ltd v Ham Manor Farm Ltd (1966) 116 L.Jo. 838, ..104
Hambrook v Stokes Bros. [1925] 1 KB 141, ...99
Hanman v Mann [1984] RTR 252, ...116
Harbutt's Plasticine Ltd v Wayne Tank & Pump Co.Ltd. [1970] 1 All ER 225, ...168
Hardcastle v South Yorkshire Ry (1859) 4 H&N 67, ...108
Harding v Hinchcliffe (1964) Times, April 8, ...21
Hardy v Motor Insurers' Bureau [1964] 2 QB 745, ...208,215
Harrington v Pinky [1989] 2 Lloyd's Rep 310, ...192
Harris v Perry & Co. [1903] 2 KB 219, ...49
Harrison v Jackson (1947) 14 LJ MCCR 242, ...120
Hartley v Birmingham City District Council [1992] 2 All ER 213, ...150
Harvey v Road Haulage Executive [1952] 1 KB 120, ...111,113
Hatch v Platt [1988] CLY 1073, ...177
Hatton v Hall [1999] Lloyd's Rep IR 313, ...186,197
Hawkyard v North Yorkshire CC (1999) 2 CL 309, ...91,94
Haydon v Kent County Council [1978] QB 343, ...86,89,90
Heath's Garage Ltd v Hodges [1916] 2 KB 370, ...121
Henderson v Henry E Jenkins & Sons [1970] AC 282, ...132,140,158
Hendy v Milton Keynes Health Authority (1992) 3 Med LR 114,150
Henley v Cameron [1949] 65 TLR 17, ...115
Henry v Santam Insurance Co Ltd 1971 (1) S.A. 466, ...19
Herbert v Railway Passengers Ass. Co. [1938] 1 All ER 650, ...192
Herschtal v Stewart & Arden Ltd [1940] 1 KB 155, ...139
Hilder v Associated Portland Cement Manufacturers Ltd [1961] 1 WLR 1434, ...110
Hill v Chief Constable of West Yorkshire [1989] AC 59, ...44,45,46
Hill v Phillips (1963) 107 Sol.Jo. 890, ...113,115,116
Hill-Venning v Beszant [1950] 2 ALL ER 1151, ...115
H.L. Motorworks (Willesden) Ltd v Alwahdi [1977] RTR 276, ..20
H.L. Pallet Services v Fairclough [1997] CLY 1794, ...175

Hoadley v Dartford District Council (1979) 123 Sol.Jo. 129, ...146
Holdack v Bullock Bros (Electrical) Ltd (1964) 108 Sol.Jo. 861, .20
Holemans v City of St. Vital [1973] 43 DLR (3rd), ...84
Holling v Yorkshire Traction Co. Ltd 2 All ER 662, ...103,104
Hoover Ltd v Depeazer (1999) CL, January, 51, ...207
Hopwood Homes Ltd v Kennerdine [1975] RTR 82, ...26
Houghton v Meares [1995] CLY 1622, ...170
Houghton v Trafalgar Insurance Co. Ltd [1954] 1 QB 247, ...48
Hougland v RR Low (Luxury Coaches) Ltd [1962] 1 QB 694, ...47
Howard v Bemrose [1973] RTR 32, ...10,27
Howart v Straver (1953), ...120
Hoy v Smith [1964] 3 All ER 670, ...76
Hucknall v Jepson [1998] CLY 1456, ...175
Hudson v Bray [1917] 1KB 520, ...106
Hughes v (1) Charlton and (2) MIB (1997) Lawtel, C00006610, 161
Hughes v Hall [1960] 2 All ER 504, ...73
Hughes v Taylor [1997] CLY 1782, ...180
Hulock v Ingliss (1963) 107 Sol.Jo, ...14
Humble v Aguis [1995] CLY 1632, ...180
Humphray v Ganson Bros 1917 S.C. 371, ...19
Humphrey v Leigh [1971] RTR 363, ...23
Hunt v Severs [1994] 2 AC 350, ...173
Hunt v Wallis [1994] PIQR 128, ...122,126
Hurley v Dyke [1979] RTR 265, ...139
Hurt v Murphy [1971] RTR 186, ...67
Hutton v Saville Tractors (Belfast) Ltd [1986] 12 MIJB, ...137
Hyman v Nye (1881) 6 QBD 685, ...131

Imrie v Clark (1939) unreported, ...120
Inwood (1974) 60 Cr App R 7, ...216

J v W [1999] New Law Digest, July 19, ...147
Jacobs v Hampshire County Council (1984) Times, May 28, .94,95
Jackson v Harrison (1978) 19 ALR 129, ...160,161
James v Preseli Pembrokeshire District Council [1993] PIQR
....114, 82,83
Jancey v Higgins (1997) CLY 589, ...254
Jaundrill v Gillett [1996] Times, January 30, ...125
Jenkins v Holt [1999[Times, May 27, ...32
Johnson v Edwards [1993] CLY 1635, ...180
Johnson v Wilson [1998] CLY 1457, ...175
Jones v Birch Bros. Ltd [1933] 2 KB 597, ...191

Jones v Boyce (1816) 1 Stark 493, ...159
Jones v Dennison [1971] RTL 174, CA, ...156
Jones v DPP [1999] RTR 1, ...186
Jones v Gravestock [1993] CLY 1412, ...178
Jones v Lawrence [1969] 3 All ER 267, ...146
Jones v Livox Quarries Limited [1952] 2 QB 608, ...144
Jones v Stroud District Council[1988] 1 All ER 5, ...165
Jones v Welsh Ins. Copr. Ltd [1937] 4 All ER 149, ...191
Jordan v North Hampshire Hire Ltd [1970] RTR 212,   115,116,117
Joseph Eva Limited v Reeves [1938] 2 KB 393, ...25,26
Jude v Edinburgh Corpn. 1943 SC 399, ...54
Jungnickel v Laing (1966) 111 Sol.Jo. 19, ...18,31

Kalinowski v Foxon [1994] CLY 1498, ...180
Karamalis v South Australian Railways Commission [1976]
SASR 432, ...33
Kay v Butterworth (1945) 175 LT 191, ...157
Kearney v London & Brighton Ry (1871) LR 6 QB 759, ...108
Keating v Elvin Reinforced Concrete Co.Ltd. [1968] 2
All ER 139, ...97
Keen v Henry [1894] 1 QB 292, ...63
Kelly v Bastible (1997) Times, Nov.15, ...151
Kerley v Downes [1973] RTR 188, ...69
Kidd v Grampian Health Board (1994) 5 Med.LR 251, ...151
Kilminster v Rule (1983) 32 SASR 39, ...147
King v London Improved Cab Company Limited (1889) 23 QBD 281,
.... 63
Kingman v Segar [1938] 1 KB 397, ...14
Kirk v Parker (1938) 60 Lloyds Law Rep.129, ...27
Kirksmith v Richardson (1992) CLY 3434, ...254
Knight v Wiper Supply Services Ltd (1965) 109 Sol.Jo 358, ...26
Knightley v Johns [1982] 1 WLR 349, ...40
Kotecka v London Borough of Harrow [1995] CLY 1812, ...96
Kozimore v Adey (1962) 106 Sol.Jo. 431, ...72
Kumar v Vernon (1994) CLY 1509, ...268

Lacey v Evans [1997] CLY 526, ...253
Laing v London Transport Executive [1957] 1 WLR 1168, ...22
Lambourn v London Brick Co. [1950] 156 Estates Gazette 146, .105
Lambert v Lowestoft Corpn [1901] 1 QB 590, ...108
Lambie v Western SMT Co Ltd [1944] SC 415, ...109
Lancaster v HB & H Transport Ltd [1979] RTR 380, ...117

Landau v Railway Executive (1949) 99 L.Jo 235, ...119
Langley v Dray & MT Motor Policies at Lloyds [1997] PIQR 508, 40
Langley v North West Water [1991] 1 WLR 607, ...84
Laurie v Raglan Building Co.[1942] 1 KB 152, ...11,28,29,70
Lavis v Kent County Council [1994] Times, November 24, ...107
Lawman v The Mayor, Aldermen and Burgesses of the London
Borough of Waltham Forest (1980) CA, January 3 unreported, ...82
Lawrence v W.N.Palmer (Excavations) Limited (1965) 109
Sol.Jo. 358, ...72
Leathley v Tatton [1980] RTR 21, ...186
Lee v Lever [1974] RTR 35, ...115
Leeson v Beavis & Tolchard Ltd [1972] RTR 373, ...20,114
Leigh & Sullivan Ltd v Aliakmon Shipping Co.Ltd, The Aliakmon
[1986] 2 All ER 145, ...168
Lester v Pearson [1952] 2 QB 668, ...73
Levine v Morris [1970] 1 WLR 71, ...107
Levy v Hockey (1961) 105 Sol.Jo. 157, ...74
Lewis v Burnett & Dunbar [1945] 1 All ER 550, ...49
Liddon v Stringer (1967) Times, April 15, ...33
Lids v Edwards [1997] CLY 1790, ...175
Liesbosch Dredger v Edison SA [1933] AC 449, ...179,180
Liffen v Watson [1940] 1 KB 556, ...28
Lightbowne v Walayet (1994) CLY 1512, ...267
Lilly v Tilling (1912) 57 SJ 57, ...140
Lister v Vergette (1964) Times, June 12, ...121
Littler v Liverpool Corporation [1968] 2 All ER 343, ...83,84
Llewellyn v McCabe [1997] CLY 1792, ...175
Lloyd v Singleton [1953] 1 QB 357, ...187
Lockie v Lawton (1959) 124 JP 24, ...73
London Transport Board v Upson [1949] AC 155, ...4
London Transport Executive v Foy Morgan & Co [1955]
CLY 743, ...176
Luddit v Ginger Coote Airway Limited [1947] AC 23, ...5,47
Ludgate v Lovett [1969] 2 All ER 1275, ...10
Ludlam v Peel (1939) Times, October 10, ...120
Lygo v Newbold (1854) 9 Ex 302, ...5,47
Lynch v Hetherington [1991] 2 IR 405, ...105
Lyons v May [1948] 2 All ER 1062, ...187

M'Knight v General Motor Carrying Co 1936 S.C. 17, ...31,32
M'Sherry v Glasgow Corp. (1917) SC 156, ...53
Mackie v Dumbartonshire County Council [1927] WN 247, ...106

Maitland v Raisbeck & RT and J Hewitt [1944] KB 689, ...112
Majeed v The Incentive Group [1999] August, unreported, ...174
Malfroot v Nozal (1935) 51 TLR 551, ...135
Malone v Rowan [1984] 3 All ER 402, ...147
Manchester Corpn v Markland [1936] AC 360, ...90,109
Manengela v Bay Passenger Transport Co. Limited 1971 (4)
SA 293, ...55
Mansfield and Another v Weetabix Limited and Another [1998] 1
WLR 1263, ...156
Marpesia (1872) LR 4 BC 212, ...158
Marples v French [1997] CLY 1793, ...175
Marshall v Osmond [1983] QB 1034, ...40
Martin v Stanborough (1924) 41 TLR 1, ...99
Martin v Zinn (1960) Times March 9, ...120
Martindale v Duncan [1973] 2 All ER 3551, ...170
Mattocks v Mann (1992) Times, 19 June, ...179
Maynard v Loveday [1994] CLY 1493, ...166,178
Maynard v Rogers [1970] RTR 392, ...71
McAlaughlin v Glasgow Corpn. 1963 SLT (ShCt) 53, ...54
McCall v Brooks [1984] RTR 99, ...174
McCauley v Hope [1998] The Independent December 21
McGorian v Hughes [1997] CLY 524, ...253
McGowan v Stott (1920) 99 LJKD 357, ...11,69
McIntyre v Coles [1965] 1 WLR 831, ...21
McKay v Borthwick (1982) SLT 265, ...145
McKenna v Scottish Omnibuses Ltd v Northumberland County
Council (1984) 134 NLJ 681, ...93,95
McKinnell v White [1971] SLT 61, ...147
McLoed v Buchanan [1940] 2 All ER 179, ...187
McLoed v Receiver of the Metropolitan Police [1971] Crim
LR 364, 39
McLoughlin v Strathclyde Regional Council [1992] SLT 959, ...85
McPhilemy v Times Newspapers Ltd [1999] Times, May 29, ...238
McReady v Miller [1979] RTR 186, ...47,133
Mediana [1900] AC 113, ...176
Meggs v Liverpool Corporation [1968] 1 WLR 689, ...83
Merchant & Manufacturers Ins. Co. v Hunt [1941] 1 KB 295, .193
Miles v Forest Rock Granite Co. (1918) 34 TLR 500, ...109
Milken v Glasgow Cpn [1918] SC 857, ...20
Miller v Evans [1975] RTR 70, ...25,26
Miller v Jackson [1977] QB 960, ...110
Mills v Barnsley Metropolitan Borough Council [1992]
PIQR 291, 81,82,83,84

Milner & Sharpe v Parcelforce [1997] CLY 1779, ...180
Minter v V&H Contractors (Cambridge) Limited (1983) Times, 30
June, ...147
Misell v Essex County Council (1995) LGR 108, ...88
Mistry v NE Computing [1997] CLY 533, ...253
Mitchell v Johnstone (1994) CLT 1507, .267
Moore v DER Ltd [1971] 3 All ER 517, .167
Moore v Maxwells of Emsworth Ltd [1968] 1 WLR 1077, .112,116
Moore v Poyner [1975] RTR 127, ...16
Morales v Eccleston [1991] RTR 151, ...147
Morris v Luton Corporation [1946] KB 114, ...7
Morris v Thyssen (GB) Ltd [1983] Arb 2418, ...88,96
Mottram v South Lancashire Transport Co.[1942] 2 All
ER 452, ...54,55
Mullans v Forrester [1921] 2 IrR 412, ...108
Mulligan v Holmes [1971] RTR 179, ...26,67
Murgatroyd v Blackburn Tramways (1887) 2 TLR 451, ...62
Murphy v Choudhery [1992] CLY 1538, ...179
Murphy v Zoological Society of London (1962) Times, November
14, ...122

Nance v British Columbia Electric Railway[1951] AC 601 at 611,
. 65,70
National Farmers Union Mutual Ins. Society v Dawson [1941] 2
KB 424, ...191
Nayeri (Payman) v Yorkshire Traction Co (1994) CLY 1517, . . .269
Neal v Bedford [1966] 1 QB 505, ...73
Nettleship v Weston [1971] 2 QB 691, ...4,50
Newberry v Bristol Tramways and Carriage Co. Ltd, ...131,140
Newcress v ARC Limited [1997] CLY 522, ...253
Newsome v Darton Urban District Council [1998] 2 All ER 93, . .98
Nicholson v Goddard (1954) 118 JB 394, ...55
Nicholson & Ward v Fleming [1997] CLY 1809, ...175
Noble v Harrison [1926] 2 KB 332, ...104,108
Norman v Selvey [1999] CL July 207, .174
Norris v Greatbatch [1998] CLY 1461, .174
Norris v Tennant-Smith (1998) Lawtel C8400241, ...67
Nugent v Smith (1876) 1 CPD 423, ...155

O'Connell v Jackson [1972] 1 QB 270, .146
O'Grady v Westminster Scaffolding Limited [1962] 2 Lloyds
Rep. 238, ...166

O'Hara v Central Scottish Motor Traction Co. Ltd [1941]
SC 363. 10,59
O'Mahoney v Joliffe [1999] Lloyds Rep 321, ...186,197
O'Sullivan v Williams [1992] 3 All ER 385, ...168
Owen v De Winston [1894] 58 JP 833, .87
Owens v Brimmell [1977] QB 859, ...147

P&S Motors v South [1995] CLY 1621, ...178
Parish v Judd [1960] 3 All ER 33, ...112
Parker v Miller [1926] 42 TLR 408, ...100
Parkinson v Liverpool Corp [1950] 1 All ER 367, ...58,59,128
Parkinson v Parkinson [1973] RTR CA, 68
Parnell v Metropolitan Police District Receiver [1976] RTR 201, .17
Parrish v Judd [1960] 1 WLR 867, ... 100
Pasternack v Poulton [1973] 1 WLR 476, ...47,48
Paszyn v Mather (1994) CLY 1506, ...265
Patel v Edwards [1970] RTR 425, ...24
Paul Farrah Sound Ltd v Rookledge (1996) CLY 4431, ...23
Payton v Brooks [1974] RTL 169, ...167
Pearsons v Coleman (1948) 1 KB 359, .122
Penn v Anwar [1994] CLY 1499, ...180
Pennant v Sparks [1999] CL January, 44, ...253
Perkins v Glyn (1976) CLY 1883, ...104
Perry v Sidney Phillips & Co [1982] 1 WLR 1297, ...179
Person v London County Buses [1974] 1 All ER 1251, ...205,208
Petrou v Kuti [1997] CLY 1803, ...175
Phelan v Austin [1994] CLY 1501, ...180
Phillips v Britannia Hygienic Laundry [1923] 2 KB 832, ...130
Pickering v Belfast Corp [1911] 2 IrR 224, ...61
Pilmore v Northern Trawlers Limited [1986] 1 Lloyds Rep 552, 151
Pitts v Hunt [1991] 1 QB 24, ...143,148,160,161
Police v Okoukwo [1954] CrimLR 869, .53
Post Office v Norwich Union Fire Insurance Society [1967]
2 QB 363, ...154
Potter v Blamey (1997), September 1992, ...255
Potter v Carlisle & Cliftonville Golf Club Ltd [1939] NI 114, . .110
Powell v Moody (1966) 110 Sol.Jo. 215, ...19
Powell v Phillips [1972] 3 All ER 864, ...16,68
Pratt v Bloom (1958) Times, October 21, ...30
Prescott v Hamnett [1998] CLY 1459, .175
Prescott v Lancashire United Transport Co. Limited [1953] 1
WLR 232, ...57

Price v Zaman [1996] CLY 213, ...180
Pridham v Hemel Hempstead Corporation [1970] 69 LGR 523, .95
Purves v Muir [1948] JC 122, ...196

Quigley v Stokes [1977] 1 WLR 434, ...217
Quinn v Scott [1965] 2 All ER 588, .14,105

R v Bezzina [1994] 3 All ER 964, ...127
R v Clark (1950) Daily Telegraph, 30 May, ...51
R v Hammersmith Coroner, ex p. Peach [1980] 2 WLR 496, . . .230
R v Spurge [1961] 2 QB 205, ...131
Radburn v Kemp [1971] 1 WLR 1582, ...25,26
Radley v London Passenger Transport Board [1942] 1 All
ER 433, ...59,60,106
Rae v Mars (UK) Ltd (1989) Times, February 15, ...96
Ramoo S/O Erul Aran v Gan Soo Swee [1971] 1 WLR 1014, ...25
Ramsden v Lee [1992] 2 All ER 204, ...150,151
Randall v Motor Insurers' Bureau [1969] 1 All ER 21, ...196,206
Randall v Tarrant [1955] 1 All ER 600, .11
Readhead v Midland Railway Co (1869) (4) QB 379, ...5,47,129
Reed v Dean [1949] 1 KB 188, ...139
Rees v Saville [1983] RTR 332, ...132,135
Reid v British Telecommunications (1987) Times, June 27, ...98
Reid v MacNichol (1958) SLT 42, ...53
Revill v Newberry (1995) Times, November 3, ...160
Richards v Thomas [1997] CLT 1777, .168
Richley v Faull [1965] 3 All ER 109, ...11,28
Rider v Metropolitan Water Board [1949]2 KB 378, ...98
Rider v Rider [1973] QB 505, ... 81,82,86,94
Riella v McLaughlin (1994) CLY 1508, ...265
Ritchie v Western Scottish MT Co (1935) SLT 13, ...131
Ritchies' Car Hire Limited v Bailey (1958) 108
L.Jo. 348, ...28,128,158
Roberts v Ramsbottom [1980] 1 AllER 7, ...157
Rogers v Night Riders [1983] RTR 324, ...63
Rogers v Parish (Scarborough) Limited (9187) QB 933, ...137
Rollingson v Kerr [1958] CLY 2427, ...103
Rowe v Clark (1998) Lawtel C8400268, ...147
Rowlands v Street (1962) Times, November 22, ...18
Rowley v Chatham [1970] RTR 462, ...134,135
Rubie v Faulkner [1940] 1 KB 571, .4,50
Ryan v Youngs [1978] 1 All ER 522, ...155
Ryland v Russell (1997) CLY 597, 255

Saledem v Drake [1993] PIQR 129, ...16
Salmon v Newland (1983) Times, May 16, ...145
Saper v Hungate Builders Limited [1972] RTR 380, ...101
Saville v Bache (1969) 113 Sol.Jo. 228, ...112
Saville v Mustaq [1997] CLT 1809, ...175
Scandle v Skeen [1976] RTR 281, ...50
Scher v Policyholders' Protection Board [1993] 3 All ER 384, . .189
Scott v Clint (1960) Times, October 28, ...73
Scott v London and St Katherine Docks Co. (1865) 3 H&C 586, .10
Scott v Warren [1974] RTR 104, ...17
Searle v Wallbank [1947] AC 341, ...119,120,121,125
Sedleigh-Denfield v O'Callaghan [1940] AC 880, ...107
Seth-Smith v Worrall [1997] CLY 1454, ...175
Shapland v Palmer [1999] PIQR 249, ...151
Sharp v Avery and Kirkwood [1938] 4 All ER 85, ...18
Shepherd v H. West & Son Ltd [1962] Sol.Jo. 391, ...19,69
Shine v General Guarantee Corpn. Ltd [1988] 1 All ER 911, ...137
Shire v Mainline Group [1997] CLY 1788, ...175
Shirvill v Hackwood Estates Ltd [1938] 2 KB 577, ...105
Sieghart v British Transport Commission (1956) 106 LJO 185, .112
Simon v The London General Omnibus Co. Limited (1987) 23
TLR 463, ...61
Singh v Eagle Star Direct (1998) CLY 461, ...255
Skipper v Perry [1995] CLY 1627, ...180
Skolimowski v Haynes [1983] CLY 2525, ...75
Slater v Worthingtons' Cash Store Ltd [1941] 1 KB 488, ...108
Sleight v Sandretto (UK) Ltd [1996] CLY 2145, ...175
Smith v Ainger (1990) Times, June 5, ...123,124,126
Smith v Bogan & Sons Limited [1997] CLT 571, ...252
Smith v Cribben [1994] PIQR 218, ...20
Smith v Goss (1996) CLY 4432, ...23
Smith v Harris [1939] 3 All ER 960, ...18
Smith v Prendergast [1984] Times, October 18, ...126
Smith, Ireland& McNay v Sunseeker Leisure (1993) CLY 3167, 255
Smithers v H&M Transport (Oxford) Ltd and Hodgkinson
(1983) 22 NLJ 558, ...26
Solent Insulation Services and Craig v Thorne (Leslie) (1994)
CLY 1519, ...270
Spear v Self Motoring Ltd (1947) S No 27, ...139
Squires v Automobile Assurance [1994] CLY 1497, ...180
Steele v Belfast Corp [1920] 2 IrR 125, ...54
Stennett v Hancock and Peters [1959] 2 All ER 578, ...135

Stevens v Kelland [1970] RTR 445, ...99
Stewart v Reavle's Garage [1952] 2 KB 545, ...133
Stimpson v Peat [1962] 2 QB 24, ...24
Stinton v Stinton [1995] RTR 167, ...186,197
Stratham v Gladstone 1937 JC 11, ...38
Sudds v Hanscombe [1971] RTR 212, ...25
Swain v Southern Railway [1939] 2 KB 560, ...34
Swift v Spence [1982] RTR 116, ...112

Tan Chye Choo v Ching Kew Moi [1970] 1 All ER, 6, ...130
Tarrant v Rowlands [1979] RTR 144, ...87,89
Tarry v Ashton (1876) 1 QBD 314, ...108
Taylor v Allon [1966] 1 QB 304, ...189
Taylor v Kiddey (1968) 118 MLJ 134, ...134
Taylor v Leslie (1998) Lawtel C0007277, ...161
Terry v Trafalgar Insurance Co. [1970] 1 Ll Rep 524, ...191
The Ferdinand Rezlaff [1972] 2 Lloyds Rep 120, ...181
The Gazelle [1844[2 W Rob (Adm) 279, ...167
The Greta Holme [1897] AC 596, ...176
The Hebridian Co [1961] AC 545, ...176
The Marpessa [1987] AC 241, ...176
The Merchant Prince [1892] 179, ...158
Thomas v Dando [1951] 1 All ER 1010, ...196
Thomas v Fuller (1977) unreported, but see Bingham's Motor Claims
Cases, ...147
Thomas v Hooper [1986] RTR 1, ...186
Thompson v Brown Construction (Ebbw Vale) Ltd [1981] 1
WLR 747, ...150,151
Thompson v Lodwick [1983] RTR 76, ...187
Thompson v Spedding [1973] RTR 312, ...17
Thompson v Stone [1997] CLY 1796, ...175
Thorn v Denby [1997] CLY 1809, ...175
Thorp v King Bros (1957) Times, Feb 23, ...121
Tingle Jacobs & Co v Kennedy [1964] 1 WLR 638, ...25
Tocci v Hankard (1966) 110 Sol.Jo. 835, ...19,158
Travers v Stych (1997) CLY 598, ...254
Traynor v Donovan [1978] CLY 2612, ...147
Tremayne v Shell (1986) Time, December 11, ...75
Tribe v Jones (1961) 105 Sol.Jo 932, ...14
Trinder v Great Western Railway Co. (1990) 35 TLR 291, ...60
Truscott v McLaren [1981] RTR 34, ...23
Usher v Crowder [1994] CLY 1494, ...170

Vaughan Transport Systems v Facrell [1997] CLY 1810, ...169

Wadsworth v Gillespie [1978] CLY 2534, ...31
Walker v Midland Fox Limited [1997] CLY 595, ...254
Walkley v Procession Forgings Ltd [1979] 1 WLR 606, ...151
Wall v Walwyn [1974] RTR 24, ...77
Wallace v Newton [1982] 2 All ER 106, .123
Waller v Levoi [1968] 112 Sol.Jo. 165, ...99
Walsh v Redfern [1970] RTR 201, ...22
Wand M Wood (Haulage) Ltd v Redpath [1967] 2 QB 520, ...10
Ward v London County Council [1938] 2 All ER 341, ... 41
Wardell-Yarburgh v Surrey County Council [1973]
RTR 462, 5,36,43
Warwick Motor Auctions v Bennett [1997] CLY 1815, ...167
Watkins v Moffat [1970] RTR 205, ...22
Watkins v O'Shaughnessy[1939] 1 All ER 385, ...187
Watson v Thomas S. Whitney & Co. Ltd [1966] 1 All ER 122, . . .11
Watson Norie Ltd v Shaw and Nelson [1967] 1 Lloyds Rep. 5, . .169
Watt v Glasgow Corp 1919 SC 300, ...54
Waugh v James K. Allen Limited [1964] 2 Lloyds Rep 1, ...156
Webb v Crane [1988] RTR 204, ...146
Weir v Field [1997] 1786, ...181
Welch v O'Leary [1998] CLY 3911, ...128
Wells v Metropolitan Water Board [1937] All ER 639, ...98
Wells v Woodward (1956) 54 LGL 142, ...25
West v Buckinghamshire County Council [1984] RTR 306, ...107
Western Scottish Motor Traction v Allam [1943] 2 All
ER 742, ...58,59
Wheelan & Wheelan v Hughes [1997] CLY 1802, ...171
White v Glass (1989) Times, February 18, ...151
White v London Transport Executive [1971] 2 QB 721, ...208
Whitfield v Faulkner [1998] CLY 457, ...253
Whiting v Hillingdon London Borough Council (1970) 114
Sol.Jo., ...95
Whybrow v Kentich Bus & Coach Co Ltd (1999) CL,
January 50, ...254
Widowson v Newgate Meat Corp. [1998] PIQR 138, ...10
Wilkie v L.P.T.B. [1947] 1 All ER 258, ...54
Wilkinson v Sealey [1996] CLY 2150, ...180,270
Willbye v Gibbons (1997) Lawtel C9000165, ...147
Williams v Fullerton (1961) 105 Sol Jo 208, ...22,23
Williams v Hoggins [1996] CLY 2148, .169

Williams v Needham[1972] RTR 387, ...67,72
Wills v TF Martin (Roof Contractors) Ltd [1972] RTR 368, ...102
Windle v Dunning & Son Ltd [1968] 2 All ER 46, ...186
Winnick v Dick (1984) SLT 185, ...148
Winnipeg Electric Co. v Geel [1992] AC 690, ...158
Winter v Cardiff RDC [1950] 1 All ER 819, ...6,130
Wintle v British Tramways and Carriage Co. Ltd. (1917) 86
LJKB 240, ...111
Withington v Bolton Borough Council [1937] 3 All ER 108, ...98
Wood v Richards [1977] RTR 210, ...36
Woodfall v Knowsley Borough Council (1992) Times, June 26, .109
Woodgate v Stafantos (1997) CLY 591, .254
Woods v Klarnet [1995] CLY 1630, ...178
Wooller v London Transport [1976] RTR 207, ...18,58
Worsfold v Howe [1980] 1 All ER 1028, ...20,21
Wragg v Grout and London Passenger Transport Board
(1966) 116 LJO, ...59
Wringe v Cohen [1940] 1 KB 229, ...108
Wyngrove v Scottish Omnibuses 1966 SC 47, ...54

Young v Chester [1973] RTR. 113
Yuen v Campbell-White (19940 CLY 1514, ...266

Zubair v Younis [1995] CLY 1625, ...179
Zurich General Accident Corp v Shuttleworth (1938) 60
LlRep 301, ...193

Table of Statutes

Animals Act 1971, ...119,121,122,126
   s2(1), ...121
   s2(2), ...122
   s2(2)(b), ...123
   s2(2)(c), ...124
   s5(1), ...125
   s5(2, ...125
   s5(3), ...125
   s6(2), ...121
   s6(3), ...123
   s6(4), ...123
   s8, ...121
   s8(2), ...125
   s10, ...124

Banking and Financial Dealings Act 1971, ...291

Civil Evidence Act 1968, ...245
   s11, ...8
Civil Evidence Act 1995
   s2(1), ...245
   s2(2)(a), ...245
   s2(4), ...245
Consumer Credit Act1974, ...172,173,175
   ss8–11, ...173
   s61(1)(a), ...173
Consumer Protection Act 1987
   ss1–9, ...139
County Courts Act 1984
   s69, ...206

Dangerous Dogs Act 1991, ...119,126
   s1, ...127
   s3, ...127
Diplomatic Privileges Act 1964, ...153
Dogs Act 1871, ...126

s2, ...127
Dogs Act 1906, ...126
Dogs (Amendment) Act 1928, ...126

Employer's Liability (Compulsory Insurance) Act 1969, ...189

Highway Act 1835
   s78, ...8
Highways Act 1959, ...79
Highways Act 1980, ...81
   s1, ...80
   s36(6), ...80
   s36(7), ...81
   s41(1), ...79,89,96,97,98
   s50(2), ...80
   s58, ...79
   s58(1), ...93
   s58(2), ...93,96
   s58(s)(a), ...93
   s58(s)(b), ...93
   s58(s)(c), ...93
   s58(s)(d), ...93
   s58(s)(3), ...94
   s96, ...106
   s96(6), ...106
   s139, ...103,
   s140, ...103
   Part 1 of Schedule 7, ...80
Highways (Miscellaneous Provisions) Act 1961, ...79,81

Insolvency Act 1986
   s285(iii), ...154
   s382(iii), ...154
   s412, ...154

Law Reform (Contributory Negligence) Act 1945, ...124,
   s1(1), ...143
Level Crossings Act 1983, ...34
Limitation Act 1980, ...148
   s2, ...149
   s5, ...149
   s11(5), ...149

s12(2), ...149
s14, ...149
s28(1), ...149
s33, ...148,149,151
s33(3), ...149
s38, ...149
London Hackney Carriages Act 1843, ...63

Magistrates' Courts Act 1980
s40(1), ...216

National Health Service Act 1977, ...188
New Roads and Street Works Act 1991, ...97
s49(1), ...97
s65, ...97
s70, ...97
s72, ...97

Occupiers Liability Act 1957, ...129
s1(3)(a), ...130
s2, ...130
s2(2), ...140
s2(4)(a), ...96,133
s5(1), ...140

Policyholders Protection Act 1975, ...302
Powers of the Criminal Courts Act 1973
s35(1), ...215
s35(3), ...216
Public Utilities Street Works Act 1950, ...97

Railway Clauses Consolidation Act 1845
s47, ...34
Road Traffic Act 1972
s151, ...274
Part VI, ...272,274,275
Road Traffic Act 1988, ...6,126
s3, ...8
s14, ...144
s15, ...144,146
s16, ...146
s17, ...146

s27(1), ...127
s27(2)-(8), ...127
s35, ...27
s36, ...27
s38(7), ...6
s41, ...129
s43, ...134
ss45–48, ...231
ss49–53, ...231
ss143–154, ...185
s143, ...185
s143(1), ...189
s143(2), ...185
s143(4), ...188
s144(1), ...187,188,294
s144(2), ...187,188
s145, ...188,190
s145(4), ...189
s147(1), ...190,191
ss148–152, ...190
s148, ...190,193
s148(5), ...191
s149, ...148
s149(4), ...189
s151, ...191
s151(3), ...191
s151(4), ...191
s151(7), ...192
s151(8), ...192
s152, ...192,193
s154, ...199,230
s154(1), ...193,201,300
s157, ...209
s161(3), ...189
s183, ...187
s185(1), ...196
s192(1), ...187,195
s193, ...188
Part VI, ...185,188,198,203,278,295
Road Traffic (NHS Charges) Act 1999, ...152,209–211
Road Traffic Regulation Act 1984
s25, ...71

s26, ...71,76
s64, ...107
s65(1), ...107
s80, ...107
s81, ...14,38
s28, ...77
s86, ...14,38
s87, ...38
s89, ...14,38
s95, ...77
Schedule 6, ...14,38

Sale of Goods Act 1979
s14, ...136
s14(2), ...136
s14(2)(b), ...137
Sale of Goods Act 1994, ...136
s13, ...138
s14, ...138
State Immunity Act 1978
s20, ...154
Supply of Goods and Services Act 1982
s13, ...134
Supreme Court Act 1981
s35A, ...206

Theft Act 1968, ...217
Third Party's (Rights Against Insurers) Act 1930, ...154
Town Police Clauses Act 1847
s37–68, ...63
Transport Act
ss97,97A,97B, ...230

Vehicle (Excise) Act 1971, ...190

Working Time Regulations 1998, ...9,22,33
Workplace (Health, Safety and Welfare) Regulations 1992, ...22

Table of Regulations

Consumer Credit (Exempt Agreements) Order 1989, ...174

Drivers Hours (Goods Vehicles)(Keeping of Records)
Regulations 1987 (SI 1421), ...231

Goods Vehicles (Plating and Testing Regulations 1988
(SI 1478), ...231

Lay Representatives (Rights of Audience) Order 1999
(SI 1225), ...249

Motor Cycles (Protective Helmets) Regulations 1998
(SI 1807), ...146
Motor Vehicles (Compulsory Insurance) Regulations 1987
(SI 2171), ...272
Motor Vehicles (Tests) Regulations 1981, ...134
Motor Vehicles (Third Party Risks) Regulations 1972
(SI 1972), ...190
Motor Vehicles (Wearing of Seat Belts) Regulations
1993 (SI 176), ...144,145,146
Motor Vehicles (Wearing of Seat Belts by Children in Front Seats)
Regulations 1993, (SI 31), ...48,144,146
Motor Vehicles (Wearing of Seat Belts by Children in Rear Seats)
Regulations 1989, ...48

Pelican Pedestrian Crossing Regulations and General Directions 1969
(SI 888), ...71
Public Service Vehicles (Conduct of Driver, Inspectors, Conductors
and Passengers) Regulations 1990 (SI 1020), ...53,55,57

Road Traffic (NHS Charges) Reviews and Appeals Regulations 1999
(SI 78), ...210
Road Vehicles (Construction and Use) Regulations 1986
(SI 1073), ...49,62,129
Road Vehicles Lighting Regulations 1989 (SI 1796), ..111,112,117

Traffic Signs Regulations and General Directions 1994
(SI 1994 1519), ...41,42,76

Zebra, Pedestrian Crossing Regulations 1971 (SI 1525), ...71
Zebra, Pelican and Puffin Pedestrian Crossing Regulations and
General Directions 1997 (SI 2400), ...41,42,71,72,73,74,75

Preface

"Of all things I dread having to write a narrative and I am wholly doubtful of my capacity; in any event if I have to do it, it will take me a long time".

Captain R. F. Scott, Polar Explorer

I have been involved in road traffic accident litigation for over ten years. I have never had recourse to a comprehensive textbook solely devoted to the subject. I have long been surprised at this omission, as RTA claims make up one of, if I not the largest area, of modern civil practice. So this little book is designed, however imperfectly, to fill a gap and provide my fellow practitioners with an inclusive guide to liability, recovery and, with some trepidation, post-Woolf civil practice. It was written over the course of a year – 1999 – in the gaps afforded by my practice and ever active young family. But my research will necessarily continue and, to this end, I am open to any advice, suggestion or comment that might improve the second edition.

I owe a debt to my colleagues and instructing solicitors. Piers Martin, in particular, never failed to courteously demonstrate an intimate knowledge of both RTA claims and Microsoft Word. Appendix 1 was kindly compiled by Jose Vazquez. I am grateful to Doreen Collins, Carol and Clair (of CnC Typing) and Beverely Blythe for typing the manuscript.

I have endeavoured to state the law as at 1 December 1999.

Mark Whalan
January 2000

Part I

Liability

Chapter 1

General Principles of Liability

The principle cause of action in road traffic accident claims is negligence. There may also be a statute which gives rise to a separate cause of action, or alternatively a claim in nuisance or contract. Nonetheless in most cases it will be necessary to prove:

- a duty and standard of care;
- breach;
- consequent injury, loss or damage.

Duty of Care

A motorist (meaning a person who either drives or rides a vehicle on a highway) owes a duty of care to other road users, pedestrians and persons occupying property adjacent to the highway. Numerous attempts have been made to provide a universal formula or definition applicable to claims in negligence. Most efforts can be traced back to the classic pronouncement of Lord Atkin in *Donoghue* v *Stevenson* [1932] AC 562 (at 580):

> "You must take reasonable care to avoid acts or omissions which you can reasonably foresee would be likely to injure your neighbour. Who, then, in law is my neighbour? The answer seems to be – persons who are so closely and directly affected by my act that I ought reasonably to have them in contemplation as being so affected when I am directing my mind to the acts or omissions which are called in question".

In *Bourhill* v *Young* [1943] AC 92 a case involving a collision between a motor cycle and a tram, Lord Macmillan stated (at 104) that:

> "The duty to take care is the duty to avoid doing or omitting to do anything which may have as its reasonable and probable consequence the injury to others, and the duty is owed to those to whom injury may reasonably and probably be anticipated if the duty is not observed".

Standard of Care

Reasonable care means the care which an ordinary skilful driver would have exercised – the care, in short, of an average motorist. What is reasonable necessarily varies from case to case. A driver is "not bound to foresee every extremity or folly which occurs on the road": *London Passenger Transport Board* v *Upson* [1949] AC 155. Equally he is not entitled to assume that other users of the highway will always exercise reasonable care. Teaching and experience leads to an acquaintance with common acts of negligence and these must be foreseen and avoided: *Berrill* v *Road Haulage Executive* [1952] 2 Lloyds' Rep. 490.

Learner Drivers

A learner driver owes a duty to drive with that degree of skill and care to be expected of a competent and experienced driver. The standard of care is not lowered by reason of the instructor's capability or the learner's lack of experience and skill: *Nettleship* v *Weston* [1971] 2 Q.B. 691.

Instructors

An instructor has a responsibility of care jointly with the learner driver to other road users in relation to the safe conduct and control of the car on the road. This means, in practice, that the instructor and the learner each have a responsibility to the other in the exercise of control over the car. This duty was summed up in *Rubie* v *Faulkner* [1940] 1 K.B. 571 (at 575) by Hilbery J:

> "It is the supervisor's duty, when necessary, to do whatever can reasonably be expected to be done by persons supervising the acts of another to prevent that other from acting unskilfully or carelessly or in a manner likely to cause danger to others, and to this extent to participate in the driving".

The control or intervention to be expected from an instructor will vary from case to case and the comparative blameworthiness between a supervisor and his pupil can vary between 0 and 100%. In *Gibbons* v *Priestley* [1979] RTR 4, the pupil let the clutch in too fast, lost control and crashed into a tree. The whole incident from start to stop lasted about five seconds. The court held that in the short time available the instructor could not reasonably have done more than he did, namely to shout "brake brake" and put on the hand brake. He was not negligent.

Examiners

An examiner is in a different position to an instructor: he is there for the sole purpose of observing and assessing the driver's competence. He should not interfere with the driver except where it is essential in the interests of safety: *British School of Motoring Ltd* v *Simms* [1971] 1 All ER 317.

Passengers

A motorist who agrees to carry a passenger in a vehicle owes a duty to exercise reasonable care and skill for the safety of that person: *Lygo* v *Newbold* (1854) 9 Ex.302, *Redhead* v *Midland Railway Co.* (1869) (4) Q.B. 379 and *Luddit* v *Ginger Coote Airway Limited* [1947] AC 233.

Pedestrians

Pedestrians and motorists owe each other a concomitant duty to exercise reasonable care for the safety of each other: *Baker* v *Willoughby* [1970] A.C. 467.

Emergency Services

A police officer is to be judged in exactly the same way as any other driver. He owes a duty to drive with due care and attention and without exposing members of the public to undue danger: *Gaynor* v *Allen* [1959] 2 Q.B. 403. By the same token, a driver of a fire tender owes the same duty of care as any other driver: *Wardell-Yarburgh* v *Surrey County Council* [1973] RTR 462.

Breach

In every case the court must apply the test of the reasonable driver to the facts of the accident in order to determine whether negligence is made out. The relevant questions are

(1) has there been a breach of duty? and
(2) was it partly or wholly causative of the accident?

Evidence of breach can be gleaned from reference to the following:

- statutory duty
- the Highway Code

- reported cases
- criminal convictions
- the "rule of the road"
- the DSA Driving Manuals

Statutes and Regulations

There are statutes and regulations (often made under the Road Traffic Act 1988) to control the conduct of motorists, passengers (particularly on public transport), pedestrians and highway authorities. Others regulate the construction and use of motor vehicles. Some breaches of statutory duty give rise to a separate cause of action in civil proceedings. Others do not – particularly those whose main purpose is to create a criminal offence: see, for example, *Barkway* v *South Wales Transport Co. Ltd* [1950] AC 185, *Tan Chye Choo* v *Ching Kew Moi* [1970] 1 All ER 266 and *Coote* v *Stone* [1970] 1 WLR 279. But the question of contravention invariably merges with the issue of negligence and proof of breach can be cited as evidence of a failure to take reasonable care: *Winter* v *Cardiff RDC* [1950] 1 All ER 819.

The Highway Code

The latest edition of the Highway Code was published in 1999. It comprises, in its current form, 278 rules (with designated sections relating to pedestrians, cyclists, motor cyclists and animals), an additional section devoted to signals, traffic signs, road and vehicle markings, and seven annexes concerned with vehicle (and bicycle) maintenance, license and legal requirements, and first aid for the road. It is (or at least the rules are) issued with the authority of Parliament and its effect is outlined in the Road Traffic Act 1988, section 38(7) which provides:

> "A failure on the part of a person to observe a provision of the Highway Code shall not of itself render that person liable to criminal proceedings of any kind, but any such failure may in any proceedings (whether civil or criminal) be relied upon by any party to the proceedings as tending to establish or to negative any liability which is in question in those proceedings".

A failure to comply with the provisions of the Code is usually, but not invariably, evidence of negligence. In *Croston* v *Vaughan* [1938] 1 KB 540, in which one motorist collided with the rear of another vehicle which had "pulled up" abruptly and without "giving a hand signal of intention", Greer LJ stated (at 551–522) that:

"The Highway Code is not binding as a statutory regulation; it is only something which may be regarded as information and advice to drivers. It does not follow that, if they fail to carry out any provisions of the Highway Code, they are necessarily negligent. The Road Traffic Act provides that a failure to observe any provision of the Code may in any proceedings be relied upon as tending to establish or rebut any liability which is in question in those proceedings. Nor is it sufficient excuse for any person to say, in answer to a claim of negligence, that he carried out every provision of the Code".

Reported Cases

No two road traffic accidents are exactly alike. Accordingly, whilst some useful guidance can be obtained from reported cases, few purport to lay down a binding (or even persuasive) authority. Each case turns on its own facts.

This was recognised over 50 years ago in *Morris* v *Luton Corporation* [1946] K.B. 114 where Lord Greene stated (at 115) that:

"There is sometimes a temptation for judges in dealing with these traffic cases to decide questions of fact in language which appears to lay down some rule which users of the road must observe. That is a habit into which one perhaps sometimes slips unconsciously – I may have done it myself for all I know – but it is much to be deprecated, because they are questions of fact dependent on the circumstances of each case".

In *Foskitt* v *Mistry* [1974] RTR 1 a child "ran straight out into the road" and collided with the nearside of the defendant's car. The Court of Appeal heard detailed argument from Counsel as to the respective fault of the parties. May LJ expressed his opinion (at 4) in terms of brusque unambiguity:

"It was a simple enough running down claim in all conscious. We were, nevertheless, referred to at least two authorities. For my part, not only do I think that reference to authority in this kind of case is unnecessary, but I would deprecate its repetition in similar simple cases in the future".

But this is, perhaps, to unreasonably discourage the use of reported cases in road traffic claims. The vast majority (statistically over 90%) of claims settle at a comparatively early stage of the pre-action or interlocutory process. The introduction of the Civil Procedure Rules in 1999 (and particularly the Pre-Action Protocol for Personal Injury Claims) should lead to a further increase in the incidence of pre-trial compromise. Such settlements are effected – even in complicated cases – by practitioners whose recourse to reported cases is both common place and well advised.

Criminal Convictions

Proof of a criminal conviction (most commonly careless driving contrary to the Road Traffic Act 1988, section 3) can be adduced as evidence of a motorist's negligence: Civil Evidence Act 1968, section 11. A conviction will settle the issue of primary liability (but not necessarily the question of contributory negligence) in the majority of cases. However, section 11(2) allows a defendant to challenge his conviction if he has good reason to do so and can satisfy the onus of proof in the civil standard. Where, on the basis of an expert's report, a defendant wishes to maintain such a challenge, it is not appropriate for the court to entertain an application for summary judgment under CPR Part 24: *McCauley* v *Hope* [1998] The Independent, December 21.

The "Rule of the Road"

The rule of the road provides that every vehicle shall keep to the left or near side of the highway. It derives from an old common law rule that was adopted into statute by The Highway Act 1835, section 78. It is now incorporated into the Highway Code at rule 136. Breach of the rule is prima facie evidence of negligence: *Chaplin* v *Hawes* (1828) 3 C&P 554. That is not to say that non observance will invariably conclude the issue of liability: the Highway Code envisages a number of circumstances (such as overtaking, turning right, passing parked vehicles or pedestrians in the road) when it may be reasonable to depart from the ordinary practice. But it does place upon the contra-vening party the evidential burden of proving what those circum-stances were.

The DSA Driving Manuals

The Driving Standards Agency (an executive agency of the Department of the Environment, Transport and the Regions) publishes a number of driving manuals:

- The Driving Manual
- The Motor Cycle Manual
- The Bus and Coach Driving Manual
- The Goods Vehicle Driving Manual

Full details of texts are provided in Sources and References page 00

All provide detailed guidance for drivers and motor cyclists. The primary aim of the DSA, according to Robin Cummins, the Chief Driving Examiner, is "to promote road safety through the advancement of driving standards". The manuals purport, with some justification, to be "essential reference books for every motorist, regardless of experience, and instructors too". Interestingly the 1993 edition of the Highway Code incorporated a reference to the Driving and Motor Cycle Manuals at rule 27/28, an inclusion which raised the arguable possibility that section 38(7) of the 1988 Act might apply. The reference is not reproduced in the 1999 edition. Yet, either way, these publications provide an extremely useful source of guidance as to correct driving practice.

Causation

Next the claimant must prove that the defendant's negligence or breach caused the accident and the loss and damage complained of. Often the facts (and causation is essentially a question of fact) speak for themselves. Sometimes the matter is shrouded.

Particular complication attaches to the drunken driver. Where his intoxication is such that he is unable to control either the vehicle or its safe passage along the highway, his conduct, in the event of an accident, will undoubtedly be a causal effect. Where the accident was one which not even a sober driver could have avoided, he will not be liable. Such is the approbrium that attaches to drinking and driving that the subtleties of this distinction are often lost on both practitioners and judges alike. But it is always important to look behind the superficial facts in order to separate that which is of causal relevance from that which is merely indicative of a general culpability.

Even when it can be proved that the defendant's negligence led to an accident, it does not necessarily follow that this fault automatically caused all the damage alleged by the claimant. Quite apart from the general question of remoteness of loss (an issue which is beyond the scope of this book), it is quite common for a motorist to claim that at least some of the damage to the other vehicle was a result of a previous incident or general wear and tear.

Res ipsa loquitur

General principle

The doctrine, which constitutes a rule of evidence and not a principle of law, stems from the judgment in *Scott* v *London and St. Katherine*

Docks Co. (1865) 3 H&C 586. Earle CJ held that where the 'thing' which inflicted the damage was shown to be under the management or control of the defendant, and the accident is such that as in the ordinary course of events does not happen without negligence, it affords reasonable evidence, in the absence of explanation by the defendant, that the accident arose from want of care. The evidential presumption is, therefore, rebuttable. The burden of proof is on the defendant to show that the accident occurred without fault on his part: *Cole v De Trafford* (No.2) [1918] 2 KB 523. It is not enough, in this regard, for the defendant to merely deny that he had done anything negligent. The onus is on him to show that he took all reasonable precaution and was not negligent: *Ludgate v Lovett* [1969] 2 All ER 1275. Res ipsa loquitor depends on a complete absence of evidence as to why or how the accident took place: where such evidence exists the question of liability must be determined on that testimony.

Examples

It has recently been held that "it is not common" to establish liability in a road traffic accident using the maxim res ipsa loquitur: *Widowson v Newgate Meat Corp.* [1998] PIQR 138. Nonetheless there are a number of common situations (both actual and evidential) where the rule is of potential application.

Car veering into the path of oncoming traffic

Where a car veers into the opposite lane hitting another vehicle the inference of negligence is likely to arise: *Davis v Burn* (1936) 56 C.L.R. 246. Where it is impossible to say whether one driver was more to blame than the other (because, for example, both vehicles were hugging the centre of the road) the inference was that both drivers were negligent and liability should be apportioned equally: *Baker v Market Harborough Co-operative Society Ltd* [1953] 1 WLR 1472. This situation can arise where either or both of the drivers are killed (see *Wand M Wood (Haulage) Ltd v Redpath* [1967] 2 QB 520), where the parties have no memory or recollection of the accident (see *Howard v Bemrose* [1973] RTR 32), or simply where it is impossible to distinguish between the evidence of the protagonists (see *Davison v Leggett* (1969) 133 JP 552).

Sudden stop or swerve

Pulling up suddenly and violently is prima facie evidence of negligence: *O'Hara v Central Scottish Motor Traction Co. Ltd* [1941] SC

363. The inference will be rebutted if the defendant gives an explanation which is consistent with the conduct of an ordinary, reasonable, careful driver: *Parkinson* v *Liverpool Corpn* [1950] 1 All ER 367.

Skidding

An unexplained and violent skid is in itself evidence of negligence. A defendant will fail unless he can prove that the skid happened without his default: *Richley* v *Faull* [1965] 3 All ER 109. (This judgment supersedes the earlier case of *Laurie* v *Raglan Building Co.* [1942] 1 KB 152 where Lord Greene reasoned that a skid by itself is neutral and may or may not have been due to negligence).

Vehicle mounting/overhanging the pavement

Where a vehicle mounts a pavement this fact, in the absence of explanation, constitutes evidence of negligence: *Ellor* v *Selfridge & Co. Ltd* (1930) 46 TLR 236, *McGowan* v *Stott* (1920) 99 LJKD 357. The same applies where a vehicle overhangs or 'projects over' the pavement: *Laurie* v *Raglan Building Co. Ltd* (ibid). No blame attaches to a pedestrian who walks close to the edge of a footway: *Watson* v *Thomas S. Whitney & Co. Ltd* [1966] 1 All ER 122. Indeed a pedestrian standing on a kerb is not guilty of negligence if he leans out or even if he goes 'an inch or two' into the roadway: *Chapman* v *Post Office* [1982] RTR 165.

Collision with a stationary vehicle

Where there is a collision between a moving vehicle and a stationary vehicle which is plainly visible, the onus is on the driver to show that he has taken all reasonable care: *Randall* v *Tarrant* [1955] 1 All ER 600.

Chapter 2

The Driver

Most road traffic accidents are caused by the negligence of one or more of the drivers embroiled in the collision. The Driving Manual begins with a cautionary reference to this truism:

"No matter how good, how fast, how expensive or how efficient your vehicle is, it's you, THE DRIVER, who determines whether it's a safe means of transport".

No two accidents are exactly alike and it is impossible to provide an all embracing guide to liability. This chapter will accordingly concentrate on the more common accident circumstances, namely:

- Speed
- Line of moving traffic
- Overtaking
- Road junctions: major and minor roads
- Traffic lights
- Crossing the centre of the road
- Skidding
- Signals
- Turning round
- Reversing
- Railway level crossings

Speed

Highway Code

The Code provides:

"103. You MUST NOT exceed the maximum speed limits for the road and for your vehicle. Street lights usually mean that there is a 30mph speed limit unless there are signs showing another limit.

104. The speed limit is the absolute maximum and does not mean it is safe to drive at that speed irrespective of conditions. Driving at speeds too fast for the road and traffic conditions can be dangerous. You should always reduce your speed when:

- the road layout or condition presents hazards, such as bends
- sharing the road with pedestrians and cyclists, particularly children, and motorcyclists
- weather conditions make it safe to do so
- driving at night as it is harder to see other road users."

The maximum speed limits are prescribed by the Road Traffic Regulation Act 1984, sections 81, 86, 89 and schedule 6. The table opposite is reproduced from the Highway Code at page 26.

Discussion

Excessive speed generally

Exceeding the speed limit (or merely driving at a "fast speed") will not automatically constitute negligence: *Tribe* v *Jones* (1961) 105 Sol.Jo. 932. By the same token, a conviction for speeding will not in itself impose civil liability: *Barna* v *Hudes Merchandising Corpn.* (1962) 106 Sol.Jo. 124. Nonetheless excessive speed will "most probably" pose a danger to other road users: *Kingman* v *Seagar* [1938] 1 KB 397.

In *Bracegirdle* v *Oxley* [1947] 1 All ER 126 Lord Goddard C.J. stated (at 128) that the court:

> "... must take into consideration all the circumstances of the case, because a speed which is too fast on one road in certain circumstances may not be dangerous when driving on another road in other circumstances."

Twenty years later, in *Quinn* v *Scott* [1965] 2 All ER 588, this reasoning was followed (per Glyn-Jones at 590) in the Queen's Bench Division:

> "There are a number of makers of motor cars who ....make their motor cars for the express purpose that, in appropriate conditions, they may safely be driven at high speeds – higher, indeed, than seventy-five mph. High speed alone is not evidence of negligence unless the particular conditions at the time preclude it."

Evidence of excessive speed will, at the very least, call for an explanation from the culpable motorist: *Hulock* v *Ingliss* (1963) 107 Sol.Jo. Here the Defendant drove at a speed in excess of 100 mph when he lost control of his car and collided with the claimant's lorry. In the absence of a satisfactory explanation of his "extraordinary behaviour" the court concluded that he must have been negligent.

Excessive speed in a built up area will undoubtably raise an evidential presumption of negligence. The motorist's chances of being confronted by other road users and/or pedestrians (particularly

Speed Limits

Type of vehicle	Built-up areas*	Elsewhere		Motorways
		Single carriage-ways	Dual carriage-ways	
	MPH	MPH	MPH	MPH
Cars & motorcycles (including car derived vans up to 2 tonnes maximum laden weight)	30	60	70	70
Cars towing caravans or trailers (including car derived vans and motorcycles)	30	50	60	60
Buses & coaches (not exceeding 12 metres in overall length)	30	50	60	70
Goods vehicles (not exceeding 7.5 tonnes maximum laden weight)	30	50	60	70†
Goods vehicles (exceeding 7.5 tonnes maximum laden weight)	30	40	50	60

These are the national speed limits and apply to all roads unless signs show otherwise.

*The 30 mph limit applies to all traffic on all roads in England and Wales (and Class C and unclassified roads in Scotland) with street lighting unless signs show otherwise.

†60 if articulated or towing a trailer

children) are greatly increased. In *Moore* v *Poyner* [1975] RTR 127, a case in which a car travelling at 25 to 30 mph struck a boy of 6 who had suddenly emerged from the roadside kerb, Buckley L.J. summarised (at 132) the duty as follows:

> "I think one can formulate the appropriate test ... in these terms: would it have been apparent to a reasonable man, armed with common sense and experience in the way pedestrians, particularly children, are likely to behave in the circumstances such as were known . . . that there was a possibility of a danger emerging, to avoid which he should slow down or sound his horn, or both."

In *Saledem* v *Drake* [1993] PIQR 129, a case founded on very similar facts to those in *Moore*, the Court of Appeal held that the duty was to slow down so as to "stop instantaneously if a child ran into the road" (per Croom-Johnson at 134), but that a driver need not sound his horn on seeing a child (or children) playing on a pavement. However, where children could be seen "hovering" in the middle of the road, a driver must reduce his speed and "make his presence felt by sounding his horn": *Armstrong* v *Cottrell* [1993] PIQR 109, at 112.

Speed and pedestrians

Rule 104 warns that a driver "should always" reduce his speed when sharing the road with pedestrians. This is so when the pedestrian is either walking along or crossing the highway: see, for example, *Powell* v *Phillips* [1972] 3 All ER 864 and *Baker* v *Willoughby* [1970] A.C. 467. Nor should a motorist automatically presume that a pedestrian will be able to move at a normal speed. Various factors – such as age or infirmity – must be allowed for. Thus, in *Daly* v *Liverpool Corp.* [1939] 2 All ER 142, a case where a motorist collided with an elderly pedestrian, Stable J. commented (at 143) that:

> "I cannot believe that the law is quite so absurd as to say that, if the pedestrian happens to be old and slow and a little stupid, and does not possess the skill of the hypothetical pedestrian, he or she can only walk about his or her native country at his or her own risk."

Line of moving traffic

Highway Code

Rule 105 provides:

> "**Stopping distances**
> Drive at a speed that will allow you to stop well within the distance you can see to be clear. You should:

- leave enough space between you and the vehicle in front so that you can pull up safely if it suddenly slows down or stops. The safe rule is never to get closer than the overall stopping distance (see Typical Stopping Distances diagram, reproduced at Appendix ...).
- allow for at least a 2-second gap between you and the vehicle in front on roads carrying fast traffic. The gap should be at least doubled on wet roads and increased still further on icy roads.
- remember, large vehicles and motorcycles need a greater distance to stop."

(See also rule 129, **Slow moving traffic.**)

Discussion

Duty of following driver

A driver following another vehicle in traffic must keep a sufficient distance between the vehicles in which to respond to all traffic exigencies reasonably to be anticipated. The obligation was succinctly expressed in *Brown & Lynn* v *Western SMT Co Ltd*, 1945 S.C. 31 where Lord Cooper stated (at 35) that:

> "The distance which should separate two vehicles travelling one behind the other must depend upon many variable factors – the speed, the nature of the locality, the other traffic present or to be expected, the opportunity available to the following driver of commanding a view ahead of the leading vehicle, the distance within which the following vehicle can be pulled up and many other things. The following driver is, in my view, bound, so far as is reasonably possible, to take up such a position, and to drive in such a fashion, as will enable him to deal with all traffic exigencies reasonably to be anticipated: but whether he has fulfilled this duty must in every case be a question of fact, just as it is a question of fact whether, on any emergency disclosing itself, the following driver acted within the alertness, skill and judgment reasonably to be expected in the circumstances".

Exigencies "reasonably to be anticipated" includes a foreseeable emergency: *Thompson* v *Spedding* [1973] RTR 312. It does not invariably extend to a situation where the leading vehicle "makes an emergency stop in a dire emergency of some kind": *Scott* v *Warren* [1974] RTR 104 (per Lord Widgery CJ at 106). Nor does it mean that a public service driver should travel so far behind a leading vehicle when a pedestrian crossing is being approached so that, even if a pedestrian should cause that vehicle to brake suddenly, the following vehicle can be pulled up behind it without having to brake sharply: *Parnell* v *Metropolitan Police District Receiver* [1976] RTR 201. Such a proposition, as Edmund Davies LJ noted in the analogous case of *Wooller* v *London Transport* [1976] RTR 207, was a counsel of perfection that ignored modern traffic conditions.

Duty of leading vehicle

Where a leading vehicle brakes suddenly the evidential burden of proof lies on the driver to explain his conduct: *Elizabeth* v *Motor Insurers' Bureau* [1981] RTR 405. If a driver is going to make a sudden, heavy stop, he is under a duty to signal traffic behind him of his intention: *Jungnickel* v *Laing (1966)* 111 Sol.Jo. 19. But a driver is under no duty to give a warning when it is merely his intention to decelerate his speed. Thus, where a leading vehicle came to a gradual halt as a result of a mechanical breakdown, with the result that it was struck by the following vehicle, it was held that the driver of the following vehicle was negligent in failing to anticipate such a fore-seeable emergency: *Rowlands* v *Street* (1962) Times, November 22. By way of an exception to the general rule, where the driver of one vehicle has specifically undertaken to lead or direct the driver of another, he will be liable in negligence if his faulty navigation obliges him to brake hard, whether or not the leading vehicle comes to a complete halt: *Sharp* v *Avery and Kirkwood* [1938] 4 All ER 85 and *Smith* v *Harris* [1939] 3 All ER 960.

Overtaking

Highway Code

Overtaking is regulated by rules 138 to 145 of the Highway Code. Specifically the rules cover the following: 138 (*Before overtaking*), 139 (*Safe method of overtaking*), 140 (*Overtaking large vehicles*), 141, 142 and 143 (*Prohibition on overtaking*), 144 (*Being overtaken*), and 145 (*The duty of slow moving vehicles to pull over*).

Discussion

When to overtake

A driver MUST NOT overtake where his vehicle would have to cross or straddle double white lines with an unbroken line nearest to him (rule 107), in contravention of a "no overtaking" sign, within the confines of a pedestrian crossing (rule 167), or if the maneuvre will involve entering a lane reserved for buses, trams or cycles. Overtaking

SHOULD NOT be attempted at (or during the approach to) a corner, bend or junction: *Tocci v Hankard* (1966) 110 Sol.Jo. 835. Nor should a driver proceeding along a dual carriageway overtake if it means pulling out into a lane that is already occupied by (or congested with) traffic: *Goke v Willett* [1973] RTR 422. A hump bridge or hill will invariably mean that a driver cannot see far enough ahead to be sure that it is safe to overtake. As to overtaking at traffic lights: "To pass a stationary vehicle under such circumstances was a dangerous practice; the danger ought to be realised by all motorists": *Shepherd v H. West & Son Ltd* [1962] Sol.Jo. 391 (per Paull J. at 392).

How to overtake

A driver should look and signal before any change in speed or direction. Overtaking should only be attempted when it can be undertaken without causing inconvenience or danger to other road users: see, for example, *Humphray v Ganson Bros,* 1917 S.C. 371. A driver who is overtaking should always "allow plenty of room" between his vehicle and the vehicle overtaken (rule 139). Where a motorist is overtaking a bicycle he should allow for some lateral movement on the part of the cyclist, particularly when the road surface is loose or uneven: *Henry v Santam Insurance Co Ltd,* 1971 (1) S.A. 466. But a driver is entitled to assume that he can overtake without danger if what he is overtaking gives "not the slightest sign that it was going to do something other than what another careful motorist might expect": *Clark v Wakelin* (1965) 109 Sol.Jo. 295 (per Roskill J). Having passed the other vehicle the overtaking driver should move back to the left "as soon as he can" but should not "cut in" (rule 139).

Overtaking a line of stationary traffic

A motorist who overtakes a line of stationary or slow moving traffic must drive at a speed and in such a way that will enable him to deal with an emergency: *Clarke v Winchurch* [1966] 1 WLR 69.

Sometimes a vehicle on the inside lane will give way to traffic waiting to emerge from a side road. Often the emerging vehicle will be invited (by either a wave or a flick of headlights) to drive through a gap in the main road's traffic by one or more of the stationary vehicles. In *Powell v Moody* (1966) 110 Sol.Jo. 215 a collision occurred between the claimant, who was overtaking a line of stationary traffic and the defendant who, at the beckon of another driver, was emerging from a side road. Contributory negligence was assessed at 80%. Sellers LJ stated that:

"Any road user who jumped a queue of stationary vehicles by going on the outside of a lane of stationary vehicles in front of him was undertaking an operation fraught with great hazard. Such an operation had to be carried out with great care because it was always difficult to see from the offside of the queue of stationary vehicle's gap in the queue on its nearside from which traffic might emerge".

In *Garston Warehousing Co Ltd v O.F. Smart (Liverpool) Ltd* [1973] RTR 377 the overtaking driver's contributory fault was assessed at two thirds, whilst in *H.L. Motorworks (Willesden) Ltd v Alwahdi* [1977] RTR 276, where the overtaking vehicle crossed onto the wrong side of the road, the emerging motorist was completely exonerated.

A driver of a motorcycle or bicycle must exercise particular care when overtaking stationary traffic. In *Clarke v Winchurch* (ibid) Phillimore LJ stated (at 72) that:

"If you have a small vehicle like a bicycle or motorcycle, you are in the fortunate position of taking up so little road space that you can slide along the offside, but if you choose to do this, it does seem to me to warrant a very, very high degree of care indeed because you are blinded, to a great extent, to what goes on on the left-hand side of the road."

In *Worsfold v Howe* [1980] 1 All ER 1028, where a motorcyclist overtaking two stationary tankers waiting at traffic lights collided with a car emerging from a side entrance, the Court of Appeal held that each party was equally to blame. Similarly, in *Leeson v Beavis & Tolchard Ltd* [1972] RTR 373 the overtaking motorcyclists contributory liability was again assessed at 50%.

The driver of an overtaking vehicle should always show consideration for the safety of pedestrians and, where the stationary traffic includes a bus or taxi, he should anticipate that passengers are likely to be alighting: *Christie v Glasgow Corp*, [1927] SC 273. He should always keep "a good look out" for pedestrians (particularly children) emerging suddenly from behind an ice-cream van: *Gambino v De Leo* [1971] 7 DLR 167.

Duty of driver being overtaken

A driver being overtaken should not accelerate, swerve outward or change his course without warning: *Milken v Glasgow Cpn*, [1918] SC 857 and *Holdack v Bullock Bros (Electrical) Ltd* (1964) 108 Sol Jo 861. But a driver is entitled to "drive normally at a proper speed and on a proper course" where a dangerous situation is created by the overtaking vehicle: *Smith v Cribben* [1994] PIQR 218. In this case the overtaking driver drove at an excessive speed in an attempt to complete an overtaking manoeuvre before the end of a dual carriageway. The driver being overtaken, who maintained a steady speed even when the overtaking driver braked, lost control of her car and collided with two oncoming vehicles, was not negligent. He could "not be expected to anticipate that the following driver will drive dangerously and extricate that driver that driver from the dangerous situation he creates" (per Roach LJ at 229).

Road junctions : major and minor roads

Highway Code

Road junctions are governed by rules 146 to 159 of the Code.

Discussion

Duty of driver emerging from minor road

When emerging from a minor road into a major road a driver should always wait for a safe gap in the traffic before commencing his manoeuvre.

Even when his vision is obscured (to an extent that he is effectively blind) he is not entitled to "inch forward" into the path of traffic on the major road: *Worsfold* v *Howe* [1980] 1 WLR 1175. This decision was followed at first instance in *Dowling* v *Dargue* (1997) CLY 3769. Where, by the same token, the waiting driver's vision is partly blocked by the presence of a large bus or lorry on the major road, he should always wait the few extra seconds necessary to ensure against the possibility of another or motorcycle being masked by the large vehicle: *Harding* v *Hinchcliffe* (1964) Times, April 8. (See also *Garston Warehousing Co* v *Smart (Liverpool) Ltd* (ibid)). Sometimes junctions are unmarked or there remains a doubt as to priority. In these circumstances it is "a well-recognised and conventional practice rather than a rule" that the vehicle which has the other on its right hand side is the give-way vehicle: *McIntyre* v *Coles* [1965] 1 WLR 831 (per Sellers LJ at 834).

Duty of driver proceeding along major road

What is the position when a motorist emerges from a side road, either at speed or without maintaining an adequate lookout, and drives across the path of traffic on the major road? What precautions, if any, must a driver on the main road take as he approaches a junction?

It is clear that a driver on a major road is under a duty "to take reasonable precautions": *Laing* v *London Transport Executive* [1957] 1 WLR 1168. This can involve, depending on the circumstances, keeping a repeated observation on the minor road and a precautionary reduction in speed. Thus, in *Williams* v *Fullerton* (1961) 105 Sol Jo 208, where a motorist emerged from a minor road at an "excessive speed", the driver of the vehicle on the major road was found to be 25% liable on the ground that had he kept a proper look-out the accident might have been avoided. A comparable set of facts led to an identical judgment in *Butters* v *J.A. Fenner & Co. Ltd* (1967) 117 MLJ 213.

These cases were considered in *Walsh* v *Redfern* [1970] RTR 201. The duty applilcable to a motorist on a main road was summarised by Lyell LJ (at 203) who stated:

> "It has been held in a number of cases that a driver on a major road is not entitled to drive on, relying on the fact that he is on a major road, and ignore the conduct of a driver approaching along a minor road which joins the major road. If the driver on the major road can see, from the way the driver is proceeding, that he is not going to give way, it is the duty of the main road driver to give way if he can, and so avoid an accident."

It may well be the case, however, that these (somewhat elderly) decisions exaggerate the burden befalling the driver on a major road. It has always been accepted that a vehicle will sometimes emerge at such a speed that the motorist on the main road, keeping a reasonable look out on both sides of the carriageway, will still not see it: *Watkins* v *Moffat* [1970] RTR 205. In this case Sachs LJ stated (at 207) that:

> "Often, Laing's case is used in argument as a sort of charter for those emerging at high speeds from side roads onto main roads ... Whether or not Laing's case was correctly decided on its own facts (a matter on which I would wish to reserve my own judgment), it is clear that it is no such charter as is often urged. Such a charter would entail a somewhat unrealistic view of the way that reasonably driven traffic use main roads, would assume a general slowing down of that traffic which has no relation to modern conditions, and would denegrate from the general responsibility upon those emerging from side roads in relation to that main road traffic."

Perhaps of more significance is the fact that many of the older cases were decided at a time when minor roads were usually marked with a sign and/or the words "Slow, major road ahead", which, when compared with the modern "Stop" or "Give Way" sign or marking constitutes a somewhat equivocal prohibition.

It is submitted, therefore, that more confidence should now be placed on cases such as *Humphrey v Leigh* [1971] RTR 363. The motorist was proceeding along a main road keeping a proper look out at a speed not exceeding 30 mph when he was struck by another vehicle which had emerged from a side road at a speed of 20 mph without stopping. The Court of Appeal (having doubted the decision in *Williams v Fullerton* as obiter dictum) stated that a motorist had no duty when driving along a main road to take his foot off the accelerator and poise it over the brake so as to be prepared to stop short in case a car driven dangerously came out of a side road. As Russell LJ pointed out (at 365): "Otherwise, you would approach a situation in which no traffic moves about the country at any reasonable speed whatsoever".

This approach was slightly refined in the subsequent case of *Truscott v McLaren* [1981] RTR 34. This time claimant on a main road was travelling at 40mph when, about 50 yards from a junction, he saw the defendant approaching from a side road at 50 to 55mph. He drove "steadily on" without paying attention to the other vehicle. They collided. The Court of Appeal acknowledged that there are many cases where a driver on a major road is entitled to assume that other vehicles approaching on a side road will not disregard all signs and emerge at speed. However, a finding of negligence could be made against a driver on a major road where "it should have been reasonably apparent that there was danger emerging" and where there was "something more than a mere possibility of danger". The claimant was held to be 20% liable for the accident.

Where a driver on a major road is travelling at an excessive speed, he can expect to be found to be between 20% and 30% liable for a collision with a vehicle emerging from a side road: see three recent decisions from the Court of Appeal, namely *Dolby v Milner* (1996) CLY 4430, *Paul Farrah Sound Ltd v Rookledge* (1996) CLY 4431 and *Smith v Goss* (1996) CLY 4432.

It is appropriate to conclude this section with a short extract from The Driving Manual (at 157):

> **"Passing minor roads**
> Look out for road signs indicating minor roads, even if you are not turning off.
> What out for emerging vehicles. Their view is often obscured at junctions. A vehicle might pull out in front of you.

If this happens, and you are not sure the driver has seen you, slow down. Be prepared to stop.
Be tolerant and don't harass the other driver by sounding your horn aggressively or driving too close.
Remember
Two wrongs don't make a right!".

Duty of driver turning into a minor road

A motorist turning left should "keep well to the left, about 1 metre from the kerb" (The Driving Manual, 156). He should give a left turn signal "well before" the junction and watch out for traffic (particularly cyclists and motorcyclists) on his nearside (rule 158). He should not overtake "just before" the turn: *Challoner* v *Williams & Ironby* [1975] RTR 425.

A right turn invariably involves steering a route across the highway and the motorist, aside from taking up a correct position on the carriageway and giving an appropriate signal, should always wait until there is a safe gap in the oncoming traffic: *Stimpson* v *Peat* [1962] 2 QB 24. Even where one vehicle (or line of vehicles) has stopped, a turning driver should ensure that his way is clear before commencing his maneouvre: *Patel* v *Edwards* [1970] RTR 425.

Traffic Lights

Highway Code

The Code provides:

> "*Junctions controlled by traffic lights*
> 151. You MUST stop behind the white "Stop" line across your side of the road unless the light is green. If the amber light appears you may go on only if you have already crossed the stop line or are so close to it that to stop might cause an accident."

> 152. You MUST NOT move forward over the white line when the red light is showing. Only go forward when the traffic lights are green if there is room for you to clear the junction safely or you are taking up a position to turn right. If the traffic lights are not working, proceed with caution."

(See also rules 153 *Green filter arrow* and 154 *Advanced stop lines*). Rules 151 and 152 reflect and reproduce a general prohibition contained in the Road Traffic Act 1988, section 36, which states that it is an offence for any driver or cyclist to disobey a traffic signal.

Discussion

Presumption that lights are working properly
In *Wells v Woodward (1956) 54 LGL 142* Lord Goddard C.J. held (at 143) that where the evidence suggested that traffic lights were showing green in one direction it could be "legitimately inferred" that they were showing red in the other direction. This dictum was taken one step further in *Tingle Jacobs & Co v Kennedy* [1964] 1 WLR 638 where Lord Denning M.R. concluded (at 639/640) that the presumption should be that traffic lights are in proper working order unless there is evidence to the contary.

What if traffic lights are not operating properly?
Where traffic lights fail a motorist should "proceed with caution" and "treat the situation as (he) would an unmarked junction" (rule 152 and The Driving Manual, page 102). Should a driver unreasonably fail to realise that the lights are out of order the court "will be justified" in finding him guilty of negligence: *Ramoo S/O Erul Aran v Gan Soo Swee* [1971] 1 WLR 1014.

Crossing a green light
A green light means "go if the way is clear". A motorist entering a junction from a road while the traffic lights are at green can properly assume that no fresh traffic will enter it from a road at which the lights are at red and his "sole duty" is to look out for traffic already in the junction which he could reasonably expect might obstruct him: *Sudds v Hanscombe* [1971] RTR 212. He is under no obligation to "assume" that the driver of another vehicle may be entering the junction in contravention of a red light: *Joseph Eva Limited v Reeves* [1938] 2 KB 393. Nor is a motorist – being a "reasonable and careful individual with normal experience exercising proper common sense" – obliged to suppose that a vehicle travelling towards a junction at speed might be unable to stop in obedience to a red light: *Miller v Evans* [1975] RTR 70. But that is not to say that a driver is entitled to pass a green light "in the face of evident danger": *Davis v Hassan* (1967) Times, January 13. Thus, even where traffic lights are green, a driver is under a duty to traffic already lawfully in the junction prior to the change of lights, which he should reasonably foresee might still be crossing, not to enter the junction until it is safe to do so: *Godsmark v Knight Brothers (Brighton) Ltd* (1960) Times, May 12, followed in *Radburn v Kemp* [1971] 1 WLR 1582. By the same token, a driver who crosses a green light will not escape a finding of fault if other aspects of his

driving (such as his speed or whether he was keeping a proper look out) demonstrably fell below the standard of a reasonable motorist: *Mulligan* v *Holmes* [1971] RTR 179.

Crossing a red light

Crossing a red light will amount to negligence. A driver who enters a junction in contravention of a red light will almost invariably be "solely liable" for any consequent accident: *Joseph Eva Limited* v *Reeves* (ibid) and *Knight* v *Wiper Supply Services Ltd* (1965) 109 Sol.Jo 358.

Turning right

A motorist who turns right across the path of an oncoming vehicle at a light controlled junction is entitled to assume that that vehicle will stop at lights showing red against him: *Hopwood Homes Ltd* v *Kennerdine* [1975] RTR 82. (See also *Miller* v *Evans* (ibid)). However, where a driver executed his turn too early, with the result that he collided with an oncoming motorcyclist who had entered the junction with traffic lights in his favour, he was wholly responsible in negligence: *Smithers* v *H & M Transport (Oxford) Ltd and Hodgkinson* (1983) 22 NLJ 558.

Duty when lights are changing

When the amber light appears a motorist may only go on if he has already crossed the stop line or is so close to it that pulling up might cause an accident (rule 151 and The Driving Manual, page 101). In *Godsmark* v *Knight Brothers (Brighon) Ltd* (ibid) a lorry driver elected to proceed through the stop light even though he could have just stopped had he immediately applied his brakes when the traffic lights changed to amber. (Nonetheless it was not entirely clear that he could have stopped in safety). He collided with a car whose driver pulled away immediately the lights showed green against him. Liability was apportioned two-thirds and one-third between the driver of the lorry and the car. (See also *Radburn* v *Kemp* (ibid) and *Smithers* v *H & M Transport* (ibid)).

Crossing the centre of the road

Highway Code

Lines and lane markings on the road are considered at various places in the Code. Specific reference can be made to rules 106 to 111 and the diagrams shown on page 78 of the 1999 edition.

Discussion

When a collision occurs in the centre of the road the normal inference is that one or both of the drivers is to blame.

If the evidence shows that the point of impact was on one side of the centre markings the collision prima facie calls for an explanation from the driver who was on the wrong side of the road: *Howard* v *Bemrose* [1973] RTR 33. It may sometimes be necessary to draw a distinction between a dotted or single white line and a double white line: crossing the former is usually permissible whereas non-compliance with the latter will almost invariably constitute an offence: sections 35 and 36 of the Road Traffic Act 1988. It can be even more difficult to infer negligence when there is no (or an "imaginary") central white line: *Kirk* v *Parker* (1938) 60 Lloyds Law Rep. 129. But blame will generally lie with the motorist driving on the wrong side (or straddling both sides) of the road. Where, for instance, a driver allowed his car to cross about 3 to 4 feet over the wrong side of the central line, with the result that it collided with an oncoming vehicle, his negligence was found to be "a substantial cause" of the accident: *Day* v *Smith* (1983) 133 NLJ 726.

Where it is clear that the collision occurred in the middle of the road but there is no evidence that will enable the court to draw a distinction between the motorists, the proper course is to apportion blame equally: *Baker* v *Market Harborough Industrial Co-Operative Society Ltd* [1953] 1 WLR 1472. Lord Denning explained (at 1476) the "practice of the court" and stated that it should " unhesitatingly hold that both were to blame". This situation can arise where both drivers are killed, where neither has a recollection of the collision or simply because it is impossible to say whether it was one vehicle that was to blame or both of them. Rarely, if ever, is it appropriate to make no finding of negligence: *Bray* v *Palmer* [1953] 1 WLR 1455. This is so even where "it is perfectly feasible that neither was negligent": *Davidson* v *Leggett* [1969] 113 Sol.Jo. 409.

Skidding

Highway Code

Rule 99 provides:

> "**Skids.** Skidding is caused by the driver braking, accelerating or steering too harshly or driving too fast for the road conditions. If skidding occurs, ease off the brake or accelerate and try to steer smoothly in the

direction of the skid. For example, if the rear of the vehicle skids to the right, steer quickly and smoothly to the right to recover".

(See also rule 100, **ABS**).

Skidding can often occur when the road is wet or icy. Rule 206 provides:

"**Drive** extremely **carefully** when roads are icy. Avoid sudden actions as these could cause a skid. You should

- drive at a slow speed in as high a gear as possible; accelerate and brake very gently
- drive particularly slowly on bends where skids are more likely. Brake progressively on the straight before you reach a bend. Having slowed down, steer smoothly round the bend, avoiding sudden actions
- check your grip on the road surface when there is snow or ice by choosing a safe place to brake gently. If the steering feels unresponsive this may indicate ice and your vehicle losing its grip on the road. When travelling on ice, tyres make virtually no noise."

Discussion

Historically it was assumed that a skid was a "neutral event" that may or may not have been due to negligence: *Laurie* v *Raglan Building Co, Limited* [1942] 1 KB 152. That was not to say that, where the facts permitted, a skid could not be interpreted as evidence of negligence: see, for example, *Browne* v *De Luxe Care Services* [1941] 1 KB 549 and *Ritchies' Car Hire Limited* v *Bailey* (1958) 108 L.Jo. 348. Regardless of the particular facts, it would usually behove a motorist to proffer an explanation for a skid or sudden swerve: *Liffen* v *Watson* [1940] 1 KB 556. Essentially, however, no presumption of either culpability or exoneration would ensue.

This proposition (and these cases) must now be considered in the light of the judgment in *Richley* v *Faull* [1965] 1 WLR 1454. A collision occurred between two cars being driven in opposite directions on the bend of a wet road. MacKenna J. stated (at 1457) that:

"I respectfully disagree with the statement that the skid by itself is neutral. I think that the unexplained and violent skid is in itself evidence of negligence".

The presumption of negligence can be rebutted by proof that the skid happened without the driver's default. This will often present the defendant motorist with an almost insurmountable challenge.

Rule 99, after all, particularises the causes of skidding in terms that almost exclusively relate to the conduct of the driver. The presumption has nonetheless been displaced where there is snow or the road is icy. In *Custins* v *Nottingham Corporation* [1970] RTR 365 a bus driver proceeding very slowly, and having seen a pedestrian a long way off, applied his brakes slowly and managed to pull up the vehicle without difficulty. Unfortunately the bus then ran out of control and struck the claimant. Salmon L.J. stated (at 368) that:

> "It is common knowledge that if you are unlucky when you are driving on an icy road, whatever care you may take, it sometimes by misfortune occurs that the vehicle does slide and gets out of control. In these circumstances, it does not mean that there is any negligence on the part of the driver so that he can be blamed in any way for the bus getting out of control."

Conversely, in *Laurie* v *Raglan Building Co, Limited* (ibid) a driver was negligent in driving a 10-wheeled lorry at 10–12mph without chains on a road surface that was "snowed and frozen and like glass".

Signals

Highway Code

The Code provides:

Signals

"85. Signals warn and inform other road users, including pedestrians, of your intended actions.

You should

- give clear signals in plenty of time, having checked it is not misleading to signal at that time
- use them, if necessary, before changing course or direction, stopping or moving off
- cancel them after use
- make sure your signals will not confuse others. If, for instance, you want to stop after a side road, do not signal until you are passing the road. If you signal earlier it may give the impression that you intend turning into the road. Your brake lights will warn the traffic behind you that you are slowing down

- use an arm signal to emphasise or reinforce your signal if necessary. Remember that signalling will not give you priority.

86. You should also

- watch out for signals given by other road users and proceed only when you are satisfied that it is safe
- be aware that an indicator on another vehicle may not have been cancelled."

Discussion

Failure to perform any of the requirements outlined in rules 85 and 96 will constitute prima facie evidence of negligence which, in the event of a collision, can be interpreted as being either partly or wholly causative of the accident: *Daborn v Bath Tramways Motor Co. Limited and Smithey* [1946] 2 All ER 333. It was held in *Pratt v Bloom* (1958) Times, October 21, that the duty of a driver changing direction is firstly to signal, and secondly to see that no-one was incommoded by is change of direction, and the duty is greater if he first gives a wrong signal and then changes it.

Misleading signals

In *Goke v Willett* [1973] RTR 422 the defendant approached a service station on his offside with two entrances situated some 50 metres apart. He activated his right indicator but, instead of turning into the first entrance, continued to the second turning, whereupon he slowed and suddenly applied his brakes. A following vehicle, whose driver was evidently confused by the defendant's signal, collided with the rear of his vehicle. The Court of Appeal found that there was "abundant evidence" to justify a finding of negligence against the defendant. Edmund Davies LJ echoed the findings of the trial judge and stated (at 428) that:

> " . . . . it is the duty of a driver who intends to turn to the right, . . . to indicate without ambiguity by hand signal (a) his intention to slow down, and (b) his intention to turn to the right".

Where a motorist driving along a main road gives a misleading signal (either because he fails to cancel an earlier signal or the indicator is accidentally activated), with the result that another motorist pulls put of a side road and across his path, he will invariably be at least partly to blame for the accident. In *Another v Probert* [1968] Crim.L.R. 564 the Divisional Court held that it was "clearly careless" to give such a misleading signal and the offending motorist was convicted of careless driving. In *Wadsworth* v *Gillespie* [1978] CLY 2534 the driver giving a misleading signal was held to be one-third liable.

Hand signals

Hand signals are not usually deemed to be necessary where a vehicle slows down or stops in the normal way: *Flack* v *Withers* (1960) Times, March 22. Indeed, rule 85 of the Highway Code confirms that: "Your brake lights will warn traffic behind you that you are slowing down." Nonetheless the application of brake-lights does not absolve the driver of a vehicle from the necessity of giving a hand signal of his intention to stop or slow down, when the circumstances, such as the need to execute a sudden or unexpected stop, render it necessary to do so: see *Goke* v *Willett* (ibid), *Croston* v *Vaaghan* [1938] 1 KB 540 and *Gussman* v *Grattan-Storey* (1968) 112 Sol.Jo. 884. In *Jungnickel* v *Laing* (1966) 111 Sol.Jo.19, the Court of Appeal drew a distinction between a "stop" and a "sudden reduction" of speed. Davies LJ stated:

> "If a driver was going to make a sudden, heavy stop, he was under a duty to signal traffic behind him of his intention: but a driver, even on the M1, was under no duty to give a warning of his intention merely because he decelerated his speed".

Turning round

There are three methods of turning round:

- using a side road
- making a u-turn
- turning in the road

Using a side road

Recognised as the safest method of turning round, a motorist must nevertheless keep a continuing look-out for other vehicles and pedestrians, particularly when reversing into a side road on the right. Reversing into a main road from a side road will almost invariably constitute negligence – The Driving Manual states (at 79) that such a manoeuvre should *never* be attempted. This general pronouncement was supported in *M'Knight* v *General Motor Carrying Co* 1936, S.C. 17.

U-turn

A U-turn means turning the car right round without any reversing. It should never be undertaken on a motorway, in a one way street or wherever a road sign forbids it. Described by The Driving Manual (at 184) as a "potentially dangerous manoeuvre", it demands that a driver maintains a good all-round observation. A motorist will be negligent if he "creates the danger of a collision" by not keeping a proper look out before executing a U-turn: *Jenkins* v *Holt* [1999] Times, May 27.

Turning in the road

The Driving Manual states (at 183) that:

> "The secret of this manoeuvre is to keep the vehicle moving slowing whilst steering briskly. Close control of the clutch is essential."

All-round observation "is essential throughout the manoeuvre" and a motorist should always give way to passing vehicles.

Reversing

Highway Code

Reversing is governed by rules 176 to 179 of the Highway Code. Rule 177 provides "Do not reverse from a side road into a main road. When using a driveway, reverse in and drive out if you can". Rule 178 stresses the importance of maintaining a good all-round observation:
"Look carefully before you start reversing. You should

- use all your mirrors
- check the "blind spot" behind you (the part of the road you cannot see easily in the mirrors)
- check there are no pedestrians, particularly children, cyclists, or obstructions in the road behind you
- look mainly through the rear window
- check all around you before you start to turn and be aware that the front of your vehicle will swing out as you turn
- get someone to guide to you if you cannot see clearly".

Discussion

Whilst a motorist should always endeavour to avoid reversing from a side road into a major road, the use of the words "if you can" in rule 177 suggests something other than an absolute prohibition, at least in relation to a driveway. Indeed, in *M'Knight* v *General Motor Carrying Co*, 1936, S.C. 17, a case where a cyclist travelling along a main road was struck by a bus that reversed from a cul-de-sac, liability was established on the basis of excessive speed rather than the mere act of emerging backwards, which Lord Hunter described (at 22) as a "perfectly proper manoeuvre". It can be argued, however, that modern traffic conditions probably demand a more strict observance.

When a driver engages another person (be it either his passenger or a pedestrian) to guide his manoeuvre, he should ensure that those "eyes" are in a position to keep an adequate observation. Thus, in *Liddon* v *Stringer* (1967) Times, April 15, a bus driver was liable when his conductor, in an effort to guide the vehicle backwards, maintained a position that was level with the back of the bus, with the result that he was unable to see a pedestrian attempting to cross from behind the back of the vehicle.

Railway level crossings

Highway Code

Rules 265 to 272 should be referred to in respect of railway level crossings. These rules outline the basic provisions applicable to motorists and, where relevant, pedestrians. (Specific guidance for pedestrians can also be found at rule 32). There are three types of crossings: controlled crossings (rules 266 to 268), user-operated crossings (rules 269 to 270) and open crossings (rule 270). Rule 272 outlines the correct practice to be adopted in the event of accidents and breakdowns.

Discussion

Duty of Drivers
The Highway Code outlines a detailed scheme of practice for motorists, much of which, understandably, turns on the notion of precedence. None of this obviates the basic requirement that a person crossing a railway line should continue to look and listen for an approaching train. This obligation is of particular effect where the line is straight and the motorist/pedestrian has an uninterrupted view: see, for example, *Karamalis* v *South Australian Railways Commissioner* [1976] 14 S.A.S.R. 432.

Duty of railway authorities
Railway authorities – essentially Railtrack – owe a duty to traffic to keep the crossing in a state of proper repair. Particular emphasis is placed on the comparative height of the rails and the surrounding

roadway, and the condition of any inclined approaches leading to the crossing: see, for example, *Guilfoyle* v *Port of London Authority* [1932] 1 KB 336 and *Swain* v *Southern Railway* [1939] 2 KB 560. The Railway Clauses Consolidation Act 1845, section 47 and, sometimes the Level Crossings Act 1983, impose additional requirements in relation to the provision, design and maintenance of gates, stiles and other protective equipment.

Chapter 3

The Emergency Services

The emergency services – essentially the police, fire and ambulance authorities – perform a unique role in protecting the public from peril. Vehicles answering 999 calls are subject to extraordinary pressures, not least a need to get to (and sometimes from) the scene of an emergency as quickly as possible. Other motorists, by convention, regard emergency vehicles as being in a privileged position, an impression reinforced by the Highway Code (see, for example, rule 194) and various statutory and regulatory provisions. Yet, no emergency will justify the driver of a police vehicle, fire engine or ambulance taking the risk of a collision with another vehicle.

This chapter is concerned with the liability of the emergency services and will consider:

- General duty
- Training and assessment of emergency drivers
- Speed
- Police pursuit of a stolen vehicle
- Compliance with traffic lights and signs
- Duty of other motorists to emergency vehicles
- Duty of the police to protect or warn against hazards on the highway
- Stationary and parked emergency vehicles.

General duty

The driver of an emergency vehicle owes the same duty of care as any other driver. Despite a number of statutory exemptions applicable to various highway prohibitions, speed and traffic lights included, a police officer, fire fighter or ambulance driver is subject to the same general standard appropriate to other motorists.

The nature of this concomitant duty was outlined in *Gaynor* v *Allen* [1959] 2 All ER 644. The claimant, while crossing a dual carriageway, was knocked down by a police motorcycle. The police officer was travelling at a speed of approximately 60 mph. The statutory speed limit was 40 mph. McNair J. held that the officer was negligent. He stated (at 646) that:

"In my judgment the driver of the police motorcycle, on this occasion as regards civil liability must be judged in exactly the same way as any other driver of a motorcycle on that occasion. He, like any other driver of a motor vehicle, on that occasion owed a duty to the public to drive with due care and attention and without exposing the members of the public to unnecessary danger".

That the same duty applies to the other emergency services was confirmed in *Wardell-Yerburgh* v *Surrey County Council* [1973] RTR 462. The defendant's fire engine was driving in the centre lane (of three) at 50mph in fog when it collided with a mini-van being driven by the claimant's husband. Giving judgment against the local authority, and following *Gaynor* v *Allen*, Brubin J. stated (at 464) that the driver of the emergency vehicle owed to the public the same duty of care as any other driver.

'Wood v Richards [1977] RTR 201 subsequently provided a clear example of the nature and operation of the duty and standard applicable to the emergency services. The defendant, a police patrol driver on a motorway, received an emergency call. The state of the traffic led him to decide to drive on the hard shoulder. His view of the hard shoulder was unfortunately blocked by a "large continental lorry" so that, almost as soon as he moved to his nearside, he collided with a stationary lorry parked by an emergency telephone box. The police officer was convicted of careless driving. His appeal was dismissed. Eveleigh J. expressed his conclusion (at 204) in terms of uninpeachable clarity:

"I find it impossible to say that a special standard should be applied in the case of a police officer. The test must be: what is due care and attention in all the circumstances of the case?"

Training and assessment of emergency drivers

Police

The Metropolitan Police Force recognises three categories of police driver:

- "Basic" drivers, who fulfil a patrol function within the constraints of the Highway Code;
- "Response" drivers, who are trained to respond to emergency calls, and
- "Advanced" drivers, who respond to 999 calls and are specially trained for pursuit driving.

(It is understood that other forces follow a broadly similar system of categorisation.)

During 1998 Metropolitan Police vehicles were involved in 5,937 accidents: police drivers were deemed blameworthy in 40% of these collisions. Nationally, 22 people were killed by police vehicles between March 1998 and April 1999. Of those who died, 17 were as a result of high speed pursuits of suspected criminals, whilst the others were killed by cars answering emergency calls.

Increased efforts directed at improving these statistics are promised for 1999/2000, with the stated aim of reducing the number of collisions involving police vehicles "by at least ten per cent" by Summer 2000. A new Safe Driving Policy, launched in July 1999, promises the following:

- A new permit which contains details of driver classification and dates of last driver assessment and eye tests.
- Driving assessments every three years.
- Driving records to be part of annual appraisals.
- Intervention by supervisors if drivers have six points on their police driving record.
- Automatic suspension for drivers who attain 10 points on their police driving record.
- Fitting of black boxes to immediate response and armed response vehicles. It is anticipated that the first black box will be fitted in early 2000: disclosure of the automatic record will obviously form an increasingly important part of the evidence in cases involving police vehicles.
- Education of officers through leaflets, posters and a training video.
- One member of each senior management team to take specific responsibility for the driving of officers.

Police drivers can meanwhile refer to the Metropolitan Police Instruction Manual, section 8, which deals with police driving and vehicles, and an ancillary guide entitled "Advice on Use of Blue Lights and Sirens".

Fire service

The London Fire Brigade (in a system that almost certainly reflects that favoured by most other brigades) classifies its drivers as follows:

- "Light" drivers, who are confined to general purpose vehicles and
- "Emergency Fire Appliance" drivers.

Light driving requires nothing more than an ordinary driving licence and compliance with the standard laid down in the Highway Code. Emergency drivers must be at least 23 years of age, have held an ordinary driving licence for three years and completed a similar period of operational experience. Candidates are then required to obtain an ordinary LGV licence: training for this (known as Part 1) involves an intensive nine day course. Successful candidates then undertake a two week "response" course (or Part 2), which involves one day of skid training, three days progressive driving in a car and four days "blue light" training in a fire appliance, as well as instruction in relevant driving theory. Fire fighters who pass the course are qualified to drive "on the bell".

The London Fire Brigade has no system of refresher instruction or re-assessment, although it may be that such courses are introduced in the future. Other brigades, with fewer drivers to manage and assess, may well have a limited system of continuing training. Nonetheless all drivers have recourse to an Emergency Fire Appliance Driving Manual.

Investigations are carried out on all accidents involving fire appliances: the precise method of examination depends on the severity of the incident under consideration. Most are considered under the line management established within each Fire Station. Some, of course, are remitted to the Police/Crown Prosecution Service.

Speed

Maximum speed limits are prescribed by the Road Traffic Regulation Act 1984, sections 81, 86, 89 and Schedule 6 (see Chapter 2, pages 13–16). Section 87 provides a qualified exemption for fire brigade, ambulance and police vehicles:

> "No statutory provision imposing a speed limit on motor vehicles shall apply to any vehicle on an occasion when it is being used for fire brigade, ambulance or police purposes, if the observance of that provision would be likely to hinder the use of the vehicle for the purpose for which it is being used on that occasion."

Note that the exemption specifically attaches to the emergency services and not services performed in (a real or perceived) emergency. Thus, "police purposes" does not include law enforcement by a private individual: see *Stratham* v *Gladstone* 1937 JC 11 where, ironically, a motorist followed a police car in order to obtain evidence to prosecute the police driver for speeding.

The driver of an emergency vehicle travelling at speed must also exercise appropriate care and skill proportionate to his speed. Compliance with this duty can often require either a tactical reduction in speed or the appropriate use of an effective warning to other road users. In *Dyer* v *Bannell* (1965) 109 Sol.Jo. 216 the claimant, an "experienced driver", was struck by a police patrol car being driven at 45mph in a road where the statutory limit was 30mph. The constable flashed his headlamps but gave no audible warning of his approach. Judgment was entered for the claimant. The court found that the police officer would not have been negligent "if there was nothing against him" except his speed. However:

> "If he found it necessary to drive so fast he must exercise a degree of care and skill proportionate to his speed, and remember that the ordinary road user in a built up area would not expect motor vehicles to drive at that speed. It was desirable that particular care should be taken to give audible warning of approach or otherwise to make known the police car's presence"

This case was followed in *McLeod* v *Receiver of the Metropolitan Police* [1971] Crim LR 364 and *Cox* v *Dixon* (1994) 134 NLJ 236. In both cases it was held that in certain circumstances excessive speed could, of itself, constitute negligence. In *McLeod* a police car being driven at 70mph in answer to an emergency call skidded into a collision with another car. It was held that whilst the police driver was not to be criticised for driving fast in answering an emergency, he should not have driven at such a speed that he lost control of his vehicle. Similarly, in *Cox* a police officer was driving an unmarked car at 60mph on a dual carriageway in a built up area that was subject to a 30mph speed limit, when he collided with a car that emerged from a side road. It was held that the exercise of police duty was, in the circumstances of the material incident, "no excuse whatsoever" for driving at 60mph. (See also *Gaynor v Allen* (ibid).)

Police pursuit of a stolen vehicle

Many accidents occur in the pressurised environment created by a high speed pursuit of a stolen vehicle. Statistics suggest that, in this regard, innocent motorists and bystanders are as vulnerable as the police driver and criminal suspect. Once again, however, the duty owed by the participating motorists broadly accords to that owed by other road users.

Duty of police drivers

In *Marshall* v *Osmond* [1983] QB 1034 a police officer was engaged in a pursuit of a car he correctly believed to have been stolen by a gang of youths. As the officer attempted to drive alongside the stolen vehicle he braked, skidded and a collision ensued. The Court of Appeal held that:

- the duty owed by a police officer driving a vehicle in pursuit of a suspected criminal was the same as that owed to anyone else, namely, to exercise such care and skill as was reasonable in all the circumstances;
- the "vital words" in this proposition of law are "in all the circumstances". This means that allowance must be made for the fact that the officer was driving in stressful circumstances in an attempt to arrest somebody engaged in a criminal activity. Thus, even though he "no doubt made an error of judgement", his conduct did not amount to negligence.

Accordingly, whilst the general duty owed by the pursuing officer is the same as that owed by any driver, the reality of the pursuit means that he will, in practice, be allowed a little more latitude than that accorded to the ordinary motorist.

Duty of the driver of the stolen vehicle

A person who drives a vehicle taken without the owner's consent owes a duty of care to all lawful users of the highway, including a pursuing police officer. This principle originally derived from the judgment in *Knightley* v *Johns* [1982] 1 WLR 349, a case where the police responded to a motorist's negligence, rather than his criminal activity. It was held that a motorist ought to foresee that if he is negligent and creates an emergency other people, particularly police officers, fire fighters and ambulance drivers, are likely to be put at risk.

In *Langley* v *Dray & M.T. Motor Policies at Lloyds* [1997] PIQR 508 this proposition was developed and applied to the apprehension of a criminal activity. A police officer sustained injury in the course of a pursuit of a car driven by a young man who had taken it without the owner's consent. The chase, which endured for four to five miles, involved speeds of 70mph (in a 30mph limit), driving the wrong way down one way streets, crossing junctions controlled by traffic lights when the lights showed red and narrowly missing a collision with at least one pedestrian. The court outlined the duty of the suspect driver to the police driver as follows:

"In my judgment, the duty of care owed by the first defendant to the claimant was the ordinary duty to drive with the skill and care of the ordinary driver so as to minimise the risk of reasonably foreseeable injury to others using the highway lawfully: or negatively, not to drive without the skill and care of the ordinary driver so as to cause reasonably foreseeable injury to others using the highway lawfully. The duty is owed to all and not to a particular or limited class of people

The circumstances in which a driver can be liable to police officers can, I believe, be stated thus. If by careless or reckless driving a defendant creates circumstances in which he foresees, or should foresee, that he will be pursued by police officers in a manner which increases the risk of injury to those police officers, or other road users, and he is pursued in that manner without negligence on the part of the pursuer, then, if in consequence injury is caused to a pursuing officer or other road user, the defendant will be liable."

Compliance with traffic lights and signs

The Traffic Signs Regulations and General Directions 1994 (S.I. 1994 1519) outline several exemptions applicable to the emergency services. Regulation 15(2), in relation to compliance with traffic signs, provides:

"On an occasion where a vehicle is being used for fire brigade, ambulance or police purposes and the observance of the requirement (to comply with traffic signs) would be likely to hinder the use of that vehicle for one of the purposes then, that requirement conveyed by the sign in question shall be that the vehicle shall not proceed beyond that sign in such a manner or at such a time as to be likely to endanger any person."

Regulation 33(b) stipulates an identical exemption in relation to traffic lights.

The Zebra, Pelican and Puffin Pedestrian Crossing Regulations and General Directions 1997, regulations 12(1)(e) and 13(1)(f), similarly dispense with strict compliance with the requirements of pelican and puffin crossings. Interestingly, in addition to the police, fire and ambulance authorities, the regulation also exempts vehicles operated by the national blood service.

It should again be noted that these provisions confer a qualified exemption. The understandable desire to get to the scene of an emergency as quickly as possible is always outweighed by the necessity of avoiding any action likely to endanger other road users. In *Ward* v *London County Council* [1938] 2 All ER 341, a case which obviously pre-dated the existing regulatory framework, it was held that whilst the driver of a fire engine "must get to the scene of the fire as quickly as possible", he had "no business charging into other cars" that did not drive aside and accord him precedence at lights that were otherwise red against him.

More recently, in *Aldridge* v *Metropolitan Police Commissioner* [1998], unreported, the Court of Appeal considered the application of regulation 15(2) in the context of a rapid response police officer driving on the wrong side of the carriageway. It was held, following the precise wording of the exemption, that such driving was permissible as long as it was undertaken in a manner that was not likely to endanger any person. The officer, in this instance, erred in proceeding at a speed (25mph) that would not have allowed him to stop in the event that a pedestrian walked out in front of him, a misfortune that actually occurred a matter of seconds after he commenced the manoeuvre.

Regulation 33(1)(b) was similarly considered in *Griffin* v *Mersey Regional Ambulance* [1998] PIQR 34. The claimant drove across a junction controlled by traffic lights at a speed of 25mph when the lights were green in his favour. He was involved in a collision with the defendant's ambulance that had entered the junction against a red signal. The Court of Appeal upheld a finding of negligence against the defendant. It stated that whilst there was no absolute bar to the ambulance crossing on red, the duty on the emergency driver was a high one. Regulation 33(1)(b) had the effect of converting the red light into a "give way" sign rather than an absolute prohibition.

Duty of other motorists to emergency vehicles

Rule 194 of the Highway Code (repeated in slightly fuller form on page 112 of The Driving Manual) governs the manner in which other motorists should respond to the approach (be it audible or visual, or both) of an emergency vehicle:

> "You should look and listen for ambulances, fire engines, police or other emergency vehicles using flashing blue, red or green lights, headlights or sirens. When one approaches do not panic. Consider the route of the emergency vehicle and take appropriate action to let it pass. If necessary, pull to the side of the road and stop, but do not endanger other road users."

Modern sirens and flashing lights, if deployed properly, are capable of denoting the approach of an emergency vehicle from some considerable distance. Moreover, in many cases the other motorist is obliged to acknowledge and negotiate exactly the same traffic or weather condition that confront the emergency driver. It is of no great surprise, therefore, that in many of the reported cases findings contributory negligence were made against the ordinary motorist.

For example:

- *Gaynor* v *Allen* (ibid); the pedestrian claimant stepped off the kerb and walked across the road without taking another look to her right. Had she done so she would have noticed the approach the police motorcycle. Contributory negligence was assessed at one-third.
- *Wardell-Yerburgh* v *Surrey County Council* (ibid) ; the claimant, like the driver of the fire engine, drove at an excessive speed and failed to keep a proper look out in fog. Both parties equally to blame.
- *Cox* v *Dixon* (ibid); the claimant, as an experienced driver, "must have known perfectly well" that another motorist might enter the junction at speed. Held to be one-third to blame for the collision.
- *Griffin* v *Mersey Regional Ambulance* (ibid): the claimant could and should have seen and heard the ambulance, and he should have realised that a van that had come to a halt ahead of him had done so to let the ambulance through. Contributory negligence was assessed at sixty percent.

Duty of the police to protect or warn against hazards on the highway

Do the police owe a duty of care to protect road users from or to warn them of hazards discovered whilst going about their duties on the highway?

This is an area of law that is, perhaps, characterised by a certain flux. Historically the position was clear: police officers did not owe a duty of care to motorists confronted by hazards such as accident debris, oil of the carriageway or malfunctioning traffic lights. This was so even if the constabulary had been alerted to the presence of the hazard some time prior to the material accident. But the certainty of this proposition has recently been challenged (albeit by a case arising under Scots law) in a way that requires, at the very least, a cautious reassessment of the relationship existing between the police and road users.

The case of *Hill v Chief Constable of West Yorkshire* [1989] AC 59 marks an appropriate starting point. The Court of Appeal, in considering the role of the police in the context of a criminal investigation, concluded that no duty of care was owed to individual members of the public. Lord Keith (at 59) said:

> ". . . a chief officer of the police has a wide discretion as to the manner in which the duty is discharged. It is for him to decide how available resources should be deployed, whether particular lines of inquiry should or should not be followed and even whether or not certain crimes should be prosecuted. It is only if his decision on such matters is such as no reasonable chief officer of police would arrive at and that someone with an interest to do so may be in a position to have recourse to judicial review. So the common law, while laying on chief officers of police an obligation to enforce the law, makes no specific requirements as to the manner in which the obligation is to be discharged. That is not a situation where there can be readily inferred an intention of the common law to create a duty towards individual members of the public."

This case was followed in *Ancell v McDermott* [1993] 4 All ER 385. A motorist inadvertently deposited a trail of diesel fuel on a road in Bedfordshire. The presence of the hazard came to the notice of officers from the Hertfordshire and Bedfordshire police forces. Indeed the police visited the scene of the spillage on at least one occasion. The matter was reported to the Bedfordshire highways department. Otherwise no protective or remedial action was taken. Shortly after the police left the scene the claimant skidded on the diesel fuel, lost control of her car and collided head-on with an oncoming lorry.

The Court of Appeal concluded that the action brought against the Chief Constables of the two constabularies should be struck out as disclosing no cause of action. The police were under no duty of care to protect road users from, or to warn them of hazards discovered by the police while going about their duties on the highway. No special relationship existed between motorists and the police giving rise to an exceptional duty to prevent harm from dangers created by another. The extreme width and scope of such a duty of care would impose on a police force potential liability of almost unlimited scope. It would also be against public policy because it would direct extensive police resources and manpower from, and hamper the performance of, ordinary police duties.

Clough v Bussan (West Yorkshire Police Authority) [1990] 1 All ER 430 concerned a similar set of facts. A collision occurred at a junction controlled by automatic traffic lights. The evidence suggested that traffic lights were not functioning properly and it was common ground that the police had been informed of the malfunction sometime prior to the accident. It was contended that the police had negligently failed to respond to the failure of the lights as they should have done.

It was held, at first instance (QBD sitting at Leeds), that nothing had occurred in the circumstances to impose on the police a particular duty of care to the motorists in collision. Although the police were under a duty to preserve law and order and to protect life and property the fact that a police station received information that traffic lights at a particular junction were malfunctioning was not sufficient to establish a special relationship.

Then, in *Gibson v Chief Constable of Strathclyde Police* (1999), Times May 11 it was suggested that the police could owe a duty of care to road users where the officers, having "taken control" of a hazardous road traffic situation, later left the hazard unattended. It is important, from the outset, to note that this case arose in the Outer House of the Court of Session in Scotland. It is of no direct authority in England and Wales, although in that the Court necessarily considered and distinguished various English authorities, it must be considered to be of persuasive relevance.

The police attended and took control of a hazardous road traffic situation, namely a collapsed bridge, but later left the scene unattended and without having put up cones, barriers or other signs. Shortly thereafter a driver (the pursuer) collided with the hazard.

Lord Hamilton concluded that a duty was established. He held that:

- once a constable has taken charge of a road traffic situation which, without control by him, presented a grave and immediate risk of death or serious injury to road users likely to be affected by the particular hazard, it seemed consistent with the underlying principle of neighbourhood for the law to recognise him as being in such a relationship with road users as to satisfy the requisite element of proximity;
- *Hill v Chief Constable of West Yorkshire* could be distinguished as the relevant observations were made in the context of criminal investigations. There was no close analogy between the exercise of the police of their function of investigating and suppressing crime and the exercise by them of their function of performing tasks concerned with safety on the roads.

It is respectfully submitted that the second assertion, namely the distinction of *Hill*, is almost certainly wrong. The Court made a brief reference to the judgments in *Ancell* and *Clough* without, it would appear, acknowledging the fact that both cases clearly applied the ratio and reasoning of *Hill* to the performance of tasks concerned with road safety. Nonetheless the first proposition undoubtedly adds something to the existing case law. It is quite easy to perceive a distinction between cases where the police, being aware of a hazard, reasonably exercised an operational discretion not to deploy resources and those cases where officers determined to "take control" of the situation. Such direct involvement, it is submitted, necessarily creates a proximity between the police and the public, whether one invokes the language of "special relationship" or "exceptional duty" expressed in *Ancell* and *Clough*, or the reference to the "underlying principle of neighbourhood" favoured by Lord Hamilton.

Stationary and parked emergency vehicles

Emergency vehicles are often pulled up or parked in inconvenient or dangerous places on or by the carriageway. It is recognised that the duty to protect the public from peril will usually assume priority over the niceties of safe parking practice: *Amos v Glamorgan County Council* (1967) 66 LGR 166. Precaution must still be taken to give other motorists an adequate indication that "there was something unusual there and keep clear" (*Amos*, 168).

This will particularly apply to heavy goods vehicles, such as fire tenders, although the principle necessarily extends to all vehicles whose stationary position is determined by the occurrence of an emergency. What constitutes an "adequate indication" will depend on the individual circumstances of each case. In daylight and on a reasonably straight stretch of road the flashing light itself ought to constitute a sufficient warning of danger. Where a vehicle such as a fire engine is parked just round a bend an "earlier warning (such as a red side light), even in daylight, might well be desirable" (*Amos*, 169).

Chapter 4

Passengers (1): Private Motor Vehicles

This chapter will examine the duty owed to and by passengers in private motor vehicles.

Duty to Passengers

A motorist who agrees to carry a passenger in a vehicle owes a duty to exercise reasonable care and skill for the safety of that person. This liability was originally settled in *Lygo v Newbold* (1854) 9 Ex. 302, confirmed in *Readhead v Midland Railway Co.* (1869) (4) QB 379 and followed in *Luddit v Ginger Coote Airway Limited* [1947] AC 233. It applies whether the carriage is undertaken for reward or gratuitously; *Lygo (ibid,* per Parke B, 305). It extends to the luggage and belongings of the passenger: see, for example, *Houghland v R.R. Low (Luxury Coaches) Ltd* [1962] 1 QB 694.

In most cases the question of liability will turn on the manner and care with which the driver managed and controlled the vehicle. However, there are three other areas of particular interest, namely (i) the use of seat belts, (ii) overcrowding and (iii) specific warnings to be given to the passengers.

Seat belts

Is the driver under an obligation to encourage, insist or ensure that his passenger wears a seat belt? Different considerations apply depending on whether the passenger is an adult or a child.

Adults

In *Pasternack v Poulton* [1973] 1 WLR 476, it was suggested that the driver was under a duty to "take some step" directed to seeing that his passenger wore the seat belt provided. A number of subsequent cases lent tacit approval to this proposition: see, for example, *McReady v Miller* [1979] RTR 186 and *Gibbons v Priestley* [1979] RTR 4.

But any such notion was implicitly rejected in *Froom* v *Butcher* [1976] QB 286 where Lord Denning stated (at 296) that:

> "Everyone knows, or ought to know, that when he goes out in a car he should fasten the seat belt. Under the Highway Code a driver may have a duty to invite his passenger to fasten his seat belt: but adult passengers possessed of their faculties should not need telling what to do."

More recently, in *Eastman* v *South West Thames Regional Health Authority* [1991] RTR 389, the Court of Appeal firmly disapproved of the proposition that there is any general duty imposed upon the driver to exhort his passenger to wear a seat belt.

It is, nevertheless, possible that the duty suggested in *Pasternack* may still survive in certain limited situations. In *Eastman* the court repeatedly noted that "each case has its own special facts" and Russell L.J. entertained (at 393) the notion that the driver would owe such a duty "in very special circumstances such as the infancy of the claimant". It is easy to envisage a similar conclusion where, for example, the passenger was either physically or mentally impaired or where, by some quirk or social circumstance, he had little or no previous experience of a modern motor vehicle. It is submitted that if the facts reported in *Gibbons* v *Priestley* (ibid) were repeated (namely if a driving instructor failed to ensure that his pupil wore a seat belt), the carrier would almost certainly be found to be liable in negligence.

Children

The driver must ensure that all children under 14 years of age wear a seat belt or sit in an approved child restraint: Motor Vehicles (Wearing of Seat Belts by Children in Front Seats) Regulations 1993, Motor Vehicles (Wearing of Seat Belts by Children in Rear Seats) Regulations 1989 and the Highway Code, rule 76.

Overcrowding

A motorist is bound to ensure that his vehicle does not become overcrowded and, if too many passengers are carried, he will be liable for any damage resulting therefrom. In *Houghton* v *Trafalgar Insurance Co. Ltd* [1954] 1 QB 247 an accident occurred at a time when six people were being conveyed in a car that was designed to carry a driver and four passengers. The Court of Appeal dismissed the submission (effectively from the driver's insurance company) that the vehicle was thereby unroadworthy. Lord Denning observed (at 249) that it "would surprise most motor-car owners" to be told that they would be negligent "if they squeezed in an extra passenger, one more than the ordinary seating capacity". But in *Clarke v National Insurance & Guarantee Corpn. Ltd.* [1964] 1 QB 199, where a four-seater car was found to contain nine adults, a capacity that "seriously impaired" its steering, braking and control, with the result that it collided with another car whilst descending a steep hill, it was held that the vehicle was "so grossly overloaded that it was unroadworthy".

Specific warnings

It would seem that in some circumstances the driver has a duty to give warning of specific dangers known to him before the passenger enters the vehicle and/or during the course of the journey. In *Harris v Perry & Co.* [1903] 2 KB 219, a case concerning the London Underground Railway, it was suggested that a passenger's rights extended to a warning of danger to be met with on the journey. This approach was followed in *Lewis v Burnett & Dunbar* [1945] 1 All E.R.550. The defendants, a lorry driver and his mate, offered a soldier a lift in the back of their lorry. Their intended route passed beneath a bridge which, to their knowledge, but not that of their passenger, had a very low headroom. The defendants failed to warn the passenger of the danger ahead and when the lorry passed under the bridge his head was struck and he received fatal injuries. Croom-Johnson J., having noted that the degree of care must vary according to the circumstances and that it is impossible to define exactly, concluded that the defendants should have warned the passenger about the presence and condition of the bridge before he actually entered the vehicle.

Duty of Passengers

Passengers owe a duty to take reasonable care for the safety of each other, other road users and, of course, their driver. Particular mention should be made of (i) the opening of vehicle doors and (ii) a number of miscellaneous situations wherein the passenger may be held to be under a duty to assist the driver.

Opening doors

It is an offence under the Road Vehicles (Construction and Use) Regulations, reg. 105 (SI No. 1073) to open a door of a motor vehicle on a road so as to cause injury or danger to any other persons.

Unfortunately for a claimant a breach of such a statutory regulation does not give rise to a civil remedy: see *Barkway* v *South Wales Transport* [1950] 1 All E.R. 392. But the negligence of a passenger who opens a door usually speaks for itself. Earlier editions of the Highway Code exhorted passengers to "make sure that (the door) will not hit anyone passing on the road or pavement" (1993, rule 137). Rule 214 of the 1999 Code adopts a wording that complements the mandatory nature of the regulatory/criminal sanction: "You MUST ensure that you do not hit anyone when you open your door". In *Brown* v *Roberts* [1982] 2 All E.R. 263 a pedestrian was struck and injured by a van door opened by a passenger in the vehicle. Megaw J. was satisfied (at 265) that the defendant "opened the door without taking due and proper care for pedestrians on the pavement".

Assisting the driver

When, if ever, does a passenger owe a duty to assist the driver? Passengers habitually perform a multitude of tasks, such as keeping a look-out, map reading and giving directions, and guiding the vehicle into and out of narrow spaces. Sometimes this assistance is proffered spontaneously, on other occasions it occurs at the instigation of the driver.

Rarely, however, will the court conclude that a finding of negligence should be made against a passenger. In *Scandle* v *Skeen* [1976] RTR 281 a driver and his passenger were killed when their vehicle was struck by a train as it crossed an unmanned level crossing. The suggestion that the passenger should have got out of the vehicle and guided the driver across was firmly rejected. Latey J. stated (at 292) that:

> "It is to me a novel proposition that a passenger in a car has a duty of care and no case was cited to support it. And the reason, I think, is a simple one. Decisions are in the hands of the driver. If they were not, much worse hazards of various kinds would be likely to arise. One does not interfere with the man at the wheel . . .".

The exception to the general rule is, once again, provided by the duty owed to a learner by his instructor or supervising driver. It has been held that a supervising driver (whether or not he is a professional instructor) and learner are jointly concerned in driving the car and together must maintain the same measure of control over the vehicle as an experienced and skilful driver: *Nettleship* v *Weston* [1971] 2 KB 691. In *Rubie* v *Faulkner* [1940] 1 KB 571 the supervising driver was able to see that the learner was about to overtake another vehicle on the bend of a road but, alas, neither said nor did anything to prevent it. An accident occurred. Hilbery J. concluded (at 575) that:

> ". . . it is the supervisor's duty, when necessary, to do what ever can reasonably be expected to be done by a person supervising the acts of another to prevent that other from acting unskilfully or carelessly or in a manner likely to cause danger to others, and to this extent, to participate in the driving."

Analogous reference can also be made to *R* v *Clark* (1950) Daily Telegraph, 30 May and *Gibbons* v *Priestley* [1979] RTR 4.

Chapter 5

Passengers (2): Public Service Vehicles; Buses, Mini-buses, Coaches and Taxis

The general duties outlined at pages xx apply (albeit with appropriate adaptation) to public service vehicles. Additional reference can be made to The Public Service Vehicles (Conduct of Drivers, Inspectors, Conductors and Passengers) Regulations 1990 (SI No. 1020). These provisions re-enact with amendments the similarly titled regulations issued in 1936, 1946, 1975 and 1980, to which allusion is often made in the reported cases.

Boarding and Alighting

The Public Service Vehicles (Conduct of Drivers, Inspectors, Conductors and Passengers) Regs. 1990, regulation 5 (1), provide that:

> "A driver and conductor shall take all reasonable precautions to ensure the safety of passengers who are on, or who are entering or leaving, the vehicle."

See also reg. 5 (5) (Chapter 6 page 3).

The Highway Code, rule 30, imposes a similar obligation on passengers:

> "Get on or off a bus only when it has stopped to allow you to do so. Watch out for cyclists when you are getting off."

Passengers

A passenger who attempts to board or alight from a moving vehicle does so at his own risk: see *Police* v *Okoukwo* [1954] Crim.L.R.869 and *Reid* v *MacNichol* (1958) S.L.T. 42 *(re: boarding)* and *M'Sherry* v *Glasgow Corp.* (1917) S.C. 156 *(re: alighting)*. A finding of contributory negligence will, at the very least, almost invariably follow. In *Guinnear* v *London Passenger Transport Board* (1948) 92 Sol.Jo. 350, a passenger attempted to board a bus that was still moving at 3–4 m.p.h. The bus then accelerated before the passenger had an opportunity to find a seat or take a firm hold. He fell from the vehicle into the road and sustained personal injury. It was held that each party was equally to blame: the claimant was negligent in boarding a moving bus and the defendant's driver was negligent in accelerating before he had made sure of the passengers' safety.

A passenger may also be at fault if he takes steps that are preparatory to alighting (such as standing or moving towards the door/rear platform) from a moving bus: see *Jude* v *Edinburgh Corpn.* 1943 S.C. 399 and *Wyngrove* v *Scottish Omnibuses* 1966 S.C. 47. But a finding of contributory negligence can often be avoided if his decision to stand or walk towards the door of a moving vehicle occurred after the signal to stop had been given: *Hall* v *London Tramways* (1896) RTLR 611, *Watt* v *Glasgow Corp* 1919 S.C. 300 and *Anderson* v *Belfast Corp* [1943] N.I. 34.

Driver/conductor

A bus driver will be negligent if he moves off while a passenger is still in the act of climbing aboard: *Steele* v *Belfast Corp* [1920] 2 IrR 125 and *Wilkie* v *L.P.T.B.* [1947] 1 All E.R. 258. This will still be the case where a driver only pulls away after the conductor had given him a signal to proceed: *McAlaughlin* v *Glasgow Corpn.* 1963 SLT (ShCt) 53 (at 54):

> "In my view, a bell from the conductor only authorises the driver to proceed, but does not absolve him from a duty to exercise reasonable care. So far as he is able from his position and with the assistance of his mirrors he must still take care."

In *Mottram* v *South Lancashire Transport Co.* [1942] 2 All ER 452 the claimant was one step behind a passenger who sounded the bell to proceed as he stepped off the bus. The bus immediately gathered speed causing the claimant to fall and sustain injury. It was held that it was putting the duty of a conductress (who was collecting fares on the upper deck) too high to say that she should have descended to the lower deck to see passengers off in safety.

But in *Davies* v *Liverpool Corp* [1949] 2 All ER 175 the bell was also rung by an unidentified and unauthorised passenger. The claimant, who had one foot on the step when the vehicle moved away, fell and sustained injury. She recovered against the defendant on the grounds that the conductor showed "a gross indifference" to the safety of passengers by not descending from the upper deck whilst the vehicle was at a stopping place. He might reasonably have foreseen such mischief had he come down more quickly.

Insofar as it is possible to reconcile these decisions, it is apparent that, as ever, each case turns on its own particular facts. Thus, whilst in *Davies* the vehicle stopped for an "appreciable time", so that it was unreasonable for the conductor not to have come down, in *Mottram* the timing afforded no reasonable opportunity for such action.

Neither the driver nor the conductor should cause the door to be opened before the vehicle stops; *Nicholson* v *Goddard* (1954) 118 J.B. 394.

Stopping and starting

The Public Service Vehicles (Conduct of Drivers, Inspectors, Conductors and Passengers) Regs. 1990, regulation 5, (5) provide that:

> "A driver shall, when picking up or setting down passengers, stop the vehicle as close as is reasonably practicable to the left or nearside of the road."

See also reg. 5 (1) (ibid)

Discussion

Public service vehicles must be stopped and started with reasonable care and skill. Quite what the application of this duty demands of a driver, and particularly the precautions to be taken before starting off, is, in the light of the reported decisions, a matter of some ambiguity.

In *Manengela* v *Bay Passenger Transport Co. Limited* 1971 (4) S.A. 293, a South African case, a bus belonging to the defendant pulled away from the terminus as the claimant was still in the act of climbing aboard. His claim for damages for personal injury succeeded. Hart A.J. held (at 295) that:

> "A passenger in a moving bus ought to know or to foresee that many contingencies might arise in a busy street or roadway. For example, the sudden appearance of a pedestrian or child or animal or even another vehicle which could require the bus driver in the interests of safety to swerve or even to stop suddenly. Such considerations, however, do not arise in the case of a passenger in the act of mounting a stationary bus. He is entitled to expect that the driver will act reasonably and not start the bus in such a way as to dislodge him and endanger his safety. I agree entirely that absolute smoothness in starting a bus is a standard of perfection which cannot be expected, particularly in regard to so large a vehicle, but, on the other hand, the bus driver is required to take ordinary precautions in starting his vehicle and to observe due care, particularly to passengers in the act of mounting the bus. Any unusual or untoward jerks in such circumstances in my view constitutes an act of negligence, rendering the owner of the bus liable for any resultant damage."

Accordingly the driver, before starting off, should keep a visual check on passengers to see that (insofar as conditions will allow) they have sat down or have grasped a hand hold.

This case echoed an earlier decision, *Geeves v London General Omnibus Co.* (1901) 17 T.L.R. 249, where a passenger successfully sued the bus operator when his fall was caused by the vehicle starting with a "jerk and swerve".

Then, in *Azzupardi v State Transport Authority* [1982] 30 S.A.S.R. 434, a case from South Australia, where a passenger fell as the bus started suddenly and as she was still walking down the aisle towards a seat in the centre of the vehicle, Chief Justice King held that:

> "I do not think, however, that a bus driver's duty to exercise reasonable care for the safety of his passengers requires that he wait until they are seated before putting the bus in motion. It is common experience that passenger buses move off from bus stops while passengers are making their way to their seats. There are, as the Judge observed "the exigencies of time tables." If executed with ordinary smoothness, the manoeuvre presents no problem to passengers. Most passengers cope with the movement of the bus simply by positioning their feet and balancing, perhaps place a hand on a seat or other hand hold as the movement of the bus is felt. The occasional passenger may feel the need to grasp a hand hold securely. In ordinary experience, passengers do not fall if the bus is driven with ordinary care and skill. It seems to me that in the absence of some indication that a particular passenger is specially vulnerable or if some other special factor, the bus driver is not required to wait until all passengers are seated or have otherwise stationed themselves. Nevertheless the decision of the bus driver to move off before all passengers are seated or have otherwise taken up a stationary position in the bus, place an obligation on him to ensure that the manner of the movement of the bus is not such as to constitute a danger to the passengers."

In *Gardner v United Counties Omnibus Co. Limited* [1996] CLY 4477 a 78 year old claimant, who "had not been properly seated", was thrown from her position as the bus negotiated a bend. It was held that the driver was not obliged to check that the passengers were properly and appropriately seated and safeguarded before a journey commenced. To expect as much would place an "impossible burden" on the defendant.

More recently, in *Fletcher v United Counties Omnibus Co. Limited* [1998] PIQR P154, a 22 year old claimant boarded a single operator double decker bus. She walked "at a perfectly reasonable pace" down the aisle to a seat in the middle of the vehicle. The bus driver "pulled out gently and at a reasonable speed", having consciously chosen to do so without waiting for the claimant to take her seat. He was not behind schedule. After "a few seconds", by which time the bus had travelled about 100 yards from the bus stop, the driver was obliged to do an emergency stop. He "was in no way open to criticism on that account". The claimant, meanwhile, could not reasonably have been expected to reach her seat by the time of the emergency stop. Her claim, nevertheless, was dismissed. Simon Brown L.J. stated (at 159/160) that:

> "Really, it seems to me no more than a matter of commonsense to recognise that drivers of public buses cannot sensibly be expected to wait for all boarding passengers to take their seat wherever they may choose to sit, before they can properly drive away the bus from the stop. Of course bus companies and bus drivers must take steps to ensure the reasonable safety of their passengers, but, as it seems to me, that duty is satisfied by the provision within all these public buses of appropriate safety support. No doubt if elderly or infirm passenger come aboard, or even indeed passengers encumbered by luggage, children or whatever else, may expose them to some particular risk of accident, then special steps may need to be taken on their account. But one only has to imagine the consequences of the driver routinely having (to wait for all passengers to sit down before moving off) to recognise the impossibility of accepting that that is indeed the driver's basic obligation".

It might well be observed that, in the context of modern bus design and the pressures of an increasingly congested road network, the courts are becoming more and more sympathetic to bus operators. And yet it is possible to reconcile these decisions. Essentially, once a passenger has successfully boarded the vehicle, a driver does not ordinarily have to wait and/or ensure that he has taken a seat before properly driving away. A passenger will only recover damages where the bus moves off with a sudden and unreasonable jerk or swerve, or where the driver should be aware, either because of a passenger's age, disability or encumbrance, that it would be unreasonable to begin the journey before he is secured and/or seated.

Sometimes traffic and/or highway conditions make it impossible for a bus to halt at the authorised stop and/or in a manner demanded by regulation 5 (5). Where this happens, it is the duty of the driver/conductor to "control the whole situation", meaning that, in practical terms, he should ensure that passengers are given an appropriate warning and/or the vehicle does not move off again before it is safe to do so: *Prescott v Lancashire United Transport Co. Limited* [1953] 1 WLR 232.

Driving and collisions

The driver of a public conveyance owes a duty of care to passengers to "act with the skill and care of a reasonable driver": *Glasgow Corp* v *Sutherland* [1951] 95 Sol.Jo. 204 This duty is owed to *all* passengers. In *Western Scottish Motor Traction* v *Allam* [1943] 2 All E.R. 742 Viscount Simon L.C. noted (at 743) that:

> "There may well be cases – the case of a person, for example, with a baby in his arms – in which a standing passenger has no free hands with which to anchor against the consequences of a sudden and pronounced swerve, and I agree with the view that the duty of reasonable care owed by the driver to those on board extends to all passengers whether they are "holding on" or not."

Sudden application of brakes

Where a passenger is injured as a result of the sudden application of the vehicle's brakes there is a prima facie inference of negligence. This can be refuted by an explanation that is consistent with the action of an "ordinary, reasonable, careful driver": *Parkinson* v *Liverpool Corp* [1950] 1 All E.R. 367. In this case a dog ran into the road when a bus was only 5–6 yards away. The driver applied his brakes "with some suddenness" causing an elderly passenger (who had risen from her seat in order to alight) to be thrown to the floor. The driver gave evidence that when confronted with such an emergency he would try to save the animal's life without endangering anybody else. It was held that the driver, in the context of a split second decision demanded by an unforeseen emergency, had properly applied his mind to the respective safety of the animal and his passengers. There was no negligence.

A bus driver was also exonerated when the emergency braking was necessitated by the sudden emergence of a pedestrian: *Wooller* v *London Transport Board* [1976] RTR 206. Interestingly, Edmund Davies L.J. observed (at 207 (L) to 208 (A)) that to demand that a bus should proceed in a manner that would allow it to pull up without having to brake suddenly was a counsel of perfection which ignored modern traffic conditions.

These decisions can be contrasted with the outcome in *Glasgow Corp* v *Sutherland* (ibid). As a tramcar moved away from a stopping place, the driver was forced to suddenly apply his magnetic brake when a dog darted in front of the vehicle. A passenger, who had not had time to take his seat, was thrown to the ground and injured. It was held that the driver had not acted with reasonable skill and care. It was of some significance that the passenger, to the driver's certain knowledge, had not had time to get to his seat, and that the magnetic brake was known to have an extremely sudden effect. This opinion did not, in the judgment of Lord Simmons (at 204), either doubt or affirm the decision in *Parkinson (ibid)*. As ever, therefore, each case presents its own particular questions of fact.

Sudden swerve

Evidence of an extra-ordinary swerve or sway might well be suggestive of negligence on the basis of res ipsa loquitur: *Wragg* v *Grout and London Passenger Transport Board* (1966) 116 L.J.O. (See also *O'Hara* v *Scottish M.T. Co.* 1941 S.C. 363 and *Doonan* v *S.M.T. Co.* 1950 S.C. 136.) However, "extra-ordinary" means in practice that the swerve, movement or sway must be associated with the vehicle travelling at an excessive speed or some other wholly exceptional occurrence, in the absence of which there will be no grounds for holding the driver negligent: *Western Scottish Motor Traction* v *Allam* (ibid).

Collisions

Liability depends, as in virtually every road traffic accident, on the negligence and/or breach of statutory duty of the drivers of the vehicles involved. The passenger may, of course, retain a right of action against the owner of the vehicle in which he was travelling, even though the accident may have been partly (or even largely) caused by another motorist.

Passenger struck by a roadside object

General Duty

The requisite duty of care was succinctly expressed in *Radley* v *London Passenger Transport Board* [1942] 1 All E.R. 433 by Humphreys L.J. who stated (at 434) that:

> "The duty upon the defendants, the owners of the omnibus, is clearly a duty to take at least reasonable care that the passengers shall not be injured when they are in an omnibus. It is common knowledge that one of the things which leads to accidents is the omnibus running into some obstruction".

The mere fact of the collision is prima facie evidence of negligence. This presumption of fact is rebutted if the defendant adduces evidence to prove that the accident occurred without negligence.

Overhanging Trees

In *Radley (ibid)* the infant claimant was a passenger of the top deck of a bus belonging to the defendants. While it was proceeding along a country road, its upper part brushed against branches of a tree over-hanging the carriageway, and some of the windows were broken. The infant claimant sustained injury when a splinter of glass penetrated her eye. The claim succeeded. Humphreys J., having outlined the general duty of care, noted (at 434) that:

> "The question I have to ask myself is this: whether there is any evidence, one way or the other, to explain why the driver, driving along this road at mid-day, did not see this obstruction which was clearly visible. There is no evidence with regard to that, and I can only assume that the driver did not, in fact, see the overhanging branch."

Each case, of course, turns on its particular facts, a reality Humphreys J. was keen to emphasise. He continued:

> "I do not want my judgment to be misunderstood or that it should be assumed that it goes one whit further than the facts of the present case. I can well imagine circumstances in which the defendants might be able to prove that, although omnibuses had come into collision with branches, it was really no fault of the driver that he did not notice the particular branch which was the cause of the accident. In a high gale, a branch may break in an instant and topple down. If that had happened here and it had been proved that, when it happened, the omnibus was perhaps only 20 feet away, it might have been a perfectly good answer for the defendants to say that it was an act of God which could not have been prevented by reasonable care on the driver's part."

In *Hale v Hants & Dorset Motor Services Limited* [1947] 2 All E.R. 628, a case founded on identical facts to those in *Radley*, judgment was also entered against the defendants, notwithstanding the fact that it was dark and the overhang was very slight. The driver had formed the opinion that the tree was a potential source of danger, but failed to give it a wide berth and could not be absolved from responsibility for the ensuing collision. By way of contrast, in *Trinder v Great Western Railway Co.* (1990) 35 T.L.R. 291, another case where a passenger travelling on the upper deck of a bus was struck in the face by an over-hanging branch, the claim failed as there was no evidence to suggest that the driver was driving too near the trees or that he had any reason to suspect that they were overhanging.

Lamp-posts

In *Simon* v *The London General Omnibus Co. Limited* (1987) 23 T.L.R. 463 the claimant was a passenger on the top of the defendants' omnibus. As it travelled around a corner, the claimant's arm, which protruded from the vehicle, struck the horizontal arm of a lamp-post. The passenger's claim was dismissed. Mr. Justice Ridley stated (at 464) that:

> "If it could have been shown that there was an obstruction of such a nature that with reasonable care the driver ought to have seen it and ought to have realised the fact that it would or might hit a passenger on the omnibus, there might have been evidence of negligence. No such evidence was given."

It would appear, however, that the fact that the claimant's arm was hanging out of the window was not a fact that contributed to the failure of the action. Presumably the defendant should have foreseen that passengers would reasonably act in this manner. Indeed, in *Bohlen* v *Perdue* [1956] 1 W.W.R. 364, a case from the Alberta Supreme Court, where an infant's protruding arm struck a roadside pole, the defendant was found to have been negligent. The driver, who was probably driving too close to the kerb, ought reasonably to have foreseen the possibility of such an occurrence.

Intra-passenger injury

Overcrowding

Public conveyances must not become overcrowded. This means, in practical terms, that the driver/conductor must take reasonable steps to prevent more passengers boarding a vehicle that is already full to capacity: *Pickering* v *Belfast Corp* [1911] 2 IrR 224. Whether this standard, originally articulated before the start of the First World War, can be reasonably upheld in the light of modern commuter travel is, perhaps, a matter of some debate. Nevertheless all buses and coaches are licensed to carry a certain number of sitting and/or standing passengers, and breach of this limitation (particularly given that most buses now operate a single means of access adjacent to the driver's seat) will render the vehicle owner prima facie liable for any damage resulting therefrom.

Violent and/or drunken passengers

A vehicle operator will not be liable for the unforeseen negligence and/or wilful violence of its passengers. But where it is apparent to the driver/conductor that a passenger is likely to be a danger to other passengers, whether by reason of his physical or mental condition, drunkenness or any other outward manifestation of violence or threat, he is under a duty to take reasonable steps to prevent that person from entering the vehicle. This duty, it is submitted, also extends to an obligation to remove disorderly passengers.

In *Murgatroyd* v *Blackburn Tramways* (1887) 2 T.L.R. 451, a man who was obviously in a drunken condition was allowed to enter a tramcar, whereupon he pushed a woman and her child so that she was injured and the infant was killed. Lord Esher M.R. stated:

> "The man was so drunk that it was idle for the defendant to (suggest otherwise) If the conductor did not see the drunken man go up to the top of the car he ought to have seen him go up. If he was inside collecting fares, the company ought to have as many servants as were necessary for the purpose of saving the passengers from unreasonable risk."

Seat-belts

The law governing the fitting of seat belts in coaches and mini-buses can be found in the RV (Construction and Use) Regulations 1986 (SI No. 1078) as (repeatedly) amended. Coaches and mini-buses (but not "large buses") first used on or after 1st October 1988 must have seat belts fitted. Coaches and mini-buses wholly or mainly used for the carriage of "three or more" children must provide a "properly equipped" seat/seat belt for each child carried, regardless of the date of manufacture, although coaches used before 1st October 1988 were not obliged to comply until 10th February 1998. Regulation 46 outlines both the general provision(s) and the (almost inevitable) list of exemptions.

Defective Vehicles

Refer to chapter 10, page 129.

Taxis

A taxi driver, like all motorists and carriers, owes a duty to take reasonable care and skill for the safety of his passengers, as well as any luggage or belongings brought into the vehicle.

This liability can also vicariously attach to the registered and/or actual proprietor of the vehicle. The precise nature and ambit of this duty depends on whether the vehicle is licensed as a hackney carriage (and whether the same operates within or outside London) or a minicab.

Hackney carriages

London

Under the London Hackney Carriages Act 1843, the registered proprietor, and also the actual proprietor of a hackney carriage is liable for the acts of the driver while he is plying for hire, whether or not the relationship of employer and employee exists between them: *Gates* v *Bill* [1902] 2 KB 38. Thus, in *Venebles* v *Smith* (1877) 2 QB D 279, where the claimant was run over "through furious driving on the part of the cab driver" and *King* v *London Improved Cab Company Limited* (1889) 23 QBD 281, a case where a passenger in a horse and cab was injured as a result of the negligence of the driver, successful actions were brought against the registered proprietors.

Outside London

The Town Police Clauses Act 1847, sections 37 – 68, provide that the registered proprietor must be treated as the employer of the driver for the purpose of claims by third parties in respect of damage caused by the negligence of the driver while plying for hire. In *Bygraves* v *Dicker* [1923] 2 KB 585 Lush J., having reviewed and affirmed the earlier case of *Keen* v *Henry* [1894] 1 QB 292, concluded that the Act of 1847 created "the same artificial relationship" as that established by the Act of 1843 for hackney carriages in London.

Minicabs

Much depends on the ownership and management of the vehicle, the precise service offered to the public and whether the passenger knows, or ought to be aware, of the nature of the defendant's business. In *Rogers* v *Night Riders* [1983] RTR 324 the defendants were a firm operating a minibus service. The claimant, believing them to be a car hire firm, arranged to be taken to Euston Station. During the course of the journey she sustained injury when a door flew open, struck a parked vehicle and bounced back. The defendants argued that as the car belonged to the driver, who was not their employee, and as they had no control over the management of the car, the driver was an independent contractor for whose negligence they were not liable. The Court of Appeal disagreed and gave judgment for the claimant. The defendants had undertaken to provide a car and driver to take the claimant to her destination and they owed her a duty to take care to see that the vehicle was safe and reasonably fit for that purpose. It was not a case of vicarious liability: it was a case of a primary and non-delegable duty. Dunn L.J. (at 331) stated:

> "There was no suggestion in the evidence in the court below, and it was never put to the claimant, that she was told of the true position of the firm, that is to say, the car did not belong to them and that the firm was no more than a booking agent for owner-driven cars over which they had no control. If there had been such evidence and if the true nature of the defendant's business had been known to the claimant, the situation would have been different, but so far as the claimant was concerned, she was dealing with a car-hire firm, not a mere booking agency and, accordingly, the defendants were under a primary duty to her."

Chapter 6

Pedestrians

Pedestrians and motorists owe each other a reciprocal duty of care. In *Boss* v *Litton* (1832) 5 C & P 407 Denman C.J. (at 409) stated that: "All persons, paralytic as well as others, have a right to walk on the road and are entitled to the exercise of reasonable care on the part of persons driving along it". This was followed by *Craig* v *Glasgow Corporation* (1919) 35 TLR 214 where it was held (at 216) that: "A man has an absolute right to be (on the road) and it is the duty of drivers of vehicles not to run him down". As to a pedestrian's obligation to other road users: "When a man steps from the kerb into the roadway, he owes a duty to traffic which is approaching him with risk of collision to exercise due care": *Nance* v *British Columbia Electric Railway* [1951] AC 601 at 611.

Yet this is also to acknowledge that the duties of pedestrians and motorists are necessarily different. In *Baker* v *Willoughby* [1970] AC 467 Lord Reid (at 490) stated:

> "A pedestrian has to look to both sides as well as forwards. He is going at perhaps 3 m.p.h. At that speed he is rarely a danger to anyone else. The motorist has not got to look sideways though he may have to observe over a wide angle ahead; and if he is going at a considerable speed, he must not relax his observation, for the consequences may be disastrous, and it sometimes happens that he sees the pedestrian is not looking his way and takes a chance the pedestrian would not stop and that he can safely pass behind him. In my opinion, it is quite possible that the motorist may be very much more to blame than the pedestrian."

In the Highway Code a pedestrian's duties are outlined at rules 1–33 and a driver's obligations appear at rules 180–186. (Reference can also be made to rules 85, 130, 141, 146, 156, 167–175 and 178.)

Pedestrian stepping out into the path of a motorist

The Highway Code

Rule 7 expressly incorporates "The Green Cross Code":

> "7. *THE GREEN CROSS CODE.* The advice given below on crossing the road is for all pedestrians. Children should be taught the Code

and should not be allowed out alone until they can understand and use it properly. The age when they can do this is different for each child. Many children cannot judge how fast vehicles are going or how far away they are. Children learn by example, so parents and carers should always use the Code in full when out with their children. They are responsible for deciding at what age children can use it safely by themselves.

A. **First find a safe place to cross.** It is safer to cross using the subway, a foot-bridge, an island, a zebra, a pelican, toucan, or puffin crossing, or where there is a crossing point controlled by police officers, a school crossing patrol or a traffic warden. Where there is a crossing nearby, use it. Otherwise choose a place where you can see clearly in all directions. Try to avoid crossing between parked cars (see Rule 14) and on blind bends and brows of hills. Move to a space where drivers can see you clearly.

B. **Stop before you get to the kerb,** where you can see if anything is coming. Do not get too close to the traffic. If there is no pavement, keep back from the edge of the road but make sure you can still see approaching traffic.

C. **Look all around for traffic and listen.** Traffic could come from any direction. Listen as well, because you can sometimes hear traffic before you see it.

D. **If traffic is coming, let it pass.** Look all around again and listen. But do not cross until there is a safe gap in the traffic and you are certain that there is plenty of time. Remember, even if traffic is a long way off, it may be approaching very quickly.

E. **When it is safe, go straight across the road – do not run.** Keep looking and listening for traffic while you cross, in case there is any traffic you did not see, or in case any traffic appears suddenly."

Discussion

When establishing the respective fault of the pedestrian and/or approaching motorist, reference can be made to the following factors:

- The extent and clarity of the view(s) afforded to the pedestrian;
- Whether the pedestrian looked to both his off-side and nearside before stepping off the kerb;
- Whether the pedestrian continued to keep a look-out as he crossed the highway;
- Whether the pedestrian was accompanied by a companion in whose observation he was entitled to rely;

- Whether the pedestrian elected to cross at an appropriate place and, particularly, whether he should have used a crossing situated nearby;
- The distance between the pedestrian and the vehicle at the moment he stepped out;
- Whether the vehicle was displaying lights that should have been visible to the pedestrian;
- Whether the driver sounded his horn;
- The vehicle's speed;
- Whether the motorist had seen, or ought to have seen and acknowledged the fact that the pedestrian had failed to look in his direction before stepping off the kerb.

Where a motorist drove at an excessive speed and/or failed to keep a proper look-out, and where the pedestrian's only fault was a failure to look again as she crossed the road, liability was decided on an 80: 20 apportionment in favour of the pedestrian: *Hurt* v *Murphy* [1971] RTR 186. Where a pedestrian merely failed to acknowledge (from the vehicle's headlights) that an approaching motorist was driving at an excessive speed, her contributory negligence was similarly limited to approximately 20%: *Mulligan* v *Holmes* [1971] RTR 179.

Conversely, where a driver's failure was limited to not noting that a pedestrian might be about to cross without looking in his direction, liability was split 30: 70 in favour of the motorist: *Williams* v *Needham* [1972] RTR 387.

It is quite possible for both parties to be equally to blame for the accident. In *Fitzgerald* v *Lane* [1988] 2 All E.R. 961 a pedestrian elected to cross at lights showing green in favour of approaching traffic. A motorist was travelling at an excessive speed and was not keeping a proper look-out for pedestrians. The House of Lords held that responsibility should be evenly shared between the parties.

It is abundantly clear, however, that where a pedestrian unreasonably steps into the path of a vehicle or at a point when the motorist has no opportunity to take any (or any effective) avoiding action, the court is entitled to conclude that the pedestrian was entirely the author of his own misfortune. Recent examples are provided by the cases of *Bateman* v *Goodman* (1998) Lawtel C8400 125 (pedestrian stepped into the path of a car about 1.5 seconds before impact) and *Norris* v *Tennant-Smith* (1998) Lawtel C8400241 (motorist only had 1 to 1.5 seconds to react).

Not walking on the pavement

The Highway Code

Rules 1 and 2 provide:

> "1. **Pavements or footpaths** should be used where provided. Where possible, avoid walking next to the kerb with your back to the traffic. If you have to step into the road, look both ways first.
> 2. **If there is no pavement or footpath**, walk on the right hand side of the road so that you can see oncoming traffic. You should take extra care and
>   - be prepared to walk in single file, especially on narrow roads or in poor light.
>   - keep close to the side of the road.
>
> It may be safer to cross the road well before a sharp right-hand bend (so that oncoming traffic has a better chance of seeing you) cross back after the bend."

Discussion

A pedestrian will not be at fault if, in order to avoid an obstruction such as a projecting building, he momentarily steps off the pavement: *Adamson* v *Roberts* (1951) SC 681. Inclement weather can also provide a justification for walking along the roadway rather than the pavement. Thus, in *Powell* v *Phillips* [1972] 3 All E.R. 864 a pedestrian was entitled to walk to a few feet out in the road for about 20 yards when the pavement was covered in snow and slush.

Indeed the reported cases go further than providing for isolated exceptions to the general rule that a pedestrian must stick to the pavement. In *Parkinson* v *Parkinson* [1973] RTR CA two pedestrians walking at night elected to proceed along the road as the off-side pavement was overhung by trees and "not in a very attractive condition". Both were struck by a car: one died, the other was seriously injured. Pearson L.J., in absolving the pedestrians of negligence, stated (at 196) that:

> "It may be said also that, in pursuance of the recommendation in the Highway Code (1959 ed, rule 3), it would have been better if they had been walking on the other side of the road. But it is depriving pedestrians of their natural rights as highway users too much to say that they must go on the off-side of the road and that they are not entitled to walk on the nearside".

This reasoning was upheld in *Kerley* v *Downes* [1973] RTR 188 where two pedestrians were struck as they walked with their backs to the traffic along an unlit country road.

Pedestrians crossing at traffic lights

The Highway Code

Rule 21 provides:

> "**At traffic lights.** There may be special signals for pedestrians. You should only start to cross the road when the green figure shows. If you started to cross the road and the green figure goes out, you should still have time to reach the other side, but do not delay. If no pedestrian signals have been provided, watch carefully and do not cross until the traffic lights are red and the traffic has stopped. Keep looking and check for traffic that may be turning the corner. Remember that traffic lights may let traffic move in some lanes while traffic in other lanes have stopped."

Discussion

In *Shephard* v *H West & Son Limited* (1962) 106 Sol.Jo. 391 the claimant attempted to cross a road at a junction controlled by traffic lights. Having ensured that the lights were showing red, she began to cross in front of stationary traffic. As she did so the lights changed to red-amber. She was struck by a lorry overtaking a stationary bus. The lights had changed as the lorry approached and the driver had not been compelled to bring his vehicle to a halt. The Court of Appeal held that the lorry driver was entirely to blame for the accident. Paull J. stated (at 392) that:

> "I have no hesitation in saying that the lorry driver was negligent A reasonable driver in such circumstances would not have let the front wheels of his lorry get level with the bus until the bus had got half way across the crossing. To pass a stationary vehicle under such circumstances was a dangerous practice."

See also *Fitzgerald* v *Lane* (ibid).

Standing on the pavement

(i) Vehicle mounting the pavement

Where a vehicle mounts the pavement and strikes a pedestrian it is likely that res ipsa loquitur will apply: *McGowan* v *Stott* (1920) 99

LJKB 357 and *Ellor* v *Selfridge & Co. Limited* (1930) 46 TLR 336. The vehicle, put bluntly, is in "a position where it has no right to be": *Laurie* v *Raglan Building Company Limited* [1942] 1 KB 152.

(ii) Vehicle overhanging the pavement

In *Chapman* v *Post Office* [1982] RTR 165 the claimant was standing on the kerb of a pavement at a bus stop when she was hit by the wing mirror of a Post Office van passing along the road. Lord Denning M.R. stated (at 166) that:

> "I see no reason why a person standing on the kerb is guilty of negligence at all; even if she leans out or has her back turned to the oncoming traffic. Even if she went an inch or two into the roadway, I cannot see that would amount to negligence in the slightest. The very fact that a van driver hits with his wing mirror a lady standing legitimately on the kerbside means that he is at fault and she is not".

Children as Pedestrians

See Chapter 11 , pages 146 to 147.

Pedestrian liable to motorist

A pedestrian owes a duty to other traffic to exercise due care. (This is, of course, one aspect of the "Rules for pedestrians" at rules 1 to 33 of the Highway Code). In *Nance* v *British Columbia Electric Railway Co. Limited* (ibid), a case where a pedestrian stepped blindly into the path of a tram, Viscount Simon offered (at 611) the following proposition:

> "Generally speaking, when two parties are moving in relation to one another as to involve risk of collision, each owes to the other a duty to move with due care, and this is true whether they are both in control of vehicles, or both proceeding on foot, or where one is on foot and the other controlling a moving vehicle".

Otherwise, and quite predictably, most of the reported cases reflect the particular vulnerability of motor cyclists. In *Eames* v *Cunningham & Capps* (1948) 92 Sol. Jo. 314 and *Barry* v *MacDonald* (1966) 110 Sol.Jo. 56, both cases where a pedestrian stepped off the kerb without looking, with fatal consequences to an approaching motor cyclist, the motorist was found to be entirely blameless and judgment was entered against the pedestrian.

Sometimes a pedestrian's culpability is crystal clear. In *Gilmour's Curator Bonis* v *Wynn* (1995) The Times, September 18, a pedestrian stood in the road in order to throw stones, a piece of wood and a half brick at a passing car. The driver panicked, lost control and collided with his young assailant, who subsequently brought a claim against the motorist. It was held that the claimant was entirely "the author of his own misfortune" and (by implication) liable to the motorist.

Crossings

There are (in the context of the pedestrian road user) three types of crossing: the zebra (or "uncontrolled") crossing, the pelican/puffin/ toucan (or "controlled") crossing and school crossings. (Railway level crossings are considered separately in Chapter 2, pages 33 to 34). They are all the creation of statute (essentially sections 25 and 28 of the Road Traffic Regulation Act 1984) and, since 15th December 1997, have been regulated by The Zebra, Pelican and Puffin Pedestrian Crossings Regulations and General Directions 1997 (SI 1997 No. 2400). (For incidents occurring prior to this date, reference should be made to The Zebra, Pedestrian Crossing Regulations 1971 (SI No. 1525) and The Pelican Pedestrian Crossing Regulations and General Directions 1969 (SI No. 888, as amended). The Highway Code replicates and/or re-enforces many of the regulations: see rules 19, 20, 22, 23, 27, 87, 171, 173, 174, 184 and 186.

(i) Zebra ("Uncontrolled") Crossings

Pedestrians
The Highway Code, rule 19, provides:

> "**Zebra crossings.** Give traffic plenty of time to see and to stop before you start to cross. Vehicles will need more time when the road is slippery. Remember that traffic does not have to stop until someone has moved on to the crossing. Wait until the traffic has stopped from both directions or the road is clear before crossing. Keep looking both ways, and listening, in case a driver or rider has not seen you and attempts to overtake the vehicle that has stopped."

In *Maynard* v *Rogers* [1970] RTR 392 the claimant stepped onto an uncontrolled crossing without first looking to her right and was struck by the defendant's car coming from that direction. The claimant "must have been able to see the car if she had looked". Mocatta J. stated (at 394) that:

"(The) evidence does indicate that the defendant had very little opportunity of doing much to avoid this accident – unless, of course, one is expected to slow down to a snail's pace whenever one sees anybody using the pavement at the side of a road where there is a pedestrian crossing anywhere in the vicinity. On the other hand, I think, though I hesitate to use such a serious word as "negligent", that there might have been a substantial chance at the last moment of the claimant checking her course or jumping backwards or avoiding this car, had the defendant sounded his horn. It is difficult to blame oneself with any degree of seriousness for not having done so on the spur of the moment, but this is the type of accident for the avoidance of which, in particular, motor vehicles are equipped with horns, though people are very reluctant to use them these days. Taking all these various considerations into account, I think that the right conclusion here is to hold the plaintiff two-thirds and the defendant one-third to blame for this accident."

A similar conclusion followed in *Williams* v *Needham* (ibid): again the pedestrian was held to be two-thirds liable for failing to look before crossing.

Nonetheless in *Lawrence* v *W.N. Palmer (Excavations) Limited* (1965) 109 Sol.Jo. 358, where a pedestrian "proceeded without regard to whether there was other traffic on the road", her contributory negligence was limited to one-third. Similarly, in *Clifford* v *Drymond* [1976] RTR 134, where a pedestrian failed to look to her right (where she would have seen the defendant's vehicle travelling at approximately 30 m.p.h. and positioned about 75 feet away) before stepping onto the crossing, it was held that the claimant should only bear 20 percent of the blame.

The Zebra, Pelican and Puffin Pedestrian Crossings Regulations and General Directions 1997, regulation 19, additionally state that:

> **"Pedestrians not to delay on crossings**
> No pedestrian shall remain on the carriageway within the limits of a crossing longer than it is necessary for that pedestrian to pass over the crossing with reasonable despatch."

This does not mean that a pedestrian can run blindly on to (or across) a crossing. In *Kozimore* v *Adey* (1962) 106 Sol.Jo. 431 the claimant did just that before being struck by the defendant's car. (The defendant, meanwhile, failed to anticipate and provide against so unexpected an occurrence, and failed to accord precedence.) Responsibility was apportioned 75% to the claimant and 25% to the defendant.

Motorists

The Zebra, Pelican and Puffin Pedestrian Crossings Regulations and General Directions 1997 lay down three important rules governing the movement of traffic at zebra crossings:

> "18 **Prohibition against the stopping of vehicle on crossings**
>
> The driver of a vehicle shall not cause the vehicle or any part of it to stop within the limits of a crossing unless he is prevented from proceeding by circumstances beyond his control or it is necessary for him to stop to avoid injury or damage to persons or property.
>
> 24. **Prohibition against vehicles overtaking at crossings**
>
> (1) Whilst any motor vehicle (in this regulation called "the approaching vehicle") or any part of it is within limits of a controlled area and is proceeding towards the crossing, the driver of the vehicle shall not cause it or any part of it -
>
> (a) to pass ahead of the foremost part of any other motor vehicle proceeding in the same direction; or
>
> (b) to pass ahead of the foremost part of a vehicle which is stationary
>
> 25. **Precedence of Pedestrians over vehicles at Zebra crossings**
>
> (1) Every pedestrian, if he is on the carriageway within limits of a zebra cross, which is not for the time being controlled by a constable in uniform or traffic warden, before any part of a vehicle has entered those limits, shall have precedence within those limits over that vehicle and the driver of the vehicle shall accord such precedence to any such pedestrian.
>
> (2) Where there is a refuge for pedestrians or central reservation Zebra crossing, the parts of the crossing situated on each side of the refuge for pedestrians or central reservation shall, for the purposes of this regulation, be treated as separate crossings."

Reference should also be made to rules 167 – 171 of the Highway Code.

Regulation 25 (in various historical guises since its initial introduction in 1951) has provoked some debate as to whether it creates an absolute liability or a qualified duty dependant on negligence or a failure to take reasonable care. Many of the reported cases reflect this confusion. In *Scott* v *Clint* (1960) Times, October 28, *Hughes* v *Hall* [1960] 2 All E.R. 504 and *Neal* v *Bedford* [1966] 1 QB 505, it was held that the (comparable) regulation imposed an absolute duty, so that a driver must accord a pedestrian precedence, however unexpectedly or suddenly he crosses, and that it was quite immaterial whether there was any evidence of negligence or failure to take reasonable care. But in *Lester* v *Pearson* [1952] 2 QB 668, *Lockie* v *Lawton* (1959) 124 JP

24 and *Burns* v *Bidder* [1967] 2 QB 227 it was held that the duty was only to take reasonable steps to let the pedestrian have precedence. It is not easy to reconcile these conflicting strands of opinion. It is submitted that (given the relatively inflexible nature of the concurrent criminal liability) the duty imposed by regulation 25 is (for all practical purposes) absolute. Of course this does not preclude a finding (in appropriate circumstances) of contributory negligence. Nor, perhaps, does it mean that in one limited situation – namely where a driver's control of his vehicle is removed by an occurrence (such as an act of God or latent defect) which is outside his possible or reasonable control – a motorist may still avoid a finding of fault: see *Levy* v *Hockey* (1961) 105 Sol.Jo.157 and *Burns* v *Bidder* (ibid).

A person who is walking across a pedestrian crossing pushing a bicycle having started on the pavement on one side on foot and pushing the bicycle with both feet on the ground is a "foot passenger" within the meaning of the regulations: *Crank* v *Brooks* [1980] RTR 441.

(ii) Pelican ("Controlled") Crossings

Pedestrians
The Highway Code, rules 22 – 24, provide:

> "**22. Pelican crossings.** These are signal-controlled crossings operated by pedestrians. Push the control button to activate the traffic signals. When the red figure shows, do not cross. When a steady green figure shows, check the traffic has stopped and then cross with care. When the green figure begins to flash, you should not start to cross. If you have already started you should have time to finish crossing safely.
> **23.** At some pelican crossings there is a beeping sound to indicate to blind or partially sighted people when the steady green figure is showing, and there may be a tactile signal to help deafblind people.
> **24.** When the road is congested, traffic on your side of the road may be forced to stop even though the lights are green. Traffic may still be moving on the other side of the road, so press the button and wait for the signal to cross."

(Reference should also be made to rule 25. ***Puffin and toucan crossings*** and rule 26, ***Staggered pelican or puffin crossings***)

Pedestrian passage is likewise governed by regulation 15 of The Zebra, Pelican and Puffin Pedestrian Crossings Regulations and General Directions 1997. The provision, like rule 22 of the Highway Code (above), outlines the significance of the red and green pedestrian light signals and explains when, in the interests of safety, pedestrians should and should not cross the carriageway. Regulation 19 (**Pedestrians not to delay on crossing**) similarly applies to pelican and puffin crossings.

Pedestrians must, of course, maintain an appropriate (and continuing) look-out for traffic. But this does not necessarily extend to a duty to keep a look-out for motorists entering the junction against a red traffic light. In *Tremayne v Shell* (1986) Times, December 11, a pedestrian negotiating a complicated multiple road junction at night was struck by a car that had passed the stop line against red traffic lights. The Court of Appeal held that proceeding against the red traffic light was conclusive against the motorist. The pedestrian, whether or not he looked in the direction of the oncoming car, was entitled to assume that traffic would stop on the light turning red.

Motorists

Regulation 12 of the Zebra, Pelican and Puffin Pedestrian Crossings Regulations and General Directions 1997 outlines the "significance of the vehicular light signals at pelican crossings". Essentially:

- the green light indicates that vehicles may proceed beyond the stop line and cross the crossing; 12(1)(a),
- the red light prohibits vehicles from crossing the stop line or, if the stop line is not visible, beyond the post "or other structure" on which the light is mounted; 12(1)(d) and (3),
- the steady amber light conveys the same prohibition as the red signal, save that a vehicle may continue if it so close to the stop line when the lights change that it cannot safely be stopped without proceeding beyond the stop line; 12(1)(c),
- the flashing amber light provides that traffic may proceed subject to the precedence to pedestrians already on the crossing; 12(1)(f).

(See also regulations 13 re. **Significance of the vehicular light signal at puffin crossings**).

Regulation 18 (**prohibition against stopping**) and 24 (**prohibition against overtaking**) similarly apply to pelican and puffin crossings (see page 73). Regulation 24, in particular, gives statutory effect to a principal previously recognised at common law. In *Skolimowski v Haynes* [1983] CLY 2525 a "slightly disabled" foreign pedestrian started to cross when the "green man" was lit, and was still crossing when the "red man" came on. Traffic on the inside lanes stopped to allow her to cross. She was struck by a vehicle which overtook on the outside lane.

It was held, at first instance, that the motorist was liable, although the pedestrian's contributory negligence was assessed at one-third. Precedence of pedestrians is governed by regulation 26 which provides:

> "When the vehicular light signals at a Pelican Crossing are showing the flashing amber signal, every pedestrian, if he on the carriageway or a central reservation within the limits of the crossing (but not if he is on a central reservation which forms part of a system of staggered crossings) before any part of a vehicle has entered those limits, shall have precedence within those limits over that vehicle, and the driver of the vehicle shall accord such precedence to any such pedestrians."

A motorist is entitled to rely on a green light in his favour. In *Carter v Sheath* [1990] RTR12 an infant pedestrian (aged 13) ignored the prohibition of the "red man" and was struck by a "good, careful driver". No finding of negligence was made against the motorist. Nonetheless a driver must still keep a lookout for pedestrians liable to cross without looking. Thus, in *Fitzgerald v Lane* (ibid), a case where two cars struck a pedestrian crossing the road at a pelican crossing with the light showing red for pedestrians and green for traffic, all parties were held to be equally to blame for the accident.

(iii) School Crossings

Section 26 of the Road Traffic Regulation Act 1984 provides that "authorities" (principally county councils or the Commissioner of Police in the Metropolis) are empowered to arrange for the patrolling of crossings used by children on their way to or from school or on their way from one part of the school to another.

School crossings are essentially indicated by a "school crossing patrol" (known by children across the land as a "lollipop man/ woman") wearing a uniform and exhibiting a prescribed sign: section 28 (1) of the 1984 Act. Some crossings are additionally marked by the erection of warning lights, although provision of the same is discretionary: see regulation 39 (2) of the Traffic Signs Regulations and General Directions 1994 (SI 1994 No 1519). The uniform, according to Home Office circular 3/89, should comprise a peaked cap, beret or yellow turban and a white raincoat, dustcoat or other white coat. The prescribed sign reads "STOP: Children". It should be exhibited in such a way that the approaching driver can see the words on the sign but it need not be full faced to oncoming traffic: *Hoy v Smith* [1964] 3All ER670.

Section 28 of the 1984 Act outlines the circumstances under which vehicles can be required to stop by a school crossing petrol. Sub-section 28 (2) reads:

> "He shall cause the vehicle to stop before reaching the place where the children are crossing or seeking to cross and so as not to stop or impede their crossing, and the vehicle shall not be put in motion again so as to reach the place in question so long as the sign continues to be exhibited."

The requirement at section 28 is absolute: the driver must stop. It is no defence in criminal proceedings (sub-section 28 (2) (a) and (b)) to show that no one was impeded by the motorists failure to stop: see *Franklin* v *Langdown* [1971] 3All ER 662 and *Wall* v *Walwyn* [1974] RTR24.

Traffic wardens (appointed under section 95 of the 1984 Act) may act as a school crossing patrol. When undertaking this role they may wear an approved traffic warden's uniform (rather than the usual white coat and peaked cap), but they must still display the prescribed sign.

Chapter 7

The Highway

Many road traffic accidents are caused or contributed to by the configuration, condition or obsruction of the highway. Potential defendants include central government (including the Department of the Environment, Transport and the Regions, and the Welsh Office), local authorities, various statutory undertakers (particularly those acting for or on behalf of the 'public utilities'), owners and occupiers. Motorists, as ever, bear a continuing responsibility for the control and management of their vehicles.

This chapter will consider the following:

- Highway maintenance
- Streetworks and the public utilities
- Highway obstruction
- Liability for dangers adjoining the highway

Highway Maintenance

The primary cause of action lies against the 'highway authority' for breach of the statutory obligation to "maintain" the highway under section 41(1) of the Highways Act 1980. The duty to maintain, which includes, where appropriate, an obligation to "repair", only applies to highways "maintainable at public expense". Section 58 of the Act provides a potential defence so that the highway authority will escape liability if it can prove that it took such care as in all the circumstances was reasonably required to secure that part of the highway to which the action relates was not dangerous for traffic.

The statutory duty

Section 41(1) of the Highways Act 1980 (HA 1980) provides:

> "The authority who are for the time being the highway authority for the highway maintainable at the public expense are under a duty . . . to maintain the highway."

The Act of 1980 consolidated the provisions of two other statutes, the Highways Act 1959 and the Highways (Miscellaneous Provisions) Act

1961, and many of the cases decided under the original regulatory framework are still relevant to an interpretation of the existing statutory obligation.

The "highway authority"

In most cases the highway authority is the county or metropolitan district council. The main exceptions to the generality of this rule are as follows:

- **London**
  The highway authority is the council of the London borough or, in the case of the City of London, the Common Council.

- **Non-metropolitan district councils**
  Non-metropolitan district councils can, on giving notice to the county council, opt to undertake the maintenance of certain highways within the district, subject to an obligation to indemnify the county council in respect of any claim arising out of a failure to maintain: section 50(2) and Part 1 of Schedule 7 of the HA 1980. The power of maintenance extends to footpaths, bridleways and urban roads which are neither trunk nor classified roads.

- **The Secretary of State for the Environment, Transport and the Regions**
  The Secretary of State is the highway authority for:
  (i) any trunk road, section 1, HA 1980;
  (ii) any road in respect of which he is appointed highway authority by statutory instrument;
  (iii) any other highway constructed by him, save where the obligation is delegated to the local highway authority.

Highway "maintainable at public expense"

The statutory duty to maintain only applies to highways "maintainable at public expense". Other roads and walkways remain the responsibility of private or corporate owners, or comprise one of he (comparatively small) number of highways which no-one is liable to maintain. A detailed consideration of the complex system of classification created by the HA 1980 is beyond the scope of this book. Suffice to state that the Act, by section 36(6), obliges the council of every county and London borough (including the Common Council of the City of

London) to keep an up-to-date list of all streets in their area which are so maintainable. Any practitioner (or indeed any person) wishing to confirm the status of a particular accident locus can inspect the list, which must be deposited at the office of the council, during all reasonable hours, free of charge: section 36(7).

The court's approach

In *Burnside* v *Emerson* [1968] 1 WLR 1490 (a case decided under the Highways (Miscellaneous Provisions) Act 1961) Lord Denning MR stated (at 1493/94) that an action against a highway authority involves three stages:

> "First: The claimant must show that the road was in such a condition as to be dangerous for traffic. In seeing whether it is dangerous, foreseeability is an essential element. The state of affairs must be such that injury may reasonably be anticipated to persons using the highway . . .
> Second: The claimant must prove that the dangerous condition was due to a failure to maintain, which includes a failure to repair the highway . . .
> Third: If there is a failure to maintain, the highway authority is prima facie liable for any damage resulting therefrom. It can only escape liability if it proves that it took such care as in all the circumstances was reasonable . . ."

This approach, which, it is submitted, equally applies to actions brought under the Highways Act 1980, has been followed in numerous subsequent cases, most recently in *Mills* v *Barnsley Metropolitan Borough Council* [1992] PIQR 291 (per Steyn LJ at 293).

Danger to traffic

Each case turns on its own facts

It is important to preface any consideration of the caselaw with a reference to the acknowledged rule that each case turns on its own facts. In *Rider* v *Rider* [1973] QB 505 Sachs LJ stated (at 514/515) that:

> "In every case it is a question of fact and degree whether any particular state of disrepair entails danger to traffic being driven in the way normally expected on that highway. The test is an objective one. To define that degree by using words or phrases suited to a particular case can end by putting an unwarranted gloss on the duty."

Lord Lawton LJ, commenting in the same case, applied (at 518) a practical gloss to the general principle:

"In most cases proof that there were bumps or small holes in a road, or slight unevenness in flagstones on a pavement, will not amount to proof of a danger for traffic through failure to maintain. It does not follow, however, that such conditions can never be a danger for traffic. A stretch of uneven paving outside a factory probably would not be a danger for traffic, but a similar stretch outside an old people's home, and much used by the inmates to the knowledge of the highway authority, might be."

In *Mills* v *Barnsley Metropolitan Borough Council* (ibid) Steyn LJ (at 294) similarly disavowed "such mechanical jurisprudence" as to say "that a depression of less than one inch will never be dangerous but one above will always be dangerous". He concluded:

"All that one can say is that the test of dangerous is one of reasonable foresight of harm to users of the highway and that each case will turn on its own facts."

"Defect" and "danger"

It can be argued, with some logic, that any "defect" in the highway, however slight, may cause an injury, but this is not what is meant by "dangerous" in the context of the statutory duty. In *Rider* v *Rider* (ibid) Lord Denning MR (who obviously felt that the courts had been "too much inclined to find a danger where there was none" (1494)), stated that in seeing whether a highway was dangerous "foreseeability is an essential element". Subsequent cases have, if anything, applied a more selective classification. In *Lawman* v *The Mayor, Aldermen and Burgesses of the London Borough of Waltham Forest* (1980),CA January 3, unreported Stephenson LJ suggested that even the urgent necessity of repair would not, of itself, identify a defect as being dangerous. This conclusion was reiterated in *James* v *Preseli Pembrokeshire District Council* [1993] PIQR 114 where it was held (per Ralph Gibson LJ at 119) that:

". . . the standard of care imposed by the law upon highway authorities is not to remove or repair all and any defect arising from a failure to maintain . . . which might foreseeably cause a person using the carriageway or footpath to fall and suffer injury, but only those which are properly to be classified as causing danger to pedestrians."

It would seem, however, that whilst foreseeability of injury must still be "an essential element" it can no longer be viewed as a talismanic mark of distinction between a "danger" and a mere "defect". It would also appear that the impetus for such a shift in emphasis (however subtle) is the perceived need to maximise increasingly scarce resources in an age of rapidly rising demand on highway authorities. In both *Mills* and *James* the Court of Appeal repeatedly referred to the need to strike a balance between cases of urgent need and the burden of an unreasonably high general standard.

"Dangerous" – examples

In *Griffiths* v *Liverpool Corporation* [1967] 1 QB 374 the claimant fell over a "ridge of a flagstone" which projected half an inch above the adjoining flagstone. The judge, at first instance, held that the pavement was dangerous, and this finding of fact was not challenged by the defendant in the Court of Appeal. Nevertheless Sellers LJ cast a great deal of doubt on the veracity of the original judgment:

> "We are all of us accustomed to walk on uneven and irregular surfaces and we can all of us trip on cobblestones, cats-eyes, studs marking pedestrian crossings, as well as other projections.
> If the finding that the half-inch projection of a solitary flagstone in a wide pavement has to be accepted as a danger because of the technicalities of this case, as my brethren think, I have perhaps said enough to indicate that it is a standard which in my view should not become a precedent or guide in ordinary circumstances."

This approach was approved in *Meggs* v *Liverpool Corporation* [1968] 1 WLR 689. A 74 year old woman, whilst walking along a pavement of a busy road, tripped on a flagstone that had sunk about three quarters of an inch. Lord Denning MR upheld the finding of the County Court Judge that such a discrepancy did not make the pavement dangerous. He stated (at 692) that:

> "It seems to me, using ordinary knowledge of pavements, that everyone must take account of the fact that there may be unevenness here and there. There may be a ridge of half an inch or three quarters of an inch occasionally, but that is not the sort of thing which makes it dangerous or not reasonably safe."

In *Littler* v *Liverpool Corporation* [1968] 2 All ER 343, a case in which the claimant tripped on an 80 year old footway which exhibited "some cracks" and a "raised lip of pavement" of approximately half an inch, Cumming-Bruce J stated (at 345) that:

> "The test in relation to a length of pavement is reasonable foreseeability of danger. A length of pavement is only dangerous if, in the ordinary course of human affairs, danger may reasonably be anticipated from its continued use by the public who usually pass over it. It is a mistake to isolate and emphasise a particular difference in levels between flagstones unless that difference is such that a reasonable person who

noticed and considered it would regard it as presenting a real source of danger. Uneven surfaces and differences in levels between flagstones of about an inch may cause a pedestrian who temporarily lost balance to trip and stumble, but such characteristics have to be accepted. A highway is not to be criticised by the standards of a bowling green."

Similar judgments followed in *Ford* v *Liverpool Corporation* (1972) 117 Sol. Jo. 167, where it was held that a raised step in a carriageway of just over an inch was not a defect that attracted liability, and *Mills* v *Barnsley Metropolitan Borough Council* (ibid), where a triangular hole measuring two inches across and one and a quarter inches deep was held not to constitute a danger.

It is a little difficult to derive a firm and consistent lead from these authorities. Again, every case turns on the objective particularity of its own facts. Nor, perhaps, was the cause of leading precedent assisted by the fact that most of the reported cases concerned claims brought in Liverpool. The 1960s and 70s apparently saw a vast increase in claims brought against the highway authority for Liverpool, so much so that Liverpool County Court felt obliged to introduce special local practice directions for highway maintenance actions: see, for example, *Langley* v *North West Water* [1991] 1 WLR 697. The prevalence of such litigation (combined, no doubt, with the example it afforded to other areas of the country) clearly appalled the Court of Appeal. In *Littler's* case, for example, Cumming-Bruce J railed (at 345) that "the sooner the importance of the decision in *Meggs'* case is appreciated in Liverpool by the profession and, in particular, those sitting on legal aid committees, the better".

It is appropriate to acknowledge, therefore, that the canon of reported decisions is not entirely devoid of cases where the hazard was an inch or less and where the judgment nonetheless favoured the claimant. Thus, in *Holemans* v *City of St. Vital* [1973] 43 DLR (3rd), a Canadian case, it was held that a one-inch depression accompanied by cracking in the surface of a pavement constituted a breach of the (almost identical) statutory duty of care.

Motor vehicles and the carriageway

The cases referred to above essentially concentrate on pedestrians walking on a footway or pavement. How can the principles outlined in these judgments be applied to traffic on the carriageway?

It is important to initially acknowledge that, with regard to pedestrian traffic, the application of the foreseeability of danger test often prompts the conclusion that the standard to be applied to carriageways is lower than that applying to pavements. Thus, in

McLoughlin v *Strathclyde Regional Council* [1992] SLT 959, the highway authority was found not liable to a claimant who had tripped on a depression of one and a quarter inches whilst crossing a road, notwithstanding the fact that the road had remained in this state for years. (See also *Ford* v *Liverpool Corporation* (ibid)).

It is submitted, however, that this assumption will not necessarily attach to cases involving motor traffic. Indeed it can be argued – with, it is submitted, some force – that carriageways often demand and require a higher standard of maintenance and repair. Motor vehicles are not as manoeuvrable or adaptable as pedestrians, they can be deflected by comparatively minor defects in the road surface and the consequences of an accident can be much more wide reaching and severe.

The Driving Manual repeatedly warns against the effect of road surface conditions and, in particular, uneven, loose or slippery surfaces: see pages 69, 74, 157, 172 and 206. Motor cyclists are known to be particularly vulnerable. The Motorcycling Manual devotes a whole section (at 71) to the potential prejudice of highway disrepair:

"The Road Surface

The state of the road surface is very important to motor cyclists. Only a small part of the motor cycle tyre makes contact with the road. Any change in the surface can therefore affect the stability of your motor-cycle.
Be on the lookout for poor road surfaces.
  Look out for

- loose surfaces, such as chippings, gravel, mud and leaves
- pot-holes and uneven surfaces
- . . .
- any shiny road surface. At junctions, frequent braking and acceleration can polish the surface.

If you can safely avoid riding on slippery surfaces then do so. If you have to ride on a slippery surface slow down well in advance. Don't swerve suddenly to avoid a poor surface.
If you find yourself on a slippery surface check the traffic, then gradually slow down."

Three cases illustrate the application of the statutory duty to the passage of motor vehicles on the carriageway:

- *Bramwell* v *Shaw* [1971] RTR 167: the claimant lost control of his vehicle when he drove across a pothole that was three feet in diameter and up to six inches deep. It was held that the condition of the road was such as to be dangerous to traffic and as that condition was due to a failure to repair, the highway authority were in breach of their statutory duty. Clearly, had such disrepair been confined to the pavement, it would still have rendered the defendant liable. But the court also added that an "extremely high standard of maintenance was necessary" where a road that was used to carry heavy traffic was old and likely to break up.
- *Bright* v *Attorney-General* [1971] 2 Lloyd's Rep. 68: the claimant, a motorcyclist, was thrown from his vehicle when it struck a "rough patch of road", comprising a "groove" of compacted chippings, deposited by workmen employed by Hertfordshire County Council. It was held that there was "ample evidence" to support the view that the road was "seriously and foreseeably dangerous" to traffic, so that the local authority was vicariously liable for the negligence of its workmen. It is hard to see that such a defect would have rendered the authority liable if it had been simply present on a pavement.
- *Rider* v *Rider* (ibid): the claimant was a passenger in a vehicle which ran out of control after driving across the "unsupported, broken and uneven" edges of a narrow unclassified road. It was held that there was "ample evidence" on which to find that the condition of the road was foreseeably dangerous to reasonable drivers. Again, from the description of the road provided in the report, it could not be said with any degree of confidence that the highway authority would have been liable if the disrepair had been restricted to the pavement.

Maintenance

Maintenance "includes repair and maintain and maintainable are to be construed accordingly.": HA 1980, section 329(1). In *Haydon* v *Kent County Council* [1978] QB 343, a case where the claimant slipped on a path covered with impacted snow and ice, Lord Denning MR stated (at 357) that the duty is "confined to a duty to repair and keep in repair". Goff LJ (at 361/62) and Shaw LJ (at 364) meanwhile entertained a wider definition and application:

"... the ordinary meaning of 'to maintain' is to keep something in existence in a state which enables it to serve the purpose for which it exists. In the case of a highway that purpose is to provide a means of passage for pedestrians or vehicles or both (according to the character of the highway). To keep that purpose the test involves more than repairing or keeping in repair ...

... there may be extreme cases in special circumstances were a liability for failure to maintain not related to want of repair may arise. Such cases are not readily brought to mind although I would not wish to exclude them by confining the scope of maintenance to matters of repair and keeping in repair ...."

Maintenance and improvement are distinct: highway authorities owe no duty of improvement. But where a highway authority undertakes works of improvement, it must continue to maintain the highway to the higher standard: *Owen* v *De Winston* [1894] 58 JP 833.

Flooding and mud

Duty of the highway authority

The mere presence of water on a road surface, whether after heavy rainfall or as a result of some other form of flooding, does not, of itself, indicate a failure to maintain or repair the highway. Something more has to be proved for a breach of duty to be established, and this will normally require evidence that either the sewers or system of drainage had broken down.

In *Burnside* v *Emerson* (ibid) the claimant was driving at a safe speed in a torrential rainstorm when he was suddenly confronted by a pool of storm-water across the road. His vehicle ran into the flood, lost control and veered into the path of another vehicle. Lord Denning MR, having referred to flooding as "a transient danger due to the elements", stated (at 1494) that:

"So I would say that ... an occasional flood at any time is not in itself evidence of a failure to maintain. We all know that in time of heavy rain our highways do from time to time get flooded. Leaves and debris and all sorts of things may be swept in and cause flooding for a time without any failure to repair at all."

Nonetheless the presence of water was undoubtably a danger to traffic and, as the evidence established a failure to maintain a satisfactory system of drainage, liability was established against the highway authority.

Tarrant v *Rowlands* [1979] RTR 144 involved an almost identical set of facts: a motorist driving on a main road on a wet day lost control of his vehicle when it ran into a pool of water on the near side of the road. It was established that on wet days there was usually a pool of water at that part of the road and that the highway authority could reasonably have been expected to know about it, so that a failure to make special provision to drain the pool amounted to a failure to maintain. (See also *Morris* v *Thyssen (GB) Ltd* [1983] Arb 2418).

But in *Pritchard* v *Clwyd County Council* [1973] PIQR 21, a case where the claimant fell whilst riding along a flooded street under several inches of water following a heavy storm, it was held that there was no evidence that the system of drainage was inadequate.

Of course, each case turns on its own particular facts. But it can again be stated, as a general observation, that the courts, when balancing the needs of motorists and pedestrians, expect road surfaces to be kept in a better standard of maintenance and repair than pavements or footways.

Mud on a road surface presents an analogous assortment of legal and evidential issues. In *Misell* v *Essex County Council* (1995) LGR 108 the claimant, whilst negotiating the corner of a country road, fell from his motorcycle because of the presence of wet mud which had been placed on the road during its use by heavy vehicles operating from an adjoining quarry. The coating comprised "a layer of wet and slippery mud" interspersed with "lumps of wet mud from fist-size upwards scattered about on the surface". It was held that the accumulation of mud, described as a continuous problem, required a regular system of inspection and cleaning. It was common ground that draining the highway and the taking of physical steps to remove the mud or prevent its accumulation amounted to "maintenance" for the purposes of the statutory duty.

Duty of the motorist

The Highway Code, at rules 201 to 212, contains a section entitled: "Driving in adverse weather conditions". The section is specifically designated to the hazards manifest by, amongst other things, rain and flooding.

Rule 202 provides:

"Wet weather
In wet weather, stopping distances will be at least double those required for stopping on dry roads. This is because your tyres have less grip on the road. In wet weather

- you should keep well back from the vehicle in front. This will increase your ability to see and plan ahead.

- if your steering becomes unresponsive, it probably means that water is preventing the tyres from gripping the road. Ease off the accelerator and slow down gradually. The rain and spray from vehicles may make it difficult to see and be seen."

The Driving Manual affords additional guidance at pages 239 (Rain), 240 (Driving on wet roads, Aquaplaning), 241 (Spray, Dealing with floods), and 242 (Driving through floodwater). Breach of these provisions (or any of them) will constitute prima facie evidence of negligence. In virtually all the reported cases, even where liability has been established against the highway authority, some blame has attached to the motorist. In *Burnside* Lord Denning referred (at 1496) to the fact that the claimant was driving "far too fast in the circumstances" and found him to be two-thirds to blame for the accident. Similarly, in *Tarrant* Cantley J. found (at 154) that a motorist was under a duty to drive in such a way that he could reasonably expect to see obstructions which would be expected, such as floods on roads in wet weather, and that where he failed to see such an obstruction because his speed was excessive in the circumstances, he could not be exempted from responsibility for a resulting accident. Liability was apportioned equally between the motorist and the highway authority.

Snow and ice

Duty of the highway authority

Snow and ice present a different set of problems for highway authorities. In *Cross* v *Kirklees Metropolitan Borough Council* [1997] Times, July 9 the Court of Appeal noted that:

"They affect the surface of the highway and create a foreseeable risk of injury, but cannot be prevented or guarded against by the proper design and construction of the road, as flooding can by the construction of drains."

It has long been recognised that – at least in theory- highway authorities can be liable under section 41(1) of the HA 1980 for either the accumulation of ice and snow or a failure to clear the same from the highway. In *Haydon* v *Kent County Council* (ibid) Goff LJ stated (at 363) that:

"In my judgment the claimant must prove either as in *Burnside* v *Emerson* [1968] 1 WLR 1490 that the highway authority is at fault apart from merely failing to take steps to deal with the ice, or . . . that, having regard to the nature and importance of the highway, sufficient time has elapsed to make it prima facie unreasonable for the authority to have failed to take remedial measures. Then the authority is liable unless it is able to make out the statutory defence . . . ".

In practice, it is necessary to examine two distinct factual situations:

- where ice has accumulated due to excessive surface water which should not have been allowed to accumulate or remain on the highway;
- where snow and ice falls, settles and accumulates as an entirely natural and unpreventable phenomenon.

Frozen rain

In the "special case" where ice forms from excessive water, the principles outlined in "Flooding and mud" (pages 87 to 89) apply: see *Cross* v *Kirklees MBC* (ibid) (per Lord Justice Evans at 371). In *Manchester Corpn* v *Markland* [1936] AC 360 a service pipe in a road burst and caused a pool of water to form on the carriageway. Three days later a frost occurred, the water froze and ice formed. A fatal accident occurred when a vehicle skidded on the ice and collided with a pedestrian. It was held that the Corporation, who were responsible for the supply of water, were liable for not having taken prompt steps to attend to the leak and so prevent the road from becoming dangerous to traffic.

Snow and ice

In *Haydon* v *Kent C.C.* (ibid) the majority (comprising Goff and Shaw LJJ) held that whilst the duty to maintain could extend to winter maintenance, the mere presence of snow and ice on the highway does not, of itself, establish a breach of statutory duty. Nor – as far as Shaw LJ was concerned (at 365) – would a failure to deal "immediately or promptly" with an icy patch on a footway give rise to a liability on the part of the highway authority.

In *Cross* v *Kirklees MBC* (ibid) a 77 year old woman slipped and fell on an icy pavement. Her claim against the highway authority was dismissed. But the Court of Appeal, in affirming the decision in *Haydon*, additionally stated that a prima facie case could be established under section 41 if the highway authority failed to deal with the snow and ice "within a reasonable time". Lord Justice Evans suggested that it was appropriate to pose the following:

" . . . correct and more limited question: Did the evidence establish that sufficient time had elapsed to make it prima facie unreasonable for the authority to have failed to take remedial measures?"

No specific guidance was given as to the length of time which would have to elapse before the delay was classed as "unreasonable". In *Cross* it was held that it was not unreasonable to leave a busy shopping area untreated by 9.30am. However, the court may have been influenced by the weather forecast available to the authority which predicted that temperatures would quickly rise above freezing.

More recently, in *Hawkyard v North Yorkshire C.C.* (1999) 2 CL 309, a case heard at Leeds County Court, the claimant slipped and fell on an icy footpath whilst on her way to work at about 7a.m. The judge, in dismissing the claim, held that the defendant had a "comprehensive winter maintenance plan" and that, irrespective of the reasonable system of prioritisation, it would not have been practicable to have salted the footway by 7am.

In these cases the question in issue was the duty to be applied to pavements and footways. It is important to recognise that the highway authority must give greater priority to carriageways. In *Cross* Evans LJ explained why:

> "The driver of the motor vehicle on an ungritted and icy carriageway may have less chance of perceiving the presence of ice; he may come to that point by roads which were not icy; and if his vehicle skids, it may hurt more people in addition to himself, and may inflict on them more serious injury."

This view was re-affirmed by the judge in *Hawkyard*:

> "North Yorkshire C.C. gave priority to major carriageways. There was a risk of serious accidents on roads carrying vehicular traffic which should be regarded as greater than the risk of accidents occurring on footways."

The most recent consideration of the duties applicable to snow and ice on the carriageway is to be found in the controversial judgment in *Goodes v East Sussex County Council* (1999) Times, January 7. This case, in variance to the previous authorities, concerned a failure to take preventative rather than remedial measures. The claimant was driving along a main road at about 7.10am when his vehicle skidded on the road surface and left the carriageway. The defendant had previously received a weather forecast which contained a warning of frost. It arranged for the road to be pre-salted in an operation timed to start at 5.30am. The lorry would have reached the accident locus within about 15 minutes of its occurrence. The Court of Appeal held that the relevant question should be:

"Had the authority, once they became aware of what it accepted was a need to take preventative measures, acted with, prima facie, appropriate diligence in implementing those measures? If they had, there would be no breach of duty. If they had not they would be thrown back on their statutory defence."

It was common ground that pre-salting was intended to prevent the formation of ice on the road surface rather than disperse ice already there. The majority (comprising Hutchison and Morritt) concluded that, in these circumstances, "logic and proper performance of the duty" dictated that the salting vehicles should be ordered out at such a time that they would be able to complete their rounds by the time the frost was such as to give rise to a real risk of icy patches on the road. Lord Justice Hutchison stated that:

"Where the decision was that what was called for was pre-salting as a preventative action, and there was no impediment to it being started at a time which would have achieved that objective, a breach of duty could be said to be established."

Specifically, in so far as the evidence suggested that there was a likelihood of ice forming from around 6am and, since the object of the exercise was to prevent that happening, the vehicles should have been sent out not later than 4am.

It is unlikely that *Goodes* will mark the last judicial word on this subject. Lord Justice Hutchison concluded his judgment by observing that "the law as it at present appeared to be in that area, (was) less than satisfactory and ripe for review". It is understood, at the time of writing, that the case awaits a final determination by the House of Lords.

Duty of the motorist

Reference can again be made to rules 203 to 206 of the Highway Code. Rule 206 provides:

"Drive extremely carefully when the roads are icy. Avoid sudden actions as these could cause a skid. You should

- drive at a slow speed in as high a gear as possible; accelerate and brake very gently
- drive particularly slowly on bends where skids are more likely. Brake progressively on the straight before you reach the bend. Having slowed down, steer smoothly round the bend, avoiding sudden actions
- check your grip on the road surface when there is snow or ice by choosing a safe place to brake gently. If the steering feels unresponsive this may indicate ice and your vehicle losing it's grip on the road. When travelling on ice, tyres make virtually no noise."

More detailed guidance can be found in The Driving Manual at pages 248 to 251.

The importance of these requirements is illustrated by the case of *McKenna* v *Scottish Omnibuses Ltd* v *Northumberland County Council* (1984) 134 NLJ 681. A coach, travelling at about 5.15am, skidded on black ice, mounted the verge and overturned. Three allegations of negligence were upheld against the first defendant:

(i) black ice was an ordinary incidence of weather conditions in Northumberland and any driver at night should have in mind the possibility of encountering a patch of black ice;

(ii) the driver had failed to acknowledge a torch signal given by the driver of another vehicle who had run back to warn him of the presence of the ice; and

(iii) he had driven too fast and/or failed to reduce his speed sufficiently on receiving the signal.

The statutory defence

Section 58(1) of the HA 1980 states:

"In an action against a highway authority in respect of damage resulting from their failure to maintain a highway maintainable at the public expense it is a defence (without prejudice to an other defence or the application of the law relating to contributory negligence) to prove that the authority had taken such care as in all the circumstances was reasonably required to secure that the part of the highway to which the action relates was not dangerous for traffic."

It is only necessary to consider the statutory offence when the claimant has first established a prima facie breach of the statutory obligation to maintain. It operates alongside "any other defence" (see Chapter 11) and co-exists with the law relating to contributory negligence.

Matters to which the court is to have regard

Section 58(2) sets out a number of criteria (which are neither exclusive nor exhaustive) to which the court "shall (i.e. consideration is mandatory) have particular regard:

"(a) the character of the highway, and the traffic which was reasonably to be expected to use it;

(b) the standard of maintenance appropriate for a highway of that character and used by such traffic;

(c) the state of repair in which a reasonable person would have expected to find the highway;

(d) whether the highway authority knew, or could reasonably have been expected to know, that the condition of the part of the highway to which the action relates was likely to cause danger to users of the highway;

(e) where the highway authority could not reasonably have been expected to repair that part of the highway before the cause of action arose, what warning notices of its condition have been displayed . . ."

S. 58(2)(a) and (b)

Highway authorities are entitled (even obliged) to classify and prioritise each road according to its size, location, age, construction and frequency of usage. (The need for a "hierarchy of treatment" was emphasised in cases such as *Cross v Kirklees MBC* and *Hawkyard v North Yorkshire C.C.* (ibid).) In *Bramwell v Shaw* [1971] RTR 167 it was held that a higher standard of maintenance was required (to an extent that the carriageway should have been inspected "pretty well daily") where a much used road was old and liable to break up. The "design" of the road can be a relevant factor. Where, for example, the road comprises "tarmac adjoining cobbles at the edge", so that it was particularly susceptible to water penetration, a six-monthly inspection did not amount to taking such care as was required to secure that it was not dangerous for traffic: *Jacobs v Hampshire County Council* (1984) Times, May 28.

S.58(2)(c)

This criterion touches on a number of primary issues. First, the statutory duty is only owed to the normal (i.e. reasonable) run of drivers to be found on the highway: *Rider v Rider* (ibid) (per Sachs LJ at 514). Secondly, as has already been noted, reasonable forseeability is an important, even essential element in the classification of a defect as being "dangerous" (*Rider v Rider* (ibid) considered at page 82). Reasonable people, in short, expect (and are entitled to expect) that the highway will be maintained in a manner that guards against the creation or retention of a foreseeable danger.

S58(2)(d)

The question of the highway authority's knowledge (actual or that reasonably inferred) turns on the adequacy of its inspection system and the success with which it entertains and records warnings given and complaints made by other bodies or individuals. (Warnings and complaints are particularly relevant to temporary or transient phenomenon such as snow and ice: see, for example, *McKenna* v *Scottish Omnibus* (ibid)).

The leading case on regularity of inspection is *Pridham* v *Hemel Hempstead Corporation* [1970] 69 LGR 523. The Claimant, an elderly woman, tripped and fell on a "tarmacadam footpath" constructed as part of the new town of Hemel Hempstead. Evidence adduced by the defendant revealed that the highways in the borough were divided into different classes:

> ". . . those on which a lot of traffic would normally be expected to travel, both vehicular and pedestrian, were to be examined monthly, 12 times a year; the less frequented roads would have been inspected once every 2 months; still less frequented roads were to be examined quarterly; and there was another class (such as) field paths, which were only to be inspected once a year."

It was held that:

(i)   the highway authority must prove that they had exercised such care as was "reasonably required", and not that said to be "reasonably practicable": it was, in the words of Davies LJ. (at 529) " wrong to detract from the words of the section";

(ii) since the authority had decided, after careful consideration, on a quarterly inspection of residential roads and had maintained the additional check of a complaints book, they had in all the circumstances, made out a statutory defence.

Other illustrative cases include:

- *Whiting* v *Hillingdon London Borough Council* (1970) 114 Sol. Jo.; held, in relation to a footpath, that an inspection held in February reasonably protected a highway authority in relation to a danger that development between the date of the survey and an accident that occurred in April of the same year;

- *Jacobs* v *Hampshire County Council* (1984) Times, May 28; a road "susceptible to water penetration" had to be inspected more than once every six months. Frequency of inspection should reflect the fact that the water penetration was capable of causing damage within two months.

S58(2)(e)

It is submitted that this criterion requires the Court to consider whether, on the facts of a particular case, the warning is such as to enable traffic to proceed in reasonable safety. The sub-section concedes that the material defect cannot reasonably be repaired (by reason, perhaps, of its nature, the manner or speed of its creation, or the priority afforded to the carriageway) prior to the accrual of the complainant's cause of action. Factors relevant to the existence or sufficiency of warning notices include, therefore, the magnitude of the defect and the volume of traffic using that part of the highway. The greater the danger, the more obvious and specific the warning of it must be. (See, by way of analogy, *Rae v Mars (UK) Ltd* (1989) Times, February 15, *a* case decided under the corresponding provision under section 2(4)(a) of the Occupiers Liability Act 1957.)

In *Morris v Thyssen (GB) Ltd* [1983] Arb 2418 the claimant lost control of his van when it hit a large pool of water on the road caused by flooding. It was held, at first instance, that the flooding was a foreseeable danger to traffic, of which hazard the authority had been notified by the police and their own employees. One flood sign displayed in a nearby lay-by "was not an adequate warning".

Where a highway authority, in pursuance of its statutory duty, carries out works of resurfacing, with the consequence that traffic signs and/or road markings are temporarily obliterated, temporary warning signs should be provided in order to remove the danger or minimise the risk to traffic: *Bird v Pearce and Somerset County Council* [1978] RTR 290 and *Kotecka v London Borough of Harrow* [1995] CLY 1812.

Independent contractors

The duty to maintain the highway under section 41(1) of the HA 1980 is, as a statutory obligation, absolute and cannot be delegated. This rule is specifically enshrined in the final part of section 58(2) which states:

> "For the purposes of (the statutory) defence is not relevant to prove that the highway authority had arranged for a confident person to carry out or supervise the maintenance of the part of the highway to which the action relates unless it is also proved that the authority have given him proper instructions with regard to the maintenance of the highway and that he had carried out the instructions."

The highway authority may, in turn, be entitled to an indemnity against the contractors. Aside from establishing the fact of responsibility for the negligent act or omission, the authority will have to show that it exercised reasonable care in appointing competent contractors.

Street works and public utilities

Various "statutory undertakers", such as the gas, electricity, water and telecommunications authorities, regularly interfere with our roads and pavements. Such "street works" are governed by the New Roads and Street Works Act 1991, which came into force on 1st January 1993, and which repealed and replaced the Public Utilities Street Works Act 1950.

The New Roads and Street Works Act 1991

Specific reference can be made to the provisions regulating the conduct of the work and the reinstatement of the "street".

Execution of works

Section 65 requires the provision of adequate guards, lighting and traffic signs, including directions to pedestrians and having regard, in particular, to the needs of the disabled. Section 66 provides that the works must be supervised by an appropriately qualified person and be completed "with all dispatch as is reasonably practicable".

Reinstatement

Section 70 provides that the undertaker "shall" reinstate the street, and do so "as soon after the completion of any part of the street works as is reasonably practicable". Section 72 empowers the "street authority" (almost invariably the highway authority: section 49(1)) to enforce compliance and, in the event of a continuing failure, to do the works itself and recover the cost of reinstatement from the undertaker. It is a provision of some importance as a failure by the highway authority to pursue reinstatement can, it is submitted, lead to a concurrent liability under section 41 of the Highways Act 1980.

Civil cause of action?

Breach of the statutory provisions will not confer a civil cause of action: *Keating* v *Elvin Reinforced Concrete Co. Ltd.* [1968] 2 All ER 139. However, undertakers undeniably owe a duty of care to road users and non-compliance can be cited as evidence of negligence.

Standard of works and reinstatement

Such authority (binding, persuasive or otherwise) as exists suggests that the work of statutory undertakers will be judged according to a standard that equates to that applied to highway authorities under section 41(1) of the HA 1980. In *Cohen* v *British Gas Corp.* [1978] CLR 2053 the claimant fell on an excavation which had sunk by about an inch. It was held, in an echo of "the Liverpool cases" (see page 83), that in a road one finds undulations, so that the surface is not to be judged by the standard of a bowling green, and a depression of one inch was not dangerous.

Inspection

A statutory undertaker's obligation to inspect its work and installations can be reasonably discharged by a reliance on the highway authority's six monthly road inspection. But, as such, the undertaker will be taken to have the same knowledge that it would have had if it had carried out its own contemporaneous inspection: *Reid* v *British Telecommunication* (1987) Times, June 27.

Continuing duty of care and maintenance

Openings, drains, manhole covers, gratings, stopcocks and hydrants are, as a general rule, the responsibility of the body which owns or operates the installation. Such 'things on the road' must be installed and maintained in a manner that ensures that they do not become a source of danger to users of the highway.

Examples of breach include:

- the installation of a raised stopcock that constituted a "danger on the highway"; *Rider* v *Metropolitan Water Board* [1949] 2 KB 378;
- an infield trench which, by reason of subsequent shrinkage of materials, constituted a danger to motorists; *Newsome* v *Darton Urban District Council* [1998] 2 All ER 93;
- the installation of a raised cover-plate of a valve box that, when opened, was a danger to traffic; *Wells* v *Metropolitan Water Board* [1937] All ER 639.

Responsibility is not always clear cut and it is often necessary to carefully examine the nature or 'mechanism' of the defect before the correct defendant can be identified. Thus, whilst a raised cover or grate may well be the responsibility of the relevant utility, attention will necessarily switch to the highway authority if the projection was the result of the wearing away of the surrounding highway: see, for example, *Withington* v *Bolton Borough Council* [1937] 3 All ER 108.

Highway Obstruction

It is proposed to consider the following:

- Parked vehicles
- Builders skips
- Smoke
- Trees
- Traffic signs.

Parked vehicles

Parking is governed by rules 214 to 226 of the Highway Code. (Reference can also be made to rule 275, in relation to parking on tramways). The Driving Manual lends additional guidance at pages 185 to 9. (See also pages 230, Motorways, 247, Fog and 264, At night.)

Liability can be established in negligence and/or nuisance.

Negligence

"Bad" parking generally
There is no rule of law for the proposition that "bad parking" could never, of itself give rise to liability in negligence. In *Chop Seng Heng* v *The Vannasan son of Sinnapam* [1976] RTR 193, a case where a lorry driver parked his vehicle too close to a bend, the Court of Appeal held (at 198) that it was necessary to "eschew excessive legalism" and "apportion blame according to the circumstances".

Parking on a bend
In *Waller* v *Levoi* [1968] 112 Sol. Jo. 165 parking on a bend was held to be "unwise" and negligent. It matters little whether the vehicle is left on either the inside or the outside of the bend: it still constitutes "a potential cause of danger": *Stevens* v *Kelland* [1970] RTR 445 (per Waller J. at 448).

Parking on a hill
It is clearly negligent to leave a vehicle unattended on a gradient when:

- the engine is still running; *Hambrook* v *Stokes Bros.* [1925] 1 KB 141, and
- the handbrake was out of order and it was only kept in position by a block of wood underneath one of the wheels; *Martin* v *Stanborough* (1924) 41 TLR 1.

In *Parker* v *Miller* [1926] 42 TLR 408 the Court of Appeal additionally held that the mere fact that a car ran down a hill by itself when it was left unattended was "sufficient evidence of negligence", even though the precise cause or failure was left unexplained.

Unlighted vehicles
See Chapter 8, pages 111 to 117.

Nuisance

In *Dymond* v *Pearce* [1972] 1 QB 496 the defendant parked his lorry on the outside of a shallow bend on an urban road. The vehicle was seven feet wide, parked with its lights on under a street lamp and was visible from some 200 yards. A motorcyclist, looking round at someone on the pavement, failed to see the parked vehicle and collided with the back of a lorry.

It was accepted, both at first instance and on appeal, that the lorry was not negligently parked. The primary issue concerning the Court of Appeal's consideration was the concomitant claim in nuisance. It is necessary, in this regard, to study the distinctive majority judgments of Sachs LJ. and Edmund Davies LJ.:

- Lord Justice Sachs stated (at 502) that;

"The leaving of a large vehicle on a highway for any purpose for a considerable period (it is always a matter of degree) otherwise than in an lay-by prima facie results in a nuisance being created, for it narrows the highway . . .

But the mere fact that a lorry was a nuisance does not render its driver or owner liable to the claimant in damages unless its being in that position was a cause of the accident."

In essence, therefore, he considered that there were two categories of nuisance: either an obstruction which is not dangerous, or one which was.

- Lord Justice Edmund Davies stated (at 504) that:

"Where a vehicle has been left parked on the highway for such a length of time or in such other circumstances as constitute it as an obstruction amounting to a public nuisance, I remain of the view I expressed in *Parish* v *Judd* [1960] 1 WLR 867 that, in order that a claimant in such proceedings as the present may recover compensation for personal injuries caused by a collision with that obstruction, he must establish that the obstruction constituted a danger."

In short: an obstruction on a highway did not become a nuisance unless it was shown to be dangerous.

Both judges agreed that the sole cause of the accident was the motorcyclist's negligence and so, on either formulation, the claim against the lorry driver was dismissed.

It is claimed that the judgment in *Dymond* leaves alive the vexed issue as to whether fault is a necessary ingredient of nuisance. Theoretically the law is clear – fault is not required. The Court of Appeal undoubtedly perceived danger in terms of the reasonable foreseeability (or anticipation) of injury. But in practice it will be rare for liability to be established in nuisance without there being some kind of culpability of fault. As Sachs LJ. stated (at 503):

> "It (i.e. the finding that the sole cause of the accident was the motorcyclist's negligence) entails a parallel consideration once negligence on the part of the driver of a stationary vehicle is negatived, for only then which was found not to be a foreseeable cause of an accident also be found to have been in law the actual cause of it."

Builder's skips

Skips or "hoppers" may pose a particularly hazardous obstruction. Habitually positioned on roads or footpaths, constructed from heavy, angular steel plate and, when ladden, commanding a mass of several tons, they constitute an immobile threat to the unwary motorist.

Liability is again based on negligence and/or nuisance. Three cases, each following *Dymond* v *Pearce* (ibid), illustrate the Court's approach to the liability of those who "deposit" skips on the highway, and the concurrent duty of the motorist:

- *Saper v Hungate Builders Limited [1972] RTR 380*
  The defendants placed a skip outside a house at a point on the highway that was 60 yards from the blind crest of the hill, with its nearside on the kerb so that it projected four feet into the road. Although the skip was painted yellow, placed under a street light and illuminated with two lighted builder's laps, the claimant, who was driving a car up the hill, failed to see it and collided with the same. Two other motorists passing the skip two or three hours before the accident had seen the skip only just in time to swerve and avoid it.

  The court, at first instance, gave judgment against the defendant on the grounds of negligence and nuisance, but assessed the claimant's contributory negligence at 40%. Cantley J. stated (at 383) that:

"A motorist must be alert driving at night, in a residential area, for such thing as motor cars parked without lights, and not always parked wisely. But persons who put obstructions in the carriageway should take reasonable care to give warning of their presence. The putting on the top of this skip of 2 lamps which so many persons looking in that direction failed to see was not, in my view, adequate lighting. An object like this is very dangerous unless proper warning of it is given: and by "proper warning", I mean warning by lighting which will be readily and instantly apparent to a motorist who does not know of the existence of the object or suspect to be there."

- *Drury* v *Camden LBC* [1972] RTR 391.
  The defendant, carrying out building work in houses on a one-way street some 35 ft wide, deposited a skip on the road way adjacent to the nearside pavement and occupying some 6 or 7 ft of the carriageway. The skip was dirty, much the same colour as the road surface, and unlit. The claimant, riding his motorscooter in the nearside lane, failed to see the skip until about 15 ft away and, although he swerved, he collided with the same.

  Liability was established in nuisance and negligence: the Court held that the skip constituted both an obstruction and a source of danger. The claimant, meanwhile, had not been keeping as good a lookout as he ought to have kept, and contributory negligence was assessed at 50%.

- *Wills* v *TF Martin (Roof Contractors) Ltd* [1972] RTR 368.
  The claimant, driving at night along a poorly lit residential road, collided with the defendant's skip that had been placed on the road "close to the kerb". The evidence, which was somewhat equivocal, suggested that the skip could not be said to have been "unlit". The claimant, who was endeavouring to "pedal start" his moped, was not displaying a light.

  The court, at first instance, dismissed the claim. The deposit of the skip, properly lit, did not amount to negligence. Further, whilst the skip was obviously a nuisance, regardless of whether it was lit, it was the claimant's failure to look where he was going that was the sole cause of the accident.

It is important to note, particularly when considering issues of negligence, that the criminal canon contains legislation designed to control the siting, repositioning and lighting of skips. Specific reference can be made to the following:

- Section 139 of the Highways Act 1980; makes provision for the depositing of builders' skips on the highway and provides that the "permission" may be subject to conditions relating to the siting, dimensions, colour, lighting and warning of the skip.
- Section 140 of the HA 1980; allows a highway authority or a policeman in uniform to require the owner of the skip to remove or reposition it.

Non-compliance with (any of) these provisions constitutes a criminal offence. This will not, of itself, confer a civil cause of action, although proof of the breach will amount to prima facie evidence of negligence.

Smoke

Smoke, like patches of fog, can amount to a transient but nonetheless injurious hazard for road users. Problems essentially occur when smoke drifts across the carriageway from land or property adjoining the highway.

There are a number of distinctive, but ultimately reconcilable decisions:

- In *Holling* v *Yorkshire Traction Co. Ltd* [1948] 2 All ER 662, the defendant owned and operated a coke oven situate 50 yards from a main road. The process of manufacturing coke involved periodic production of clouds of smoke and steam. (This was a by-product of the "essential" operation of the coke being quenched with water.) A fatal accident occurred when a car and a bus travelling on the main road collided amidst one of the clouds of smoke. It was held, at first instance, that the motorist's claim should succeed in nuisance and negligence. The "flooding of the road with an impenetrable fog of smoke and steam" was not a lawful use and constituted a nuisance. The defendant was also negligent in not positioning a man at each end of the area affected to warn approaching vehicles as soon as discharge was imminent.

  This judgment was followed in *Rollingson* v *Kerr* [1958] CLY 2427, a case where a collision occurred amidst a dense cloud of smoke that blew across the road from the defendant's bonfire of hedge clippings. It was held, at first instance, that the defendant was guilty of negligence and nuisance, and neither driver was guilty of contributory negligence.

- In *Hall & Co. Ltd* v *Ham Manor Farms Ltd* (1966) 116 L. Jo. 838, a collision occurred as a result of "dense smoke"drifting from the defendant's land where stubble was being burned. The claimant's action was dismissed. It was held, at first instance, that the smoke was not a nuisance, as the burning of stubble was a "necessary one and in accordance with normal agricultural practice". Nor were the defendants negligent as their servants had taken all reasonable precautions to avoid any danger.

  This judgment was followed, on almost identical facts, in *Perkins* v *Glyn* (1976) CLY 1883. The court held, at first instance, that "a motorist on the highway had to expect to be obstructed occasionally".

It has been mooted, with some conviction, that as the quenching of coke and the burning of stubble are both activities properly incidental to normal industrial or agricultural usage, the decisions in *Holling* and *Hall* are infuriatingly inconsistent. Essentially, however, each case turns on its particular facts. In *Hall* the smoke was found to be unforseen, of short duration and capable of being seen by those travelling along the road. Similarly, in *Perkins* case the smoke "could be seen by motorists from more than a mile away". Thus could the judge in *Hall* conclude that the "facts were wholly different" from those in *Holling*.

Trees

The occupier of land adjoining the highway owes a duty, as a prudent landowner, to prevent his trees from being a danger to persons on the highway. Trees can overhang the road, fall onto the carriageway and, on occasions, discharge sap, pollen, leaves, twigs or branches which, when deposited on the road surface, can pose a threat to motorists.

Knowledge that tree is unsafe

Liability will not be established unless it can be proved that the occupier knew, or had reasonable grounds for knowing that the tree was unsafe.

In *Noble* v *Harrison* [1926] 2 KB 332, a motorist collided with a branch that suddenly broke away from a tree overhanging the highway. The Court of Appeal held that the defendant was not liable on the ground that the fracture was due to a latent defect not discoverable by any reasonably careful inspection. The occupier, in other words, had no knowledge, actual or imputed, of the danger. By the

same token, in *Cunliffe v Banks* [1945] 1 All ER 459, a case where a
motorcyclist collided with a 50 year old elm tree which had fallen
across the road, the cause was traced back to an attack of honeyfungus.
The defendant's servant had carried out an annual inspection but the
tree had exhibited no signs of danger. It was held that there was no
evidence of negligence or nuisance. The defendant, who had not
caused or allowed the tree to be or remain in a vulnerable state, had no
knowledge of the danger. (See also *Shirvill v Hackwood Estates Ltd*
[1938] 2 KB 577 and *Lambourn v London Brick Co.* [1950] 156
Estates Gazette 146.)

Similar principles apply where the danger derives not so much from
the condition of the tree itself but from a 'fortuitous confluence of
vehicles on the highway'. In *British Road Services Ltd v Slater* [1964] 1
All ER 816, two lorries met at night on a narrow roadway. One lorry,
in an attempt to manoeuvre past the oncoming vehicle, collided with
the "stout branch" of an old oak tree that just impinged on the
highway. The Court of Appeal held that whilst the overhanging branch
was, when looked at objectively, a nuisance, no-one had ever thought
of it as a hazard and the accident only occurred because of a fortuitous
circumstance that two heavy lorries happened to meet on the highway.
The defendant was not liable.

Examination, inspection and maintenance

Most trees demand regular (often biannual) attention in the form
of lopping, topping or pruning. Periodic inspection may also
be necessary, particularly if the tree is old or showing signs of
disease.

No liability will lie against a landowner who carries out a sufficiently regular and detailed inspection of his tree: see *Lynch v
Hetherington* [1991] 2 IR 405. Otherwise an occupier is not obliged
to call in an expert unless he has reason to believe that the tree is
unsafe: *Caminer v Northern & London Investment Trust Ltd* [1951]
AC 88.

By way of contrast, a landowner will be liable where:

- the danger is apparent, not only to an expert but to the
  ordinary layman, but he ignores or chooses not to notice the
  same; *Brown v Harrison* [1947] WN 191; and
- having obtained the advice of an expert, he unreasonably fails
  to carry out the (or any) steps recommended by the same:
  Quinn v Scott [1965] 2 All ER 588.

Duty to light and/or warn of an obstruction

A landowner is under no obligation to light or warn of a tree fallen on the highway when the obstruction arises without fault or negligence on his part: *Hudson v Bray* [1917] 1 KB 520. Conversely, where the danger is caused, either wholly or in part, by his act or misfeasance, his duty can extend to the issue of an appropriate warning: see *Mackie v Dumbartonshire County Council* [1927] WN 247.

Local authorities

Section 96 of the Highways Act 1980 authorises a highway authority (and sometimes a local authority that it is not a highway authority) to remove, alter, maintain or guard grass verges. The power includes an entitlement to plant trees and shrubs. However, the statutory power specifically prohibits, at sub-section 96(6), either the creation or continuation of a nuisance:

> "No tree, shrub, grass verge, guard or fence shall be planted, laid out or erected under this section, or, if planted, laid out or erected under this section, allowed to remain in such a situation as to hinder the reasonable use of the highway by any person entitled to use it, or so as to be a nuisance or injurious to the owner or occupier of premises adjacent to the highway."

It was held in *Hale v Hants & Dorset Motor Services Ltd* [1947] 2 All ER 628 that a local authority was liable when, having planted trees near the highway, it failed to cut them back, with the result that a bus collided with an overhanging branch.

Negligence of the motorist

The Highway Code, at rule 124, warns motorists to: "Be prepared for unexpected or difficult situations". The Driving Manual additionally advises (at 127) that: "The secret of dealing with an obstruction lies in looking and planning well ahead".

Failure to see and avoid an obstruction such as a fallen or over-hanging tree can, depending on the circumstances, lead to a finding of negligence (or contributory fault) against the motorist. In *Radley v London Passenger Transport Board* [1942] 1 All ER 433 a bus collided with the overhanging branch of a tree. It was held that the driver was negligent as the accident occurred at midday and the tree was clearly visible to approaching motorists. In *Hale v Hants & Dorset Motor Services Ltd* (ibid), a case founded on virtually identical facts, the bus driver was found to be one-third to blame for the collision.

Traffic signs

Traffic signs are regulated by sections 64 and 80 of the Road Traffic Regulation Act 1984. Essentially, by section 65(1), a highway authority is empowered, at its discretion, to erect traffic signs.

In so far as it is a matter of discretion for a highway authority whether to erect a road sign, a decision not to do so or a failure to consider doing so does not establish negligence unless it can be proved, on the balance of probabilities, that a competent road engineer, exercising reasonable care and skill, would have directed that a sign be placed on the road and that the absence of the sign caused or was a contributory cause of the material accident: *Lavis* v *Kent County Council* [1994] Times, November 24. (See also *West* v *Buckinghamshire County Council* [1984] RTR 306.)

Care must be exercised in the design, construction and erection of road signs. In *Levine* v *Morris* [1970] 1 WLR 71 it was held that the highway authority (in this case the Ministry of Transport) owed a duty of care to motorists in the siting of road signs. A fatal accident occurred when a vehicle skidded on a bend, left the road and collided with a large road sign mounted on four concrete columns and sited about four feet in from the nearside of the carriageway. The Court of Appeal held that

(i) when there were two sites equally good as regards visibility, the highway authority should not select one that involved materially greater hazard to motorists, and

(ii) the road sign constituted a hazard and had been sited without any consideration of an appropriate position.

Danger Adjoining the Highway

Occupiers of land or premises adjoining the highway must maintain their property in a manner that avoids either the creation or continuance of a danger to road users. Liability is essentially based on nuisance although, as has been previously noted (see page 101) it will be comparatively rare to establish liability in circumstances where there is not some form of concomitant negligence.

Dangerous buildings, fences and boundary walls

In *Sedleigh-Denfield* v *O'Callaghan* [1940] AC 880, the Court of Appeal expressed an occupier's liability in terms of his "creation", "continuance" or "adoption" of a nuisance. A nuisance can be created by either a positive act (e.g. the erection of a dangerous structure) or, more commonly, by omission (e.g. a failure to maintain or repair the premises). An occupier continues a nuisance if, with knowledge or presumed knowledge of its existence, he fails to take reasonable steps to bring it to an end when he has ample time to do so. He adopts it if he makes use of the erection or artificial structure which constitutes the nuisance.

Liability was established where:

- a brick fell onto the highway from a recently constructed railway bridge; *Kearney* v *London & Brighton Ry* (1871) LR 6 QB 759,
- a wall collapsed onto the highway; *Mullans* v *Forrester* [1921] 2 Ir. R. 412 and *Noble* v *Harrison* [1926] 2 KB 332,
- a lamp became detached from a house and fell onto the highway; *Tarry* v *Ashton* (1876) 1 QBD 314.

No liability was established where:

- the danger (namely the collapsing gable end of a house) was the result of a latent defect which was not discoverable by the exercise of reasonable care and skill; *Wringe* v *Cohen* [1940] 1 KB 229. (See also *Lambert* v *Lowestoft Corpn.* [1901] 1 QB 590).
- the danger was created by a trespasser; *Barker* v *Herbert* [1911] 2 KB 633.

As has been noted, an occupier can be liable for the continuance of a nuisance for which he originally bore no responsibility. In *Slater* v *Worthingtons' Cash Stores Ltd* [1941] 1 KB 488, snow fell and accumulated on the roof of the defendant's premises. Four days later, having become dislodged by reason of its sheer mass, it fell onto the highway. It was held, at first instance, that the defendant had erred in failing to clear the snow within a reasonable period.

Works and excavations adjoining the highway

An occupier will be liable if he creates, continues or adopts any works or excavations which constitute a danger to users of the highway. Proximity (i.e. the distance between the works and the carriageway) is a crucial factor. Thus, in *Hardcastle* v *South Yorkshire Ry* (1859) 4 H&N 67, it was held (per Pollock CB) that:

"We think that the proper and true test of legal liability is, whether the excavation be substantially adjoining the way in every case it is (a matter of fact) whether the excavation was sufficiently near to the highway to be dangerous."

In practice, pedestrians are necessarily more vulnerable than motorists. Nonetheless, where the excavation undermines the structure of the road and leads to the formation of a surface defect, an occupier can be liable to vehicular traffic.

Egress of water and the formation of ice

Water can flow from premises onto the highway and, in certain circumstances, collect as a flood or form patches of ice. Two cases illustrate an occupier's potential liability:

- *Lambie* v *Western S.M.T. Co. Ltd* [1944] SC 415; the washing of motor vehicles in a garage caused water to flow onto the highway where it subsequently formed as ice. The garage proprietors were liable for failing to take precautions to prevent the formation of the hazard.
- *Manchester Corp.* v *Markland* [1936] AC 360; water from a burst pipe caused a pool of water to collect in the roadway. Three days later, a frost occurred and ice formed. A vehicle skidded, left the carriageway and killed a pedestrian. Liability was established on the grounds that the defendant had failed to take prompt action to attend to the leak in order to prevent the road from becoming dangerous to traffic.

Roadside activity

The occupier's duty to take care extends to an obligation to avoid activity likely to injure persons on the highway.

Industrial usage

In *Miles* v *Forest Rock Granite Co.* (1918) 34 TLR 500, the occupier of a quarry was liable when blasting operations caused injury to a person passing on the highway. By the same token, a local authority was liable when it failed to clear burning rubbish from a tip, with the result that a road user was struck by a fragment of exploding aerosol can: *Woodfall* v *Knowsley Borough Council* (1992) Times, June 26.

Sporting activities

Numerous cases attest to the danger posed by cricket, golf or even footballs bouncing onto the highway. Liability (of either the individual sportsman or, more appropriately, the occupying club) will essentially depend on the propensity or frequency of the 'emission' and, accordingly, the magnitude of any foreseeable risk of injury.

Liability was established where:

- the hole of a golf course was positioned in a way that lead to players "habitually" driving balls onto an adjoining road; *Castle* v *St. Augustin's Links* (1921) 28 TLR 615;
- footballs were "regularly" kicked onto the road with the result, in the material instance, that a motorcyclist fell off and sustained fatal injuries; *Hilder* v *Associated Portland Cement Manufacturers Ltd* [1961] 1 WLR 1434;
- cricket balls were hit out of the club grounds on "fairly frequent occasions"; *Miller* v *Jackson* [1977] QB 960.

Liability was not established where:

- cricket balls emerged on "only rare occasions"; *Bolton* v *Stone* [1951] AC 850;
- a golf club took reasonable care to prevent balls straying onto the highway; *Potter* v *Carlisle & Cliftonville Golf Club Ltd* [1939] NI 114.

Chapter 8

Lights

Lights on vehicles perform three main functions. They:

- denote the position of the vehicle;
- indicate the direction (and sometimes the speed) of a moving vehicle;
- allow the driver to see where he is going.

This chapter will examine the various regimens relating to the lighting of both moving and stationary vehicles. Primary reference should be made to the Highway Code, rules 90, 93–96, 214 and 222–225, and the Road Vehicles Lighting Regulations 1989 (SI No. 1796).

Headlamps and headlights

General requirement

Headlights must be used during the "*hours of darkness*" (defined as the period "*between sunset and sunrise*") and whilst visibility is "*severely reduced*": RVLR 1989, reg. 24 and the Highway Code, rule 93. These provisions regularised a general requirement long recognised at common law. Thus, in *Wintle* v *British Tramways and Carriage Co. Ltd.* (1917) 86 LJKB 240 it was held (at 242) that:

> "a driver must make allowance for the appearance on the road of lorries and other vehicles, and he must exercise common prudence by showing such an amount of light as would warn an approaching vehicle of the driver and his trolley . . .".

Non-compliance

Driving in the dark and/or severely reduced visibility without proper lights is prima facie evidence of negligence: *Baker* v *E. Longhurst & Sons Limited* [1933] 2 K.B.461 (at 464). In *Burgess* v *Heard* [1965] Guardian, 25 March, the Court of Appeal held that a motor cyclist was negligent in not having dipped headlights on whilst travelling at 15 mph in thick fog with visibility of 10–15 yards. (See also *Harvey* v

Road Haulage Executive [1952] 1 K.B.120). Use of side lights only does not constitute a compliance with the regulations: *Swift* v *Spence* [1982] RTR 116. In the words (at 119) of Donaldson L.J.: "It is dipped headlights or nothing".

Malfunctioning lights

Where a vehicle's lights become extinguished or fail completely, unbeknown to the driver and through no fault on his part, the presumption of negligence will be rebutted. In *Maitland v Raisbeck & R.T. and J. Hewitt Limited* [1944] K.B. 689 a bus collided with the back of a slow moving lorry whose rear light had gone out. The Court of Appeal rejected the bus driver's submission that it was immaterial whether or not the lorry driver knew that the rear light was out. He was not negligent nor liable in nuisance. "Accidents can happen". . ., observed (at 693) Lord Greene M.R., ". . . when both parties have been reasonable and neither having misused the highway". Similarly, in *Parish* v *Judd* [1960] 3 All E.R. 33 the defendant was driving along a main road at 10 mph when the lighting system of his car failed completely. It was held that, although the presence on a dark road at night of a wholly unlit vehicle is prima facie evidence of negligence, the lights failed without negligence on his part. Nor was the fact that an unlighted vehicle was found at night on a road sufficient to constitute a nuisance: there must also be some fault on the part of the person responsible for the vehicle. The cases of *Sieghart v British Transport Commission* (1956) 106 L.J.O 185 and *Moore v Maxwells of Emsworth Ltd* [1968] 1 WLR 1077 provide further examples of this dictum.

Dipped headlights

A motorist must not use any lights that would dazzle or cause discomfort to other road users. Headlights should always be dipped when overtaking, where there is oncoming traffic and in built up areas: RVLR 1989, reg. 27 and the Highway Code, rules 94 and 95. In *Saville v Bache* (1969) 113 Sol. Jo. 228 the claimant, a cyclist, was struck by a vehicle whose driver had been dazzled by the lights of an oncoming car. The court found that this motorist had switched his headlights to main beam as the vehicles approached one another. He was negligent. Nevertheless this requirement, although mandatory, does not impose an absolute duty. Widgery L.J. (at 229) acknowledged that: "there could be circumstances when a driver had to resort to the full beam whilst approaching another car". He would not be negligent if "he had some good reason" for doing so.

Limit of vision

A driver should always proceed at a speed and in a manner that will allow him to pull up and stop in the limit of his vision: the Highway Code rules 105 and 210.

In *Young v Chester* [1973] RTR a motorist was driving a van at night with dipped headlights at a speed of some 40–50 mph. He negligently collided with the rear of the car in front. O'Connor J. stated (at 324) that:

> "if on a dark night a motorist chooses to drive on dipped headlights for the convenience of those who may be coming in the opposite direction, he is bound to travel at a speed which will enable him to cope with the ordinary trials that occur on the highway."

Further examples are provided by *Baker v E. Longhurst & Sons Limited* [1933] 2 K.B. 461 (re: darkness) and *Harvey v Road Haulage Executive* (ibid) (re: fog).

In *Hill v Phillips* (1963) 107 Sol.Jo. 890 the Court of Appeal recognised the particular difficulties associated with driving in rural or isolated areas. Upjohn L.J. stated that:

> "So long as motorists drive with dipped headlights in country roads they must drive in a manner as to see unlighted obstructions. Everyone knows that there are cyclists who ride their bicycles without lights, or men in dark clothes in country roads, and motorists must appreciate their presence."

Flashing headlights

Rules 90 and 91 of the Highway Code provide:

> "**90. Flashing headlights.** Only flash your headlights to let other road users know that you are there. Do not flash your headlights in an attempt to intimidate other road users.
>
> 91. If another driver flashes his headlights never assume that it is a signal to go. Use your own judgment and proceed carefully."

Common usage can unfortunately prompt the interpretation that a motorist who flashes his lights to beckon another driver thereby provides a warranty of safe passage. So when, if ever, is a driver who gives such a signal liable to one who acts on the same?

In *Clarke v Winchurch* [1969] 1 WLR 69 a bus driver flashed his lights at another motorist who took it as an invitation to cross the road. Unfortunately his vehicle was then struck by another car. The Court of Appeal held that the bus driver, by flashing his lights, meant only "Come on so far as I am concerned", and he was under no duty of care to the motorist who responded to the signal. Russell L.J., in explaining the reasoning behind the decision, stated (at 76) that to impose such a duty on a driver who "flicks his headlights at another vehicle" would "operate as a serious impediment to the courtesies of the road and the proper flow of traffic".

This approach was followed in *Leeson* v *Beavis & Tolchard Ltd* [1972] RTR 373. The driver of a lorry flashed his lights at a van waiting to emerge from a garage entrance. As the van slowly moved forward it collided with a motor cyclist. Stamp J. stated (at 379/380) that:

> "I do think it important to emphasise that if a driver in one way or another gives the driver of another vehicle or a pedestrian an indication that he, the driver, is going to stop, or is stopping, or has stopped, and will give the other party passage in front of his vehicle, he is merely telling him that he, the driver, is not going to run over him or run into him, he does not thereby indicate that, if the other party crosses beyond the shelter of his vehicle, he will be safe."

In *Worsfold* v *Howe* [1980] 1 WLR 1175 a tanker driver indicated that a car driver could emerge from a side turning, whereupon it collided with a motorist travelling on the main road. Again, no action was brought against the tanker driver. (This is a slightly confusing case as the leading judgment of Browne L.J. made it clear that *Clarke* v *Winchurch* was a decision on its own facts and laid down no principle of law. But this dictum applied to the apportionment of liability between the emerging driver and the injured motorist, and not the liability of the signalling driver).

There is, however, an apparent exception to the general rule. In *Clarke* v *Winchurch* (ibid) Phillimore L.J. and Russell L.J. both noted (at 73 and 76) that if the driver who flashed his lights had noted the presence and approach of the vehicle who collided with the emerging motorist, this case would "give rise to different considerations". If, in other words, the driver who gave the signal realised that a collision might subsequently ensue, he would then owe the emerging motorist "a duty to do his best to stop him". Presumably, in certain circumstances, it would also be negligent to give the signal in the first place.

Parked and stationary vehicles

Unlighted vehicles

Rule 223 of the Highway Code provides:

> "All vehicles MUST display parking lights when parked on a road or lay-by on a road with a speed limit greater than 30 mph."

In *Hill-Venning* v *Beszant* [1950] 2 All E.R.1151 Denning L.J. stated (at 1153) that:

"The presence of an unlighted vehicle in a road is prima facie evidence of negligence on the part of the driver, and it is for him to explain how it came to be unlighted and why he could not move it out of the way or give warning to oncoming traffic."

Numerous cases attest to the presumption of negligence:

- *Fotheringham* v *Prudence* (1962) Times, 16 May. The defendant was driving along in the dark when one wheel came off and he was obliged to pull into the nearside of the road. The vehicle displayed no rear lights or reflectors. The claimant approached on his motor cycle at 10–12 mph and collided with the rear of the lorry. The Court of Appeal held that there was "ample evidence of negligence and causation".
- *Barber* v *British Road Services* (1964) Times, 18 November. The defendant attempted to execute a "U" turn on the Oxford-Banbury Road at 3 a.m. on a dark and rainy morning. At a point when the vehicle (which displayed no lateral lights) was at right angles to the road, it was struck by the claimant's lorry. It was held that the defendant driver had given no sufficient explanation to rebut the presumption of negligence.
- *Jordan* v *North Hampshire Hire Ltd* [1970] RTR 212. The defendant's articulated lorry, which was 35 ft. long, emerged from a driveway and crossed the highway. The vehicle had reflectors but no lights on its side. It was struck by the claimant's vehicle driving at 60 mph along the northbound lane. The Court of Appeal concluded that the lorry, to the certain knowledge of the defendant's driver, was inadequately lit to give proper warning to approaching motorists.

This does not, of course, preclude a finding of contributory negligence. The fact that a motorist runs into a stationary unlighted vehicle does not establish that the driver or keeper of the motionless vehicle was solely to blame. It is a question of fact depending on the particular circumstances: *Henley* v *Cameron* [1949] 65 TLR 17, per Tucker L.J. at 18/19.

In *Hill* v *Phillips* [1963] 107 Sol.Jo. 890 and *Lee* v *Lever* [1974] RTR 35, both cases were stationary unlit vehicles were struck by other traffic, liability was apportioned equally on the grounds of the claimant's "failure to keep a good look-out". Similarly, in *Drew* v

Western Scottish Motor Traction Co. (1947) SC 222, where a bus collided with a van whose rear light was obscured by the lower half of the open back door, contributory negligence was assessed at 50%. Lord Mackay referred (at 232) to the bus driver's "lack of vigilance". In *Hanman v Mann* [1984] RTR 252 the claimant motor cyclist collided with a car parked without lights just before a junction. The Court of Appeal upheld a finding of 75% contributory negligence.

It is also possible for the evidence to entirely rebut the presumption of negligence. In *Butland v Coxhead* (1968) 112 Sol.Jo. 465 the defendant's appropriately lit lorry broke down and could not be moved from the side of the road. The claimant, a learner, drove his scooter into a collision with the rear of the lorry. The defendants were not liable. In *Moore v Maxwells of Emsworth Limited* (ibid) 1 WLR 1077 the claimant collided with the defendant's parked and unlit trailer. The claimant failed to prove any liability as the trailer's lights had fused shortly before the collision and the driver, as he attempted to mend the lights, had sent his mate to the rear of the vehicle to warn traffic. In *Dymond v Pearce* [1972] 1 All E.R. 1142 a motor cyclist collided with a lorry that was parked on a dual carriageway. The Court of Appeal held that the sole cause of the accident was the negligence of the motor cyclist who, in the words of the trial judge, (at 1147): "was watching the attractive young ladies on the pavement instead of looking ahead of him to see what conditions he was about to encounter".

Various other means of exoneration are hinted at in the reported cases:

- *Barber v British Road Services* (ibid). The Court of Appeal observed that "some lateral light could have been shown".
- *Jordan v North Hampshire Plant Hire Ltd* (ibid). Sachs L.J. indicated (at 215) that "the lorry driver's mate could have flashed a torch as a warning" and suggested that liability could have been avoided had he done so.
- *Hill v Phillips* (ibid). A lighted lorry was parked in front of an unlighted trailer. Upjohn L.J. suggested that the defendant driver would have taken adequate precaution had he reversed the lorry behind the trailer and left the lorry's lights on.

Lighted vehicles

Rule 214 of the Highway Code provides:
   "**Parking**
- You MUST switch off the . . . headlights and foglights."

To park a lorry on the wrong side of the road with its headlights still illuminated was "plain and obvious negligence": *Chisman* v *Electromotion (Export) Ltd* (1969) 113 Sol.Jo. 246.

Side marker lamps and reflectors

RV Lighting Regs 1989

Regulations 21 and 22 (and Schedules 9 and 17) make complex provision for the illumination of long/heavy goods vehicles (particularly by means of additional side marker lamps), and those carrying projecting or overhanging loads. (See also the Highway Code, rule 224).

Discussion

Although most of the reported cases predate the inception and passage of the 1989 regulations, they serve to highlight the importance of additional illumination for large vehicles and (by implication in negligence) the consequences of non-compliance with the regulatory regime. Reference has already been made to *Barber* v *British Road Services* (pages 115 and 116) and *Jordan* v *North Hampshire Plant Hire Ltd* (pages 115 and 116). In *Lancaster* v *HB & H Transport Ltd* [1979] RTR 380 the defendant driver guided a "very large articulated lorry" across the A1 early on a February morning as it "was still getting light". The side of the vehicle only displayed a small marker light and orange reflector. The claimant was killed when his car crashed into the underneath of the lorry. Liability was essentially founded on the conclusion that the defendant driver should never have embarked on a manoeuvre that, given the prevailing conditions, was "little short of lethal" (per Lane L.J. at 385). One reason for such poor visibility was, of course, the comparative paucity of the illumination to the side of the defendant's vehicle.

Chapter 9

Animals on the highway

At common law an owner of an animal is only liable in the event that it strays onto the highway if:

- having brought it onto the highway, he fails to take reasonable care to prevent damage to other parties; or
- being aware of its "peculiar propensities", he allows it to stray onto the highway from adjoining pasture.

There is no general duty to restrain or control an animal and no duty to fence land adjoining a highway so as to prevent an animal straying onto it. These exceptions to the general principles of negligence, known as the rule in *Searle v Wallbank*, were codified (and partly abolished) in the Animals Act 1971. Additional reference can be made to the Dangerous Dogs Act 1991.

Common law

Searle v Wallbank [1947] AC 341

A cyclist was injured when a horse strayed from a field adjoining the highway through a gap in the perimeter hedge, It was held that:

> "The owner of a field abutting on the highway is under no prima facie legal obligation to users of the highway so to keep and maintain his hedges and gates along the highway as to prevent his animals straying onto it nor is he under any duty as between himself and users of the highway to take reasonable care to prevent any of his animals, not known to be dangerous, from straying onto the highway."

Care of animals brought onto the highway

In *Deen v Davies* [1935] 2 KB 282 the court of Appeal held that where the owner himself had brought the animal onto the highway, he had a duty to take reasonable care that the animal does not damage other parties.

This duty was not discharged where an animal was incorrectly tethered (*Deen*), where the owner failed to keep a dog on a lead (*Gomberg v Smith* [1963] 1 QB 25), where a horse was left unattended for five minutes (*Landau v Railway Executive* (1949) 99 L.Jo. 235), where a farmer attempted to drive cattle along a highway in the absence of a man placed at the head of the herd (*Harrison* v *Jackson* (1947) 14 LJ MCCR 242), where a farmer entrusted the job to his inexperienced 17 year old son (*Friend* v *Facey* (1963) Times, March 19) and where a farmer failed to provide his men with lights (*Andrews* v *Watts* [1971] RTR 484).

Where, however, an owner employed a competent drover, there was no evidence of failure to take reasonable care: *Ludlam* v *Peel* (1939) Times, October 10 and *Imrie* v *Clark* (1939) (unreported, cited in *Binghams Motor Claims Cases*, 243). Where a defendant stationed himself by the gateway of his farm and illuminated the highway with a hand held lamp, he was not liable when a motor cycle collided with one of his cows: *Martin* v *Zinn* (1960) Times, March 9).

The Highway Code, rule 44, provides specific guidance on the herding of animals:

> "**Animals being herded.** These should be kept under control at all times. You should, if possible, send another person along the road in front to warn other road users, especially at a bend or the brow of a hill. It is safer not to move animals after dark, but if you do, then wear reflective clothing and ensure that lights are carried (white at the front and red at the rear of the herd)."

In *Bativala* v *West* [1970] 1 QB 716, a case which immediately preceded the introduction of the Animals Act 1971, the exception was further developed. Where a pony competing in a gymkhana lost both its saddle and young rider, causing it to dash into the path of a vehicle, it was held that each link in the chain of causation was reasonably foreseeable. The court concluded that when an animal escaped from a situation in which it was under direct human control, the facts would be decided in accordance with the ordinary principles of negligence.

Straying animals with "peculiar propensities"

In *Fitzgerald* v *E.D. & A.D. Cooke Bourne (Farms) Ltd* [1964] 1 QB, following *Searle* v *Wallbank* (ibid), the court found that a horse was not vicious but had a natural propensity to gallop up to nearby pedestrians. In these circumstances it was reasonably foreseeable that it might cause injury were it to stray onto the highway and the owner was liable. Evidence that a dog was not vicious in the ordinary sense of the term, but that its "frolicsome disposition" prompted it to run into cyclists, provided no defence for its hapless owner: *Howarth* v *Straver* (1953) (cited in *Binghams Motor Claims Cases*, 241). However, where the owner was not aware of a dog's "unwelcome attitude to users of the highway", the claimant's action failed: *Lister* v *Vergette* (1964) Times, June 12. A similar result occurred in *Thorp* v *King Bros* (1957) Times Feb. 23, where a cow "which had never shown any sign of vice" had been frightened by people shouting and waving their arms in Guildford Market. Some animals, such as sheep, were almost immune to a finding of "unnatural tendencies": see, for example, *Heath's Garage Ltd* v *Hodges* [1916] 2 KB 370.

The Animals Act 1971

The Act expressly abolished the rule in *Searle* v *Wallbank*. Otherwise it retained and codified many of the existing common law principles and reference to the previous case law can still illustrate and illuminate the statutory provisions. The sections of relevance to road traffic accidents are as follows:

Section 8: Duty to take care to prevent damage from animals straying onto the highway
Section 8 (1) provides:

> "So much of the rules of the common law relating to liability for negligence as excludes or restricts the duty which a person might owe to others to take such care as is reasonable to see that damage is not caused by animals straying onto a highway is hereby abolished."

The exception laid down in *Searle* v *Wallbank* is, therefore, abolished and, in respect of damage caused by animals straying onto the highway, the owner, or the person having control of the animal will be liable to the extent that the damage was caused as a result of his failure to take reasonable care.

Section 2; Liability for damage done by dangerous animals
Section 2 (1) provides:

> "Where any damage is caused by an animal which belongs to a dangerous species, any person who is a keeper of the animal is liable for the damage, except as otherwise provided by this Act."

Dangerous species
In section 6 (2) a "dangerous species" is defined as a species -

> "(a)   which is not commonly domesticated in the British Islands; and
>
> (b)   whose fully grown animal normally has such characteristics that they are likely, unless restrained, to cause severe damage or that any damage they may cause is likely to be severe."

Classification is purely a question of law. It has been held to include bears (*Pearsons v Coleman* (1948) 1 KB 359), elephants (*Behrens v Bertram Mills Circus Ltd* [1957] 2 QB 1) and lions (*Murphy v Zoological Society of London* (1962) Times, November 14). The Schedule to the Dangerous Wild Animals Act 1976 contains a detailed, (but perhaps incomplete) list of species. The provision attracts strict liability, whether or not "the damage" is of a kind associated with the animal in question.

Non-dangerous species
Section 2 (2) provides for liability:

"Where damage is caused by an animal which does not belong to a dangerous species, a keeper of the animal is liable for the damage, except as otherwise provided by this Act, if

(a) the damage is of a kind to which the animal, unless restrained, was likely to cause or which, if caused by the animal, was likely to be severe; and

(b) the likelihood of the damage or of its being severe was due to characteristics of the animal which are not normally found in animals of the same species or are not normally so found except at particular times or in particular circumstances; and

(c) those characteristics were known to that keeper or were at any time known to a person who at that time had charge of the animal as that keeper's servant or, where that keeper is head of a household, or known to another keeper of the animal who is a member of that household and under the age of 16."

The court's approach
In *Curtis v Betts* [1990] 1 WLR 459 Stuart-Smith L.J., having noted that the provision was "not easy to construe", stated (at 471) that:

"In my view it is desirable, when judge's have to decide cases under section 2 (2), that they should consider each part of the sub-section in turn and satisfy themselves that the claimant has made out his case on one or other of the limbs of each part."

This "step by step approach" was subsequently followed in *Hunt v Wallis* [1994] PIQR 128. The court must also (perhaps as an initial step) determine whether the defendant is a keeper of the animal.

"Keeper"

By section 6 (3) a person is a keeper of an animal if:

"(a) he owns the animal or has it in his possession; or
 (b) he is the head of a household of which a member under the age of 16 owns the animal or has it in his possession; and if at any time an animal ceases to be owned by or to be in the possession of a person, any person immediately before that time was the keeper thereof by virtue of the preceding provisions of this sub-section continues to be the keeper of the animal until another person becomes a keeper thereof by virtue of both provisions."

Section 6 (4) provides an exception:

"Where an animal is taken into and kept in possession for the purpose of preventing it from causing damage or of restoring it to its owner, a person is not a keeper of it by virtue only of that possession."

More than one person can, therefore, be simultaneously liable for the same animal. A person with the custody of the animal under contract with the owner, such as a trainer, livery man or dog walker, is a keeper and will potentially (subject to his knowledge) be subject to the same liability as the owner.

"Damage"

It is not necessary to show that the severity of the damage was caused by the abnormal characteristics of the animal, but simply that the damage caused by the animal was likely to be severe. In *Smith* v *Ainger* (1990) Times, June 5, a case where a pedestrian on the highway was knocked down by an aggressive dog, Neill L.J. outlined the material issues:

"(1) Was personal injury to a human a kind of damage which the defendant's dog, unless restrained, was likely to cause?
 (2) Was personal injury to a human, if caused by that dog, likely to be severe?"

"Characteristics"

A claimant need not demonstrate that the animal has a vicious tendency to injure people by attacking them: it is sufficient to show that it has characteristics of the kind not normally found in its species or breed: *Wallace* v *Newton* [1982] 2 All E.R. 106. Section 2 (2) (b) specifically contemplates both permanent and temporary characteristics. Thus, in *Curtis* v *Betts* (ibid), a bull mastiff was territorially possessive but only at particular times or in certain circumstances.

"Knowledge"

The Act requires knowledge of the animal's characteristics. Knowledge means "actual knowledge": it is not sufficient that the keeper should have knowledge, but, as a matter of fact, did not. The knowledge is either that of the keeper or that imputed by a servant or another keeper in the same household: S.2 (2) (c). Such knowledge may be acquired by incidence of past damage or, as in *Smith* v *Ainger* (ibid), the apparent propensity of the animal to do the harm in fact caused.

Defences

The Act provides the keeper with certain defences. The wording of section 2 (which imposes liability "except as otherwise provided") suggests that other defences previously available at common law are no longer of validity.

(i) Fault and contributory negligence of the claimant

Section 5 (1) provides:

> "A person is not liable under ss 2-4 of this Act for any damage which is due wholly to the fault of the person suffering it."

Section 10 applies the provisions of the Law Reform (Contributory Negligence) Act 1945, so that the court may apportion liability where the claimant is held to be partly to blame for the damage.

The Highway Code contains various provisions by which a motorist's conduct can be assessed:

> "**190. Animals.** When passing animals, drive slowly. Give them plenty of room and be ready to stop. Do not scare animals by sounding your horn or revving your engine. Look out for animals being led or ridden on the road and take extra care and keep your speed down at left hand bends and/or narrow country roads. If a road is blocked by a herd of animals, stop and switch off your engine until they have left the road. Watch out for animals on unfenced roads.
>
> **191. Horse riders.** Be particularly careful of horses and riders, especially when overtaking. Always pass wide and slow. Horse riders are often children, so take extra care and remember riders may ride in double file when escorting a young or inexperienced horse rider. Look out for horse riders' signals and heed a request to slow or stop. Treat all horses as a potential hazard and take great care."

(ii) Claimant voluntarily accepting the risk
Section 5 (2) provides:

"A person is not liable under s 2 of this Act for any damage suffered by a person who has voluntarily accepted the risk thereof."

It is difficult, though not impossible, to entertain much practical relevance to road traffic accident claims. But where, for example, a motorist drives across property he knows to be populated by animals, he could reasonably expect this defence to be levied against him.

(iii) Claimant as trespasser
Section 5 (3) provides that a person is not liable under section 2 to trespassers where the animal is "reasonably kept" for "the protection of personal property". Again, this "guard dog's defence" is of little application to motor claims.

(iv) Common land
Section 8 (2) provides:

"Where damage is caused by animals straying from unfenced land to a highway a person who placed them on the land should not be regarded as having committed a breach of the duty to take care by reason only of placing them there if–
a) the land is common land, or is land situated in an area where fencing is not customary, or is a town or village green; and
b) he had a right to place the animals on that land."

This provision – which, in relation to "common land", effectively preserves the spirit (if not the rule) of *Searle* v *Wallbank* – constitutes an important exception to the ambit of statutory liability. There must be many areas nationwide (such as moorland) where fencing "is not customary." A claimant must, therefore, take great care to identify the status and nature of the land from where the animal strayed.

(v) Release by malicious third party
In *Jaundrill* v *Gillett* [1996] Times, January 30 the claimant's vehicle collided with a number of riderless horses. It was common ground that the horses had escaped from a field because a malicious intruder had opened the gate and driven them onto an unlit road. Russell L.J. suggested that if it could be shown that the defendant had failed to take reasonable care then he could still be liable under the Act. However, as the cause of the damage was not a "characteristic" of the horses, but the release of the animals by a third party, judgment was entered for the defendant. Whilst not, therefore, amounting to a

defence as such, it is clear that liability will be negated if the keeper can show that he took reasonable care and the damage was entirely caused by the intervention of a third party.

Dogs

Liability for damage caused by dogs can be founded in the tort of negligence or under the provisions of the Animals Act 1971 – see above. Threat can be posed to motorists and, in particular, pedestrians. The Highway Code gives guidance to both:

> "**42. Dogs.** Do not let a dog out on a road on its own. Keep it on a short lead when walking on the pavement, road or path shared with cyclists.
> "**43.** When in a vehicle, make sure dogs or other animals are suitably restrained so that they cannot distract you while you are driving or injure you if you stop quickly."

Examples from the reported cases include the following:

- *Gomberg* v *Smith* [1963] 1 QB 25; the defendant was liable for a large St. Bernard which "shot out" into the road and collided with the claimant's van.
- *Draper* v *Hodder* [1972] 2 QB 556; the defendant was liable for Jack Russell terrier puppies which "attacked as a pack."
- *Smith* v *Prendergast* [1984] Times, October 18; the defendant was liable for an "adopted stray" Alsatian dog which attacked an infant pedestrian.
- *Smith* v *Ainger* (1990) Times, June 5; the defendant was liable for an Alsatian which knocked over and injured the pedestrian claimant.
- *Curtis* v *Betts* [1990] 1 WLR 459; the defendant was liable for a "territorially possessive" bull mastiff which savaged the infant claimant.
- *Hunt* v *Wallis* [1994] PIQR 128; the claimant was injured by a "comparatively large and potentially fast-moving" Border Collie.

Reference can also be made to three other statutes:
(1) the Dogs Act 1871 (as amended by the Dogs Act 1906 and the Dogs (Amendment) Act 1928),
(2) the Road Traffic Act 1988 and
(3) the Dangerous Dogs Act 1991.

Dogs Act 1871

Section 2 provides for the "control or destruction" of a dog that is "dangerous." "Dangerous" should be construed by reference to its ordinary everyday meaning and the danger presented can be to human beings as well as livestock such as sheep, cattle, horses or poultry: *Briscoe* v *Shattock* [1998] Times, October 12.

Road Traffic Act 1988

Section 27 states:

> "(1) A person who causes or permits a dog to be on a designated road without the dog being held on a lead is guilty of an offence."

Sub-sections (2) to (8) define a "designated road" and "local authority" and provide for a number of exceptions to liability.

Dangerous Dogs Act 1991

The Act, according to its preamble, is designed to "prohibit persons from having in their possession or custody dogs belonging to types bred for fighting" and "enable restrictions to be imposed in relation to other types of dog which present a serious danger to the public." Thus:

- **Section 1. Dogs bred for fighting**, prohibits the breeding of dogs for fighting and requires such dogs to be muzzled/kept on a lead whilst in a public place;
- **Section 3. Keeping dogs under proper control**, imposes strict (criminal) liability on the owners of dogs of all breeds which are in a public place and which are "dangerously out of control": see *R* v *Bezzina* [1994] 3 All E.R. 964. Liability under section 3 can be established by acts of omission (such as a failure to properly chain or tether the dog) as well as those of commission: *Greener* v *DPP* [1996] Times, February 15.

Civil liability?

Breach of these statutory provisions does not give rise to a separate cause of action in civil proceedings: the purpose of all three Acts is to provide for criminal sanction. Nonetheless, a conviction (or mere proof of breach) will constitute evidence of negligence. It is appropriate (insofar as CPR Part 16 either demands or allows for voluminous particularity) for reference to be made to the relevant statute in the Particulars of Claim.

Wild animals on the highway

How should a motorist react to the sudden or unexpected appearance of a wild animal on the highway?

The reported cases, on balance, support the driver who instinctively attempts to avoid the animal, even at the expense of another road user.

In *Parkinson* v *Liverpool Corporation* [1950] 1 All E.R. 367 an omnibus driver executed an emergency stop when an unattended dog suddenly emerged into his path. The claimant, a passenger, was thrown to the floor and sustained personal injury. The Court of Appeal held that the driver, faced with a sudden emergency, had acted as an ordinary and careful driver ought to act in such circumstances.

In *Ritchie's Car Hire Ltd* v *Bailey* [1958] LJ 348 a motorist instinctively swerved to avoid a cat that suddenly ran out from the nearside of the road. Judge Gordon Clarke stated (at first instance) that:

> "There might be a school of thought which said that a driver should subordinate the interests of animals to the safety of his passengers, or even of a vehicle, but such a doctrine had never been expressed by Parliament or in the Highway Code. Nowhere is it stated that a driver was at fault in swerving to avoid an animal. The defendant had apparently had no time for thought, but it could not be said that his action would have been a correct one had he had time to reflect on it, yet in the particular circumstances it could not also be said that what the defendant did was unreasonable."

But in *Gussman* v *Gratton-Storey* (1968) CLY 2676 the Court of Appeal upheld "as a matter of law" a finding of negligence against a driver who had applied his brakes violently to avoid a pheasant which ran in front of her car. It should be noted that the report of this case is very brief and the court's reasons are not readily apparent. It is assumed that the decision turned on its particular (even esoteric) facts.

This conclusion is supported by the more recent case of *Welch* v *O'Leary* [1998] CLY 3911. The claimant was forced to make an emergency stop to avoid some ducks that had waddled onto the highway. The defendant, who was riding a motor cycle and about to overtake the claimant, was unable to avoid a collision. The defendant contended that the driver should subordinate the interests of wild animals to those of human road users. He also sought to draw a distinction between *Parkinson* and *Ritchie's* cases, which involved domestic animals and *Gussman*, where the offending beast was a wild bird. Nonetheless the court (albeit at first instance) gave judgment for the claimant and held that the defendant was wholly responsible for the accident.

Chapter 10

Defective vehicles

Sometimes a road traffic accident is caused by a fault or defect in one of the vehicles involved in the collision. Not only can this lead to a claim (or a Part 20 claim) against the owner of the vehicle, but action may also be contemplated against those responsible for its maintenance, repair and, in certain circumstances, sale and manufacture. Passengers in a public conveyance may similarly look to recover against the operator or carrier. This chapter will examine the potential liability of:

- Owners and drivers
- Garages, repairers and examiners
- Sellers: commercial retailers and private vendors
- Manufacturers
- Hirers
- Public service carriers

Owners and drivers

A motorist must take reasonable care to provide a safe vehicle. In *Readhead* v *The Midland Railway Company* [1869] 4 QB 379 it was stated (at 393) that:

> ""Due care" undoubtedly means ... a high degree of care, and casts on carriers the duty of exercising all vigilance to see whatever is required for the safe conveyance of their passengers is in fit and proper order."

The duty will arise in tort or be implied into the contract for hire or carriage. Reference can be made to The Road Vehicles (Construction and Use) Regulations 1986 and The Occupiers' Liability Act 1957.

The Road Vehicles (Construction and Use) Regulations 1986

The regulations (made under the Road Traffic Act 1988, section 41) impose numerous obligations concerning the condition and maintenance of vehicles. Breach of the regulations does not give rise to a civil cause of action: *Phillips* v *Britannia Hygienic Laundry* [1923] 2 KB 832, *Barkway* v *South Wales Transport Co. Ltd.* [1950] AC 185 and *Tan Chye Choo* v *Ching Kew Moi* [1970] 1 All E.R. 266. But the question of contravention invariably merges with the issue of negligence and proof of breach can be cited as evidence of a failure to take reasonable care: *Winter* v *Cardiff R.D.C.* [1950] 1 All E.R. 819. Indeed, the Highway Code, rule 72, requires that motorists "MUST" comply with the "full requirements" of the regulations.

The Occupiers' Liability Act 1957

An occupier of premises includes a person having control over any vehicle: section 1 (3) (a). Section 2 provides:

> **Extent of occupier's ordinary duty**
> (1) An occupier of premises owes the same duty, the "common duty of care," to all his visitors, except in so far as he is free to and does extend a strict, or exclude his duty to any visitor or visitors by agreement or otherwise.
> (2) The common duty of care is a duty to take such care as in all the circumstances of the case is reasonable to see that the visitor will be reasonably safe in using the premises for the purposes for which he is invited or permitted by the occupier to be there.
> (3) The circumstances relevant for the present purpose includes the degree of care, and of want of care, which would ordinarily be looked for in such a visitor, so that (for example) in proper cases –
> (a) an occupier must be prepared for children to be less careful than adults; and
> (b) an occupier may expect that a person, in the exercise of his calling, will appreciate and guard against any special risks ordinarily in incident to it, so far as the occupier leaves him free to do so.
> (4) In determining whether the occupier of premises has discharged the common duty of care to a visitor, regard is to be had to all the circumstances, so that (for example) –
> (a) where damage is caused to a visitor by a danger of which he has been warned by the occupier, the warning is not to be treated without more as absolving the occupier from liability, unless in all the circumstances it was enough to enable the visitor to be reasonably safe; and
> (b) where damage is caused to a visitor by a danger due to the faulty execution of any work of construction, maintenance or repair by an independent contractor employed by the occupier, the occupier is not to be treated without more as answerable for the danger if in all the circumstances he had acted reasonably in

entrusting the work to an independent contractor and taken such steps (if any) as he reasonably ought in order to satisfy himself that the contractor was competent and that the work had been properly done.

(5) The common duty of care does not impose on an occupier any obligation to a visitor in respect of risks willing accepted as his by the visitor (the question whether risk was so accepted to be decided on the same principles as in other cases in which one person owes a duty of care to another).

(6) ...."

Reasonable care and "latent damage"

A motorist will not be held liable for a defect that could not have been detected with reasonable care and skill. This much was confirmed over one hundred and fifty years ago in *Readhead* v *Midland Railway Company* (ibid. at 393):

"But the duty to take due care, however widely construed or however vigorously enforced, will not, as the present action seeks to do, subject the defendants to the plain injustice of being compelled by the law to make reparation for a disaster arising from a latent defect in the machinery which they are obliged to use, which no human skill or care could either have prevented or detected."

Other examples include:

- Carriage "upset" when a bolt on the underside broke causing the splinter bar to become displaced – defendant liable; *Hyman* v *Nye* (1881) 6 QBD 685.
- Passenger injured when the trolley arm of an electric tramcar became entangled in the overhead gear – defendant not liable; *Newberry* v *Bristol Tramways and Carriage Co. Ltd* (1912) 29 TLR 177.
- Bus overturned owing to deflated tyre caused by a defect in the metal of the flange under the tyre – defendant liable; *Ritchie* v *Western Scottish MT Co.* (1935) S.L.T. 13.

In *R* v *Spurge* [1961] 2 QB 205 the defendant, who had taken delivery of a sports car a few days before, drove the vehicle around a very sharp and dangerous left hand bend. As he did so the car crossed the centre white line and collided with an oncoming motor scooter. Expert witnesses suggested that the brakes were in a very bad condition and that vigorous application at 30 mph pulled the car violently to its off-side. It was held (obiter) that there is no distinction between a man being suddenly deprived of all control of a motor car by some sudden affliction to his person and being so deprived by some defect suddenly manifesting itself in the motor car.

The leading case is now *Henderson* v *Henry E. Jenkins & Sons* [1970] AC 282. A lorry was descending a hill when the brakes failed and it struck another motorist who had just alighted from his vehicle. The failure was due to the sudden escape of brake fluid from a hole in a pipe in the hydraulic braking system resulting from corrosion of that pipe. The House of Lords (by a 3 to 2 majority) held that:

(1) The (evidential) burden of proving "latent defect" rested on the defendants;
(2) The defence could not be made out unless the defendants showed that they had taken all reasonable care in the circumstances. This demanded that they adduce evidence of the past history of the vehicle, where it had been, what had been carried and in what conditions it had operated.

To what extent – if at all – is a motorist entitled to place reliance on a valid MOT Certificate? In *Rees* v *Saville* [1983] RTR 332 the defendant's vehicle suddenly swerved to the right and struck the claimant's parked car. The accident was caused by a failure or bad joint on the steering mechanism of the front off-side wheel of the defendant's car. The defendant had owned the vehicle for just over a month. It had passed an MOT test 3–4 months prior to the purchase. Expert evidence was that the condition of the ball joint was not easily discernible on inspection, but should have been detected during the MOT test. It was held that there was no negligence on the part of the defendant. The Court of Appeal accepted that the legislation which imposed a duty on motorists owning cars more than three years old to submit them for examination did not relieve the owner of any personal obligation to use reasonable care in relation to the maintenance of his vehicle. Nonetheless, in relation to matters which are the subject of the test, the submission for a test is a way of performing the common law duty of care and that if a purchaser received a valid MOT certificate then, provided that the certificate was not too old, it is a factor that must be taken into account in deciding whether the owner was obliged to subject the car to an expert for inspection.

Section 2 (4) (a) and "warnings"

A warning by the motorist (as "occupier") does not absolve him from liability unless, in all the circumstances, it was enough to enable the passenger (the "visitor") to be reasonably safe.

This should not be interpreted as an obligation to issue a warning to beware of "well known hazards." In *Donn* v *Schacter* [1975] RTR 238 the claimant tripped and fell when her foot became entangled in the loop of a seat belt as she alighted from the rear seat of the defendant's car. Phillips J. stated (at 242) that:

> "I do not think that there is an obligation on the driver, every time he or she gets in or out of the car with a passenger, to make a visual check of the seat belt ... (or) to issue a warning to the passenger to look to make sure that the seat belts are satisfactory."

This judgment can be contrasted with the decision in *McReady* v *Miller* [1979] RTR 186. Again the passenger tripped and fell on the trailing end of a seat belt. This time the Court of Appeal held that the driver was in breach of the common duty of care. The facts were necessarily distinctive: the defendant was a mini-cab driver, the claimant was unfamiliar with the car and no internal light was provided.

Garages and repairers

Liability for a defective repair can arise in either contract or tort.

Contract

Three cases illustrate (at least historically) the nature and extent of a repairer's obligation:

- *G.H. Myers & Co.* v *Brent Cross Service Co.* [1934] 1 KB 46; a garage fitted six connecting rods to a car engine, one of which subsequently broke causing extensive damage. It was held that the repairer was liable to use material that was "reasonably fit for its purpose."
- *Stewart* v *Reavel's Garage* [1952] 2 KB 545; the defendants, experienced care repairers, fitted a faulty off-side front brake-drum lining to a Bentley. The next day the fault caused an accident and the car was damaged. It was held that the repairer's duty was to provide a good workmanship, materials of good quality and a braking system reasonably fit for its purpose.

- *Taylor* v *Kiddey* (1968) 118 MLJ 134; an accident was caused when the nearside of the front wheel of the claimant's vehicle became detached. Two months before the defendants had carried out a routine service. It was held that the defendants were liable as the service should have included a check on the front wheels to ensure that the securing bolts were tight.

Reference can now be made to the Supply of Goods and Services Act 1982, section 13, which provides that where the repairer is "acting in the course of a business" (which will almost invariably be the case where a garage is involved) the repairs must be carried out "with reasonable care and skill."

MOT test

The Motor Vehicles (Tests) Regulations 1981, SI 1694 (made under the Road Traffic Act 1988, section 43) provide for the examination of vehicles every three years and the issue of test certificates. Regulation 14 is deservous of particular mention:

"14 (1) Where a motor vehicle has been submitted for an examination … the examiner … shall have the same responsibility for –

(a) loss of or damage to the vehicle, its equipment or accessories occurring in connection with the carrying out of examination during any period where the vehicle is, in connection with the carrying out of the examination, in the custody of the examiner, … and

(b) loss of or damage to any other property or personal injury (whether fatal or not) being loss, damage or injury arising out of the use of the vehicle in connection with the carrying out of the examination,

as would rest on a person who, having the same facilities for carrying out the examination as are available to the person who is to carry out the examination, an undertaking for payment to accept the custody of the vehicle and to carry out the same examination under a contract making no express provision with respect to the incidents of liabilities between the parties thereto for any such loss, damage or injury."

This provision applies to the actual performance of the examination. To what extent –if at all – will an examiner be liable for the condition of the vehicle once the test has been competed?

In *Rowley* v *Chatham* [1970] RTR 462 the steering column of a van broke down 25 days after the vehicle had undergone an MOT test. It was held, as a matter of fact, that the examination had been properly carried out and would not have revealed that there was a fault or defect in the steering. The duty owed by the examiner is limited to certifying the condition of the vehicle at the date of the examination. Any representation expressed or implicit in the certificate cannot be relied on some months later. Shaw J. expressed his reasoning (at 470) in terms of brutal clarity: "The purpose of ... the regulations in regard to test certificates is not to benefit motorists in general by providing them with an inexpensive means of satisfying themselves that their ageing vehicles remain roadworthy."

This case was followed by *Artingstoll v Hewen's Garages Limited* [1973] RTR 197. Here the period between the MOT test and the subsequent accident was five weeks. Again, the defect concerned a fault in the steering column. Kerr J. confirmed that whilst there is a duty on a examiner to carry out the test with reasonable care and skill, the issue of a certificate merely imports a warranty that the regulations were complied with at the date of the examination. But, in a subtle departure from *Rowley*, he also concluded that there was no reason in principle why a claimant should not succeed where it could be proved that the examination was not carried out with reasonable care and skill that a test certificate should not have been issued, although lapse of time would always present an obstacle to recovery.

With the more recent case of *Rees v Saville* (ibid) (see page 132) it is apparent that, where the facts allow, the MOT test can be a factor in determining the liability for a road traffic accident caused by defects in the vehicle.

Tort

The principles of negligence enunciated in *Donoghue v Stevenson* [1932] AC 562 apply: see, for example, *Malfroot v Nozal* (1935) 51 TLR 551 and *Stennett v Hancock and Peters* [1959] 2 All E.R. 578.

In *Aspin v J. Bretherton & Son* (1947) (unreported, cited in *Bingham's Motor Claims Cases*, 220) the front off-side wheel of a lorry became detached causing the vehicle to collide with a bus. The repairers – who had negligently carried out works of repair and maintenance to the lorry – were liable to a passenger in the bus.

Sellers

The liability of a seller will depend on whether the transaction involved a commercial retailer or a private lender.

Commercial retailers

The Sale of Goods Act 1979, section 14 contains the following (relevant) provisions:

> **"Implied terms about quality or fitness**
>
> (1) Except as provided by the section and section 15 below and subject to any other enactment, there is no implied [term] about the quality or fitness for any particular purpose of goods supplied under a contract of sale.
>
> (2) Where the seller sells goods in the course of a business, there is an implied terms that the goods supplied under the contract are of satisfactory quality.
>
> (2A) For the purposes of this Act, goods are of satisfactory quality if they meet the standard that a reasonable person would regard as satisfactory, taking account of any description of the goods, the price (if relevant) and all other relevant circumstances.
>
> (2B) For the purposes of this Act, the quality of goods includes their state and condition and the following (among others) are in appropriate cases aspects of the quality of the goods –
>
>   (a) fitness for all the purposes for which the goods of the kind in question are commonly supplied;
>
>   (b) appearance and finish;
>
>   (c) freedom from minor defects,
>
>   (d) safety and
>
>   (e) durability
>
> (2C) The term implied by sub-section (2) above does not extend to any matter making the quality of goods unsatisfactory –
>
>   (a) which is specifically drawn to the buyer's attention before the contract is made,
>
>   (b) where the buyer examines the goods before the contract is made, which that examination ought to reveal or
>
>   (c) in the case of a contract for sale by sample which would have been apparent on a reasonable examination of the sample."

Section 14 (2) was amended by the Sale of Goods Act 1994: the words "satisfactory quality" replace the original requirement of "merchantable quality."

New vehicles

In *Bernstein* v *Pamson Motors (Golders Green) Limited* [1987] 2 All E.R. 220 it was suggested that consideration should be given to three main factors:

- First, the nature and consequences of the defect; minor defects can still have very serious consequences.
- Secondly, the car should be safe to drive.
- Thirdly, the ease and cost of a satisfactory repair.

The court should not merely consider a vehicle as a means of transport, but look at the whole range of expectations flowing from the purchase: *Rogers v Parish (Scarborough) Limited* [1987] QB 933. Mustin L.J. defined (at 944) a buyer's entitlement in terms of a vehicle's functional and non-functional aspects:

> "Starting with the purpose for which "goods of that kind" are commonly bought, one would include in respect of any passenger vehicle not merely the buyer's purpose of driving the car from one place to another, but of doing so with the appropriate degree of comfort, ease of handling and reliability and, one might add, of pride in the vehicle's outward and interior appearance."

Section 14 (2B) includes "freedom from minor defects" amongst the list of indicators which a court must consider in determining whether the vehicle is of satisfactory quality. The courts have long accepted that a multitude of minor defects can render a car unfit for its purpose: see *Farnworth Finance Facilities v Attryde* [1970] 1 WLR 1053.

Second-hand vehicles

The test to be applied to a second-hand car is precisely the same as that applicable to a new vehicle: both must be of "satisfactory quality"; see *Business Appliances Specialists Ltd v Nationwide Credit Corpn. Ltd* [1988] RTR 332. Nonetheless it is accepted that it is unreasonable to expect a second-hand vehicle sold at a lesser price to be as good as a new vehicle sold at a higher price.

It is a little difficult to fit the case law into an entirely consistent judicial framework. Some decisions favour the buyer, others serve to limit the expectations of a reasonable purchaser.

Cases favourable to the buyer

In *Hutton v Saville Tractors (Belfast) Ltd* [1986] 12 MIJB it was held that a second-hand car should be "reliable and capable of giving good service and fair performance." In *Shine v General Guarantee Corpn. Ltd* [1988] 1 All E.R. 911 the car had been classed as an insurance company "write-off" after being submerged in water for 24 hours. Although there was no evidence of specific defect, and the car appeared to be generally useable, it was still held to be (under the old statutory provision) "unmerchantable."

Perhaps the most favourable decision to the buyer concerned the case of *Crowther* v *Shannon Motor Co.* [1975] 1 All E.R. 139. The claimant bought a second-hand Jaguar which had covered over 82 000 miles for the price of £390. Three weeks later, after the car had done a further 2000 miles, it required a reconditioned engine after the original seized up. The evidence suggested that the engine was "clapped out" when the defendant sold the car to the claimant. The Court of Appeal awarded £460 damages – more than the claimant had paid for the vehicle in the first place!

Cases favourable to the seller

In *Bartlett* v *Sydney Marcus Ltd* [1965] 1 WLR 1013 the claimant bought a second-hand car from the defendant knowing that the clutch was defective. A post-purchase inspection revealed the defect to be much more severe than originally thought. The Court of Appeal acknowledged that if a new car was sold with a defective clutch it would be "unmerchantable" (now "unsatisfactory"). But where the car was sold under a description which referred to a defective clutch it could not be said to be unmerchantable because the defect proved to be more serious than expected.

In *Business Appliances Specialists Ltd* v *Nationwide Credit Corpn. Ltd* (ibid) a second-hand Mercedes developed serious wear in the valves, valve guides and oil seal after covering 37 000 miles. Expert evidence was produced to suggest that such wear was very unusual on a Mercedes of that age and mileage. Nevertheless it was held that second-hand cars must be expected to have some defect and ordinary wear and tear. There was no breach of the requirement that the car of merchantable quality.

Private vendor

Goods sold privately by a seller are not within the ambit of section 14 of the 1994 Act. Nonetheless section 13, which requires conformity with description, does apply. Thus, a person who sells a second-hand vehicle as a "Herald, convertible, white 1962," impliedly provides that it is a 1961 Herald (and not, as was actually the case, two cars welded together, only one of which was a 1961 model), though he does not impliedly promise that it is of any particular quality. The general rules of contract also apply to a private seller of a motor vehicle. A buyer could, therefore, bring a claim in negligent misrepresentation or for repudiatory breach of contract.

Otherwise there are circumstances in which the buyer will be entitled to rely on the tort of negligence. Where, for example, a seller knows that the vehicle is in a dangerous condition, he will be in breach of the duty of care owed to the buyer if he fails to give an appropriate warning: *Hurley* v *Dyke* [1979] RTR 265.

Manufacturers

Under the Consumer Protection Act 1987, sections 1–9, a "producer" (section 1) of goods (essentially, but not exclusively, the manufacturer) is liable (section 2) for "death or personal injury or any loss or damage to any property" (section 5) caused by a "defect" (section 3) in the product. Section 4 provides certain defences to liability under the Act.

The tort of negligence, based on the principles outlined in *Donoghue* v *Stevenson* [1932] AC 562, is also applicable. To this end it is not necessary for the claimant to identify any particular individual as being responsible for the defect or for any particular act of negligence to be specified. In *Carroll* v *Fearon* [1998] Times January 26 the Court of Appeal found that a tyre was subject to an "immediate and catastrophic" disintegration as a result of "something that had gone wrong in the manufacturing process," and the manufacturers, Dunlop, were liable for the resulting accident.

Hirers

A contract for hire contains an implied warranty that the vehicle is fit for the purpose for which it is hired. The hirer owes a concurrent duty to take reasonable care to keep the vehicle in a safe condition: see *Spear* v *Self Motoring Ltd* (1947) S No. 27 and *Reed* v *Dean* [1949] 1 KB 188. In *Herschtal* v *Stewart & Arden Ltd* [1940] 1 KB 155 the claimant suffered injury when the nearside rear wheel came off his hire car. The defendant argued that at the time of delivery the claimant had signed a receipt stating that the car was accepted as being in good condition and as seen, tested and approved. The court held that whilst the receipt might affect the contractual liability, it did not protect the defendant in a claim in negligence.

Public service carriers

The duty of those who are in charge of public conveyances is similar to that owed by the private motorist. Reasonable care and skill must be taken for the safety of passengers and the "common duty of care" under the Occupiers Liability Act 1957, section 2(2) applies. Section 5(1) additionally provides that where the contract of carriage is silent on the question the carrier's liability for the safety of the vehicle the duty implied shall be the common duty of care.

The existence of a defect will amount to prima facie evidence of negligence: *Lilly* v *Tilling Ltd* (1912) 57 S.J.57. Such evidential presumption will be rebutted if the carrier can show that it had exercised reasonable care and skill in detecting and remedying defects: *Newberry* v *Bristol Tramways & Co* (1912) 107 L.T.801. Over the years the standard of reasonable care expected from carriers has undoubtedly developed and the 'evidential burden of proof' now establishes an onerous threshold: *Henderson* v *Henry E Jenkins & Sons* [1970] AC 281.

Part II

Defences and Conditions of No Liability

Chapter 11

Defences

This chapter will examine a number of defences of general application. Defences applicable to a specific statutory duty are outlined at the appropriate chapter. Consideration will be given to the following:

- Contributory negligence;
- Volenti non fit injuria;
- Limitation;
- Individual immunity.

Contributory Negligence

Responsibility for an accident may be shared between the parties and in these circumstances damages should be apportioned between them.

The Law Reform (Contributory Negligence) Act 1945, section 1 (1) provides:

> "Where any person suffers damage as the result partly of his own fault and partly of the fault of any other person or persons, a claim in respect of that damage shall not be defeated by reason of the fault of the persons suffering the damage, but the damages recoverable in respect thereof shall be reduced to such an extent as the court thinks just and equitable having regard to the claimant's share in the responsibility for the damage."

Negligence, in this context, means any careless act or omission which materially contributed to the claimant's injury or damage: it does not depend on the breach of a legal duty to take care.

100% contributory negligence?

A claimant cannot be found to be 100% contributory negligent. Such a finding is logically unsupportable as the Act of 1945 operates on the premise that there is causal fault on the part of both parties so that responsibility must be shared: *Pitts v Hunt* [1991] 1 QB 24. Instead, where a claimant is the sole cause of his loss and damage, he will fail to establish causation and the claim will be dismissed.

Application in road traffic accident claims

In *Davies* v *Swan Motor Co.* [1949] 2 KB 291 Denning L.J.(at 326) outlined the following approach:

> "Speaking generally, therefore, the questions in road accidents are simply these: What faults were there which caused the damage? What are the proportions in which the damages should be apportioned having regard to the respective responsibilities of those in fault?"

Examples

Each case turns on its individual facts: "It is a matter of common sense depending on the evidence": *Jones* v *Livox Quarries Limited* [1952] 2 QB 608. For an indication as to the various approaches applied to drivers, passengers and pedestrians, reference should be made to chapters 2, 4, 5 and 6 respectively. In a number of particular situations, however, certain principles can be outlined:

Seat belts

In *Froom* v *Butcher* [1976] QB 286, Lord Denning M.R. stated that:

> "Everyone knows, or ought to know, that when he goes out in a car he should fasten the seat belt. It is so well known that it goes without saying, not only for the driver, but also the passenger. If either the driver or the passenger fails to wear it, and an accident happens – and the injuries would have been prevented or lessened if he had worn it – then his damages should be reduced."

There is nothing, as a matter of logic or public policy, to justify adopting a different standard in relation to rear seat belts: *Biesheuvel* v *Birrell* (1999) Lawtel, C8400282.

It is now compulsory for drivers, front and rear seat passengers to wear (where fitted) seat belts: the Road Traffic Act 1988, sections 14 and 15, the Motor Vehicles (Wearing of Seat Belts) Regulations 1993 (SI.1993/176) and the Motor Vehicles (Wearing of Seat Belts by Children in Front Seats) Regulations 1993 (SI. 1993/31).

Apportionment

In *Froom* v *Butcher*, Lord Denning M.R. (at 296) stated that:

> ". . . (where damage would have prevented altogether) . . . I would suggest that damages should be reduced by 25 per cent. . . . where the evidence will only show that the failure made a considerable difference, I would suggest that damages attributable to the failure to wear a seat belt should be reduced by 15 per cent."

Subsequent cases have, if anything, tended to slightly exceed these figures. In *Salmon* v *Newland* (1983) Times, May16, where the claimant would have sustained significantly less severe facial injuries had she worn a seat belt, a reduction of 20% was applied.

Exceptions; no contributory negligence
In *Froom* v *Butcher* Lord Denning entertained the existence of exceptions to the ordinary run of cases and referred (at 295) to the fact that a "man who is unduly fat or a woman who is pregnant may rightly be excused because, if there is an accident, the strap across the abdomen may do more harm than good". In *McKay* v *Borthwick* (1982) SLT 265 the claimant was held not to have been negligent in not wearing a seat belt on a short journey as she suffered from a hiatus hernia on which the strap would have pressed. Similarly, in *Condon* v *Condon* [1978] RTR 483, it was held that a claimant's phobia of being trapped in the event of an accident made her an "extraordinary case" so that a refusal to wear a seat belt did not constitute a failure on her part to take reasonable care of her own safety.

The Motor Vehicles (Wearing of Seat Belts) Regulations 1993, regulations 5 and 6, now provide a detailed list of approved exceptions applicable to persons aged 14 and over. They include:

- a person holding a medical certificate; i.e. a medical certificate signed by a doctor to the effect that it is inadvisable on medical grounds for him to wear a seat belt;
- a person using a vehicle constructed or adapted for the delivery of goods or mail to consumers or addressees, as the case may be, while engaged in making local rounds of deliveries or collections;
- a person driving a vehicle while performing a manoeuvre which includes reversing;
- a person driving or riding a vehicle while it is being used for Fire Brigade or police purposes or for carrying a person in lawful custody;
- a driver of a licensed taxi or private hire vehicle answering a call for hire or carrying a passenger for hire;
- a person riding in a vehicle, being used under a trade licence, for the purpose of investigating or remedying a mechanical fault in the vehicle;
- a disabled person who is wearing a disabled person's belt;
- a person riding in a vehicle while he is taking part in a procession organised by or on behalf of the Crown.

The statutory regime also provides for a number of complicated exceptions applicable to children aged 14 and under. These are outlined in: the Road Traffic Act 1988, section 15; the Motor Vehicle (Wearing of Seat Belt) Regulations 1993, regulations 9 and 10; and the Motor Vehicle (Wearing of Seat Belts by Children in Front Seats) Regulations 1993, regulation 7.

A newsagent driving to collect bundles of newspapers was not "making local rounds or deliveries" within the meaning of the exception: *Webb* v *Crane* [1988] RTR 204.

A vehicle owner is not negligent if he fails to fit seat belts in a vintage vehicle that had never contained the same: *Hoadley* v *Dartford District Council* (1979) 123 Sol. Jo. 129.

Crash Helmets

The Highway Code, rule 67, provides:

> "On all journeys, the rider and pillion passenger on a motor cycle, scooter or moped MUST wear a protective helmet. Helmets MUST comply with the Regulations and they MUST be fastened securely. It is also advisable to wear eye protectors, which MUST comply with the Regulations. Consider wearing ear protection. Strong boots, gloves and suitable clothing may help to protect you if you fall off."

The substantive law can be found in the Road Traffic Act 1988, sections 16 and 17 and the Motor Cycles (Protective Helmets) Regulations 1998 (S.I. 1998/1807).

In *O'Connell* v *Jackson* [1972] 1 QB 270 the claimant sustained a severe fracture of the skull when he was knocked off his moped. His injuries would have been less severe had he been wearing a crash helmet and his damages were consequently reduced by 15 percent. A motor cyclist who fails to properly secure his crash helmet can expect a reduction of 10 percent: *Capps* v *Miller* [1989] 1 WLR 839.

Children

When considering whether a child has taken reasonable care of his own safety, regard must be had to his age, experience and the particular circumstances of the case. In *Gough* v *Thorne* [1961] 3 All E.R. 398, Lord Denning M.R. held that a "very young child" cannot be guilty of contributory negligence. Thus, in *Abbott* v *Mackie* (1863) 33 L.J. Ex.177, *Calkin* v *McFie & Sons Limited* [1989] 3 All E.R. 613 and *Jones* v *Lawrence* [1969] 3 All E.R. 267, where the infant claimant ran from a pavement into the path of a motor cyclist, no findings of contributory negligence were made on the grounds that the claimants were all only seven years old. But in *McKinnell v White* [1971] S.L.T. 61, *Minter v V & H Contractors (Cambridge) Limited* (1983) Times, 30 June and *Morales v Eccleston* [1991] RTR 151 findings of contributory negligence were upheld against infant claimants aged five, nine and 11 respectively. In *Willbye v Gibbons* (1997) Lawtel C9000165 a claimant aged 12 was found to be 75 percent to blame when she ran into the path of a motorist. Similarly, in *Rowe v Clark* (1998) Lawtel C8400268, where a 14 year old schoolboy was injured whilst crossing a road, a finding of 50 percent contributory negligence was upheld by the Court of Appeal: "A boy aged nearly 15 must be expected to take reasonable care of himself." Nonetheless, for the defendant's liability to be reduced it has to be demonstrated that the child appreciated that his conduct would put him at risk of an accident. Where a nine year child jumped off the pavement into the road to avoid the threat of being hit by another boy, his behaviour was classed as an "involuntary action" and there was no finding of contributory negligence: *J v W* [1999] New Law Digest, July 12. In summary, therefore, whilst children are not expected to exercise the same degree of care required of a normal adult, it is clear that where circumstances allow the court will not shrink from finding fault with the conduct of infants as young as five years old.

Intoxication

Passengers

Where a passenger knowingly travels with a motorist whose ability to drive is impaired by alcohol the deduction for contributory negligence will usually be in the region of 20–25 percent: *Thomas v Fuller* (1977) and *Buckingham v D'Souza* (1978) (unreported, but cited in *Bingham & Berryman's Motor Claims Cases*, 179). (This obviously assumes that ex turpi causa non oritur actio will not apply – see Chapter 12 pages 159–161) Where a passenger is so drunk that he is unable to appreciate that the driver is unfit through drink, there will be an equivalent finding: *Owens v Brimmell* [1977] QB 859. But where there is no evidence to suggest that a sober claimant was aware of the defendant's intoxication, there should be no deduction for contributory negligence: *Traynor v Donovan* [1978] CLY 2612 and *Malone v Rowan* [1984] 3 All E.R. 402.

Pedestrians

Where an intoxicated pedestrian stepped off the pavement and was fatally struck by a car, contributory negligence was assessed at 35 percent: *Kilminster v Rule* (1983) 32 S.A.S.R.39. In another case, *Donohoe v Blundel* (1986) CLY 2254, a young man was run over by a car as he lay in the road. Such was his intoxication that he didn't even realise he had been hit, despite the fact that he had sustained multiple injuries. It was held, at first instance, that contributory negligence should be assessed at two thirds.

Volenti Non Fit Injuria

Volenti Non Fit Injuria, meaning that a person who has expressly or impliedly consented to an act cannot claim for its consequences, has no application in road traffic claims. Insofar as the maxim might negate the liability of the driver of a motor car to his passengers, it is specifically excluded by the Road Traffic Act 1988, section 149, which provides:

> "If any other person is carried in or upon the vehicle while the user is so using it, any antecedent agreement or understanding between them (whether intended to be legally binding or not) shall be of no effect so far as it purports or might be held -
> (a) to negative or restrict any such liability of the user in respect of persons carried in or upon the vehicle as is required by section 154 of this Act to be policy of insurance, or
> (b) to impose any conditions with respect to the enforcement of any such liability of the user."

The defendant may still claim the defence of contributory negligence and/or ex turpi causa non oritor actio: *Winnik* v *Dick* (1984) SLT 185, applied in *Pitts* v *Hunt* [1990] 3 All E.R. 344.

Limitation

Limitation is a procedural defence which must be specifically pleaded by the defendant: CPR, PD16.1. The Limitation Act 1980 prescribes fixed periods for the bringing of different categories of cases and effluxion of time will usually extinguish the claimant's substantive cause of action. In personal injury claims in negligence, nuisance or breach of duty the "primary limitation period" can be extended (or disapplied) if it "appears to the Court that it would be equitable to allow" the action to proceed: section 33, Limitation Act 1980.

The "primary limitation period"

The various limitation periods are well known and do not bear a detailed exposition. The following table briefly outlines the provisions likely to be applicable in motor claims.

Class of action	Limitation period
1. Personal injury claims in negligence, nuisance or breach of duty.	Three years: section 11, LA 1980
2. Other claims in tort or contract (such as "damage only" accidents)	Six years: sections 2 and 5, LA 1980.
3. Claims brought on behalf of a deceased's estate and/or for his dependents under the Law Reform (Miscellaneous Provisions) Act 1934 and/or the Fatal Accidents Act 1976	Three years from the date of death or the personal representative/dependant's date of knowledge: sections 11(5) and 12(2), LA 1980.
4. Claims brought on behalf of a "child" (see CPR 21.1)	Time runs from the claimant's 18th birthday, so that in personal injury claim proceedings should be issued before the claimant's 21st birthday: section 28(1), LA 1980.
5. Claims brought by a "patient" (see CPR 21.1)	Three years from the cessation of the disability: section 28 and 38 (4), LA 1980.

Time begins to run from the accrual of the claimant's cause of action or, in personal injury claims, his "date of knowledge": see section 14, LA 1980. In virtually all road traffic claims this means, in practice, the date of the material accident.

Discretionary extension: section 33 of the LA 1980

Section 33 empowers the court in personal injury actions to disapply the primary period of limitation if it appears equitable to do so having regard to the balance of prejudice suffered by each party.

Criteria

Section 33 (3) provides that the Court:

"... shall have regard to all the circumstances of the case and in particular to -

(a) the length of, and the reasons for, the delay on the part of the claimant:

(b) the extent to which, having regard to the delay, the evidence adduced or likely to be adduced by the claimant would be or is likely to be less cogent than if the action had been brought within the time allowed:

(c) the conduct of the defendant after the cause of action arose, including the extent (if any) to which he responded to requests reasonably made by the claimant for information or inspection for the purpose of ascertaining facts which were or might be relevant to the claimant's cause of action against the defendant;

(d) the duration of any disability of the claimant arising after the date of the accrual of the cause of action;

(e) the extent to which the claimant acted promptly and reasonably once he knew whether or not the act or admission of the defendant, to which the injury was attributable, might be capable at the time of giving rise to an action in damages;

(f) the steps, if any, taken by the claimant to obtain medical, legal or other expert advice and the nature of any such advice he may have received".

The court's discretionary power is entirely unfettered (the particular criteria are not, in other words, exhaustive) and account must be had to all the circumstances in the case: *Thompson* v *Brown Construction (Ebbw Vale) Ltd* [1981] 1 WLR 747.

Specific factors

The burden of proof falls on the claimant on questions arising out of the statutory criteria and the balance of prejudice: *Barrand* v *British Cellophane* (1995) Times, February 16. Delay, in this instance, is limited to a consideration of the time elapsed since the expiry of the primary limitation period.

In general, the shorter the delay the more likely the court is to exercise its discretion in favour of the claimant, whilst protracted delay will usually militate against allowing the action to proceed. In *Hartley* v *Birmingham City District Council* [1992] 2 All ER 213, *Hendy* v *Milton Keynes Health Authority* (1992) 3 Med. LR 114 and *Ramsden* v *Lee* [1992] 2 All ER 204 short periods of delay (measured in days) were excused. In other cases, such as *Buck* v *English Electric Co Ltd* [1978] 1 All ER 271 and *Dale* v *British Coal Corp (No.2)* (1992) 136 Sol Jo LB 199, a delay of five years of more was held to be fatal.

It is impossible, in practice, to separate the question of delay from the other factors in the case. Thus, cases of extreme delay have been allowed to proceed where either liability was not in dispute, there was no evidential prejudice or there were acceptable reasons for the delay: see *Halford* v *Brooks* [1991] 3 All ER 559 (6 years) and *Doughty* v *North Staffordshire Health Authority* (1992) 3 Med LR 81.

Significant evidential prejudice – such as the death of a witness or destruction of important documentary evidence – is likely to be fatal to an action: see *Bater* v *Newbold* (1991) LEXIS July 30 and *Pilmore* v *Northern Trawlers Limited* [1986] 1 Lloyds Rep 552. It has been held that where a case turns on the recollection of witnesses the evidence may be presumed to be less cogent after five years: *Buck* v *English Electric Co Ltd* (ibid). But, in contrast, a claim was allowed to proceed notwithstanding the fact that the defendant's main witness had had a stroke and was unable to give evidence: *Kidd* v *Grampian Health Board* (1994) 5 Med. LR 251.

Prejudice

Prejudice, unlike "delay", requires the court to look at the entire period since the accrual of the cause of action: *Donovan* v *Gwentoys Limited* [1990] 1 All ER 1018. Consideration can be given to the strengths or weaknesses of the case, the size of any award, the availability (or otherwise) of legal aid or valid insurance cover, any rights against the Motor Insurers' Bureau and whether or not the claimant might have a remedy against his solicitors: see, for example *Thompson* v *Brown Construction* (ibid), *Ramsden* v *Lee* (ibid) and *Kelly* v *Bastible* (1997) Times, Nov 15.

Second actions

If a claimant brings an action within the normal limitation period, he is not entitled to start a second action out of time in the event that the original proceedings are never served, struck out for want of prosecution or otherwise discontinued. Section 33, as a matter of statutory interpretation, does not operate where the prejudice derives not from the operation of the Act but rather from the claimant's own inaction: *Walkley* v *Procession Forgings Ltd* [1979] 1 WLR 606. Exceptionally, second actions were allowed:

- where the original writ was wholly ineffective and the proceedings were classed as a nullity; *White* v *Glass* (1989) Times, February 18, and
- in a road traffic claim where the first action was brought against a company for the negligence of its employee and the second claim was brought against the driver personally; *Shapland* v *Palmer* [1999] PIQR 249

Factors particularly relevant to road traffic claims

There are a number of commonly occurring and relevant factors that are particularly characteristic of motor claims.

From the perspective of the claimant:

- it is in the nature of a road traffic accident that both (or all) parties are immediately aware of the incident giving rise to liability, so that a proposed defendant has ample warning of the potential need to preserve evidence and otherwise protect his position;

- where the police are involved, it will usually be the case that a methodical record of the objective facts is compiled (and subsequently preserved) during the first minutes and hours post-accident;

- it is likely that all parties will make expeditious report to their insurance companies, legal expenses insurers or nominated solicitors, with the result that the relevant evidence (particularly the recollections of the parties and witnesses) will be captured and preserved at an early stage;

- over the years motor insurers have successfully created a well developed litigation support network, meaning that both sides, and especially defendants, will have the support of experienced specialists (claims advisers, legal expenses insurers, RTA solicitors) adept to protecting their interests from an early stage;

- liability is statistically less likely to be an issue (there may even have been a prosecution and conviction for a road traffic offence) so that the essential merits of the claimant's action should often be more readily apparent;

- injury and damage resulting from highway collisions tends to be well documented;

- hospitals are more likely to keep comprehensive records of attendance, given the opportunity provided by the Road Traffic (NHS Charges) Act 1999 (see chapter 16) and losses such as repair costs, hire charges and medical expenses are usually supported by clear invoices and receipts. (Some insurers actually distribute protective advice at the time the contract of insurance is entered into.)

Conversely, from the defendant's vantage:

- important issues (particularly liability) almost invariably turn on individual recollections of a split second (and necessarily shocking) incident. Memories are especially (almost uniquely) susceptible to the disorientating effect of a motor collision, with the result that delay almost always has a corrosive effect on the cogency of the evidence to be adduced by both sides;

- ignorance of the law is rarely a genuine factor. Most drivers have at least an anecdotal appreciation of the fact that road traffic accidents give rise to a potential cause of action;
- given the nature and range of the post-accident support likely to be available to a claimant, it will usually be difficult to justify or mitigate a failure to bring proceedings and/or any subsequent delay;
- assessing the potential merits of a road traffic claim constitutes, in most cases, a comparatively straightforward process, so that it is rare to see inaccurate legal advice being proffered as a convincing explanation for delay.

Individual Immunity

The law confirms immunity upon certain persons and/or bodies.

Diplomats

The relevant law is contained in the Diplomatic Privileges Act 1964 and the Vienna Convention on Diplomatic Relations of 1961. Accredited diplomatic agents (meaning the head of a mission, members of its staff having diplomatic status and members of the families forming part of the households of the same) are immune from civil jurisdiction. (There are three specific exceptions to this general rule: the only one of any import to road traffic claims concerns an act relating to any professional or commercial activities exercised by diplomatic agent outside his official functions.) Members of the administrative and technical staff of a mission are also protected, save that their immunity does not extend to acts performed outside the course of their duties. Members of the service staff are immune in respect of acts performed in the course of their duties.

The protection granted is immunity from suit and not from liability. This means that:

- if proceedings are begun at a stage where the defendant is no longer protected by his status, no immunity can be pleaded: see *Empson* v *Smith* [1966] 1 QB 426; and
- it may sometimes be possible to bring proceedings against an insurance company even though the diplomatic defendant could not be sued: see *Dickinson* v *Dell Solar* [1930] 1 KB 376.

Heads of State

By the State Immunity Act 1978, section 20, heads of state, members of their family forming part of their household and their "private servants" enjoy immunity from the jurisdiction of United Kingdom courts. But this protection is not extended to actions in respect of death, personal injury, damage to or loss of property caused by an act or omission in the United Kingdom. Accordingly, most, if not all, road traffic claims all fall outside the ambit of this immunity.

Bankruptcy

Most practitioners will have been confronted with the problem of bringing a claim against an insolvent individual or company.

Personal Insolvency

Any tort committed before the bankruptcy will be classed as a "bankruptcy debt": Insolvency Act 1986, section 382 (iii). Assuming that such debts are provable in the bankruptcy (see section 412) no claim can be brought against the property or person of the bankrupt without the leave of the court: section 285 (iii) of the 1986 Act. Any tort committed after the bankruptcy is not a bankruptcy debt and a bankrupt remains personally liable.

Corporate Insolvency

For a clear exposition of this complex subject, reference can be made to an excellent article by Andrew Pattison, entitled "Banging your head against a brick wall? – the insolvent defendant", [1997] JPIL 264.

The Third Party's (Rights Against Insurers) Act 1930

The Act provides that where a company is wound up, whether voluntarily or compulsorily, if the company had in force a policy of insurance against liabilities to third parties, then the rights of the company as against its own insurer shall become vested in the third party. Identifying the insurer, and obtaining a copy of the relevant policy, will be of paramount importance. Expeditious enquiries should be made of the liquidator and/or the Official Receiver.

No indemnity against the insurer can be pursued until judgment has been obtained (meaning that liability must be both established and quantified) against the company: *Post Office* v *Norwich Union Fire Insurance Society* [1967] 2 QB 363.

Chapter 12

Conditions of No Liability

There are a number of circumstances (which are commonly, but erroneously, subsumed within the term "defence") in which a prima facie liability is entirely negated. This chapter will examine the folllowing:

- Act of God and Involuntary Act;
- Inevitable accident;
- Agony of the moment and alternative danger;
- Ex turpi causa non oritor actio.

Act of God

Act of God is defined as a "direct, violent, sudden and inevitable act of nature, which could not, by any reasonable care, have been foreseen or resisted": *Nugent* v *Smith* (1876) 1 CPD 423. In *Greenock Corpn.* v *Caledonian Railway Company* [1917] AC 556, a Scottish case, Lord Finlay L.C. referred to "circumstances which no human foresight can provide against and which human prudence is not bound to recognise the possibility". In road traffic claims, such acts can include gusts of wind, lightning strikes, flash floods, hail and, arguably, sudden falls of snow and accumulations of ice, although in these instances a claim will often lie against the third party motorist (see chapter 2) and/or the highway authority (see chapter 8).

Involuntary Act; Death, Automatism or Sudden Illness

The reported cases naturally form three categories:

- sudden onset of symptoms;
- gradual onset of symptoms;
- sleep

Sudden onset of symptoms

The sudden and unforeseeable onset of a disabling condition will almost always absolve the defendant of any subsequent liability. In *Ryan* v *Youngs* [1978] 1 All E.R. 522 a lorry crashed after its driver suddenly collapsed and died of a cardiac arrest. He had previously appeared to be in good health and medical examination would not have disclosed a defect or liability to sudden collapse. Slesser LJ (at 524) stated:

> "To my mind, this case is what has been referred to as an Act of God. An apparently healthy, apparently competent man, in charge of a competent machine, is suddenly struck down, and that is a matter which nobody can reasonably anticipate".

Also, in *Waugh* v *James K. Allen Limited* [1964] 2 Lloyds Rep. 1, an accident occurred when a driver of a lorry suddenly succumbed to an attack of coronary thrombosis. Although he had continued to drive after feeling unwell, the court concluded that he could have reasonably ascribed this to a historical propensity to periodic gastric attacks, and so the fatal event was, at least to the driver, an unforeseen attack which absolved him of liability.

In *Jones* v *Dennison* [1971] RTL 174, CA, the defendant lost control of his vehicle following a temporary "blackout" or loss of consciousness. Six years before he had suffered from a coronary thrombosis and a slight cerebral thrombosis. The issue was whether the defendant out to have realised from what had happened in the past that he ought not to have been driving. It was held that there were no grounds for saying that he ought reasonably to have supposed that he was, or might be, subject to such an attack.

Gradual onset of symptoms

In *Mansfield and Another* v *Weetabix Limited and Another* [1998] 1 WLR 1263, the defendants' employee was unaware that he suffered from malignant insulinoma, a condition that resulted in a hypogly-caemic state which starved the brain of glucose so that he could fall into a semi-conscious state. During the course of the 40 mile journey he was involved in two incidents of driving eratically, one minor accident and, ultimately, a more serious incident that led to the claimant's action. Nevertheless it was held that the condition was such as to exhibit no physical symptoms, or "sign posts", that would have prompted a reasonable driver to abandon his journey. Leggatt LJ stated that:

> "There is no reason in principle why a driver should not escape liability when a disabling event is not sudden but gradual, provided that the driver is unaware of it. A person with (the driver's) very rare condition commonly does not appreciate that his ability is impaired, and he was no exception."

Aldous LJ added that:

> "The standard of care that (the driver) was obliged to show was that which is expected of a reasonably competent driver. He did not know and could not reasonably have known of his infirmity which was the cause of the accident. Therefore he was not at fault. His actions did not fall below the standard of care required."

This decision can be contrasted with the judgments in *Roberts* v *Ramsbottom* [1980] 1 All E.R. 7, where a 73 year old defendant crashed his vehicle after sustaining a stroke, and *Boomer* v *Penn* (1965) 52 D.L.R. 673, which concerned an accident caused by a defendant who was a diabetic. In both cases the court found that the defendant had continued to drive after becoming aware of his unfitness.

Sleep

The Highway Code, rule 80, provides:
"Driving when you are tired greatly increases your accident risk. To minimise this risk

- make sure you are fit to drive. Do not undertake a long journey (longer than an hour) if you feel tired.
- avoid undertaking long journeys between midnight and 6 a.m. when natural alertness is at a minimum.
- plan your journey to take sufficient breaks. A minimum break of at least 15 minutes after every 2 hours of driving is recommended.
- if you feel at all sleepy, stop in a safe place. Do not stop on the hard shoulder of a motorway.
- the most effective ways to counter sleepiness are to take a short nap (up to 15 minutes) or drink (for example, two cups of strong coffee) fresh air, exercise or turning up the radio may help for a short time, but are **not** as effective".

Not surprisingly, therefore, falling asleep whilst driving provides no defence. It is a driver's business to keep awake: if drowsiness overtakes him whilst at the wheel, he should stop and wait until he shakes it off and is wide awake again: *Kay* v *Butterworth* (1945) 175 LT 191.

Inevitable Accident

Inevitable accident is defined as "that which the party charged with the offence could not reasonably prevent by the exercise of ordinary care, caution and skill": *Marpesia* (1872) LR 4 BC 212. The burden of proof rests on the defendant: *The Merchant Prince* [1892] 179 per Fry L.J. at 189.

Application in road traffic accident claims

Inevitable accident is essentially a matter of fact and there are few reported cases. In *Ritchie's Car Hire Limited v Bailey* (1958) 108 L.J. 348 the defendant driver successfully established that his collision with a roadside tree had been caused by him swerving to avoid a cat which had suddenly and unforeseeably run into his path. The defence also succeeded in *Winnipeg Electric Co. v Geel* [1992] A.C. 690 where a highway collision was caused by a latent defect in one of the vehicles.

These decisions can be contrasted with the judgment in *Henderson v Henry Jenkins & Sons* [1970] AC 282, a case where a latent fault in the braking system of a lorry led to a fatal accident. It was held that a defendant cannot rely on the defence of latent defect not discoverable by the exercise of reasonable care unless it was shown that he had taken all reasonable care in the circumstances. This, in turn, demanded a consideration of the vehicle's usage and maintenance history. As the defendant failed to adduce evidence of a past history of the lorry, he could not rely on the defence for inevitable accident. Vehicle owners are now subject to a very high standard of care (see chapter 11) and it is likely that the defence of inevitable accident based on an inherent defect will be increasingly subject to a searching critique.

The defence was also not made out where a wasp entered a car and settled on the driver's eye: *Gilson v Kidman* (1938) (unreported, but cited in *Bingham and Berryman's Motor Claims Cases*, 41).

Agony of the Moment and Alternative Danger

There are two similar, but distinct principles:

Agony of the moment

Where a person is placed in danger by the wrongful act of another, he is not negligent if he exercises such care as may reasonably be expected of him in the predicament in which he is placed, even if he does "not do quite the right thing in the circumstances": *Brandon v Osborne, Garrett & Co.* [1924] 1 KB 548. In *Tocci v Hankard & Another* (1966) 110 Sol. Jo. 835, the defendant was overtaking another vehicle when it negligently swung into his path, causing the defendant, in an attempt to avoid the culpable motorist, to swerve into a collision with the claimant. Lord Denning M.R. held that the defendant was not to blame and emphasised that:

> "It has often been said that, where a dangerous situation was created such as this one, one ought not to be critical of what was done on the spur of the moment to avoid an accident".

A more recent example is provided by the case of *Clift* v *Howes & Ors.* (1998) New Law Digest, 11 December QBD. Here the second defendant suddenly braked (from 70 m.p.h. to 10 m.p.h) to avoid accident debris negligently deposited on a dual carriageway by the first defendant. Immediately thereafter the claimant collided with the rear of the second defendant. The court dismissed the claim against the second defendant. It held that any reasonable man faced with an emergency and in the frightening situation that the second defendant was in, might well have done exactly as he did and that he could not be blamed for making a less than perfect decision in the circumstances.

Alternative danger

In *Jones* v *Boyce* (1816) 1 Stark 493 the claimant was a passenger travelling on a coach. He sustained injury when, the coachman having negligently conducted the vehicle into a "perilous position", he was forced to leap from the coach. Lord Ellenborough (at 495) stated that:

> ". . . it is sufficient if he was placed by the misconduct of the defendant in such a situation as obliged him to adopt the alternative of a dangerous leap, or to remain at certain peril; if that position was occasioned by the default of the defendant, the action may be supported. On the other hand, if the claimant's act resulted from a rash apprehension of danger, which did not exist, and the injury which he sustained was to be attributed to rashness and imprudence, he is not entitled to recovery."

The basis for this defence is not, therefore, a reasonable desire to avoid another accident, but rather the permissible "prudence of self-preservation".

Ex turpi causa non oritur actio

Ex turpi, roughly translated from Latin, means that "no action arises out of a base (or an illegal or immoral) act". Historically the relevance of the maxim to a claim in tort has been the subject of some dispute: see, for example, *Revill* v *Newberry* (1995) Times, November 3. But in *Clunis* v *Camden & Islington Health Authority* [1998] 2 WLR 902, Bedlam L.J. irrefutably confirmed its applicability:

> "We do not consider that the public policy at the court will not lend its aid to a litigant who relies on his own criminal or immoral act is confined to particular causes of action."

Application in road traffic accident claims

Four cases illustrate the application of the ex turpi in road traffic accident claims:

- *Jackson* v *Harrison* (1978) 19 ALR 129: a case heard in the High Court of Australia in which the claimant and defendant were both, to the certain knowledge of the other, disqualified from holding a driving licence. The court, having noted that there was no asbolute rule that participants in a joint illegal enterprise owed no duty of care to each other, concluded that ex turpi would apply in cases where the conduct of the claimant (or in this case, both parties) was such that it was impossible to set the appropriate standard of care.

- *Pitts* v *Hunt* [1991] 1 QB 24: the claimant was a pillion passenger on the first defendant's motor cycle. The first defendant was not licenced to drive, had no insurance and, whilst in the company of the claimant, had consumed an excessive amount of alcohol. During the course of their journey the first defendant, encouraged by the claimant, had driven in a fast and haphazard manner in a deliberate attempt to frighten a number of pedestrians. Eventually the motor cycle collided with a car driven by the second defendant. The court, following *Jackson* v *Harrison*, dismissed the claimant's action against both defendants. Bingham L.J. found that:
  (i) The maxim ex turpi causa non oritor actio applied as the claimant and the first defendant were engaged in a joint illegal enterprise.
  (ii) It would be against public policy for the claimant to succeed.
  (iii) The nature of the joint enterprise was such that it precluded the court from finding that the defendant owed any duty of care to the plaintiff.

- *Hughes* v *(1) Charlton and (2) MIB* (1997) Lawtel, C0006610: the claimant was a passenger in a vehicle driven by her husband, the first defendant, who, at the time of the material accident, was engaged in a race with another motorist. It was held (obiter) that it would be fatal to a claim where a claimant "had encouraged or wanted the defendant to race on the highway and been egging him on in his folly".

- *Taylor* v *Leslie* (1998) Lawtel C0007277: a Scottish case in which the pursuer and the defendant had jointly taken a vehicle without the consent of its owner, and where the defendant had driven the same in a dangerous manner and whilst being unlicensed and uninsured. The court accepted that the defendant's conduct amounted to criminal activity in "a technical sense". However, his conduct would not have been regarded as particularly reprehensible in the community in which he lived, and was essentially "skylarking" rather than criminal. Ex turpi would not, therefore, apply, although the pursuer was found to be 50% contributorily negligent.

Insofar as these cases illustrate a common consensus (and *Taylor* obviously introduces an element of inconsistency) it is submitted that the approach in *Jackson* and *Pitts* is likely to be preferred.

Part III

The Vehicle:
Loss, Damage, Repair, Hire of a Replacement, Credit Hire and Loss of Use

Chapter 13

The Vehicle

Loss, Damage, Repairs, Hire of a Replacement, Credit Hire and Loss of Use

Loss of or damage to the vehicle constitutes a specific aspect of the claim for special damages. This chapter will examine the following:

- Repairs and loss of value;
- Hire of a replacement vehicle;
- Credit hire agreement;
- Loss of use and inconvenience.

Repairs

Many motor insurers operate a "knock-for-knock" system under which the damage to each vehicle is borne by its own insurers. Where, however, the insurer covering one of the vehicles has no such agreement, or where the policy is otherwise void, it will be necessary for the claimant to bring an action for the cost of repair or the pre-accident value of the vehicle.

There are two principles applicable:

- First, the claimant is entitled to recover as damages a sum of money that will place him in as good a position as he would have been in if the accident had not occurred.
- Secondly, the claimant must take all reasonable steps to mitigate his loss.

The application of these principles prompts a number of common problems:

What if the repairs are never carried out?

Ordinarily the court will require proof that the vehicle has been, or will be, repaired before damages will be awarded: see, for example, *Jones v Stroud District Council* [1988] 1 All ER 5. But this does not mean that a claimant is compelled to express his loss in terms of the cost of repair. An unrepaired vehicle will necessarily have incurred a diminution in its value and (subject to other matters outlined below) this "depreciation" could as easily form the basis of a sustainable claim. Thus, in *Maynard* v *Loveday* [1994] CLY 1493, where the claimant's vehicle was stolen before it could be repaired, the court awarded damages for "diminution in value".

Vehicle damaged beyond economical repair

Where the cost of repair exceeds the vehicle's market value it will be classed as a "write-off" and damages will be limited to the lesser amount. (Obviously "the loss" is the vehicle's market value at the date of the accident and not its replacement value.) One or both of the interested insurers will usually commission a report and valuation from an expert assessor. It is often worth a claimant's time and effort to contest the initial valuation. A well argued challenge (supported by a detailed service history, recent photographs and/or an informed consideration of the values published in *Glass's Guide*) can frequently prompt a modest increase in the insurer's offer.

Can a claimant ever recover the cost of repairs when they exceed the value of the vehicle?

Very rarely. In *O'Grady* v *Westminster Scaffolding Limited* [1962] 2 Lloyds Rep. 238 the claimant pleaded the cost of repairs of £253 when the vehicle was valued at £145. The vehicle was a 1938 MG which for over 13 years had received the "loving care and assiduous attention" of the claimant. It was, in short, his "pride and joy" – he even called it "Mademoiselle Hortensia". Mr. Justice Edmund Davies, having referred to a "touching tale of loyalty and devotion", held that in the circumstances the claimant acted reasonably in having the vehicle repaired.

Generally, however, the courts are reluctant to award the cost of more expensive repairs. To succeed a claimant will usually have to demonstrate that his vehicle is "unique" and not simply "rare" or "difficult to replace". In *Darbishire* v *Warran* [1963] 3 All ER 310 the claimant attempted to recover the cost of repairing a Lea Francis 1951 shooting brake. Whilst it might have been difficult to find another such vehicle on the market, other estate cars were readily available. The Court of Appeal held that as the vehicle was not an irreplaceable article, damages should be assessed on the basis of the market price and not on the higher cost of repairs.

Can the claimant ever recover the market value when this exceeds the cost of repairs?

Sometimes. Many insurance policies now undertake to replace a vehicle in the event that it is written off during the first year of registration. Questions of "special use" or "business suitability" can also lead to a higher recovery. In *Moore v D.E.R. Ltd* [1971] 3 All ER 517 the claimant, a dental surgeon, whose work demanded a reliable car, habitually bought a new vehicle every two years. When his 18 month old Rover 2000 was classed as a total loss, he purchased a new car rather than one of an equivalent age and usage. The Court of Appeal held that the course adopted by the claimant was, in all the circumstances, reasonable.

Reduced market value of repaired vehicle

A repaired car can still be worth less than its pre-accident value. Serious accident damage, even if the repairs are expertly carried out, can irremediably taint the vehicle.

If the claimant can prove a diminution in value, he is entitled, in principle, to compensation under that head. In *Paynton v Brooks* [1974] RTL 169 Edmund Davies stated (at 175) that:

> "It seems to me that the question whether loss of market value consequential on damage sustained in an accident, notwithstanding that excellent repairs have been carried out, should rank as part of the damages recoverable by the claimant must depend on the particular circumstances of each case."

It should be noted that these remarks were obiter and that on the facts of this case the claimant failed for want of evidence of loss of value. But in *Warwick Motor Auctions v Bennett* [1997] CLY 1815 the claimant successfully demonstrated that his relatively new luxury BMW had sustained a reduction in its market value notwithstanding the fact that a repair had restored it to substantially the same condition as before the accident.

Betterment

Sometimes a repair may cause an increase in the value of the vehicle:

- Where the betterment is an incidental result of repairs, which would otherwise require unreasonable steps to be taken such as exposing the claimant to some loss or burden, there is to be no reduction in damages: *The Gazelle* [1844] 2 W Rob (Adm) 279. Where, in other words, the claimant has no option but to replace a part, the proper measure of damages is the cost of replacement: *Harbutt's Plasticine Ltd v Wayne Tank & Pump Co. Ltd.* [1970] 1 All ER 225.

- Where, however, the repairs may have utilised a suitable second-hand part, there will be some allowance for betterment. Even then a defendant can face an uphill struggle. Proving the "life-span" of a particular part necessarily involves an uncertain process: see *Bacon* v *Cooper (Metals) Ltd* [1982] 1 All ER 397.

Bailment

Very often the claimant (being either the driver or injured motorist) will not be the owner or registered keep of the damaged vehicle. Can such a claimant (as bailee) sue for the cost of repairs or must the owner/keeper (the bailor) be joined as a party to the proceedings?

In *Leigh & Sullivan Ltd* v *Aliakmon Shipping Co. Ltd, The Aliakmon* [1986] 2 All ER 145 Lord Brandon stated (at 149) that:

> ". . . there is a long line of authorities for a principle of law that, in order to enable a person to claim in negligence for loss caused to him by reason of loss or damage to property, he must have either the legal ownership of or a possessory title to the property concerned at the time when the loss or damage occurred."

This reasoning was followed in *O'Sullivan* v *Williams* [1992] 3 All ER 385. In this case the claimant never had legal ownership of the car but, at the time of the material accident, was authorised to use it by her boyfriend, the registered keeper. The Court of Appeal held that the claimant was entitled to claim for both the cost of repairs and damages for loss of use. Lord Justice Fox sated (at 387) that:

> ". . . the bailee can sue a wrongdoer simply by reason of the bailee's possession. Such possession is, as against the wrongdoer, full and complete ownership. It enables the bailee to recover the full value of the chattel. He must, however, account to the bailor for the amount recovered."

In *Richards v Thomas* [1997] CLY 1777 the claimant, who at the time of the accident was driving a car borrowed from a family friend, was allowed to claim the cost of repairs, loss of use and hire charges incurred by the owner. Not only could the bailee recover all losses arising from damage to a chattel whilst in his hands, he should do so as a means of "avoiding the duplication of claims".

Hire of replacement vehicle

A claimant will often hire a substitute car pending either the repair or replacement of his vehicle. Recovery of such expenditure will depend on reasonableness and the steps taken by a claimant to mitigate his loss. Two issues commonly arise: (i) the nature of the substitute vehicle and (ii) the period of hire.

The substitute vehicle

It is generally accepted that like may be replaced with like although, in the case of a prestige vehicle, a claimant must make some enquiry as to the cost and availability of a reasonable alternative.

In *A.L. Motorworks (Willesden) Ltd* v *Alwahbi* [1977] RTR 276 the Court of Appeal held that the owner of a Rolls Royce was entitled to hire a substitute Rolls Royce during a period of 11 days when his own car was being repaired. Lord Justice Cairns observed (at 281) that the claimant was "no doubt extremely annoyed at what had happened" to his vehicle and unless the claim was "clearly exorbitant" he was entitled to recover the whole cost of hiring a replacement. In *Daily Office Cleaning Contractors Ltd* v *Shefford* [1977] RTR 361 it was held that a company director was entitled to replace an American Rambler Ambassador motor car with a Jaguar XJ6 for a period of 25 weeks. Judge Stubb could see (at 364) "no reason why the claimant should have been required to shop around in order to hire for a lesser sum a car of a lower standard from some concern with whom they did not normally deal". This reasoning was followed in *Williams* v *Hoggins* [1996] CLY 2148 where the claimant was entitled to replace a BMW 318is with a BMW 3 series at a rate of £125 plus VAT per day, and *Vaughan Transport Systems* v *Fackrell* [1997] CLY 1810 where it was reasonable for a company who needed to keep a high profile amongst its customers to replace a Mercedes 250D with a BMW 325.

Nevertheless each case turns on its own fats and a claimant must sometimes be prepared to hire a cheaper or less prestigious alternative. In *Watson Norie Ltd* v *Shaw and Nelson* [1967] 1 Lloyds Rep. 5 the Court of Appeal refused (albeit with some reluctance) to interfere with the decision of a County Court judge who found that the claimant had not acted reasonably in hiring a Rover 100 and then a Jaguar 3.8 in place of a Jenson car. Lord Justice Sellers noted (at 516/517) that the claimant company had been "casual about hiring a substitute care" and that it had unreasonably failed to query the price and make any further investigation as to suitable alternatives. More recently, in *Coyne* v

Cawley [1995] CLY 164, where a BMW 316 was replaced with another BMW at a rate of £125 per day exclusive of VAT, the court held that the claimant had failed to make any investigation into the cost of hiring other cars and had failed to mitigate her loss by hiring a cheaper Ford 2-litre car. (See also *Usher* v *Crowder* [1994] CLY 1494). Similarly, where a claimant replaced a Land Rover Discovery motor vehicle with an "entirely different vehicle" (namely a BMW at £90 per day plus VAT and insurance) she should have hired a cheaper saloon car such as a Ford Mondeo: *Gowen* v *Owens Radio & T.V.* [1995] CLY 1631. In practice, therefore, a claimant should assume that it will be necessary to demonstrate a particular business requirement or a willingness to investigate and entertain a cheaper alternative before the cost of a prestigious substitute will be allowed.

The period of hire

The principles applicable to loss of use (see pages 176 to 181) also attach to the hire of a substitute vehicle. Specific examples include the following:

Repairs

Where the defendant's insurers take time to authorise the repairs, or where there is a difficulty in obtaining parts, the hire period may be reasonably extended. But if running repairs will render a vehicle driveable, these must be undertaken in preference to hiring a substitute vehicle. This was exactly the situation that arose in *Barry* v *Phoenix* [1998] CLY 1464. Whilst the vehicle would have cost more than £1,000 to repair, running repairs would have cost just under £80 to complete. Instead the claimant hired an alternative vehicle for eight weeks at a cost of £31.50 per day. The court held that it was "wholly unreasonable" for the claimant not to have taken the "obvious course", which was to effect the running repairs, and the period of recovery was limited to two days.

Administrative delay

Where liability is in dispute, and where the defendant's insurers refuse to authorise repairs, the claimant is entitled to delay the commencement of the work and hire a substitute vehicle whilst the matters in dispute are resolved: *Martindale* v *Duncan* [1973] 2 All ER 355I. In *Houghton* v *Meares* [1995] CLY 1622 the defendants admitted liability and agreed a valuation of the vehicle, but failed to send the claimant a cheque, thereby requiring that proceedings were necessary. The court allowed hire charges for 27 weeks. In *Butler* v *Norton* [1997] CLY 1804 the defendant's insurers delayed settlement of the claim for an "excessively long" nine weeks during which period the claimant was entitled to incur hire charges. By the same token, a claimant was entitled to hire charges for a period (of over a month) during which the defendant's insurers delayed the repairs by unreasonably objecting to the work being undertaken at the claimant's local garage: *Cockburn* v *Davies and Provident Insurance plc* [1997] CLY 1805.

Impecuniosity

In *Wheelan & Wheelan* v *Hughes* [1997] CLY 1802 the first claimant was insured under a third party only policy and gave evidence of impecuniosity which prevented him from replacing the vehicle. Hire charges were allowed for a period of 31 weeks – essentially the time between the accident and entry of interlocutory judgment.

Credit Hire Agreements

The terms of a typical credit hire agreement are, in broad outline, as follows:

(1) The credit hire company ("the company") makes a car available to the motorist whilst the damaged car is under repair.

(2) The company pursues a claim against the defendant, at its own expense and employing solicitors of its choice, in the name of the motorist for loss of use of the motorist's car.

(3) The company makes a charge for the loan of the replacement car which is reimbursed from the part of the damage recovered by the motorist from the defendant or his insurers which relates to the loss of uses of the motorist's car.

(4) Until this happens, the motorist is under no obligation to pay for the use of the replacement car.

(5) The motorist is contractually obliged to co-operate in pursuing the claim and any resulting legal proceedings.

In recent years, transactions of this type have been entered into in large numbers. The benefits to the motorist are obvious: few have the time, energy and resources to go to law solely to recover the cost of a substitute vehicle and many potential claimants lack the inclination or ready cash to hire a replacement on the chance of recovering reimbursement from the defendant's insurers. The prejudice to the defendant is equally apparent: over-optimistic claims abound and in virtually every case credit hire rates are significantly higher than regular hire charges.

General principles

In *Giles* v *Thompson* [1994] 1 AC 142 the House of Lords held that credit hire agreements are neither champertous nor inviolate of any requirement of public policy. Such charges were recoverable as long as the claimant remained contractually liable for the cost of hire and could demonstrate a reasonable need for a replacement vehicle. Nevertheless judges "should look carefully at claims for hiring, both as to their duration and as to their rates" (167) as a means of discouraging the promotion of inflated or over-optimistic claims.

Dimond v Lovell [1999] 3 WLR 561

The lead case on credit hire is now *Dimond* v *Lovell* (ibid) where the judgment of the Vice Chancellor, Sir Richard Scott, was handed down on April 29th, 1999.

Facts

The defendant collided with the rear of the claimant's vehicle and did not dispute liability. The claimant hired a replacement vehicle from a credit hire company, 1st Automotive Ltd, under an agreement that allowed credit on the hire "until such time as the claim for damages has been concluded". The hiring lasted for eight days and the charge under the agreement totalled £346.63, a sum that was said to be 80% above the ordinary hire rate for a similar car. The court, at first instance, held that the agreement was enforceable and gave judgment against the defendant for the full rate charged. The defendant appealed.

Issues

The issues before the Court of Appeal were:

1. Did the agreement provide credit within the meaning of the Consumer Credit Act 1974?
2. If the agreement provided credit, was it enforceable?
3. If not enforceable, had the claimant suffered any loss?
4. Did the claimant fail to take reasonable steps to mitigate her loss?

Judgment

It was held that: -

1. The agreement was prima facie regulated by the 1974 Act. The court, considering sections 8 to 11 of the Act, gave broad construction to the term "credit". The Vice Chancellor, after a detailed consideration of both the Act and Goode's Consumer Credit Legislation (1999) stated (at para 64) that:

   > "In the present case, the agreement that Mrs Dimond's obligation to pay for the car hire would be deferred until her damages claim had been concluded was, in my judgment, an agreement allowing her 'credit' for the purposes of 1974 Act."

   It was held that debt was deferred and credit extended whenever a contract entitled the debtor to pay later than the time when payment would otherwise have been earned under the contract's express or implied terms. Further, it was held that the hire of an article involved the acquisition of a service, and accordingly the deferment of an obligation to pay hire charges constituted the provision of credit.

2. The agreement was not enforceable. Section 61(1)(a) of the Act requires compliance with a number of prescribed terms. The agreement, in leaving blank all the matters required as prescribed terms, breached this provision. It was, therefore, unenforceable against Mrs Dimond.

3. It was held that there was no loss recoverable by the claimant. Specifically:

   > "If, a claimant had received a benefit from a third party that has, in the event, met his need with no cost to himself, if there is a need for care services or a need for a replacement vehicle, the court may allow an award of damages in order to enable the claimant to recompense the third party. The claimant will then hold the amount of the award in trust for the third part. But if the circumstances of the case do not permit a trust for the third party to be imposed on the damages, the claimant cannot recover damages. He does not need to recover damages in order to meet his own loss or, in the event, he has suffered none. To allow him to recover in circumstances where the trust solution could not be applied would lead to recovery by the claimant of more than he had lost. These, in my judgment, are the principles to be applied to this case (para 88)."

   The court, as such, applied the House of Lords authority of *Hunt* v *Severs* [1994] 2 A.C. 350 and disapproved the earlier decision of the Court of Appeal in *McCall* v *Brooks* [1984] RTR 99.

4. The claimant (via her broker) was entitled to take the view that firms like 1st Automotive would provide a suitable vehicle and relieve her of the worry of having to argue with the defendant's insurers. She had acted reasonably. The issue, in any event, was a question of fact and the Recorder was entitled to conclude that there was no failure to mitigate.

See *Norman* v *Selvey* [1999] CL July 207, *Feary* v *Buckingham* [1999] CL July 208 and *Majeed* v *The Incentive Group* [1999] August, unreported, HHJ Ryder at Central London County Court for cases applying and distinguishing *Dimond*.

Exemption?

The most common means by which credit-hire companies have sought (and doubtless will in future seek) to avoid regulation under the 1974 Act is by drafting their agreement in such a way that it falls within Article 3(1) of the Consumer Credit (Exempt Agreements) Order 1989. This provides, in distilled summary, that an agreement which states that the payments are required to be made within 12 months beginning with the date of the agreement, shall not be regulated by the Act. The effect of this exemption was also specifically noted by the Vice Chancellor at paragraph 51 of the judgment in *Dimond*.

Continuing effect

No other substantive issue raised during the last few years has generated quite so much relentless concern and activity than the question of credit hire and the decision in *Dimond*. But these matters are, at least in the short term, of no more than academic interest. In October 1999 the claimant in *Dimond* successfully petitioned the House of Lords for leave to appeal. On 28th October 1999 the Vice Chancellor, in conjunction with the Master of the Rolls, advised 'Designated Civil Judges' that all pending cases (believed to number about 40,000 nationwide) should be stayed until the House of Lords decision is known, unless "there are other issues that can conveniently be dealt with at once".

Other matters

The burden of proof falls on the claimant and it is unlikely to be discharged unless the contract is disclosed in evidence: *Norris* v

Greatbatch [1998] CLY 1461. However, a failure to produce an invoice should not, of itself, invalidate a claim: *Thompson* v *Stone* [1997] CLY 1796. Where any doubt exists, the court should endeavour to look at the "commercial reality" of the situation and decide whether a charge was to be levied: *Petrou* v *Kuti* [1997] CLY 1803.

Reasonable; examples

Impecuniosity is often cited as a ground for reasonable need: *Sleight* v *Sandretto (U.K) Ltd* [1996] CLY 2145 and *Llewellyn* v *McCabe* [1997] CLY 1792. In the same way credit hire charges will be recoverable where the claimant is unable to buy or borrow a replacement: *Thorne* v *Denby* [1997] CLY 1795. But this does not mean that an ability to pay for an alternative will necessarily preclude the option of credit hire: *Saville* v *Mustaq* [1997] CLY 1809.

Other cases reflect a particular business requirement – commercial usage often demands a prestige replacement: *Marples* v *French* [1997] CLY 1793 and *Seth-Smith* v *Worrall* [1997] CLY 1454. In *Nicholson & Ward* v *Fleming* [1997] CLY 1797 the claimant entered into a credit hire agreement in order to continue his employment as a taxi driver. It was held that credit hire was a reasonable alternative to "enforced unemployment".

Unreasonable; examples

A failure to obtain a comparable quote or enquire as to rates of hire will often be held to be unreasonable conduct: *H.L. Pallet Services* v *Fairclough* [1997] CLY 1794, *Johnson* v *Wilson* [1998] CLY 1457 and *Prescott* v *Hamnett* [1998] CLY 1459.

The court may also enquire as to usage. Where a claimant only used the vehicle to periodically attend her GP and the hospital, both of which were within easy walking distance of her home, it was not reasonable for her to hire a car for any period: *Lids* v *Edwards* [1997] CLY 1790.

Where a courtesy car is available (either from the repairing garage or pursuant to a policy of insurance) this option should be preferred to credit hire: *Hucknall* v *Jepson* [1998] CLY 1456. Nor are the courts above rebuking an impecunious claimant for a failure to "live within his means": *Shire* v *Mainline Group* [1997] CLY 1788.

Loss of use and inconvenience

General principle

In the *Mediana* [1900] AC 113 the House of Lords refined a broad principle originally articulated in *The Greta Holme* [1897] AC 596 and held that a claimant is entitled to damages for the loss of the use of the damaged chattel. Lord Halsbury L.C. sated (at 116) that:

> "Where by the wrongful act of one man something belonging to another is either itself so injured as not to be capable of being used or is taken away so that it cannot be used at all, that of itself is a ground for damages."

A claimant may still recover "substantial damages" for loss of use even though he would not have used the chattel during the period of its incapacity: *Caxton Publishing Co v Sutherland Publishing Co* [1939] AC 178.

Method of assessment

In *Birmingham Corporation v Sowsbery* [1970] RTR 84, a case where the claimant lost the use of an omnibus because of a collision caused by the defendant's negligence, Lane J. noted (at 86) that "such authority as exists upon the subject" indicates that there are two possible methods of arriving at a figure for damages for loss of use:

- First, the court can take the cost of maintaining and operating the vehicle as the basis for calculation, on the assumption that this figure must represent approximately the value of the vehicle to the operator where the concern is non-profit making. This method was adopted in *The Marpessa* [1987] AC 241 and *London Transport Executive v Foy Morgan & Co* [1955] CLY 743.
- Secondly, the court can base a calculation on interest on capital value together with depreciation. This method is exemplified by *Admiralty Commissioner v Chekiang (Owners)* [1926] AC 627 and *The Hebridian Co* [1961] AC 545.

Lane J. acknowledged that neither method was entirely satisfactory. He stated (at 86/87) that:

> "The former puts a premium upon inefficiency. The higher the cost of maintenance the greater will be the damages. In other words, there can be no guarantee, if the point is contested, that the standing charge cost represents the true value of the vehicle to the claimants, and

consequently the damages may be too high. The latter method will produce unduly differing results according to the age of the vehicle and the amount by which it has depreciated at the time of the accident."

A third possible method of calculation was adopted in *The Ikala* [1929] AC 196:

- In this case the court calculated what it would have cost to hire a substitute chattel for the one which had been lost. This method was followed in *Hatch v Platt* [1988] CLY 1073 where the court (at first instance) heard evidence that it would cost approximately £60 per week to hire an alternative small vehicle to substitute for the claimant's motor cycle that was damaged beyond economic repair in a road traffic accident.

The Automobile Association (AA) produces an annual "Schedule of Motoring Costs" for all petrol cars (up to 4,500 cc), diesel cars, motor cycles, mopeds and scooters. Copies are available from The Automobile Association, Norfolk House, Priestley Road, Basingstoke, Hampshire RT24 9NY or by telephoning 01990 500600. These tables also appear in *Heads of Damage* published by CLT and "Facts & Figures: Tables for the Calculation of Damages" published by the Professional Negligence Bar Association and Sweet & Maxwell. Selected extracts are reproduced at Appendix 2. These tables are of use where calculation of the 'standing charge' for the vehicle is used as a comparable method of assessment.

Inconvenience

Despite the intricacies of these methods (or possibly because of their complexity) awards for loss of use are increasingly determined by the inconvenience experienced by the owner of a vehicle (and in some cases his family) during the period of its incapacity. Most judges can relate to the additional problems experienced during, say, a claimant's journey to and from work or the invariable interruption to his regular domestic or social activities. Strictly speaking, such assessments bear little or no relation to either the rationale or method of a traditional claim for loss of use. But an award of damages based on inconvenience undoubtedly touches the reality of a claimant's experience and in the vast majority of recently reported cases this approach has been adopted.

How much?

In *Durbin v Lewis* [1997] CLY 17892 it was noted that there was a "going rate" of about £50 per week. Higher or lower rates could be awarded to reflect the particular facts of an individual case. In practice awards vary enormously – a general scale of £10 to £80 per week (albeit with the majority of cases falling towards the upper end of the bracket) can be supported. Many reported cases appear in *Current Law Monthly Digest*. Decisions are almost invariably from the county court and the brevity of the reports must sometimes belie the detail of the evidence adduced on a claimant's behalf. Nonetheless these reports – especially when considered in number – provide an invaluable indication of likely recovery. A number of recent decisions are set out at Appendix .

It should be noted that the draft Pre-Action Protocol For Road Traffic Accidents, at 7.2.2 provides that recovery for loss of use and enjoyment of a vehicle should be calculated at £60 per week unless there are "exceptional circumstances" (see chapter 18 page 221).

Mitigation

A claimant bears a duty to mitigate his loss. He can only claim for loss actually sustained. This means that, in the context of the claim for loss of use, he must give credit for any sums saved (such as petrol or parking expenses) as a result of the unavailability of the vehicle. Nor will he be allowed to recover any losses that he might reasonably have avoided.

The onus of proving that a claimant has failed to mitigate falls on the defendant. Any such allegation should be pleaded in his Defence: see CPR Part 16.5 and PD 13.2, 15.

A number of situations commonly arise:

Vehicle driveable

If a damaged vehicle is capable of being driven, and legally fit for the road, then a claimant should continue to use it: *Appleby* v *White* [1989] CLY 1770. However, where the vehicle is unsafe (even though it may be mechanically sound) the claimant is entitled to claim for loss of use: *Jones* v *Gravestock* [1993] CLY 1412 and *Maynard* v *Loveday* [1994] CLY 1493.

Expeditious repairs

A claimant should endeavour to ensure that the repairs to his vehicle are carried out with appropriate expedition. In *Woods* v *Klarnett* [1995] CLY 1630 the claimant was penalised for entrusting the repair of his vehicle to a garage with a backlog of over two months. In *P & S Motors* v *South* [1995] CLY 1621 the claimant waited for 16 weeks for the defendant's insurers to inspect the vehicle. It was held that since the claimant was a mechanic and knew (or ought to have known) that the vehicle was a write-off, he should not have delayed before disposing of it. Conversely, where liability for an accident is in dispute, a claimant is entitled to instruct solicitors and serve a "letter of claim" before undertaking repairs at his own expense: *Gidman* v *Pure* [1994] CLY 1511.

Administrative delays

Culpable delay can emanate from either the claimant, the defendant or the insurers. In *Murphy* v *Choudhrey* [1992] CLY 1538 and *D'Costa* v *Ryan* [1994] CLY 1495 the defendant gave false details to the claimant necessitating a claim to the Motor Insurers' Bureau and a lengthy period of enquiry. Loss of use was allowed for 60 and 45 weeks respectively.

In *Griffin & Co. Ltd* v *De-la-Haye* [1968] 2 Lloyds Rep. 253 the claimant's solicitors advised the defendant that the vehicle was "believed to be a write-off" within a week of the accident. Despite repeated reminders from the claimant's solicitors, the defendant's insurers failed to inspect the vehicle until approximately six months post-accident. Paul J. held (at 254) that if insurers chose not to reply to the claimant's letters (and thereby acted in a "quite disgraceful manner") they could not complain if the claimant took steps to hire a replacement vehicle and charge it to the defendants. Another such example is provided by *Crickmore* v *Bennet Baggs* [1995] CLY 1633 where delay resulted from both the defendant's failure to inspect and "some delay" in the resultant proceedings.

Delay in receipt of insurance payments

Time will often elapse between the determination of a motor claim and the date when the claimant receives the settlement cheque. Awards for loss of use should, where appropriate, allow for this hiatus: *Zubair* v *Younis* [1995] CLY 1625 and *Davies* v *Tate* [1993] CLY 1458.

Impecunious claimant

Historically a claimant has been unable to cite his impecuniosity as a valid reason for not carrying out repairs: *Liesbosch Dredger* v *Edison SA* [1933] AC 449. But in *Perry* v *Sidney Phillips & Co* [1982] 1 WLR 1297 Lord Justice Kerr said (at 1307) that the authority of this proposition was consistently being attenuated in more recent decisions. Perhaps the best modern statement of the law applicable to motor vehicle claims is to be found in *Mattocks* v *Mann* (1992) Times 19

June. Here the claimant could not afford to finance the repairs to her "top of the range" car. It was held that a strict application of *The Liesbosch* was "insupportable in the social conditions that now prevail". Lord Justice Beldon stated (at 304) that:

> "In the varied web of affairs after an accident, only in exceptional circumstances was it possible or correct to isolate impecuniosity of the claimant as a separate cause and as terminating the consequences of a defendant's wrong. It could not be said that the claimant's inability to provide resources to pay for the repairs was the sole cause of having to incur hire charges for the additional weeks."

This approach has been followed and applied in a large number of subsequent cases: see, for example, *Barrett* v *Western* [1994] CLY 1496, *Squires* v *Automobile Assurance* [1994] CLY 1497, *Kalinowski* v *Foxon* [1994] CLY 1498, *Penn* v *Anwar* [1994] CLY 1499, *Clark* v *Davis* [1994] 1502, *Skipper* v *Perry* [1995] CLY 1627 and *Price* v *Zaman* [1996] CLY 213.

Nonetheless a claimant may still be expected to mitigate his loss by the interim use of, say, his savings, an inheritance (see *Skipper* v *Perry* (ibid)) or even by taking out a commercial loan: *Humble* v *Agius* [1995] CLY 1632. But the obligation to take out a loan does not apply where a claimant cannot satisfy the bank that he could repay the sum borrowed: *Johnson* v *Edwards* [1993] CLY 1635. Nor will the claimant be expected to take out a loan with (or in times of) high interest rates: *Wilkinson* v *Sealey* [1996] CLY 2150. In *Butta* v *Rai* [1997] CLY 1813 it was held that the claimant was not obliged to use a student grant to purchase a replacement car.

Damages limited to the value of the vehicle?

In *Phelan* v *Austin* [1994] CLY 1501 it was noted that the value of the vehicle provided a "useful guide" when calculating the award for loss of use. Indeed it would be difficult to see how the award could possibly exceed the value of the vehicle when either of the classic methods of calculation outlined in *Birmingham Corp* v *Sowsbery* (ibid) are used. Thus, in *Squires* v *Automobile Assurance* (ibid), the court specifically provided that the claim for loss of use should be limited to the value of the vehicle.

And yet, with the ascendance of "inconvenience", numerous cases attest to the court's reluctance to impose a ceiling on recovery. Reference can be made to *Milner & Sharpe* v *Parcelforce* [1997] CLY 1779 (where damages for loss of use amounted to £2,730 although the car was only worth £390), *Hughes* v *Taylor* [1997] CLY 1782 (loss of use £2,200, value of vehicle £1,500) and *Weir* v *Field* [1997] 1786 (£2,700 compared with £1,500).

Credit for the cost of running a car

The court can take into account the cost a claimant would have been put to in running his own car during the period of loss: *Blades* v *Peake* [1994] CLY 1500. A claimant should also reclaim the car tax from the moment he is informed that the vehicle is a total loss: *Ajibade* v *Leech* [1994] CLY 1505.

Loss of use extended by additional non-urgent repairs

A claimant can undertake non-urgent repairs at the same time as the accident repairs and, provided it was reasonable for the work to be done simultaneously, he can recover damages for loss of use for the entire period: *The Ferdinand Retzlaff* [1972] 2 Lloyds Rep. 120 and *Elipidoforus Shipping Corporation* v *Furniss Withay (Australia) Ltd* (1986) Times, 28 November.

Part IV

Recovery

Chapter 14

Motor Insurance

A motor vehicle policy will cover the assured (which, aside from the policy holder himself, may include other drivers) against a variety of different risks. A "comprehensive" policy will, in addition to the compulsory element of third party cover, insure the vehicle against loss and may well include a variety of ancillary risks, such as personal accident insurance, personal effects in the vehicle, destruction of or damage to the garage in which the car is kept and, increasingly, the cost of legal representation in either criminal or civil proceedings. A "third party fire and theft" policy will, as the title suggests, limit cover to the compulsory risk and those losses caused by fire or theft.

A consideration of modern motor insurance requires an examination of Part VI of the Road Traffic Act 1988. This chapter will concentrate on the provisions outlined in section 143 to 154 of the Act, namely:

- the requirement and range of compulsory cover, (sections 143 to 147);
- the nature and effect of a third party's statutory rights, (sections 148 to 153);
- the insured's duty, on the demand of a third party, to give information and details of his insurance policy (section 154.)

Other issues, such as common contractual terms, exceptions and exclusions in motor policies, are necessarily beyond the scope of this book.

Compulsory cover

General obligations

Section 143 of the Act provides that a person must not use, or cause or permit any other person to use, a motor vehicle on a road unless there is in force a valid policy of insurance. Contravention of this requirement constitutes an offence; section 143(2).

"Use"

"Use" implies an element of controlling, managing or operating the vehicle: *Brown* v *Roberts* [1965] 1 QB 15. It has been held to include the leaving of a car on a road, even though it is incapable at present of being mechanically propelled, but not a case where the vehicle was "totally immovable": *Elliott* v *Grey* [1960] 1 QB 367 and *Thomas* v *Hooper* [1986] RTR 1. The definition also extends to the case of a motorist who left his car because it had run out of fuel and caused an accident when he crossed the road for help: *Dunthorne* v *Bentley* [1996] Times, March 11.

A passenger does not, in the normal case, "use" the vehicle: *B (A Minor)* v *Knight* [1981] RTR 136. In *Brown* v *Roberts* (ibid), a case where a passenger negligently opened her door and struck a passing pedestrian, it was held that she was not using the car because she had no control over the vehicle. "Use" can occur in limited circumstances, such as where the passenger owns the vehicle, or is the driver's employer or is controlling and directing the vehicle for his own purposes: *Cobb* v *Wiliams* [1973] RTR 113, *Leathley* v *Tatton* [1980] RTR 21 and *Stinton* v *Stinton* [1995] RTR 167. It is also clear that the owner of a vehicle being driven by someone else can still use the same, whether or not he is travelling as a passenger, if the driver is his employee acting in the course of his employment: *Windle* v *Dunning & Son Ltd* [1968] 2 All ER 46, applied in *Jones* v *DPP* [1999] RTR 1.

Several recent cases have considered whether a motorcycle pillion passenger can be a user of the vehicle. In *Hatton* v *Hall* [1999] Lloyd's Rep. IR 313 Lord Justice Henry found that a pillion passenger on a motorcycle was not a user, despite the fact that, knowing that the driver was uninsured, he suggested the destination and route to a public house. But in *O'Mahoney* v *Joliffe* [1999] Lloyds Rep. 321 the Court of Appeal held that a pillion passenger was more than a mere passive passenger, so that he could properly be said to share in the joint use of the vehicle. Simon Brown LJ. identified various features that justified this conclusion, namely that the passenger had assisted in getting the motorcycle started, at one point he had driven the vehicle, all the decisions were joint and the entire enterprise was criminal in nature, with both riders knowing that there was no tax, no insurance, no MOT certificate and neither were licensed to drive.

"Causing or permitting use"

"Cause" involves an express or positive mandate to use a vehicle in a particular way, whereas "permit" is looser, and merely denotes an express or implied licence to use a vehicle, so that the other person is not told to use the vehicle in a particular way, but he is told (expressly or by inference) that he may do so if he desires: *McLeod* v *Buchanan* [1940] 2 All ER 179 (per Lord Wright at 187). The mandate or permission may be granted by one who is not the owner, but who is responsible for the care, management or control of the vehicle: *Lloyd* v *Singleton* [1953] 1 QB 357.

In *McLeod's* case, a man was held to have permitted his brother to use a vehicle when, knowing that it was insured for business use only, he failed to direct that the vehicle should not be used for private purposes. Use was also "permitted" where a motorist instructed a garage to deliver an uninsured vehicle after a repair: *Lyons* v *May* [1948] 2 All ER 1062. In contrast, in *Watkins* v *O'Shaughnessy* [1939] 1 All ER 385, an auctioneer did not cause or permit the use of a car when he allowed a purchaser to drive away a vehicle he knew to be uninsured. The Court of Appeal concluded that, having sold the vehicle, the auctioneer no longer had any control over it. In *Thompson* v *Lodwick* [1983] RTR 76 a driving instructor was held not to have caused or permitted the use of a vehicle owned and driven by his pupil.

"Road"

"Road" is defined in section 192(1) of the Act as "any highway and any other road to which the public has access". The meaning and application of this definition has been the subject of considerable case law. Many of the more important or recent decisions are considered in relation to the liability of the Motor Insurers' Bureau at pages 195 to 208.

Exceptions

Section 144(1) and (2) provide that the obligation under section 143 to insure against third party risks does not apply to certain classes of vehicles:

(i) vehicles owned by a person who has deposited and keeps deposited with the Accountant-General of the Supreme Court the sum of £500,000 at a time when the vehicle is being driven under the owner's control, (section 144(1));

(ii) vehicles owned by certain local authorities, while being driven under their control, (section 144(2)(a));

(iii) vehicles owned by a police authority or the Receiver for the Metropolitan Police District, while being driven under the owner's control, or to a vehicle at a time when it is being driven for police purposes by or under the direction of a constable, or a police employee, (section 144(2)(b));

(iv) vehicles being driven on a journey for salvage purposes under the Merchant Shipping Act 1894, or used for certain purposes under the Army or Air Force Acts 1955, (section 144(2)(d));

(v) vehicles owned by a national health service body, at a time when the vehicle is being driven under the owner's control, (section 144(2)(da));

(vi) ambulances owned by a NHS Trust at a time when the vehicle is being driven under the owner's control, (section 144(2)(db));

(vii) vehicles made available by the Secretary of State to any person, body or local authority for certain purposes under the National Health Service Act 1977, or being used on the terms on which it is made available, (section 144(2)(e)).

Certain classes of vehicles are, moreover, totally exempt from Part VI of the Act:

- invalid carriages, (section 143(4));
- tramcar or trolley vehicles operated under statutory powers, (section 193);
- vehicles in the public service of the Crown, (section 183).

Essentials of a valid policy

The essentials of a valid policy are outlined in section 145 and comprise provisions relating to both the status of the insurer and the risks against which insurance is required. First, the policy must be issued by "an authorised insurer", meaning, in broad terms, a person or body of persons carrying on motor insurance business in Great Britain and membership of the Motor Insurers' Bureau. Secondly, the required risks are:

(i)   against liability in respect of death or bodily injury to any person or damage to property caused by or arising out of the use of the vehicle on a road in Great Britain; "person" includes any passenger, but not the driver;

(ii) in the case of a vehicle normally based in the territory of another EC Member State, against any civil liability occurring as a result of an event related to the use of the vehicle in Great Britain if

(a)   the law of that Member State would require such insurance in respect of an event occurring in that country and

(b)   the cover required by that law would be higher than that required by (i) above;

(iii) in the case of a vehicle normally based in Great Britain, against any liability in respect of the use of the vehicle in the territory other than Great Britain of each of the Member States of the EC according to

(a)   the law on compulsory motor vehicle insurance of the State where the event occurred or

(b)   if it would give higher cover, the law which would apply if the place where the event occurred was in Great Britain;

(iv) against the statutory liability for payment for emergency treatment.

Insurance is not required in respect of the following:

- the liability of an employer to an employee in respect of death or bodily injury out of and in the course of his employment, when there is effective cover under the Employers' Liability (Compulsory Insurance) Act 1969 (section 149(4));
- cover in respect of property damage of more than £250,000 "caused by or arising out of, any one accident" involving the vehicle, (section 161(3));
- liability in respect of damage to the vehicle;
- liability in respect of damage to goods carried for hire or reward in or on the vehicle or in any trailer drawn by the vehicle;
- liability of a person in respect of damage to property in its custody or under his control;
- any contractual liability, (section 145(4)).

Policy "in force"

Under section 143(1) there must be "in force" at the material time a policy of insurance covering the user of the vehicle against third-party risks. In *Scher v Policyholders' Protection Board* [1993] 3 All ER 384 the Court of Appeal held that there was, in general terms, no magic in the word "policy", so that a cover note, or even an enforceable oral contract could suffice. What is important is that the agreement must be contractually binding: *Taylor v Allon* [1966] 1 QB 304. Where a policy is avoidable on the grounds of, say, misrepresentation or non-disclosure, it remains "in force" until the insurer takes such steps to avoid the policy: see, for example, *Adams v Dunne* [1988] RTR 281.

Certificate of insurance

Section 147(1) provides that the policy is of no effect "for the purposes of . . . the Act" unless and until the insurer delivers to the insured a certificate of insurance "in the prescribed form". "For the purposes . . . of the Act" means the obligation to insure the driver against the liability outlined in section 145. Regulations prescribing the form of the certificate can be found in the Motor Vehicles' (Third Party Risks) Regulations 1972, S.I. 1972 No. 1217, as amended by S.I. 1974 No. 792.

Third Parties' rights

The Act, at sections 148 to 152, operates to protect the interests of those to whom the insured is legally liable, by restricting the contractual rights of insurers.

General invalidation of certain contractual terms

Section 148(1) provides that, where a certificate of insurance has been delivered to the insured, so much of the policy as purports to restrict the insurance of the persons insured by reference to a list of specified matters is of no effect as regards insurance required under section 145. Accordingly, certain terms are of no practical validity, regardless of their contractual status or effect. The "list of matters" is outlined at section 148(2) as follows:

(a) the age or physical or mental condition of persons driving the vehicle;

(b) the condition of the vehicle;

(c) the number of persons that the vehicle carries;

(d) the weight or physical characteristic of the goods that the vehicle carries;

(e) the times at which or the areas within which the vehicle is used;

(f) the horse power or cylinder capacity of value of the vehicle;

(g) the carrying on the vehicle of any particular apparatus;

(h) the carrying on the vehicle of any particular means of identification other than any means of identification required to be carried by or under the Vehicles (Excise) Act 1971.

The list is comprehensive, but not such as to embrace all types of contractual restriction. A condition that the assured "shall use all care and diligence to avoid accidents and to employ only steady and sober drivers" does not fall within (a) and is not a condition restricting the insurance: *National Farmers Union Mutual Ins. Society* v *Dawson* [1941] 2 KB 424. By the same token, a limitation as to use (such as a condition negativing liability if the vehicle is used otherwise than for "social, domestic and pleasure purposes" or in connection with a specified business usage) is always effective against third parties: see, for example, *Jones* v *Welsh Ins. Corp. Ltd* [1937] 4 All ER 149.

Invalidity of breach of condition

Section 148(5) provides that other breaches of condition are of no effect or validity against third parties. The conditions are those relieving the insurers from liability by reason "of some specified thing being done or omitted to be done after the happening of the event giving rise to a claim under the policy". This covers a broad range of conditions precedent and subsequent, such as a clause regarding notice or particulars of loss, and even an admission of liability by the assured in breach of the standard condition: see, for example, *Terry* v *Trafalagar Insurance Co.* [1970] 1 Ll Rep. 524. An arbitration clause will almost certainly fall outside the ambit of section 148(5) (see the various views outlined in *Jones* v *Birch Bros. Ltd* [1933] 2 KB 597) although such clauses are rarely, if ever, invoked in road traffic claims.

Insurers duty to satisfy judgment

General obligation

Section 151 confers a powerful remedy upon third parties who have obtained judgment against the user of a vehicle. Provided a certificate of insurance has been delivered under section 147, and once a third party has obtained a judgment against any person insured by the policy, the whole of the judgment in respect of liability for death or personal injury, and up to £250,000 of it in respect of liability for damage to property, must be satisfied by the insurer, notwithstanding that the insurer may be entitled to avoid or cancel the policy, or may have actually done so. Further, this obligation applies in respect of persons not insured by a policy, such as persons not within the category of permitted drivers, except that in respect of liability for death or personal injury, it does not apply if the third party was allowing himself to be carried in or upon a vehicle knowing or having reason to believe that the vehicle had been stolen or unlawfully taken: (section 151(4)). A term in a policy which purports to restrict cover to drivers in possession of a valid licence is also of no validity: (section 151(3)).

Qualification upon insurers' liability

Section 152 qualifies the insurers' liability in four respects. The insurer is not liable:

(1) unless he had notice of the bringing of the proceedings in which the judgment was given, before or within seven days after their commencement: (section 152(1)(a));

(2) while execution is stayed pending an appeal: (section 152(1)(b));

(3) if the policy was cancelled before the accident, and within the period of 14 days from the cancellation either the certificate was surrendered, or the holder made a statutory declaration that it was lost or destroyed, or the insurer commenced proceedings in respect of failure to surrender it: (section 152(1)(iii));

(4) if, in an action commenced not later than three months from the commencement of the proceedings in which the judgment was given, he has obtained a declaration that he is entitled to avoid the policy for non-disclosure of a material fact or material misrepresentation, and the third party receives notice of the action for a declaration and the particulars of the non-disclosure or misrepresentation within seven days of it being commenced: (section 152(2)).

Under section 152(1)(a) the notification must be "formal", but can be affected by an unambiguous solicitors' letter, or even a "clear oral notice" of the commencement of proceedings: see *Herbert* v *Railway Passengers Ass. Co.* [1938] 1 All ER 650 and *Harrington* v *Pinky* [1989] 2 Lloyd's Rep. 310. However, an inquiry as to whether or not liability is admitted will not suffice, even where the letter infers that proceedings will be issued if liability is denied: *Weldrick* v *Essex & Sussex Equitable Ins. Society* [1950] 83 Ll. Rep. 91. Conversely, it is not necessary to identify the court where the action will be or has been commenced, nor the date of issue or service: *Ceylon Motor Ins. Association Ltd* v *Thambughla* [1953] AC 584. The obligation under section 152(1)(a) was recently reviewed in *De Souza* v *Waterlow* [1999] RTR 71. The claimant, shortly after the accident, wrote to the other motorists' insurers giving full details of the accident, the names of the witnesses and two estimates for the repair of his car. The insurers authorised the repairs, having received a report from their own engineer, but made no proposals for the other aspects of the claim, namely car hire charges and costs. On two subsequent occasions the claimant wrote to the insurers warning of his intention to sue if his claim was not met. He ultimately issued proceedings and obtained judgment against the other driver. The insurers contended that the claimant had failed to give the requisite notice of the bringing of proceedings. The Court of Appeal rejected this argument and gave judgment for the claimant. Cazalet J. stated (at 79) that the statutory obligation did not require that the notice had to be notice of the particular proceedings issued. He continued (at 81):

> "In my view, notice in any particular case is a matter of fact and degree and will turn on the extent to which the insurer has been made aware of the background circumstances and of the position of the claimant in regard to the taking of proceedings. Such notice can be given orally or in writing. The essential purpose of the requirement of notice is that the insurer is not met with information, out of the blue, that his insured has had a judgment obtained against him. Here it seems to me that the position was made overwhelmingly clear to the insurers as to the claimant's position".

Under section 152(2) the insurers have to show not only that there was a non-disclosure or misrepresentation of a material fact, but also that they were influenced or induced by the same to an extent that it could properly be said that the policy was "obtained" by the misfeasance: see, for example, *Merchants & Manufacturers Ins. Co.* v *Hunt* [1941] 1 KB 295, *Zurich General Accident & Liability Ins. Co.* v *Morrison* [1942] 2 KB 53 and *General Accident Corp.* v *Shuttleworth* (1938) 60 Ll Rep. 301.

Section 152(3) provides that where a declaration is obtained, the third party should be given seven days notice of the intention to avoid the policy, so that he can decide whether or not to oppose the declaration. He can, if he thinks fit, apply to be made a party to the action: section 152(4).

Insurers rights of recovery

The insurer compelled to pay a third party has a number of statutory remedies against the insured:

- where, but for the operation of section 148(1), an insurer would have avoided liability, any money paid to the third party can be recovered from the insured: (section 148(4));

- section 151(7) entitles an insurer to recover from the insured the amount paid out when liability is established by virtue of section 151(3), namely when the person was driving without a valid licence. The insurer also has a remedy under the subsection where the amount of the judgment exceeds the amount for which he would otherwise have been liable;
- in cases where an insurer meets a judgment against someone not insured by a policy, the liability can be recovered, under section 151(8), from either that person or from any person who was insured by the policy and who caused or permitted the use of the vehicle which gave rise to the liability.

Insured's duty to provide information regarding insurance

By section 154(1) a person against whom a claim is made in respect of damage compulsorily insurable is under a duty, on demand of the third party, to give certain information concerning his insurance. He is obliged, in short, to state whether he is insured and, if so, provide details of his insurance as are specified in his certificate of insurance. Failure to comply in the absence of reasonable excuse, and the making of a wilfully false statement in response to such a demand, constitute criminal offences.

Chapter 15

The Motor Insurers' Bureau

The Motor Insurers' Bureau ("MIB") exists to compensate the innocent victims of uninsured, untraced and foreign motorists.

There are three separate Agreements:

- Motor Insurers' Bureau (Compensation of Victims of Uninsured Drivers) Agreement 1988;
- Motor Insurers' Bureau (Compensation of Victims of Untraced Drivers) Agreement 1996;

For accidents involving uninsured drivers occurring on or after 1st October 1999, the relevant provision is;

- Motor Insurers' Bureau (Compensation of Victims of Uninsured Drivers) Agreement 1999.

The Agreements, each designed to meet a distinct prejudice, necessarily outline different schemes of compensation, although they share a number of common definitions, exclusions and procedural characteristics.

The address of the MIB is:
Motor Insurers' Bureau,
152 Silbury Boulevard,
Central Milton Keynes,
Milton Keynes, MK9 1MB,
tel: 01908 240 0000,
fax: 01908 671 681,
DX: 84753 MK 3.

The text of all three Agreements, with accompanying notes, is reproduced at Appendix 4.

Definitions

Liability under the Agreements is restricted to the use of a motor vehicle on a road.

"Road"

Road is defined in section 192 of the Road Traffic Act 1988 as "any highway and any other road to which the public has access". It is difficult, if not impossible, to provide a comprehensive interpretation of this definition and, therefore, a universal method by which a place might be identified as a road. In *Oxford* v *Austin* [1981] RTR 416 Kilner Browne J. suggested the following approach:

> "The first question which has to be asked is whether there is in fact, in the ordinary understanding of the word, a road. That is to say, whether or not there is a definable way between two points over which vehicles could pass. The second question is whether or not the public, or a section of the public, has access to that which has the appearance of a definable way. If both questions can be answered affirmatively, there is a road for the purposes of the various Road Traffic Acts and Regulations".

More recently, in *Clarke* v *Kato; Cutter* v *Eagle Star Insurance Co. Ltd* [1998] 4 All ER 417, a case where the House of Lords considered whether a car park could be classified as a road, Lord Clyde stated that " some guidance might be found by considering its physical character and the function which it existed to serve". Eventually the question "came to be a matter of fact".

The following have been held to be (or have been identified as) a road:

- a forecourt used as a short cut; *Bugge* v *Taylor* [1941] 1 KB 198;
- a farm road to which the public had access, a drive leading from a public road to a private house and a forecourt providing access to an hotel; *Purves* v *Muir* [1948] J.C. 122;
- a site cleared for building at the rear of a school; *Randall* v *Motor Insurers' Bureau* [1969] 1 All ER 21;
- a hard shoulder and, potentially, a lay-by; *Clarke* v *Kato; Cutter* v *Eagle Start Insurance Co. Ltd* (ibid).

The following cannot be classified as a road:
- an unpaved forecourt, adjoining the pavement, but forming part of a private garden; *Thomas* v *Dando* [1951] 1 All ER 1010;
- a car park "in all but some exceptional cases"; *Clarke* v *Kato; Cutter* v *Eagle Star Insurance Limited* (ibid).

"Motor vehicle"

Motor vehicle is defined in section 185(1) of the Road Traffic Act 1988 as "a mechanically propelled vehicle intended or adapted for use on roads". In *Chief Constable of Avon & Somerset* v *Fleming* [1987] 1 All ER 318 the court adopted an objective test, so that the particular use of the vehicle was considered to be irrelevant. Instead the court should ask whether a reasonable person, looking at the vehicle, would say that its general use encompassed possible general road use. By way of a different (but complementary) approach, it was suggested in *Daley v Hargreaves* [1961] 1 All ER 552 that the word "intended" in the statutory definition might be paraphrased as "suitable" or "apt".

"Use" and "User"

Use and user have the same meaning as under section 143 of the Road Traffic Act 1988. In *Hatton v Hall* [1997] RTR 212 the Court of Appeal applied the following test: "Is there a sufficient degree of control or management of the vehicle to make a claimant a user of the vehicle?".

General exclusions and limitations

There are a number of situations not covered by the Agreements.

Particular vehicles

The MIB is not liable for claims arising out of vehicles owned by, or in the possession of, the Crown, except where liability is actually covered by a contract of insurance or where some other person has undertaken responsibility for the existence of insurance cover. Nor do the Agreements apply to local authority or police vehicles, or vehicles operated by a health service body, unless the vehicle is being driven without the operator's permission or control.

Knowledge that the vehicle is stolen and/or uninsured

The MIB will not incur liability in a case where the claimant knew or believed the vehicle to be stolen or that there was no contract of insurance. Thus, where a driver and his passenger were both drunk and embarked on the "common object" of driving in an uninsured vehicle, the Bureau was entitled to an exemption from liability: *Stinton v Stinton* [1995] RTR 157. Liability was also excluded where a motor cycle pillion passenger knew that the driver was uninsured: *O'Mahoney v Joliffe*; *O'Mahoney v Motor Insurers' Bureau* [1999] PIQR 149. Enforcement of this exclusion is strict, but not absolute. A passenger in a vehicle is accordingly obliged to take "all reasonable steps" to get out of a vehicle as soon as he knows that it is stolen or uninsured.

Uninsured Drivers: The Motor Insurers' Bureau (Compensation of Victims of Uninsured Drivers) Agreement 1988

The Motor Insurers' Bureau (Compensation of Victims of Uninsured Drivers) Agreement 1988, known as "the first agreement", exists to compensate the innocent victims of negligent drivers who are not insured. (Aside from indemnifying the "man of straw", the Agreement also applies where the insurers have become insolvent or otherwise avoided the policy of insurance). The MIB will pay to a claimant any sums due under a judgment, including costs, where the judgment remains unsatisfied for seven days.

Prerequisites to the liability of the MIB

Liability

The claim must be in respect of a risk required to be covered by insurance under the Road Traffic Act 1988, Part VI. This covers claims brought by the driver and all passengers for personal injury, death, damage to property (with an excess of £175 and to a maximum in any one case of £250,000: clause 2) and loss of use of a motor vehicle.

Notice

When?

Notice must be given within seven days after the issue of proceedings: clause 5(1)(a). The Bureau can extend the seven day time limit or even waive its right to rely on the limitation, although this discretion is rarely exercised. Where any such permission or representation is given, the Bureau will be estopped from relying on clause 5(1)(a): see *Begum v Ullah* (1998) CLY 590. But neither waiver nor estoppel applied where the MIB, aside from pleading that a claimant failed to give due notice, also applied to be joined as a second defendant and continued with the proceedings: *Filberton v Goodall and Motor Insurers' Bureau* [1997] PIQR 451.

To whom?

Notice must be given:

> (a) to the MIB in the case of proceedings in respect of a relevant liability which is either not covered by a contract of insurance or covered by a contract of insurance with an insurer whose identity cannot be ascertained (clause 5(1)(a)(i)); or

(b) to the insurer, in the case of proceedings in respect of a liability which is covered by a contract of insurance with an insurer whose identity cannot be ascertained (clause 5(1)(a)(ii)).

How?

Notice must be given in writing and be accompanied by a copy of the Writ, Summons or, under the Civil Procedure Rules 1999, the Claim Form. In *Cambridge v Callaghan* (1997) Times, March 21 the Court of Appeal confirmed that notice of proceedings was a condition precedent to the liability of the MIB and held that effective notice under clause 5 required official evidence of the instigation of proceedings, either by way of a copy of the stamped Writ or the Notice of Issue of Default Summons.

Information

The Road Traffic Act 1988, section 154, requires a person against whom a claim is made to provide, on demand by or on behalf of a person making a claim, full particulars of his insurance, the name and address of the insurers and the policy number. Clause 5(1)(c) of the Agreement states that the claimant must have demanded this information, or authorised the MIB to do so on his behalf. Also, by clause 5(1)(b), the claimant must provide such information relating to the proceedings as the MIB may reasonably require.

Judgment

The MIB can require that:

(a) the claimant must (subject to a full indemnity as to costs) take all reasonable steps to obtain judgment against all persons liable in respect of the injury or death (clause 5(1)(d)); and/or

(b) the judgment obtained, and any order for costs, be assigned to the MIB or its nominee (clause 5(1)(e)).

Procedure

There is no formal procedure for making a claim – aside, of course, from the requirement of "notice". A claim can initially be made by a letter from the claimant (or his legal adviser) which should outline the facts and enclose copies of any relevant documents.

When a claim is made the Bureau will appoint one of its members to act as an agent of the MIB. (If there is in existence a policy of insurance the insurer concerned will invariably be delegated as agent). The insurer, as agent, will be authorised to investigate and settle the claim.

If the claim does not settle, the claimant must establish his case against the defendant in the usual way and must recover judgment.

Where judgment is recovered, but only part of the debt is recoverable under the Agreement, the MIB will apportion and pay the appropriate part of the debt and costs.

Uninsured Drivers: The Motor Insurers' Bureau (Compensation of Victims of Uninsured Drivers) Agreement 1999

The Motor Insurers' Bureau (Compensation of Victims of Uninsured Drivers) Agreement 1999 replaces the 1988 Agreement (or "first agreement") for all incidents occurring on or after 1st October 1999. The 1999 Agreement reproduces the basic purpose and structure of the first agreement. The MIB's obligation to satisfy judgments which fall within the terms of the Agreement (outlined in clause 5) is, as before, subject to certain exceptions (clause 6), there are a number of pre-conditions which the claimant must comply with (clauses 7 to 15) and there are some limitations to the Bureau's liability (clauses 16 and 17). Nonetheless the new Agreement introduces a number of significant changes to both the operation and effect of the MIB's liability. The main changes are as follows:

Excess

Where the claim is for property damage it is subject to a "specified excess" of £300 (increased from £175) and a cap of £250,000: clause 16.

Application form

Claims should now be made using the MIB's application form, fully completed giving "such information about the relevant proceedings" and "accompanied by such documents as the MIB may reasonably require": clause 7. The MIB "shall incur no liability" unless this condition precedent is met: clause 7(1). Copies of the form can be obtained on request made by post, telephone, fax, DX or on personal application to the MIB's offices in Milton Keynes.

Notice
When?

The claimant is now allowed 14 days in which to give the MIB notice in writing that he has commenced legal proceedings: clause 9(1). Unfortunately the new Agreement additionally imposes a number of onerous notice provisions. The claimant must:

- inform the MIB of the date of service within seven days (if served by the court or by personal service; (clause 10(3)(a)(i) and (iii)), or within 14 days of the date when service is deemed to have occurred in accordance with the Civil Procedure Rules (clause 10(3)(b))
- give the MIB notice within seven days of the filing of a Defence in the relevant proceedings, an amendment to the Statement or Particulars of Claim, the setting down of the case for trial or receipt by the claimant of a court notice notifying him of the trial date; (clause 11(1))
- give the MIB "at least" 35 days notice of an intention to apply or sign for judgment; (clause 12).

Notice
What?

Clause 9(2)(a) to (d) lists the information and/or documentation which must be supplied if "proper notice" is to be given. Normally this includes, in addition to the Claim Form, any documentation supplied with the application form, a copy of the Particulars of Claim (assuming that such a pleading is endorsed on the Claim Form) and copies of "all other documents which are required under the appropriate rules of procedure to be served on the Defendant".

Service

Service of any notice or document supplied to the MIB must now be effected by facsimile transmission or Registered or Recorded Delivery. Service is not permitted by either first class post or DX: (clause 8).

Information

Clause 13(a) reproduces the requirement that the claimant must "as soon as reasonably practicable" exercise his statutory rights under section 154(1) of the Road Traffic Act 1988. But clause 13(d) extends the obligation by stating that if the person on whom the demand is made fails to provide the "relevant particulars" of his insurance policy, the claimant must make "a formal complaint to a police officer in respect of such failure" and use "all reasonable endeavours to obtain the name and address of the registered keeper of the vehicle".

Joinder

Clause 14(b) provides that the claimant must not oppose (or refuse consent to) any application by the MIB to be joined as a party to the relevant proceedings.

Setting aside judgment

Under clause 15(b)(i) the claimant must undertake to repay to the MIB "any sum paid to him" in the event that the judgment is either wholly or partly set aside.

Repayment on receipt of payment from another source

Similarly, under clause 15(b)(ii) the claimant must undertake to reimburse the MIB upon receipt of a payment from another source that duplicates the compensation assessed by the court.

Untraced Drivers: The Motor Insurers' Bureau (Compensation of Victims of Untraced Drivers) Agreement 1996

The Motor Insurers' Bureau (Compensation of Victims of Untraced Drivers) Agreement 1996, known as "the second agreement", exists to compensate the victims of drivers who are never traced. It applies to any case "in respect of the death or bodily injury to any person caused by or arising out of the use of a motor vehicle on a road in Great Britain" (clause 1(1)). The Bureau is under no liability to pay compensation for damage to property. The agreement applies to accidents occurring on or after 1st July 1996. Accidents prior to that date are governed by "the second agreement" dated 22nd November 1972.

Prerequisites to the liability of MIB

Clause 1 requires that a number of conditions be fulfilled:

- The death or personal injury must have been caused in such circumstances that on the balance of probability the untraced person would be liable to pay damages to the claimant in respect of death or injury; (clause 1(1)(c)).

- The liability of the untraced driver to pay damages to the claimant must be one which is required to be covered by insurance or security under Part VI of the Road Traffic Act 1988, it being presumed for this purpose, in the absence of evidence to the contrary, that the vehicle was being used in circumstances in which the user was required to be insured or secured against third party risks; (clause 1(1)(d)).
- The death or personal injury must be demonstrated not to have been caused as a result of the use of the vehicle by the untraced driver in any deliberate attempt to cause injury to the claimant; (clause 1(1)(e)).
- The application must be made in writing within three years of the event giving rise to the death or injury; (clause 1(1)(f)).
- The incident must have been reported to the police within 14 days or as soon as the claimant reasonably could and the claimant must co-operate with the police; (clause 1(1)(g)).

Clause 6 imposes a number of other prerequisites to the liability of the MIB:

- The claimant must give all assistance as may reasonably be required by the MIB to enable any investigation to be carried out, including, in particular, the provision of statements and information; (clause 6(1)(a)).
- The claimant must take all steps as in the circumstances it is reasonable for the MIB to require him to obtain judgment against any person or persons in respect of their liability for the death or injury; (clause 6(1)(b)).
- If required by the MIB, the claimant must assign to it any judgment obtained by the claimant in respect of the death or injury to which the application to the MIB relates; (clause 6(1)(c)).

Procedure

There is again no formal procedure for making a claim under the second agreement. Notification of a claim is normally made by letter from the claimant or a solicitor acting on his behalf. The Bureau will arrange for a full investigation into the accident. A decision will then be made as to the merits of the claim and, if applicable, the amount of the award. The decision, either way, together with reasons and an accompanying statement, is sent to the claimant. If the claimant accepts the decision, and the amount of the award, if any, it will be paid over within six weeks from the date of notification.

Accelerated procedure

Clauses 24 to 28 of the Agreement reproduce the terms of a Supplemental Agreement, originally introduced in 1977, and provide for an "accelerated procedure" for claims arising out of accidents occurring on or after 1st July 1996.

Under this procedure the MIB, having undertaken a preliminary investigation, can make an offer to settle the claim for a specified sum: (clause 24). The claimant is then entitled to accept the offer, at which point the MIB is discharged from all liability, or reject the offer, whereupon the case will revert to the full procedure: (clause 25(2)). The accelerated procedure is designed to be both faster and less formal than the general procedure.

It does not apply to claims:

- estimated to exceed £10,000 where brought by a litigant in person or £100,000 where brought by a legal representative;
- where an identified driver is also involved;
- which present unusual features.

Appeals

The claimant may dispute either the decision of the MIB not to make an award or the amount of the same. (This right is limited to claims decided under the general procedure; a claimant who accepts an offer under the accelerated procedure foregoes the right of appeal). The appeal is made to an arbitrator (a Queen's Counsel chosen from a panel maintained by the Secretary of State and the Lord Chancellor) whose decision is final: (clause 12(a)). All statements and documents are forwarded to the arbitrator who is then entitled to ask the MIB to undertake any further investigation he considers desirable: clause 17(2)(a). The MIB, meanwhile, is entitled to review and reconsider its own decision prior to the appointment of the arbitrator. This will quite often occur where, for example, the claimant produces a supplementary medical report. The arbitrator is empowered to determine whether the MIB should make an award and, if so, the amount it should pay to the claimant: (clause 16(b)). (See also clauses 16(a) and (c) in respect of the determination of questions relating to the application of the Agreement and other disputes.) He will then notify his decision to the MIB who "shall forthwith" send a copy to the claimant: (clause 19). Each party to the appeal pays their own costs – the fee of the arbitrator is paid by the MIB: (clauses 21 and 22). A claimant cannot challenge the decision of the Bureau by either issuing proceedings against the MIB or appealing to Court: *Person* v *London County Buses* [1974] 1 All ER 1251.

Foreign motorists and the "Green Card Scheme"

Where an accident is caused by a foreign motorist in the United Kingdom, the MIB will deal with the claim brought by the victim thereof and, in most cases, proceed against the foreign insurer.

Recovery

There are, in effect, two aspects to a claim arising from the negligence of a foreign motorist:

- First, the MIB is required to satisfy any judgment under its obligation pursuant to "the first agreement": the liability outlined in clause 2 of the Agreement applies regardless of the nationality or domicile of the defendant.
- Secondly, the MIB will often be able to recover its outlay under a Multilateral Guarantee Agreement concluded in 1991. Under the scheme, insurers in each participating country (the list includes virtually all European nations) set up a Bureau, which both guarantees insurance against third party risks in other signatory countries (by the issue of international motor insurance cards known as "Green Cards"), and deals with claims brought by other Bureaux. The MIB, following settlement of the claim, will thus be able to seek an indemnity from either the foreign insurer or the Bureau which provided the green card.

Procedure

A claimant should, as soon as practicable after the accident, give notice of the claim to the MIB. He should also, if possible, forward the name of the foreign motorist, the registration number of his vehicle and the particulars of any green card.

General procedural matters

Interim payments

Interim payments can be awarded where the claim concerns an uninsured driver: *Sharp* v *Pereira* [1998] Times, July 25 and CPR 25.7(2).

The claimant should supply the MIB with the medical reports and schedules relied on and the Bureau will adopt the principles applicable in court. This means, in turn, that where a claim is (or will be) allocated to the "fast track", the MIB will rarely entertain an application.

Interest

Uninsured drivers

Interest included in the judgment debt (pursuant to either the Supreme Court Act 1981, section 35A or the County Courts Act 1984, section 69) is payable by the MIB. Interest on the judgment debt is not usually recoverable, although the authority for this (almost habitual) practice remains unclear.

Untraced drivers

Interest is not payable under the terms relating to untraced drivers: the second agreement contains no provision for such an award. But an arbitrator appointed by the MIB can award interest where he decides, in his discretion, that the Bureau has not acted with reasonable expedition, or where he concludes that the amount awarded by the Bureau was too low. Interest, in these circumstances, can be awarded on the period between the original decision and the arbitrator's review: *Evans* v *Motor Insurers' Bureau* (1997) Times, November 10.

Costs:

Uninsured drivers

The "unsatisfied judgment" payable by the MIB includes the claimant's reasonable (or assessed) costs, or such proportion of the same as is attributable to the liability of the Bureau: *Randall* v *Motor Insurers' Bureau* [1969] 1 All ER 21. The fact that the defendant has legal aid will not necessarily mean that an order for the claimant's costs is unenforceable: the fact that the MIB "stands behind" the defendant is a "circumstance relevant" to the question of costs and whether or not a full order should be made; *Godfrey* v *Smith* [1955] 2 All ER 520.

Untraced drivers

The MIB and the Law Society have reached an understanding whereby the sum of £150 plus VAT plus reasonable disbursements is payable in respect of solicitors (but not, usually, Counsel's) costs. Where one solicitor introduces more than one claimant arising from the same incident an additional fee is recoverable in the sum of £75 plus VAT for each supplementary claimant.

The MIB as defendant

There are two similar but distinct situations:

- joinder of the MIB as a defendant;
- proceedings against the MIB as a defendant.

Joinder

Uninsured Drivers
Sometimes it is appropriate for the MIB to guide or control the steps taken in the litigation. (The MIB can, for example, conduct the uninsured driver's defence, where he consents to this course of action.) Accordingly, and in order to facilitate this requirement, the MIB can be made a party to the proceedings.

The rationale for joinder was neatly expressed by Lord Denning MR in *Gurtner* v *Circuit* [1968] 1 QB 587:

> "They are directly affected, not only in their legal rights, but also in their pockets. They ought to be allowed to come in as defendants. It would be most unjust if they were bound to stand idly by watching the claimant get judgment against the defendant without saying a word when they are the people who have to foot the bill".

All the same, joinder is always within the discretion of the court. Consent has been refused (at least historically) in cases where the insurers were not members of the Motor Insurers' Bureau: *Fire Auto and Marine Insurance Co Ltd* v *Greene* [1964] 2 QB 687. The court can also grant leave for the MIB to be added as defendants but simultaneously limit its role to certain issues in the litigation. In *Baker* v *Francis* [1997] PIQR 155 the Court of Appeal restricted the MIB to issues relating to quantum, on the grounds that the Bureau's nominated insurer had previously allowed the Claimant to enter judgment in default of defence. This decision was followed (albeit at first instance) in *Hoover Ltd* v *Depeazer* (1999) CL, January, 51.

Untraced Drivers
There are no circumstances in which the MIB can be added as a defendant. Where the culpable motorist cannot be identified, proceedings are only ever issued at the behest of the Bureau and, as such, it would be inappropriate for the MIB to defend an actin it had

originally instigated: *White* v *London Transport Executive* [1971] 2
QB 721. In cases where at least one of the responsible drivers is identified, joinder of the MIB is unnecessary.

MIB sued as a defendant

Uninsured drivers
Irrespective of the liability of the uninsured driver, the MIB may
dispute liability under the Agreement: it may, for example, raise or
rely on one of the prerequisites to liability discussed at pages 198 to
199. The authorities suggest that, in these circumstances, a cause of
action will lie directly against the Bureau: see *Hardy* v *Motor Insurers'
Bureau* [1964] 2 QB 745 (per Lord Denning MR at 757) and *Albert* v
Motor Insurers' Bureau [1972] A.C. 301 (per Lord Donovan at 312).

Untraced drivers
No cause of actin will lie against the MIB under the second agreement.
Thus, in *Person* v *London County Buses* [1974] 1 All ER 1251, a case
where the claimant appealed to court against the Bureau's decision to
make no award, the Court of Appeal upheld the decision of the
District Judge to strike out the Particulars of Claim on the ground that
the pleading disclosed no cause of action.

Service by an alternative method on the MIB

Service by an alternative method (previously "substituted service")
is governed by CPR 6.8. It is necessary to look at two contrasting
situations:

- Where a driver stops and provides his name and address, but
  subsequently disappears, so that the claimant, notwithstanding
  the expenditure of all reasonable efforts to trace him, is unable
  to ascertain the identity of his insurers, the court may permit
  service of proceedings upon the MIB: *Gurtner* v *Circuit* (ibid).

- Where a driver either refuses to stop after an accident, or stops
  and provides completely fictitious information, so that he
  cannot be reliably identified or traced, "alternative service" on
  the MIB will be refused, and the claimant will be obliged to
  apply to the MIB under the second agreement: *Clarke* v *Vedel*
  [1979] RTR 26.

Chapter 16

Recovery of Charges for NHS Treatment in Road Traffic Accident Claims

Hospitals which provide care for road traffic casualties have long been able to make some recovery from insurers or certain vehicle owners for the cost of "expenses reasonably incurred in affording the treatment": Road Traffic Act 1988, section 157. But the power of restoration is capped at a low level (£2,949 for each person treated as an in-patient and £295 for each person treated as an out-patient), and this, along with the administrative complexity of the recovery process, has acted to ensure that claims are rarely progressed. The Road Traffic (NHS Charges) Act 1999, which was brought in to force on 5th April 1999, is designed to address this and provide the NHS with an effective scheme of recovery.

The Road Traffic (NHS Charges) Act 1999

The Act, in essence, removes NHS hospitals from the scope of the Road Traffic Act 1988, increases the charges and maximum sums recoverable and introduces a collection process administered by the Compensation Recovery Unit ("CRU") of the Department of Social Security.

When are charges recoverable?

Under section 1(1) of the Act charges become recoverable if:

(a) a person (the traffic casualty) has suffered injury, or has suffered injury and dies, as a result of the use of a motor vehicle on a road;

(b) a compensation payment is made in respect of that injury or death; and

(c) the traffic casualty has received NHS treatment at a health service hospital in respect of his injury.

A compensation payment is defined in section 1(3) of the Act and covers payments made by insurers, vehicle owners and payments made in pursuance of a compensation scheme (e.g. the MIB agreements) for motor accidents.

What charges are recoverable?

The Act applies to all accidents whenever occurring. (The exception to the generality of this rule concerns the liability of the MIB which only arises in respect of accidents occurring after 5th April 1999.)

The maximum amounts payable are outlined in The Road Traffic (NHS Charges) Regulations 1999, S.I. No. 785, at regulations 3 and 4, and depend on the date of the accident:

- for accidents occurring before 2nd July 1997; £295 for an out-patient, £435 per day for an in-patient, with a maximum ceiling of £3,000.
- for accidents on or after 2nd July 1997; £354 for an out-patient, £435 per day for an in-patient (as above), but with a cap at £10,000.

Recovery of charges

Collection is affected by the CRU under a "certificate scheme" set out at sections 2 to 5 of the Act. The NHS hospital providing the care must inform the CRU of the treatment it has given and the cost thereof. The compensator (either the defendant motorist, his insurers or the MIB) must (under section 2(1)) apply to the Secretary of State for a certificate attesting to the charges. The application for a certificate must be made prior to the making of the compensation payment or within 14 days thereof. Under section 4 payment to the CRU must be made within 14 days of the date of the compensation payment being made. Should the compensator fail to make prompt payment the Secretary of State may issue a demand for immediate payment and, in due course, pursue payment through the County Court.

Can the compensator challenge the sum payable to the CRU?

The Act (along with The Road Traffic (NHS Charges) Reviews and Appeals Regulations 1999, S.I. No. 78) provides for two methods by which the compensator may dispute the sum payable to the CRU:

(1) Review

Under sections 6 and 7 (see below) of the Act, a certificate may be reviewed by the Secretary of State, either on an application made for the purpose or his own initiative, whereupon he may confirm the existing certificate, issue a new certificate or revoke the certificate.

(2) Appeal

Under section 7 of the Act an appeal may be made against a certificate on the grounds that:

(a) an amount specified in the certificate as incorrect;
(b) an amount so specified takes into account treatment which is not NHS treatment;
(c) the payment on the basis of which the certificate was issued is not a compensation payment.

An appeal, which is determined by an appeal tribunal (see section 8) must be made within three months of the disposal of the claim giving rise to the compensation payment. Under section 9 there is a right of appeal to the High Court on any point of law arising from a decision of an appeal tribunal.

Chapter 17

Compensation for Criminal Injuries

This chapter will examine the availability of compensation in cases where the road traffic accident also constituted a criminal offence. Specific reference will be made to:

- The Criminal Injuries Compensation Authority;
- Compensation orders in criminal courts.

Criminal Injuries Compensation Authority

The Criminal Injuries Compensation Authority ("CICA") exists to administer a scheme of state sponsored compensation (or, at least, financial provision) for the victims of crime. The Criminal Injuries Compensation Scheme 1996, often referred to as "the new scheme", applies to all applications made on or after 1st April 1996. It replaces the 1990 Scheme, known as "the old scheme", which continues to govern applications made before that date.

Road traffic and motor vehicle offences

The scheme provides that a personal injury sustained as a result of a road traffic offence is not, in most cases, a criminal injury, so that redress cannot be obtained from the CICA. The exception to the general rule concerns cases where the vehicle is intentionally used as a weapon. Both provisions (the exclusion and the exception) are outlined at paragraph 11 of the 1996 Scheme:

"A personal injury is not a criminal injury for the purpose of this Scheme where the injury is attributable to the use of a vehicle, except where the vehicle was used so as to deliberately to inflict, or attempt to inflict, injury on any person".

(The 1990 Scheme contains, again at paragraph 11, a similar, but slightly more inclusive provision.)

"deliberately"

Reference to "deliberately" must, it is submitted, exclude recklessness. Only in cases where the vehicle was intentionally used as an agent of violence – a weapon – will the claim be allowed. This impression is confirmed in paragraph 7.21 of the CICA Guide to the 1996 Scheme (Issue Number Two (4/99), TS2 (Print S1)).

"to inflict"

Paragraph 11 refers to "the vehicle" being "used so as" to "inflict" the injury. Yet, the Scheme undoubtedly extends to cases where the damage was not inflicted by the driver of the vehicle (who may be completely innocent) but by a third party who nonetheless engages in a plan of violence which necessitates, or incorporates, the use of a vehicle. Professor David Miers, in *State Compensation for Criminal Injuries* (Blackstone Press, 1997), lists, at page 103, a number of examples taken from various Annual Reports submitted by the CICB/CICA. They include applications:

- where the victim was pushed into the path of an oncoming vehicle: CICB, 1983, para. 25;
- where the offender tied a rope across a path causing a cyclist to fall off and into the path of a following vehicle: CICB, 1986, para. 26 and 1992, para. 23.4;
- where a motor cyclist was injured when he collided, in poor visibility on an unlit road, with a pile of debris that had been deliberately placed on the carriageway: CICB, 1995, para. 6.4.

"any person"

"Any person" does not just refer to the person specifically targeted by the offender. Secondary victims can include an innocent bystander also struck by the vehicle or a person in a close relationship with the primary target who sustains mental injury attributable to the material incident.

Procedure

Application must be made in writing "on a form obtained from" the CICA (para. 17 of the 1996 Scheme) at Tay House, 300 Bath Street, Glasgow, G2 4JR. Application "should be made as soon as possible" after the material incident, and in any event within two years, although the claims officer may waive this time limit where "it is reasonable and in the interests of justice to do so" (para. 17).

Relationship between the Criminal Injuries Compensation Scheme and the Motor Insurers' Bureau

The remedies provided by the CICA and the MIB "are not necessarily mutually exclusive alternatives and were not designed to be so": *Gardner v Moore* [1984] AC 548 (per Lord Hailsham LC at 562). The MIB can be liable to the innocent victim of an uninsured driver even though the material incident constituted a criminal offence. (This, in large part, provides a justification for the general exclusion contained in paragraphs 11 of both the 1990 and the 1996 Schemes.) Liability of the MIB can even extend to cases where the uninsured driver intentionally caused injury to the claimant: see *Hardy v Motor Insurers' Bureau* [1964] 2 QB 745 and *Gardner v Moore* (ibid).

There are, however, several circumstances in which the jurisdiction of the CICA and the MIB can be said to be mutually exclusive:

- The Motor Insurers' Bureau (Compensation of Victims of Untraced Drivers) Agreement 1996 ("the second agreement"), at clause 1(e), excludes a claim against the MIB where the death or injury was caused by the untraced person deliberately using the vehicle as a weapon.
- Compensation can be payable under the Scheme where the circumstances of the incident fall outside the terms of the MIB Agreements. This can occur, for example, where one of the various exclusions or limitations to the Agreements apply, or where the incident occurred on land that could not be classified as a "road".

Compensation orders in criminal courts

Many road traffic accidents result in the culpable driver making an appearance in both the criminal and civil courts. In almost every such case the prosecution will be concluded before judgment is obtained in the civil litigation. Criminal courts have power to make compensation orders under the Powers of Criminal Courts Act 1973, section 35. Regrettably, however, there are notable restrictions applicable to compensation in respect of offences involving the use of a vehicle.

General principles

The PCCA 1973, section 35(1) provides:

"Subject to the provisions of this Part of this Act and to section 40 of the Magistrates' Courts Act 1980 (which imposes a monetary limit on the powers of a magistrates court under this section), a court by or before which a person is convicted of an offence, instead of, or in addition to dealing with him in any other way, may, on an application or otherwise, make an order (in this Act referred to as "a compensation order") requiring him to pay compensation for any personal injury, loss of damage resulting from that offence or any other offence which is taken into consideration by the court in determining sentence [or to make payments for funeral expenses or bereavement in respect of a death resulting from any such offence, other than a death due to an accident arising out the presence of a motor vehicle on a road; and a court shall give reasons, on passing sentence, if he does not make such an order in a case where this section empowers it to do so]."

In *Inwood* (1974) 60 Cr App R 7 Scarman LJ explained (at 73) the rationale and value of this provision:

"Compensation orders were introduced into our law as a convenient and rapid means of avoiding the expense of recourse to civil litigation when the criminal clearly has means which would enable the compensation to be paid".

In the magistrates court the Magistrates' Courts Act 1980, section 40(1), provides that the maximum sum which may be ordered by way of compensation for any offence is £5,000.00. In a crown court there is no limit to the amount of compensation that may be ordered, subject to a regard to the defendant's means.

Road traffic and motor vehicle offences

With regard to compensation being ordered by the court in respect of road traffic and motor vehicle offences, section 35(3) provides:

"A compensation order may only be made in respect of injury, loss or damage (other than loss suffered by a person's dependents in consequence of his death) which was due to an accident arising out of the presence of a motor vehicle on a road, if -

(a) it is in respect of damage which is treated by sub-section (2) above as resulting from an offence under the Theft Act 1968; or
(b) it is in respect of injury, loss or damage as respects which -
    (i) the offender is uninsured in relation to the use of the vehicle; and
    (ii) compensation is not payable under any arrangements to which the Secretary of State is a party;

and, where a compensation order is made in respect of injury, loss or damage due to such an accident, the amount to be paid may include an amount representing the whole or part of any loss of, or reduction in preferential rates of insurance attributable to the accident."

Claims are accordingly limited to cases:

- involving an offence under the Theft Act 1968, either where the property is not recovered, or where the property, although recovered, has sustained damage whilst it was out of the owner's possession: see *Quigley* v *Stokes* [1977] 1 WLR 434;

- where notwithstanding the fact that the offender is uninsured, a claim cannot be brought under either of the MIB agreements because, for example, one of the various exceptions or limitations apply, or where the incident occurred on land that was not a "road".

Part V

Practice & Procedure

Chapter 18

Pre-Action Procedure

Pre-action practice in road traffic accident claims is (or will be) determined by three procedural matrices:

- the Pre-Action Protocol for Road Traffic Accidents;
- the Pre-Action Protocol for Personal Injury Claims;
- the Code of Best Practice on Rehabilitation, Early Intervention and Medical Treatment in Personal Injury Claims.

What follows is no substitute for a thorough familiarity with either the Protocols, the Code or, indeed, the CPR. Instead this chapter will provide a short consideration of the relevant provisions. Then, as an early and accurate assessment of merits is always a priority, it will consider the nature and collation of the evidence upon which the claim will rely.

Pre-Action Protocol For Road Traffic Accidents

The introduction to the draft RTA Protocol sets out the following aims:

> "The objective is to set out a series of standards between the parties in respect of pre-issue conduct in handling all claims arising from a road traffic accident to involve damage only and personal injury claims. The protocol includes procedures on general matters of conduct and early exchange of information; and an agreed level of costs.
>
> The protocol is an opportunity to remove the uncertainty and mistrust between the parties, and to give stability and understanding between the parties with the common goal of improving the communication and speed of settlement of the claims handling process."

The protocol was pioneered by the members of the Moter Accidents Solicitors Society ("MASS"). Although it has been the subject of severel succesful pilot schemes, it has not yet been approved by the Head of Civil Justice or specified in the Schedule to the appropriate Practice Direction. Active consideration is now being given to a general implementation and significant progress is expected in 2000.

It is proposed to deal with each section in brief. The complete text of the draft RTA Protocol is reproduced at Appendix 6. Both the protocol and the costs shedules can also be downloaded from the MASS website at http: //www.mass.org.uk/prot.htm.

Part 1 – Standards

Solicitors (acting for claimants) and insurers (representing defendants) must both nominate a 'liaison officer' in respect of the protocol and undertake to deal with all letters, telephone calls (including voice mail messages) and e-mail correspondence in a "polite and courteous" manner within the prescribed time limits.

Part 2 – Claims Handling Procedures

Designed to "ensure the early release and exchange of information", Part 2 contains some of the most important provisions of the protocol.

Sections 3.1 to 3.5 provide for a series of initial and subsequent letters between the parties, each subject to a strict timetable, and in the form(s) outlined at Annex A to E.

Engineer's reports are governed by section 3.6. This leads on to specific provisions regarding repair (3.7) and settlement where the vehicle is damaged beyond economical repair (3.8). The protocol preserves the claimant's right to challenge the insurer's valuation of his vehicle (3.8.2). Where the vehicle is a 'write off' the insurer must obtain the owner's consent before disposing of the same in a manner that complies with the Motor Conference "Code of Practice for the Disposal of Motor Vehicle Salvage to Detect and Deter Criminal Activity" (copied at Annex H).

Section 3.9 introduces an important provision in relation to the hire of a replacement vehicle. Essentially the insurer must either:

(i) agree the hire rate, period and type of vehicle; or
(ii) provide a suitable replacement vehicle.

Storage charges are similarly provided for at section 3.10.

Section 3.12 applies to medical evidence. The RTA Protocol, like the PI Protocol, encourages the joint instruction of, and access to, medical experts. It promotes the practice of the claimant obtaining a medical report, disclosing it to the defendant who then asks questions and/or agrees it and does not obtain his own report. Again, however, the defendant is entitled to instruct his own expert, subject to the court (if proceedings are issued) subsequently deciding whether either party acted unreasonably (3.12.6).

The Protocol then outlines important provisions as to negotiation and settlement:

3.13 Claims where liability is not in dispute (non injury)
The parties must contact one another to discuss settlement of the claim within 15 working days of the 'insurer's second letter', provided that full particulars of the claim have been presented.

3.14 Claims where liability is not in dispute (injury)
Upon receipt of the claimant's medical report, the insurer must undertake either of the following:

(i)   Make an offer of settlement within 10 working days, where requested, or;

(ii) Advise the Solicitor if obtaining own medical report in accordance with the provisions set out in clause 3.12, and;

(iii) Forward a copy of the Insurer's medical report to the Solicitor within ten working days from the date of receipt, provided the Insurer intends to rely upon this report.

Sub-section 3.14.2 allows for another 14 days "continued negotiation" if the offer is not accepted.

3.15 Claims where liability is in dispute
This section alternatively provides for short periods (usually 10 days) of discussion interspersed with the obtaining and disclosure of the police report and the exchange of evidence.

All the prescribed timescales simultaneously prohibit the issue of proceedings whilst discussions and/or negotiations are continuing.

Where settlement is agreed, the insurer must forward a cheque within 20 working days (3.16.1). Non-compliance of more than 20 working days incurs interest at the punitive rate of 25% per annum on a daily rate basis.

Time Periods, Part 36 Offers, Solicitors Procedures and Insurers Procedures

The rest of the protocol outlines various procedures (including procedures for disputes and breaches of the protocol) and provisions for calculation. Of some significance is section 5.1, "Part 36 Offers", which suggests that such offers should not be made unless a claim involves parties not operating under the protocol. Costs are provided for at section 7.1 and Annex G. In addition to the prescribed costs,

VAT and "all reasonable disbursements" will be paid (7.11). Somewhat surprisingly, but no doubt to the relief of most judges, section 7.2.2 provides that claims for loss of use and enjoyment of a vehicle should be calculated at a rate of £60 per week unless there are "exceptional circumstances". The period of loss should also continue until seven working days after receipt of the settlement cheque (7.2.3).

Pre-Action Protocol For Personal Injury Claims

Given the anticipated implementation of the RTA Protocol, it is not proposed to consider the protocol for PI claims in exhaustive detail. Nonetheless it remains, at present, the primary guide to pre-action procedure in personal injury claims arising out of road traffic accidents.

The protocol, as published, divides into three sections:

1. Introduction,
2. Guidance Notes and
3. The Protocol.

There are also three Annexes that illustrate:

A. Letter of Claim,
B. Standard disclosure lists of documents and
C. Letter of instruction to medical expert.

It is designed to promote "more pre-action contact between the parties" and "better and earlier exchange of information" (1.2).

Every action should begin with the claimant sending a 'letter of claim'. Section 3 provides that the letter, which is recommended to be in "standard format" (3.3 and Annex A), should contain "sufficient information to substantiate a realistic claim before issues of quantum are addressed in detail" (3.1), including "a clear summary of the facts on which the claim is based together with an indication of the nature of any injuries suffered and of any financial loss incurred" (3.2). (Two draft letters of claim are included at Appendix . . .). The defendant must reply within "21 calendar days" of the date of posting of the letter (3.6) and has a "maximum of three months from the date of acknowledgement" (3.7) to investigate the claim.

If liability is denied, the defendant must disclose with his letter of reply all "documents in his possession which are material to the issues" (3.10). The claimant should endeavour to identify the category of relevant documents in the letter of claim (3.10). Annex B, Sections A and B – which do not purport to be exhaustive (3.11) – provide for the following standard disclosure in RTA Cases:

"SECTION A
In all cases where liability is in issue

(i) Documents identifying the nature, extent and location of damage to Defendant's vehicle where there is any dispute about the point of impact.
(ii) MOT certificate where relevant.
(iii) Maintenance records where a vehicle defect is alleged or it is alleged by Defendant that there was an unforeseen defect which caused or contributed to the accident.

SECTION B
Accident involving commercial vehicle as potential Defendant.

(i) Tachograph charts or entry from individual control book.
(ii) Maintenance and repair records required for operators licence where vehicle defect is alleged or it is alleged by Defendants that there was an unforeseen defect which caused or contributed to the accident."

Reference, in appropriate cases, can also be made to Section C, Highway Tripping Claims.

Sections 3.14 to 3.21 deal with experts and complement the provisions of CPR Part 35. The protocol encourages the joint selection of, and access to experts, both medical and non medical. It provides a mechanism and timetable by which a party should select, instruct and disclose the report of an expert. Ideally the claimant should obtain and disclose a medical report. The defendant should then either agree the report or ask questions of the expert. Nonetheless the protocol refers to "the first party" and "the second party" (rather than the claimant and defendant) so that insurers or solicitors acting for the defendant are entitled to take the initiative. Either way, the protocol retains the option for each party, in appropriate circumstances, to obtain their own expert report.

Finally, the Guidance Notes published with the protocol emphasise the desirability of a periodic "stocktake" of evidence and issues and the importance of pre-action discussions and/or negotiations:

"The protocol does not specify where or how this might be done but parties should bear in mind that the courts increasingly take the view that litigation should be a last resort, and that claims should not be issued prematurely when a settlement is a reasonable prospect."

Code of Best Practice on Rehabilitation, Early Intervention and Medical Treatment in Personal Injury Claims

The Code is the product of the combined efforts of the Association of British Insurers, the International Underwriting Association and solicitors who act for the victims of accidents. Compliance is expected to become mandatory some time in 2000.

The Code, according to paragraph 1.5 of the Introduction, aims to:

". . . ensure that those acting for claimants and those responding to
claims against the insurance industry, in acting for such persons, act in
future to ensure possible improvements in the quality of life, and the
present and long term physical and mental well-being of the claimant,
are being addressed as issues equally important as the payment of just,
full and proper compensation."

It is designed to facilitate the availability of appropriate medical treatment, counselling, re-training or the provision of aid and equipment ("rehabilitation") at the "earliest practicable opportunity". Nothing in the code affects the obligations placed on a claimant's solicitors or the insurers under the pre-action protocols (2.4 and 3.4).

The code, in distilled form, provides for an 'independent assessment' of the need for and the extent of such "intervention, rehabilitation and treatment" (4.1). It is recognised that the assessment may well be precede the commission of medical evidence (4.2). The assessment must be carried out by "those who have an appropriate qualification" (4.4).

The code encourages the claimant's solicitors and the insurers to agree the agency to be instructed. Paragraph 5.2 provides that the report should consider the following:

"1. The injuries sustained by the claimant.
2. His/her present medical condition.
3. The claimant's domestic circumstances, where relevant.
4. The injuries/disabilities in respect of which early intervention or early rehabilitation is suggested.
5. The type of intervention or treatment envisaged.
6. The likely cost.
7. The likely short/medium term benefits to the claimant."

It should not deal with diagnostic criteria, causation issues or long-term care requirements (5.3).

The report, on completion, should be sent to the claimant's solicitors and insurers simultaneously. Both parties can raise questions on the report (6.1). Neither side can rely on the contents of the report in any subsequent litigation (6.2). Payment should be made by the insurers within 28 days of receipt.

On disclosure of the report the insurer is:

". . . under a duty to consider the recommendations made and the extent to which funds which will be made available to bring about implementation of all, or some of, the recommendations. The insurer will not be required to pay for such intervention or treatment as shall be unreasonable in nature, or content or cost."

The claimant, meanwhile, is under no obligation to undergo unreasonable intervention or medical investigation (7.1). Funds made available are treated as an interim payment on account of damages.

The full text of the code appears at Appendix 7.

Evidence

Proof of Evidence

It is necessary, as a first step, to obtain a detailed proof of evidence from the client and any other witnesses to the accident. The reasons for this are, perhaps, three-fold. First, it will facilitate a realistic assessment of merits – whether, in the words of CPR 44.3(5)(b), it is "reasonable for a party to raise, pursue or contest a particular allegation or issue" – before too much time and money is spent on the litigation. Secondly, as everyone's memory fades with time, it will capture and preserve the recollections upon which the action may ultimately turn. Finally, it will provide a contemporaneous record from which the witness may subsequently refresh his memory. Consistency of expression may also, in due course, add weight to the evidence given in court, particularly if it is shown that the witness said the same thing, possibly over a number of years, to the police, the insurers, an enquiry agent or the party's legal representative.

Many solicitors ask their clients to complete a pro-forma questionnaire and this practice is to be encouraged. Aside from relieving the solicitor of the burden (and expense) of taking a dictated proof, it ensures that each matter of potential relevance is methodically covered. It will also oblige the client to sit down and crystallise his thoughts at an early stage, a process that can provide invaluable support when, in the event that proceedings are necessary, he is asked to sign a statement of truth. (Counsel of caution will also note that a completed questionnaire can serve to protect the practitioner should the passage of time ultimately bring a solicitor/client dispute as to 'who said what to whom and when'.)

Road traffic accident claims invariably require the acquisition of the following information:

- The identity of the parties.
- The make, type and registration number of every vehicle involved in the accident.
- The date and time of the accident.
- The location of the accident and a description of the directions in which the parties were travelling.
- Reference to the weather, road and traffic conditions.
- Reference to any other 'environmental factors', such as the effect of low lying/dazzling sunlight, ice or snow, overgrown trees or hedges.
- A description of how the accident happened, possibly accompanied by a sketch or plan of the incident.
- Details of any post-accident conversation(s) with either the other motorist(s), his passenger(s) or any other witnesses.
- Whether the police attended and, if so, the name/number/station of the officer involved, plus the criminal reference number, if any. In turn, whether a prosecution followed, the details and result.
- The claimant's date of birth, national insurance number, hospital reference number (if any), Inland Revenue and, if applicable, DSS reference.
- Details of any injuries, involving the name of any hospital attended and the litigant's GP.
- A preliminary description and calculation of any special damages, exhibiting any supporting documentation.

Cases involve highway disrepair or animals on the carriageway obviously demand a detailed description of the material obstruction. Fatal accident claims require confirmation of the letters of administration or grant of probate, and reference to the bereavement, funeral expenses and loss of dependency, if any.

A precedent for a questionnaire to be sent to other witnesses appears at Appendix 5.

Police report

Where the police attend the scene of an accident their involvement will be recorded in a formal report. Such reports commonly contain the Accident Report Book compiled by the attending officer, statements or witness questionnaires subsequently obtained, proof that the parties produced their driving licence, insurance certificate and MOT test certificate (which, if not presented at the roadside, will be recorded on Form HO/RT 2) and, in the more serious or fatal accidents, a report from a police accident investigator. A copy of the full report will be disclosed on payment of the appropriate fee (usually £50) and requests for disclosure should always be made where liability is in dispute. Enquiries should usually be addressed to the Chief Constable, although some constabularies permit an approach to the individual police station. Disclosure will normally be withheld where a prosecution is contemplated or pending. Reports are normally destroyed after three years unless otherwise requested. Where, for example, the accident involved injury to a child or person under a disability, efforts should always be made to ensure that the original report is preserved.

Should it be necessary or desirable to call a police officer as a witness, consideration should always be given to a preliminary interview, as this will allow an assessment of the tone, strength and weight of his evidence. Payment of a fee will again be required. But be warned: many constabularies will only allow an officer to be interviewed once, so there may be an advantage in getting in first. Where attendance at court is required, it will always be necessary to obtain and serve a subpoena or witness summons.

Coroner's documents

A coroner's inquest will be held in every case where a road traffic accident leads to a "violent or unnatural death". The coroner must, on application by a "properly interested person", supply a copy of any report of a post-mortem examination, any notes of evidence (even, it is submitted, those recorded on tape) or any documents put in evidence at an inquest: Coroners Rules 1984, rule 57(1). ("Properly interested person" is not defined in the rules but probably means a person who is entitled to be represented at the inquest. Such persons are listed at rule 20(2)(a) to (h) of the CR 1984). Disclosure is dependent on payment of "the prescribed fee": Coroners Records (Fees for Copies) Rules 1982, amended in 1990. (The fee tends to vary from court to court. Where, as is often the case, proceedings are recorded on tape, transcripts are charged at a rate of approximately £12 per one thousand words.) Requests for disclosure made prior to the inquest normally prompt a polite refusal. It is not at all clear that this represents correct practice – *Jervis on Coroners* (11th ed, Sweet & Maxwell) expresses (at

18–32) the clear view that the rules "do not restrict the time at which the copy is to be made available". By common consent, however, the obligation to disclose does not extend to documents evidencing preliminary enquiries or reports prepared by a police officer which are not put in evidence at the inquest: see *R v Hammersmith Coroner, ex p. Peach* [1980] 2 WLR 496.

Insurance

It will be necessary to determine if the other party is insured or whether recompense will be sought via the Motor Insurers Bureau. A policy holder must, on demand by the victim of a road traffic accident, provide details of his insurance: section 154 of the Road Traffic Act 1988 (see Chapter 14, page 185). Where the information has been supplied to the police, it will usually be provided to other interested parties, whether or not a formal request is made for disclosure of the police accident report.

Vehicle and driver records

There are a number of contemporaneous documentary sources that may yield valuable evidence as to the performance of both vehicle and driver.

Tachographs

A tachograph must be fitted on most goods vehicles (and some public service vehicles) whose combined weight exceeds 3.5 tonnes. The provisions relating to the installation and use of tachographs are contained in sections 97, 97A and 97B of the Transport Act 1986, as amended, which incorporates and/or makes directly applicable EC Regulation 2821/85 of December 20, 1985, as amended. The tachograph comprises an automatic record (which is reproduced on a wax coated chart) for each 'day's driving'. The chart records the start and finish of every period of 'driving', 'working' and 'resting'. Within each mode of operation the chart will record the vehicle's speed (although the graph may not record speeds below 6.6 mph) and distance travelled. It should be possible to see whether the driver worked long hours (so that his performance may have been tainted by fatigue) or drove at an excessive speed. Charts need only be preserved for 12 months and any request for disclosure should be made before the first anniversary of the accident.

Manual records

Drivers of goods vehicles exempt from the requirement of fitting a tachograph must still compile a manual record book detailing each 'working day'. The provisions relating to manual records are contained in the Drivers Hours (Goods Vehicles) (Keeping of Records) Regulations 1987 (S.I. 1987 No. 1421). A separate entry (or 'log') is required for each day worked. The log records, in fairly brief form, the time of going on and off duty as well as an estimate of the time spent driving: reg. 5 and the schedule. A driver must complete the log within seven days and the operator must ensure that the record is retained for 12 months: reg. 11.

MOT tests

Every vehicle must be tested in accordance with regulations made under sections 45 to 48 of the Road Traffic Act 1988. (See also Chapter 10, pages 134 to 135). The regulations require an examination of a vehicle's structure, lights, steering, suspension, braking, tyres and wheels, as well as a number of general matters. Nonetheless a Test Certificate will only be regarded as evidence of the condition of the vehicle (or, more specifically, the testable items) at or about the date of the test. Sometimes the MOT Inspection Report (Form VT30) will also advise of any matters that may, in the opinion of the examiner, require attention within a specific mileage or period. Disclosure of this record may, in certain cases, be of some value, although the keeper of the vehicle is under no obligation to retain or preserve the same.

Goods vehicles: testing and maintenance

Goods vehicles are generally subject to a more stringent regulatory regime. Thus, the examination must be performed at a recognised 'HGV Testing Station', more items must be tested and the requirement of an annual test begins with the date of the original registration. (See sections 49 to 53 of the RTA 1988 and the Goods Vehicles (Plating and Testing) Regulations 1988 (S.I. 1988/No. 1478, as amended)). Once again, however, the Test Certificate only evidences compliance at the time of the test.

Maps, plans, photographs and videos

Hand drawn sketches of the scene of an accident (and even the mechanics of the collision itself) often appear in the police officer's Accident Report Book, the questionnaire completed by any other witness and the insurance claim forms submitted by the parties. But these are of very limited evidential or probative value. Modern practice now admits and relies on a variety of other illustrative aids.

Maps and plans

Large scale maps can be obtained from Ordnance Survey. OS maps are, perhaps, of more value where the accident occurs in an urban area, where the largest scale is 1: 1250, rather than more remote rural regions, where the maximum scale is often 1: 10000. OS maps are widely available. Enquiries can be directed to: Information and Enquiries, Ordnance Survey, Romsey Road, Maybush, Southampton SO16 4GV, tel: 01703 792 5584, fax: 01703 792 922

Otherwise a firm of expert accident surveyors or reconstruction-alists can be instructed to produce a detailed scale plan of the accident locus. This often confers certain advantages, not least flexi-bility (features such as skid marks, the position of debris and vege-tation can be easily incorporated) and the fact that the draftsman can be simultaneously instructed to provide a set of complementary colour photographs.

Photographs

A set of colour photographs can provide an invaluable aid to the understanding of an accident. Every effort should be made to:

- capture and portray the scene visible to both (or all) the drivers involved in the accident. The camera, in other words, should often be lowered to the eye level of the seated motorist.
- record all relevant distances and mark the position of the photographer on a separate plan.
- reproduce, as far as is possible, the atmospheric, seasonal and traffic conditions that prevailed at the time of the collision. This may require more than one visit to the scene, particularly if it is said that factors such as darkness, snow, low autumnal sunlight or summer vegetation were of relevance to the occur-rence of the accident.
- acknowledge and describe any subsequent changes in road 'furniture' (signs, lights, bollards etc.) and layout.

Practitioners must always, in this regard, endeavour to balance the expedition demanded by changing conditions and, indeed, the CPR with the fact that plans and photographs will only be required in the minority of cases.

Video

Video evidence is generally restricted to claims allocated to the multi-track and, in particular, those involving fatal or catastrophic injuries. Nonetheless the medium is of use to both claimants and defendants:

- claimants adduce 'A Day in the Life' videos to demonstrate the nature and profundity of the loss of amenity experienced by the victim.
- defendants rely on clandestine surveillance videos compiled by enquiry agents to provide a realistic context to the claimant's condition and, perhaps, demonstrate that he is exaggerating or malingering.
- both parties rely on a formal reconstruction of the preamble to the accident – video re-enactment is particularly useful in cases involving extreme speed, restricted look-out or collisions on a narrow carriageway.

Disclosure

Disclosure is governed by CPR 33.6. Unless the court orders otherwise, no plan, photographs or models (or, by implication, video) are receivable at trial unless the party intending to use such material has given appropriate notice to the other parties. Where the evidence forms part of an expert's evidence, the notice should accord to the rules applicable to witness statements and expert reports. Otherwise the party adducing the evidence should give notice "at least 21 days before the hearing".

Highway Records

Highway authorities are obliged to maintain voluminous records pertaining to the classification, condition, inspection and maintenance of highways within their area. These include records of inspection, maintenance logs, records of complaints or other accidents, and the minutes of highway authority meetings where maintenance or repair policy was discussed or decided. Disclosure should be sought in all cases where it is alleged that a defect in the highway caused or contributed to the accident. Section C of Annex B to the Pre-Action Protocol for Personal Injury Claims requires disclosure of this documentation "for a period of 12 months prior to the accident".

Expert evidence

Expert evidence is governed by CPR Part 35. This provision, along with the protocols, encourages the joint selection of, and access to experts. Care should always be taken to ensure that the chosen expert has the relevant expertise and speciality. Road traffic claims often require the assistance of medical and non medical experts.

Medical experts

Most medico-legal specialists will have experience in advising in road traffic accident claims. No part of a person's physical or psychological health is completely immune from the effects of a motor collision and, in any event, RTA claims make up the vast majority of personal injury actions issued in England and Wales. Medical reports are usually directed at issues of quantum, particularly injury, treatment, causation and prognosis. However, the medical evidence occasionally assists in the determination of liability. Thus, where a pedestrian is knocked down by a car, the expert may be able to relate the injury to the vehicular damage. If the precise point of impact can be determined it may be possible to establish how far the pedestrian had crossed before being struck by the vehicle. In other cases, such as those involving an involuntary act occasioned by medical incapacity (see chapter 11 pages 145 to 146), the medical evidence will obviously be of pivotal importance to the question of liability.

Non-medical experts

Non-medical experts might include an Accident Reconstructionalist, a Consulting Engineer or a Highway Consultant. Expert reconstruction is particularly useful where one of the parties is killed (or subsequently dies), or where either or both of the protagonists have no recollection of the collision. Technical assistance will often be required in highway maintenance claims and is almost invariably necessary where it is alleged that the accident was caused or contributed to by a defect in one of the vehicles.

Topics for the non-medical expert commonly include the following:

- *Speed*
  Precise calculation of vehicle's speed will often determine (or at least assist in the attribution of) fault. Reference can be made to a basic formula: speed = distance covered ÷ time travelled. Of course, witnesses, particularly the drivers themselves, can be notoriously imprecise (or even deliberately

disingenuous) when it comes to an estimation of distance, time and, indeed, speed. The expert will accordingly place more reliance on exact measurement of distance, a consideration of the vehicle(s) type, size, power ratio and braking efficiency, and the coefficient of friction between the wheels of the vehicle and the surface of the road. Skid marks can often be interpreted in a way that calculates the minimum speed of the vehicle at the time that braking caused the wheel(s) to lock. Examination of the damage suffered by the vehicle and, occasionally, the nature or extent of the injuries sustained by its occupants, can also assist in the calculation of speed.

- *Collision at the junction of a 'major' and 'minor' road*
  Assessment of liability will often turn on the view afforded to the driver of the emerging vehicle (and the distance represented by this 'sight line') and the speed of the motorist proceeding along the major road. A motorist involved in a collision after emerging from a side road will often state that the other vehicle was not in view at the time he began his manoeuvre. This can often be either confirmed or refuted by a consideration of the views available to both drivers, with particular regard to road side walls, signs, trees, hedges (and, in this regard, the volume of foliage at different times of the year), the width of the road, an exact calculation of the speed of both vehicles and the point of impact.

- *Pedestrian struck whilst crossing the road*
  The expert will consider:
  - the distance between the kerb and the point of impact;
  - the speed of the pedestrian. This can be estimated by reference to his age, health, mobility and the accounts of any eye-witnesses. Other factors, such as intoxication, the fact that he was carrying heavy shopping or accompanied by children, are also of potential relevance;
  - the speed of the vehicle.

  From these components it should be possible to calculate the time the pedestrian spent on the road. This, in turn, will allow the court to gauge the opportunity afforded to either party to see the other and thus determine whether the conduct of either or both fell below the required standard of care.

- *Defective vehicles*

  Technical investigation may well be warranted where the accident was caused or contributed to by a defect in a vehicle. Attention will frequently focus on the tyres, wheels (should one have become detached), braking system and suspension.

Chapter 19

Pleadings

The implementation of the CPR in April 1999 heralded important changes in culture, practice and nomenclature. Proceedings are started when the court issues a Claim Form which, in most cases, must be supported by a Particulars of Claim. The defendant responds, as before, with a Defence, although the nature and requirements of this pleading are much altered. Where the defence raises a new issue the claimant will wish to file and serve a Reply. Collectively these pleadings are known as Statements of Case. Part 16 of the CPR (along with the accompanying Practice Direction) deals with pleadings. It contains extensive guidance in relation to the mandatory and discretionary content of statements of case. CPR Part 16 is, on its face, a relatively clear exposition of the formal requirements. But neither the Part nor the Practice Direction give clear guidance as to how, in practice, a litigant is to plead his case in an action arising out of a road traffic accident.

Particulars of Claim

CPR/PD

The particulars of claim should identify the matters in issue by "a concise statement of the facts on which the claimant relies": CPR 16.4(1)(a). Paragraphs 4 and 5 of the Practice Direction lay down further requirements for personal injury and fatal accident claims respectively. Certain mandatory requirements are additionally outlined at 16 PD10. Of particular relevance to motor claims is the necessity of setting out details of any criminal conviction relied on: 10.1(1). Various 'optional' provisions appear at 16 PD 16.3. A claimant may:

(1) refer in his particulars of claim to any point of law on which the claim is based,
(2) give in his particulars of claim the name of any witness whom he proposes to call, and
(3) attach to or serve with the particulars of claim a copy of any document which he considers is necessary to his claim (including any expert's report to be filed in accordance with Part 35)"

The particulars of claim must be verified by a Statement of Truth in the manner and form outlined at CPR 22.1 and 22 PD 2-1.

Discussion

The CPR rules on pleadings are accompanied by some confusion of interpretation and application. Different courts (sometimes separate judges in the same court) alternate between an exclusive or inclusive interpretation of the mandatory and discretionary requirements. Clearly the rules favour a more straightforward, narrative style that is accessible to the lay client. But does this mean that it is unnecessary (or even incorrect) to plead precise particulars of negligence or breach of statutory duty? How can a claimant, for that matter, sign a statement of truth attesting to issues (factual or legal) about which he has no direct knowledge or understanding?

Application of a restrictive interpretation would have a considerable effect on particulars of claim in road traffic accident claims. Thus, in a straightforward rear end shunt, the central body of the allegation could be expressed as follows:

> "The accident was caused by the defendant who negligently drove into a collision with the rear of the claimant's stationary car."

Reference to excessive speed, not keeping an adequate look out or a failure to brake/stop would be entirely superfluous. Instead the pleading would provide nothing more than a 'concise statement' of facts with the balance of the information required by the court being gleaned from the witness statements.

This approach undoubtably holds some attraction, with convenience, expense and administrative clarity listed amongst the perceived advantages. The case for reducing pleadings also received support from the Court of Appeal in *McPhilemy* v *Times Newspapers Ltd* [1999] Times, May 26 where Lord Woolf MR stated:

> "The need for extensive pleadings including particulars should be reduced by the requirement that witness statements were now exchanged.
>
> In the majority of proceedings identification of the documents upon which a party relies, together with copies of the parties' witness statements, would make the detail of the nature of the case the other side had to meet obvious. That would reduce the need for particulars in order to avoid being taken by surprise.
>
> That did not mean that the pleadings were now superfluous. Pleadings were still required to mark out the parameters of the case that was being advanced by each party.

In particular they were still critical to identify the issues and the extent of the dispute between the parties. What was important was that the pleadings should make clear the general nature of the case of the pleader. That was true both under the old rules and the new rules."

But all this is, perhaps, to under-estimate the value of an inclusive particulars of claim. First, a detailed pleading entirely conforms with the stated desire (expressed by Lord Woolf in his final Access to Justice Report of July 1996) to encourage "better and earlier exchange of information". This objective, otherwise described as a "cards on the table" approach, is hardly complemented by a skeletal statement of case. Second, the particulars of claim provide the claimant with an opportunity to extract a fully particularised defence. Particularity, in other words, demands a similar response. Given that the standard directions in a fast track case allow for exchange of witness statements up to 10 weeks after allocation (28 PD 3.12), the advantage of an inclusive pleading should be obvious. Third, the suggestion that nothing more than a concise statement of facts is required hardly squares with the claimant's discretionary entitlement to plead any point of law and, more particularly, the names of witnesses whom he wishes to call: 16 PD 11.3. Nor will specific breaches of statutory duty be necessarily obvious from the witness statements. It would seem to be incongruous for a pleading to refer to the regulation/statute relied on (and also the details of any probative criminal conviction) but not, say, particularised allegations of negligence. Fourth, the particulars of claim now fulfils a number of additional procedural functions. As Master Leslie has noted, in an article in *Civil Court News*, Volume 1, No.3, November 1999 (Butterworths):

> "Statements of case fulfil all of the functions previously performed by pleadings but, in addition, are also the most important aid to the procedural judge when dealing with allocation and initial case management. . . .
> Carefully considered and drafted statements of case greatly help him to discharge this function. In a borderline case, the party whose case is pleaded fully and with clarity is more likely to achieve the case allocation it seeks."

Finally, it is observed that a busy judge's pre-trial preparation (and, indeed, the opening of the case itself) can be greatly assisted by a fully particularised pleading. Convoluted explanation of the road layout, vehicles and the passage to collision can be largely avoided by a well directed statement of case. Howsoever detailed the pleading is it will almost always provide a more succinct articulation of the relevant issues than that to be gleaned from the parties' witness statements.

It is submitted, in conclusion, that the nature of the particulars of claim should be pragmatically determined by the defendant's reply to the claimant's letter of claim (or solicitor's 'final letter'). If liability is conceded, there is little point in pleading anything more than a bare allegation of negligence and/or breach. Conversely, if liability remains an issue (or the defendant attempts to obfuscate or equivocate), both the court and the cause of expeditious settlement will be best served by an inclusive particulars of claim.

Appendix contains numerous examples of both types of particulars of claim.

Defence

CPR/PD

Part 16.5(1) and (2) provides that a defendant must say:

- which allegations in a particulars of claim the defendant denies – stating his reasons for doing so and giving any different version of events from the claimant's
- which he admits; and
- which he is unable to admit or deny, but which he requires the claimant to prove.

Essentially the defence should deal specifically with each and every allegation in the particulars of claim. Where the defendant denies an allegation he must state his reasons for doing so. Should he wish to challenge the claimant's version of events he must state his own version. Nonetheless a failure to deal with an allegation will no longer be taken as an implied admission:

A defendant who -
a   fails to deal with an allegation; but
b   has set out in his defence the nature of his case in relation to the issue on which the allegation is relevant;
shall be taken to require that allegation to be proved (16 PD 5.3)

The defence must be verified by a statement of truth: 16 PD 13.1

Discussion

Such particularity, to be fair, was always a characteristic of defences filed in road traffic accident claims. Motor collisions rarely occur without negligence on the part of at least one of the drivers, so that a bare denial of a claimant's allegations would rarely suffice, with the defendant usually being compelled to particularise his allegations against either the claimant or whichever driver he blamed for the accident. The CPR merely preserves this imperative. Counter-allegations of negligence against a claimant motorist will, in most cases, deny the particularity of the claim against the defendant. However, in some cases it may also be necessary to articulate additional matters of refutation. Thus, whilst a defendant who emerged from a 'minor road' may wish to challenge the speed and look out of a claimant approaching on the 'major road', it might also behove him to plead, for example, the paucity of view afforded by the layout of the junction as context for his own denial of negligence.

Chapter 20

Trial

There is very little difference between the conduct of a road traffic accident claim and any other civil action for damages. Whilst the pre-action protocols confer the gloss of a specialist jurisdiction, and although much of the evidence is necessarily distinctive, the pre-hearing preparation and, in particular, the conduct of the trial itself reflects a common practice. This chapter is designed to give an overview of the conduct of the trial. The Civil Procedure Rules are, in this regard, largely self-explanatory and what follows is no substitute for a thorough familiarity with the relevant Parts and Practice Directions.

Witness statements

General
Witness statements are governed by CPR Part 32 and the relevant Practice Direction. A witness statement is defined as a "written statement signed by person which contains the evidence, and only that evidence, which that person would be allowed to give orally": Part 32.4(1). It is, in effect, a full proof of evidence and should, so far as possible, be expressed in the witness's own words. The witness statement will stand as the witness's evidence in chief, unless the court orders otherwise, and great care should be taken to produce a comprehensive testimony: Part 32.5(2). In RTA claims where liability is not in dispute, it is not necessary to include a detailed description of the accident, although brief allusion to the nature and severity of the collision can sometimes provide useful corroborative background to the damages claimed.

Service
The court "will order" each party to serve on the other parties the witness statements on which he intends to rely: Part 32.4(2). Fast track directions are made under Part 28.3(1)(b) and in the multi-track under Part 29.2(1). Provision can now be made for sequential (as opposed to mutual) exchange: Part 32.4(3)(a).

Form

Part 32PD 17 to 23 outlines detailed provisions concerning the heading, body, format and filing of witness statements. Particular reference should be made to 32PD17.2, which states that at the top right hand corner of the first page there should be clearly written:

(1) the party on whose behalf it is made,
(2) the initials and surname of the witness,
(3) the number of the statement in relation to that witness,
(4) the identifying initials and number of each exhibit being referred to, and
(5) the date the statement was made.

Exhibits should be produced and identified in the manner applicable to affidavits: Part 18.4/5. Every statement must specify the nature and source of the witness's information or belief (Part 18.2) and contain a statement of truth (Part 20.1). 32PD19, in addition to detailed provisions regarding "format" (meaning the numbering, pagination, binding and legibility of statements), states that it "is usually more convenient for a witness statement to follow the chronological sequence of the events or matters dealt with".

Consequence of failure to serve witness statement

If a witness statement is not served in respect of an intended witness within the time specified by the court, then the witness may not be called to give oral evidence unless the court gives permission: CPR Part 32.10.

Bundles

Trial bundles are regulated by CPR Parts 39.5 and 39PD3.1 to 3.10. Bundles must be filed "not more than seven days and not less than three days before the start of the trial": Part 39.5(2). Bundles should be indexed, paginated, separated by numbered dividers (where the total number of pages is more than 100) and should normally be contained in a ring binder or lever arch file: 39PD3.5/6. 39PD3.2 sets out in detail the copy documents to be included unless the court orders otherwise:

(1) the claim form and all statements of case,
(2) a case summary and/or chronology where appropriate,
(3) requests for further information and responses to the requests,
(4) all witness statements to be relied on as evidence,
(5) any witness summaries,

(6) any notices of intention to rely on hearsay evidence under rule 32.2

(7) any notices of intention to rely on evidence (such as a plan, photographs etc) under rule 33.6 which is not –

   (a) contained any witness statement, affidavit or expert report,

   (b) being given orally at trial,

   (c) hearsay evidence under rule 33.2,

(8) any medical reports and responses to them,

(9) any experts reports and responses to them,

(10) any order giving directions as to the conduct of the trial, and

(11) any other necessary documents.

Attendance at trial and hearsay evidence

Witnesses, as a general rule, must attend court and give oral evidence: CPR Part 32.2 The generality of this provision is subject to the court's general power to "control the evidence by giving directions": Part 32.1(1). Agreed evidence can, of course, be proffered in writing and the attendance of experts will often be excused, particularly in fast track cases. Witness attendance can be enforced by the issue of a witness summons under the provisions outlined at Part 34.2 to 6. Attendance by police officers will always require a summons. Other witnesses -often lay witnesses whose employer may be reluctant to sanction the necessary absence – may require the same facility.

Hearsay evidence is governed by CPR Part 33 (along with the relevant Practice Direction) and the Civil Evidence Act 1995. The Act, which came into force on 31 January 1997, supercedes and simplifies the hearsay provisions contained in the Civil Evidence Act 1968. Section 2(1) provides that a party proposing to adduce hearsay evidence must notify the other part of that fact. The Act makes provision (at section 2(2) (a)) for the giving of notice to be regulated by rules of court and these now appear at CPR Part 33.2. A failure to comply with the notice provisions does not affect the admissibility of the evidence but (a) may affect the weight to be attached to it (section 2) (4)), and (b) will be a fact to consider with respect to costs.

Trial

Generally

CPR Part 32.1 confers a general power on the court to control the evidence. Of particular interest is the power to "exclude evidence that would otherwise be admissible" (Part 32.1(2)) and "limit cross-exami-nation" (Part 32.1(3)). Sometimes the trial timetable (see below) will limit the time available to each party. Alternatively the court may order that the witness evidence be limited to certain issues. Either way, the rule complements various other provisions, such as those relating to the fast track (Part 28) or those applicable to experts (Part 35).

Fast track

The court will give directions for the conduct of the trial, either at the allocation stage (Part 26.5) or the listing stage (Part 28.6) and, unless the trial judge otherwise directs, the trial will be conducted in accordance with the order made: Part 28.7. Central to the conduct of a fast track trial is the principle of a 'trial timetable'. Given that each case should last a maximum of one day, or five working hours, a typical timetable is as follows:

Claimant's opening	10 min
Defendant's opening	10 min
Cross-examination of Claimant's witnesses	1 hr 10 min
Re-examination	15 min
Cross examination of Defendant's witnesses	1 hr 10 min
Re-examination	15 min
Defendant's submissions	20 min
Claimant's submissions	20 min
Judge's "thinking time" and judgment	30 min
Costs and consequential orders	20 min

28PD additionally provides that the judge may confirm or vary any timetable given previously or, where none has been given, set his own: 8.3. The trial will normally conclude with a summary assessment of costs in accordance with Part 46 8.5.

Multi-track

The 'trial timetable' – which may be fixed at either of the listing hearing (Part 29.6(3)) or pre-trial review (Part 29.7), or "as soon as practicable thereafter" (Part 29.8) – will break the action down into stages and set the time to be allocated at each stage to each party. Unless the trial judge otherwise directs, the trial will be conducted in accordance with the order made: Part 29.9. 29PD10.1.to 10.6 provides additional guidelines that essentially replicate the corresponding provisions relating to fast track trials (see 28PD, 8.1–8.6 above).

Chapter 21

RTA actions and the Small Claims Track

Every year tens of thousands of small road traffic accident claims are decided in the County Court. RTA 'arbitrations', to resurrect an outmoded term, are now allocated to the small claims track. This chapter, whilst not an exhaustive treatise on civil procedure, aims to provide a practical guide to small road traffic accident claims. It is aimed at junior solicitors, barristers and legal executives whose initial experience of practice may largely (or even exclusively) involve undertaking small 'running down' cases.

Scope of the small claims track

By CPR 26.6(1) (a) and (3) the small claims track is the normal track for:

- any claim for personal injuries where the financial value of the claim is not more than £5,000 and the financial value of any claim for damages for personal injury is not more than £1,000;
- any other claim where the financial value is not more than £5,000.

It is for the court to assess the financial value of the claim, and in doing so it will disregard any amount not in dispute, any claim for interest, costs and contributory negligence: CPR 26.8(2). When it has allocated a claim, the court will serve notice (see Form N154) on every party: CPR 26.9.

Pre-hearing preparation

After allocation the court will give the parties "at least 21 days notice" of the date fixed for the final hearing "unless the parties agree to accept less notice": CPR 27.4(2). It will also give 'standard' and any 'special' directions. In road traffic accident claims claims the court will usually give the standard directions outlined at Form B, Appendix A, PD 27 (see over).

FORM B – STANDARD DIRECTIONS FOR USE IN CLAIMS ARISING OUT OF ROAD ACCIDENTS.

THE COURT DIRECTS

1. Each party shall deliver to every other party and the court office copies of all documents on which he intends to rely at the hearing. These may include:
    *   experts reports (including medical reports where damages for personal injury are claimed),
    *   witness statements,
    *   invoices and estimates for repairs,
    *   documents which relate to other losses such as loss of earnings,
    *   sketch plans and photographs.

2. The copies shall be delivered no later than 19/20 [14 days before the hearing].

3. The original documents shall be brought to the hearing.

4. Before the date of the hearing the parties shall try to agree the cost of the repairs and any other losses claimed subject to the court's decision about whose fault the accident was.

5. Signed statements setting out the evidence of all witnesses on whom each party intends to rely shall be prepared and copies included in the documents mentioned in paragraph 1. This includes the evidence of the parties themselves and of any other witness, whether or not he is going to come to court to give evidence.

6. The parties should note that:
    (a) In deciding the case the court will find it very helpful to have a sketch plan and photographs of the place where the accident happened.
    (b) The court may decide not to take into account a document or the evidence of a witness if no copy of that document or no copy of a statement or report by that witness has been supplied to the other parties.

7. [Notice of hearing date and time and hour].

8. The court must be informed immediately if the case is settled by agreement before the hearing date.

    Judges regularly complain that these directions are not adhered to. Court offices habitually 'over list' (it is common practice in many County Courts in London to list up to 15 hours work per judge per day) and judicial preparation time is necessarily short. This means, in turn, that non-compliance can often lead to a summary resolution of either the issue in question or the action itself. In particular, paragraph 6(a) and (b), relating to sketch plans, photographs and exchange of statements/documents should be regarded as, in practice, mandatory requirements.

The Hearing

Preliminary hearing

The court may, on giving 14 days' notice to the parties, hold a preliminary hearing. This may be appropriate when it considers that special directions are necessary or where it is minded to strike out a statement of case or part of a statement on the basis that it discloses no reasonable grounds for bringing or defending the claim: see CPR 27.6. It is in the nature of road traffic accidents that, in practice, such hearings are comparatively rare and most actions proceed to a substantive hearing.

Substantive hearing

Representation

A party may present his own case or be represented by a barrister, solicitor, legal executive or lay representative. The Lay Representatives (Rights of Audience) Order 1999 (S.I. 1999 1225) allows for lay representatives to exercise rights of audience in small claims, although this does not apply where the party does not attend the hearing, at any stage after judgment or on appeal: PD 27.3.2(2). Nonetheless the court, in "exercising its general discretion to hear anybody", may still here a lay representative in circumstances excluded by the order: PD 27.3.2(3).

Venue

PD 27.4(1) states that the "general rule is that a small claim hearing will be in public". Nonetheless the hearing will normally take place in the judge's room, so that all parties will usually find themselves informally sat around a large central table. Advocates are not robed and usually remain seated when addressing the court.

What if a party fails to attend

CPR 27.9 anticipates a number of different situations:

- If a party gives the court at least seven days' written notice that he will not attend and asks the court to decide the claim in his absence, the judge will decide the case on the pleadings and documents filed with the court;
- If a claimant, without notice, does not attend the hearing the court may strike out the claim;

- If a defendant, without notice, fails to attend the hearing the court may decide the claim on the basis of the evidence of the claimant alone, even if the claimant has given notice of an intention not to attend;
- If neither party, without notice, attends the court may strike out the claim and any defence and counterclaim.

None of these provisions affect the general power of the court to adjourn a hearing where, for example, a party has "a good reason" for his non-attendance: PD 27.6.2.

Conduct of the hearing

The court is empowered to "adopt any method of proceeding at a hearing that it considers to be fair": CPR 27.8(1). Specifically:

(1) Hearings will be informal.
(2) The strict rules of evidence do not apply.
(3) The court need not take evidence on oath.
(4) The court may limit cross-examination.
(5) The court must give reasons for its decision.

The standing instructions issued to District Judges state that they should take the opportunity to read the papers before beginning a case, even if this means a short delay in the start of proceedings. Often, however, this represents a counsel of perfection and advocates should be prepared to give a short opening. Most judges will value a succinct recitation of those matters which have been agreed and those which remain in dispute. A brief description of the accident locus, with reference to the plan and/or photographs, is often appreciated. No judge will object if, at the outset, an advocate enquires whether any or all of this assistance is required.

Evidence

PD 27.4.3, with regard to witnesses of fact, provides that the judge may:

(1) ask questions of any witnesses himself before allowing any other person to do so,
(2) ask questions of all or any of the witnesses himself before allowing any person to ask questions of any witnesses,
(3) refuse to allow cross-examination of any witness until all the witnesses have given evidence in chief,

(4) limit cross-examination of a witness to a fixed time or to a particular subject or issue, or both.

Judges will often hear all the witnesses before allowing any cross-examination. Many prefer impartial inquisition to the adversarial 'cut and thrust' of an ordinary trial. Do not be surprised, therefore, if the judge takes the lead in cross-examination. Sometimes a judge will also alter or invert the usual witness running order. He may, for example, wish to hear from the defendant first, particularly if his pre-hearing reading has suggested that the claimant has an overwhelmingly strong case. (One District Judge recently commented to the author that the small claims court is "often used by insurance companies as a comparatively cheap and easy alternative to not having to tell their client that the accident was his fault", so that in a surprisingly high proportion of cases liability is almost immediately apparent.) Experience also suggests that judges, advocates and witnesses can all benefit from an impromptu 'accident reconstruction' using model cars supplied (often by the advocates) for this purpose.

No expert evidence, whether written or oral, can be given at the hearing without the permission of the court: CPR 27.5. Permission can be requested in the allocation questionnaire (N150, box F) and/or at a preliminary hearing held for the purpose of 'special' directions.

Judgment
The judge must give reasons for his decision and these should be carefully noted. Otherwise the judge is obliged to "make a note of the central reasons for his judgment" and a party is entitled to a copy of the same: PD 27.5.5(1) and 5.7. Alternatively proceedings can be tape recorded by the court and a party can obtain a transcript of such a recording on payment of the appropriate fee: PD 27.5.1.

Setting judgment aside and appeals

A party who was neither present nor represented at the hearing may, within 14 days of the date the notice of judgment was served on him, apply for the judgment to be set aside: CPR 27.11(1) and (2). The court may only grant such an application if the applicant:

- had a good reason for not attending or being represented at the hearing or giving written notice to the court; and
- has a reasonable prospect of success at the hearing.

Appeals to the circuit judge are governed by CPR 27.12 and 13, and PD 27.8. An appeal, which must be made within 14 days of service of the notice of order, can only be brought on the grounds that

(a) there was a serious irregularity affecting the proceedings; or
(b) the court made a mistake of law.

Road traffic accident claims are, of course, essentially creatures of fact and this, together with the inherent flexibility of the small claims track and the equally entrenched reluctance of insurance companies to commit additional funds to cases where costs are unlikely to be recovered, ensures that appeals are rarely made in RTA actions.

Costs

CPR 27.14 essentially provides that no costs are recoverable from an unsuccessful party except:

- the fixed costs attributable to issuing the claim;
- expenses which a party or witness has reasonably incurred in travelling to and from a hearing or in staying away from home for the purposes of attending a hearing;
- a sum "not exceeding the amount specified in the relevant practice direction" for any loss of earnings incurred by a party or witness in attending/staying away from home for the purposes of attending a hearing PD 27.7.3(1) prescribes a sum "not exceeding" £50 per day for each person;
- a sum "not exceeding the amount specified in the relevant practice direction" for an expert's fees;
- such further costs as the court may assess by the summary procedure and order to be paid by a party who has "behaved unreasonably".

Expert's fees

PD27.7.3(2) specifies "a sum not exceeding" £200 for each expert, which includes both the preparation of a report and attendance at any hearing. Significantly, in motor claims, the cost of a report dealing with the extent of the damage and/or repair to a vehicle can be recovered, but only if these matters are in issue: *Smith* v *Bogan & Sons Limited* [1997] CLY 571. Where no objection was taken to a garage repair invoice an expert report stating that the repairs were necessary was redundant and, consequently, the cost of preparing the report could not be recovered: *Mistry* v *NE Computing* [1997] CLY 533. See also *Pennant* v *Sparks* [1999] CL. January, 44, a case founded on virtually identical facts, where the judge observed that the garage estimates could have been expanded or improved to verify the claim for repairs.

'Behaved unreasonably'

The rules make no attempt to define 'unreasonable behaviour' or provide any guidance as to what may amount to the same. CPR 27.14(2)(d) is couched in almost identical terms to the corresponding provision in the County Court Rules (Ord. 19, r4(2)(c)) and reference can be made to cases decided under the old enactment. If the plethora of recent cases provide any general guidance, it is simply that the definition allows extensive scope for productive argument. Virtually all the judgments cited in this section relate to road traffic accident claims. The following propositions emerge:

(i) Defence Filed After Settlement

Numerous cases confirm that a defendant will have acted unreasonably if, having agreed settlement, he files a defence purely to have the matter referred to the small claims track. Such a defence will, in other words, serve no purpose and be an abuse of process: *Lacey* v *Evans* [1997] CLY 526, *McGorian* v *Hughes* [1997] CLY 524 and *Clark* v *Brazier* [1997] CL September 84.

(ii) Claim Filed After Settlement

Similarly, where the defendant's insurers paid the claim arising out of a road traffic accident, there was no reason for the claimant to issue proceedings and recover assessed costs: *Whitfield* v *Faulkner* [1998] CLY 457.

(iii) Defence Filed After Claim Paid in Full

Where a defence was filed after the claim had been paid in full it was "meaningless and an abuse of process" and the defendant had acted unreasonably: *Necrews* v *A.R.C. Limited* [1997] CLY 522. Interestingly the judge in that case, H.H.J. Graham Jones (Cardiff County Court) observed that the defendants and their insurers "should pay up in full before the issue of proceedings if there was no defence to the claim either as to liability or quantum".

(iv) Defence Filed but Claim Paid Prior to Hearing

In *Walker v Midland Fox Limited* [1997] CLY 595 it was held that the defendant had acted unreasonably where, having filed a defence, he paid the claim five days before the hearing. In this case the defendant's insurers argued that their driver had no knowledge of the incident, but nonetheless filed a defence citing specific acts of negligence against the claimant, before capitulating at a late stage.

(v) Defence Filed, Settlement Offered at a Late Stage

An offer of settlement proffered eight days prior to the hearing was held to constitute unreasonable conduct in *Jancey v Higgins* [1997] CLY 589. See also *Whybrow v Kentish Bus & Coach Co. Ltd* [1999] CL, January 50.

(vi) Withdrawal of Defence

A finding of unreasonable behaviour was made after a defence was withdrawn seven days prior to the hearing: *Pathan v O'Connor* [1997] CLY 596. Here the reason was not so much the late withdrawal but rather the fact that the defendant, having disputed liability, was not prepared to follow this through by attending court.

(vii) Non-Attendance at Court

A finding of unreasonable behaviour will almost invariably be made where a party fails, without written notice, to enter an appearance. In *Pathan* (ibid) costs were awarded against the defendant whilst in *Travers v Stych* [1997] CLY 598 and *Dibor v Kentish Bus & Coach Co. Ltd* [1998] CLY 458, it was the claimant who was at fault.

(viii) "Drip-Feeding" Offers of Settlement, Followed by Payment of the Claim

"Drip-feeding" conveys the impression that a defendant is not genuinely desirous of defending a case and will often be held to constitute unreasonable conduct: *Kirksmith v Richardson* [1992] CLY 3434, followed in *Woodgate v Stafantos* [1997] CLY 591. A defendant's conduct prior to the issue of proceedings will be relevant: *Jones v Donker* [1997] CLY 590.

(ix) Delay in Paying Agreed Damages

In *Calderbank v Burton* [1997] CLY 594 the defendant, having agreed quantum, delayed payment by approximately two months. Accordingly the claimant issued proceedings and successfully argued that the defendant's delay amounted to unreasonable conduct. A similar decision was reached where the defendant's delay amounted to only 28 days: *Potter* v *Blamey* [1997] CL, September, 1992.

(x) Unsupportable Defence

In *Afzel* v *Ford Motor Co.Limited* [1994] 4 All ER 720, Beldam LJ suggested that the raising of an unsupportable defence might be regarded as unreasonable conduct. Thus, in *Smith, Ireland & McNay* v *Sunseeker Leisure* [1993] CLY 3167, where the defendant took no adequate steps to examine the allegations prior to the issue of proceedings, and where his evidence was subsequently held to adduce no reason for defence, the court found that he had acted unreasonably.

(xi) Claim "Wholly Misconceived"

A claimant's failure to recognise that his claim is "wholly misconceived", even where this has been spelt out in the defendant's statement of case, will amount to unreasonable behaviour: *Singh* v *Eagle Star Direct* [1998] CLY 461.

(xii) One Party Deliberately Misleading Court

When one party gave an account which "simply could not be believed" it was accepted that he had "deliberately misled the court" and costs were awarded for unreasonable behaviour: *Ryland* v *Russell* [1997] CLY 597. This decision is potentially of great (albeit persuasive) significance as in many cases the accounts of the litigants are exclusive to an extent that the acceptance of one necessarily implies that the other was intentionally misleading. Significantly, however, in *Armstrong-James* v *Radcliffe-Smith* [1997] CLY 593 it was held that it was not unreasonable conduct to file a defence that was untrue. This case can probably be explained by the fact that the 'lie' concerned an attempt by the defendant to deceive his insurers and did not directly impinge on the issues as between himself and the claimant.

Appendices

1. Tables   259
2. AA Motoring Costs   261
3. Loss of Use: Case Summaries   264
4. Motor Insurers' Bureau Agreements   271
5. Witness Questionnaire   305
6. Pre-Action Protocol for Road Traffic Accidents   308
7. Code of Best Practice on Rehabilitation, Early Intervention
   and Medical Treatment in Personal Injury Claims   336
8. Letters of Claim   342
9. Pleadings   348
   1. Rear-end "shunt"   348
   2. Driver on major road collides with car emerging
      from minor road   351
   3. Head-on collision after negligent overtaking
      manoeuvre   354
   4. Collision after the Defendant turned right across the
      Claimant's path   357
   5. Collision at traffic lights   359
   6. Pedestrian run over while crossing the road at
      a zebra crossing   362
   7. Negligent "u" turn   365
   8. Negligent opening of vehicle door into the path
      of motorcyclist   368
   9. Pedestrian knocked down by car that mounted the
      pavement and driven by a Defendant who had
      consumed excess alcohol   370
   10. Motorcyclist injured when struck by a
       mischeivous horse   373
   11. Highway maintenance case   376
   12. Bus passenger   379
   13. Accident caused by defective repair to vehicle   382
   14. Claim against Motor Insurers' Bureau   385
   15. Standard defence to form 1   387

Tables

Conversion Table of Speed and Distance

Miles per hour	Feet per second	Metres per second
5	7.33	2.24
10	14.67	4.47
15	22.00	6.71
20	29.33	8.94
25	36.67	11.18
30	44.00	13.41
35	51.33	15.65
40	58.67	17.88
45	66.00	20.12
50	73.33	22.35
55	80.67	24.59
60	88.00	26.82
65	95.33	29.06
70	102.67	31.29
75	110.00	33.53
80	117.33	35.76
85	124.67	38.00
90	132.00	40.23
95	139.33	42.47
100	146.67	44.70
105	154.00	46.94
110	161.33	49.17

Table compiled by Jose Rafael Vazquez

Typical Stopping Distances

Speed	Thinking Distance		Braking Distance		Overall Stopping Distance	
mph	ft	m	ft	m	ft	m
20	20	6	20	6	40	12
30	30	9	45	14	75	23
40	40	12	80	24	120	36
50	50	15	125	38	175	53
60	60	18	180	55	240	73
70	70	21	245	75	315	96

These distances should be at least doubled on wet roads and increased still further on icy roads.

Table reproduced from the Highway Code, rule 105

AA Motoring Costs 1999

Petrol Cars

		Engine Capacity (cc)				
		Up to 1100	1101 to 1400	1401 to 2000	2001 to 3000	3001 to 4500
	Standing Charges per annum (£)					
A	Road Tax	100.00	155.00	155.00	155.00	155.00
B	Insurance	281.37	376.36	452.10	698.27	721.35
C	Depreciation					
	(based on 10,000 miles per annum)	1064.73	1568.31	2217.55	4008.10	5501.47
D	Subscription	74.00	74.00	74.00	74.00	74.00
	Total £	1520.10	2173.67	2898.65	4935.37	6451.82
	Standing Charges per mile (in pence)					
	5,000	30.40	43.47	57.97	98.71	129.04
	10,000	15.20	21.74	28.99	49.35	64.52
	15,000	11.55	16.58	22.28	38.25	50.35
	20,000	10.79	15.57	21.15	36.70	48.76
	25,000	10.34	14.97	20.46	35.77	47.81
	30,000	8.62	12.47	17.05	29.81	39.84
	Running Costs per mile (in pence)					
E	Petrol*	7.83	8.95	10.44	14.24	15.66
F	Oil	0.34	0.35	0.36	0.44	0.70
G	Tyres	0.74	0.96	1.17	2.25	2.92
H	Servicing	0.94	0.94	0.94	1.47	2.07
I	Repairs & Replacements	3.08	3.51	3.57	5.47	5.63
	Total Pence	12.93	14.71	16.48	23.87	26.98

* Unleaded petrol at 68.9 pence per litre.
For every penny more or less add or subtract: 0.11   0.13   0.15   0.21   0.23

	Engine Capacity (cc)				
	Up to 1100	1101 to 1400	1401 to 2000	2001 to 3000	3001 to 4500
Total of standing and running costs (in pence) based on Annual mileage of:					
5,000 miles	43.33	58.18	74.45	122.58	156.02
10,000 miles	28.13	36.45	45.47	73.22	91.50
15,000 miles	24.48	31.29	38.76	62.12	77.33
20,000 miles	23.72	30.28	37.63	60.57	75.74
25,000 miles	23.27	29.68	36.94	59.64	74.79
30,000 miles	21.55	27.18	33.53	53.68	66.82

Diesel Cars

		New Purchase Price (£)		
		Up to 11,000	11,001 to 15,000	15,001 to 20,000	Over 20,001
	Standing Charges per annum (£)				
A	Road Tax	155.00	155.00	155.00	155.00
B	Insurance	281.37	376.36	452.10	698.27
C	Depreciation				
	(based on 10,000 miles per annum)	1213.39	1739.63	2330.04	3383.65
D	Subscription	74.00	74.00	74.00	74.00
	Total £	1723.76	2344.99	3011.14	4310.92
	Standing Charges per mile (in pence)				
	5,000	34.48	46.90	60.22	86.22
	10,000	17.24	23.45	30.11	43.11
	15,000	13.11	17.95	23.18	33.25
	20,000	9.83	13.46	17.39	24.94
	25,000	8.81	12.56	16.64	24.36
	30,000	8.17	11.30	14.70	21.14
	Running Costs per mile (in pence)				
E	Diesel*	7.26	8.17	8.60	10.90
F	Oil	0.50	0.50	0.65	0.80
G	Tyres	0.74	0.96	1.17	2.25
H	Servicing	1.02	1.02	1.27	1.53
I	Repairs & Replacements	3.08	3.51	3.57	5.47
	Total Pence	12.60	14.16	15.26	20.95

* Diesel at 71.9 pence per litre.
For every penny more or less add or subtract: 0.10   0.11   0.12   0.15

	New Purchase Price (£)		
	Up to 11,000	11, 01 to 15,000	15,001 to 20,000	Over 20,001
Total of standing and running costs				
(in pence) based on Annual mileage of:				
5,000 miles	47.08	61.06	75.48	107.17
10,000 miles	29.84	37.61	45.37	64.06
15,000 miles	25.71	32.11	38.44	54.20
20,000 miles	22.43	27.62	32.65	45.89
25,000 miles	21.41	26.72	31.90	45.31
30,000 miles	20.77	25.46	29.96	42.09

Mopeds, Motorcycles and Scooters

		Engine Capacity (cc)						
		50*	50*	125	250	500	750	1000+
	Standing Charges per annum (£)							
A	Road Tax	15.00	15.00	15.00	40.00	65.00	65.00	65.00
B	Insurance	113.58	124.82	276.86	581.06	727.99	1076.94	1278.47
C	Depreciation	153.44	223.53	363.56	497.80	619.95	1114.45	1338.17
D	Helmet/Clothing	100.00	100.00	200.00	200.00	200.00	200.00	200.00
E	Subscription	40.00	40.00	40.00	40.00	40.00	40.00	40.00
	Total £	422.02	503.35	895.42	1358.86	1652.94	2496.39	2921.64
	Standing Charges per mile (in pence)							
	5,000	8.44	10.07	17.91	27.18	33.06	49.93	58.43
	10,000	4.22	5.03	8.95	13.59	16.53	24.96	29.22
	15,000	2.81	3.36	5.97	9.06	11.02	16.64	19.48
	20,000	2.11	2.52	4.48	6.79	8.26	12.48	14.61
	Running Costs per mile (in pence)							
F	Petrol**	3.13	3.48	4.18	5.22	6.26	6.96	7.83
G	Oil	0.39	0.52	0.71	0.76	0.79	1.00	1.00
H	Tyres	0.64	0.75	1.30	1.86	2.50	4.40	4.73
I	Servicing	1.62	2.16	2.78	2.78	3.12	3.52	3.52
J	Repairs & Replacements	0.75	0.95	1.13	1.41	1.88	2.83	3.77
	Total Pence	6.53	7.86	10.10	12.03	14.55	18.71	20.85

** Unleaded petrol at 68.9 pence per litre. For every penny more or less add or subtract:

		50*	50*	125	250	500	750	1000+
		0.04	0.05	0.06	0.08	0.09	0.10	0.11

* 50cc Class: The two figures represent, respectively, the lowest priced commuter mopeds and the more sophisticated motorcycles and mopeds up to 50cc.

	Engine Capacity (cc)						
	50*	50*	125	250	500	750	1000+
Total of standing and running costs (in pence) based on Annual mileage of:							
5,000 miles	14.97	17.93	28.01	39.21	47.61	68.64	79.28
10,000 miles	10.75	12.89	19.05	25.62	31.08	43.67	50.07
15,000 miles	9.34	11.22	16.07	21.09	25.57	35.35	40.33
20,000 miles	8.64	10.38	14.58	18.82	22.81	31.19	35.46

Loss of Use: Case Summaries

The case summaries in this Appendix collectively provide a useful guide to the calculation of claims for loss of use. Additional examples can be found in *Current Law Monthly Digest* (Sweet & Maxwell).

"Going rate"

DURBIN v LEWIS (1996) CLY 782

D's car was damaged beyond economical repair. He was unable to replace it for almost fifteen weeks. During this time he had the use of a company car from his work's pool. He was able to use the company car most weekends and occasionally on weekday evenings. There was no other car in the family, and when the company car was not available, D had to rely on friends and taxis for lifts. He would often walk to work, a six mile round trip. The period of loss of use was in the Winter months. The net pre-accident value of D's car was £450.

Held, that there was a "going rate" in these cases of about £50 per week. Higher or lower rates would be awarded on the particular facts of a case. Here D's case was ameliorated by the company car, but aggravated by the long walk to and from work when it was not available. It was considered that the two factors cancelled each other out, and loss of use was awarded at £50 per week. D was awarded a total of £735 with additional special damages for the taxi fares.

Inconvenience during journey to work

DAVIES (B.R.) v DAVIES (1994) CLY 1503

C's car was written off in an accident caused by D's negligence. The car was worth £300. C was without a vehicle for sixteen weeks following the accident, after which time he was able to afford to buy a new vehicle. He claimed for loss of use and inconvenience. He was able to get a lift to work for twelve out of the sixteen weeks, but for four weeks he had to travel by public transport which took one hour longer each way than by car and for which he incurred £55.60 travel expenses. C's family had no other car and suffered inconvenience. For example C's wife had to use public transport to visit her ill mother.

Held, that the total award would be £1,629.97, including £100 per week for loss of use for the four weeks when C had to travel to work by public transport and £70 per week for loss of use for the other twelve weeks.

CAMPBELL v BECK (1994) CLY 1504
C claimed damages for the loss of use of her car.

Held, that C would be awarded £75 per week to compensate her for the loss of use and inconvenience during the eight-week period between the date of the accident and the date on which her insurers settled the claim under her comprehensive insurance policy. C used the vehicle for journeys to and from work, and when she was deprived of the use of her vehicle she was forced to catch two buses each way. Furthermore, she was an active member of the local church – as a result of being deprived of the car she was unable to visit the sick and elderly in her parish. This was found to be of particular inconvenience to her and damages were accordingly awarded at the higher end of the scale. Total award: £600 for loss of use and inconvenience, and £50 excess.

PASZYN v MATHER (1994) CLY 1506
C, a middle-aged woman, was left without the use of her car for twenty-one weeks following a road traffic accident. She worked as a freelance academic researcher and needed the car to visit libraries in Central London on a regular basis. The lack of a car also disrupted her social life.

Held, that in assessing the loss of use claim, the security a car provided a single woman living in London whilst travelling at night was to be considered. C was awarded £1,050.

RIELLA v MCLAUGHLIN (1994) CLY 1508
C's motor vehicle was involved in a road traffic accident on March 31, 1993 and damaged beyond repair. C used her car to travel to and from University five days per week and for social purposes. Six weeks after the accident C purchased a cheap replacement car which took two weeks to put into a roadworthy condition. During the eight weeks that C was without a car she caught a train to and from University which put an extra two hours travelling time on her daily journey. For social purposes she relied on friends for lifts and used buses and taxis.

Held, that C recover general damages for the loss of use of her motor car of £560 (being eight weeks at £70 per week) together with the agreed written-off value of her car of £4,125, storage charges of £305 and a recovery charge of £75.

YUEN v CAMPBELL-WHITE (1994) CLY 1514

C was involved in a road traffic accident in September 1992, in which his vehicle suffered damage, requiring repair over a period of ten days. He lived in Wimbledon and worked in South Kensington and used his vehicle to drive to and from work everyday, as well as for normal domestic and social purposes. During the ten days he was without his vehicle, he relied upon the underground to go to and from work and this involved an earlier start in the morning than was ordinarily necessary. For domestic and social purposes, he relied upon a variety of forms of public transport.

Held, that C recover his special damages of £808.67 in full and general damages for loss of use of the car at a rate of £10 per day. The judge stated that he felt the daily rate was reasonable.

Disruption to social amenity

FOX v GREEN (1995) CLY 1618

C's vehicle was involved in an accident on June 3, 1994, and was off the road for one Saturday whilst repairs were carried out. C was physically handicapped and needed a large wheelchair. His vehicle was adapted to take the wheelchair, which could be harnessed in place. On Saturdays, C would usually use the vehicle to go on day trips with his carer. C was unable to "get out and about" in any other way. It was not possible to obtain a suitable alternative vehicle for use on the day the repairs were carried out. C was therefore confined to his house, which he found depressing. The court awarded a total of £255, including £30 for one day's loss of use.

DIX v RICHARD (1996) CLY 2146

D, a middle-aged woman, was involved in a road traffic accident on December 11, 1993, as a result of which damage was done to the front of the car, including the headlight. She continued to use the car after the accident, except when it was dark, until temporary repairs were carried out by a friend at the beginning of April 1994 at a cost of £175. D could not afford to have the car fully repaired (which would have cost about £1,000) as the car was only worth £350. During the period of restricted use, she had to rely on friends to take her to bingo each week, and could not baby-sit for her daughter or son unless they either picked her up or arranged for a taxi. D missed a wedding reception on the night of the accident. D was awarded general damages for loss of use of the car at £40 per week for sixteen weeks, a total of £640.

GORDON v PROCTOR (1996) CLY 2154

The 23 year old claimant suffered from spina bifida and was paralysed from the waist down, requiring a wheelchair to get around. Her specially adapted motor car was written off in an accident and provision of a suitable replacement took sixteen weeks to effect. She lived in an isolated position in the countryside and, during the period without a car, was forced to depend upon family and friends for lifts. The period included the Christmas and New Year season, during which her social life was seriously affected.

Held, she had been particularly inconvenienced by the loss of use of her car and her damages should reflect this. Total award: £2,796, of which £1,280 was damages for loss of use and inconvenience at a rate of £80 per week.

Disruption to family activities

ALZARRAD v WYATT (1994) CLY 1482

C was left without his car for thirty-four weeks and for nine of those weeks he claimed £35 per week in special damages for travelling expenses. On average C covered 75 miles per week, transporting his severely arthritic father around.

Held, that loss of use would be assessed for the first nine weeks at £15 per week and for the next twenty-five weeks, when no claim for alternative travel was made, at £50 per week. Total award: £1,385.

MITCHELL v JOHNSTON (1994) CLY 1507

C's car was written off in a road traffic accident. The vehicle was used primarily by his wife as C himself would often use another vehicle owned by him. It was ten weeks before he was able to purchase a new car.

Held, that C was entitled to damages for inconvenience in respect of loss of use of the car. Since his wife was the principal user of the car, the award should be modest. £25 per week for ten weeks giving a total of £250 would be awarded under this head of damages.

LIGHTBOWNE v WALAYET (1994) CLY 1512

C owned an S-registered Austin Mini, which was valued at £270. After an accident C left her vehicle in storage from December 18, 1992 until April 17, 1993 at a rate of £5 per day, totalling £600. C also claimed for a recovery fee of £65 and loss of use and inconvenience caused by being without the vehicle. C gave evidence that she used taxis to get to and from the shop and that she could not visit her daughter very much or her son who had cancer. C said that the journey she would normally take to the general hospital, to do two days per week voluntary work, would take ten minutes in a car whereas it was now taking her forty-five to fifty minutes on the bus, which does not help her arthritis. Prior to the hearing an offer was made to C's solicitors of £1, 500 taking into consideration all heads of claim. C rejected the offer and proceeded to the hearing.

Held, that a reasonable period of time for loss of use was thirty-five weeks and an appropriate award per week was £60. Damages were therefore assessed at £3,035 with interest at £26.04 for special damages and costs to be taxed if not agreed on county court scale 2, the particulars of claim having being limited to £5,000.

Multifarious inconvenience

KUMAR v VERNON (1994) CLY 1509

P's motorcar was involved in a road traffic accident and was damaged to the extent that it could not be driven. D agreed to undertake repair work on the motorcar, with C paying £400 in the form of a deposit. The repairs were not effected and the motorcar was partly dismantled by D whilst he had custody of it. C was deprived of the use of the car for almost twenty-two months and entirely dependent on public transport for his social life, his part-time job and for attending University some twenty miles from his home. The value of the motorcar when delivered to D, was assessed at £470 by C's insurers. Judgment in default was entered on the basis of breach of contract and conversion.

Held, that C should recover damages in full. C was awarded £400 in respect of the deposit paid for the repair work, £470 for the value of the motorcar prior to the agreement and £1,750 as a global sum to represent loss of use and inconvenience.

CANE v JAYAKODY (1995) CLY 1634

C, an agency nurse, was involved in a road traffic accident on March 30, 1992, in which her car, valued at £270, was damaged beyond economical repair. C used her car for two to three days before deciding that it was unsafe to drive further. C brought a new car for £1,400 on credit on November 14, 1992. Up until October 24, 1992, C worked as an agency nurse, on average six days a week, and had to travel by public transport for 2½ hours instead of the twenty minutes the journey had previously taken by car. C was not able to visit her ill mother in hospital during August.

Held, that liability having been agreed at 50/50, C would be awarded half of £270 for the car, £798 for travel expenses to and from work, £2,218 for loss of use from the beginning of April 1992 to October 24, 1992, and £150 for the three weeks to November 14, 1992.

DORRICOTT v VILLIERS (1997) CLY 1781

D was involved in a road traffic accident on March 9, 1995, in which his vehicle, a C registration Ford Granada, sustained substantial damage. The repairs were estimated at £1,476, which D could not afford to pay. The driver's door had been damaged and could not be opened and D kept the vehicle off the road for fifteen weeks, after which he took the vehicle to a garage to have the door freed. The vehicle was drivable thereafter. D needed his car for work and was forced to ask for lifts from his neighbours. In addition, he was unable to take his disabled 12 year old stepson on weekend trips, or on a planned two weeks holiday to Scotland. V did not contest the proceedings.

Held, that £85 per week damages for loss of use and inconvenience be paid for the full period of fifteen weeks.

Commercial 'tool of the trade'

NAYERI (PAYMAN) v YORKSHIRE TRACTION CO (1994) CLY 1517

C ran a satellite receiver and television business, whose vehicle was used in connection with collection of stock from wholesalers and delivery, installation and service to the customer. The vehicle was extensively damaged after being struck by D's bus whilst it was parked outside the shop premises. D initially suggested the vehicle swerved to avoid an oncoming vehicle. No defence was served and judgment was entered to be assessed. At the hearing damages were assessed based on C's pro forma invoice which had previously been agreed with D's insurers at £1,600, together with thirty-eight days car hire at £1,294.85. C's vehicle needed further repair to continue his business. The vehicle supplied by the hire company was not entirely satisfactory. At the assessment of damages hearing a loss of use applicator of £210 per week was awarded.

ARA SERVICES v HEWITT (T/a HEWITT HAULAGE) (1994) CLY 1518

C was a vending machine operator whose vehicle was extensively damaged in an accident in June 1991 when it was struck by a heavy goods vehicle. The Motor Insurers' Bureau dealt under the Untraced Drivers Agreement. The vehicle was off the road for a period of twelve days being repaired, during which time C was obliged to reschedule service operations, causing extensive inconvenience. At the assessment of damages hearing, £60 per week was awarded in respect of the loss of use. Repairs: £1,110.57. Policy excess: £250. Total award: £1,963.61.

SOLENT INSULATION SERVICES AND CRAIG v THORNE (LESLIE) (1994) CLY 1519

C's company's van was involved in a road traffic accident. The van was used for transporting materials and labour from C's warehouse to various sites and was required as a direct tool of the trade in order that contract work could be carried out. On average, the vehicle travelled about 750 miles per week. Evidence was not challenged that C was without the use of the van for nine weeks and that the period of time was reasonable for repairs to be effective.

Held, that C was entitled to recover loss of use for a period of nine weeks at a weekly rate of £80.

WILKINSON v SEALEY (1996) CLY 2150

W was involved in a road traffic accident on March 2, 1995 as a result of which his vehicle was written off and he claimed damages for loss of use. At the assessment of damages hearing the evidence was that W was only able to afford a replacement vehicle in the first week of January 1996. He was a self-employed painter and decorator and required his car daily. His working day commenced at 8 a.m. and ended at about 5 p.m. His closest bus stop was five minutes walk from his home from which he could then reach the Underground Train Network. He relied on public transport and lifts from friends, his social activities were curtailed and he was unable to visit his family who lived in Whetstone and Luton. He had no money and did not think he would have been credit worthy. In any event he did not attempt to take out a loan or buy a replacement vehicle.

Held, that there was no reason why W should have to take out a loan with high interest rates. As damages had been limited in the particulars of claim to £3,000, the district judge awarded W £2,430 loss of use (£3,000 less the salvage value of the vehicle of £570). This award was based upon a loss of use rate of £70 per week.

Motor Insurers' Bureau Agreements

Motor Insurers' Bureau (Compensation of Victims of Uninsured Drivers) Agreement 1988

Text of an Agreement dated the 21 December 1988 between the Secretary of State for Transport and the Motor Insurers' Bureau.

In accordance with the Agreement made on 31 December 1945 between the Minister of War Transport and insurers transacting compulsory motor vehicle insurance business in Great Britain (published by the Stationery Office under the title 'Motor Vehicle Insurance Fund') a corporation called the 'Motor Insurers' Bureau' entered into an agreement on 17 June 1946 with the Minister of Transport to give effect from 1 July 1946 to the principle recommended in July 1937 by the Departmental Committee under Sir Felix Cassel, (Cmnd 5528), to secure compensation to third party victims of road accidents in cases where, notwithstanding the provisions of the Road Traffic Acts relating to compulsory insurance, the victim is deprived of compensation by the absence of insurance, or of effective insurance. That Agreement was replaced by an Agreement which operated in respect of accidents occurring on or after 1 March 1971 which in turn was replaced by a new Agreement which operated in respect of accidents occurring on or after 1 December 1972. The Agreement of 1972 has now been replaced by a new Agreement which operates in respect of accidents occurring on or after 31 December 1988.

The text of the new agreement is as follows:

> MEMORANDUM OF AGREEMENT made the 21st day of December 1988 between the Secretary of State for Transport and the Motor Insurers' Bureau, whose registered office is at New Garden House, 78 Hatton Garden, London EC1N 8JQ (hereinafter referred to as 'MIB') SUPPLEMENTAL to an Agreement (hereinafter called 'the Principal Agreement') made the 31st Day of December 1945 between the Minister of War Transport and the insurers transacting compulsory motor insurance business in Great Britain by or on behalf of whom the said Agreement was signed and in pursuance of paragraph 1 of which MIB was incorporated.

IT IS HEREBY AGREED AS FOLLOWS–

DEFINITIONS

1. In this Agreement—
'contract of insurance' means a policy of insurance or a security;
'insurer' includes the giver of a security;
'relevant liability' means a liability in respect of which a policy of insurance must insure a person in order to comply with Part VI of the Road Traffic Act 1972,
and references to the Road Traffic Act 1972 are references to that Act as amended by the Motor Vehicles (Compulsory Insurance) Regulations 1987 (No. 2171).

SATISFACTION OF CLAIMS BY MIB

2. (1) If judgment in respect of any relevant liability is obtained against any person or persons in any Court in Great Britain whether or not such a person or persons be in fact covered by a contract of insurance and any such judgment is not satisfied in full within seven days from the date upon which the person or persons in whose favour the judgment was given became entitled to enforce it then MIB will, subject to the provisions of paragraphs (2), (3) and (4) below and to Clauses 4, 5 and 6 hereof, pay or satisfy or cause to be paid or satisfied to or to the satisfaction of the person or persons in whose favour the judgment was given any sum payable or remaining payable thereunder in respect of the relevant liability including any sum awarded by the Court in respect of interest on that sum and any taxed costs or any costs awarded by the Court without taxation (or such proportion thereof as is attributable to the relevant liability) whatever may be the cause of the failure of the judgment debtor to satisfy the judgment.

(2) Subject to paragraphs (3) and (4) below and to Clauses 4, 5 and 6 hereof, MIB shall incur liability under paragraph (1) above in respect of any sum awarded under such a judgment in respect of property damage not exceeding £250,000 or in respect of the first £250,000 of any sum so awarded exceeding that amount.

(3) Where a person in whose favour a judgment in respect of a relevant liability which includes liability in respect of damage to property has been given, has received or is entitled to receive in consequence of a claim he has made, compensation from any source in respect of that damage, MIB may deduct from the sum payable or remaining payable under paragraph (1) above an amount equal to the amount of that compensation in addition to the deduction of £175 by virtue of paragraph (4) below. The reference to compensation includes compensation under insurance arrangements.

(4) MIB shall not incur liability under paragraph (1) above in respect of any amount payable or remaining payable under the judgment in respect of property damage liability where the total of amounts so payable or remaining payable is £175 or less, or, where the total of such amounts is more than £175, in respect of the first £175 of such total.

PERIOD OF AGREEMENT

3. This Agreement shall be determinable by the Secretary of State at any time or by MIB on twelve months' notice without prejudice to the continued operation of the Agreement in respect of accidents occurring before the date of termination.

RECOVERIES

4. Nothing in this Agreement shall prevent insurers from providing by conditions in their contracts of insurance that all sums paid by them or by MIB by virtue of the Principal Agreement or this Agreement in or towards the discharge of the liability of their insured shall be recoverable by them or by MIB from the insured or from any other person.

CONDITIONS PRECEDENT TO MIB's LIABILITY

5. (1) MIB shall not incur any liability under Clause 2 of this Agreement unless—

(a) notice in writing of the bringing of the proceedings is given within seven days after the commencement of the proceedings—

(i) to MIB in the case of proceedings in respect of a relevant liability which is either not covered by a contract of insurance or covered by a contract of insurance with an insurer whose identity cannot be ascertained, or

(ii) to the insurer in the case of proceedings in respect of a relevant liability which is covered by a contract of insurance with an insurer whose identity can be ascertained;

Such notice shall be accompanied by a copy of the writ, summons or other document initiating the proceedings;

(b) the person bringing the proceedings furnishes to MIB—

(i) such information (in such form as MIB may specify) in relation thereto as MIB may reasonably require; and

(ii) such information (in such form as MIB may specify) as to any insurance covering any damage to property to which the claim or proceedings relate and any claim made in respect of that damage under the insurance or otherwise and any report which may have been made or notification which may have been given to any person in respect of that damage or the use of the vehicle giving rise thereto, as MIB may reasonably require;

(c) the person bringing the proceedings has demanded the information and, where appropriate, the particulars specified in section 151 of the Road Traffic Act 1972 in accordance with that section or, if so required by MIB, has authorised MIB to do so on his behalf;

(d) if so required by MIB and subject to full indemnity from MIB as to costs the person bringing the proceedings has taken all reasonable steps to obtain judgment against all the persons liable in respect of the injury or death or damage to property and, in the event of any such person being a servant or agent, against his principal; and

(e) the judgment referred to in Clause 2 of this Agreement and any judgment referred to in paragraph (d) of this Clause which has been obtained (whether or not either judgment includes an amount in respect of a liability other than a relevant liability) and any order for costs are assigned to MIB or their nominee.

(2) In the event of any dispute as to the reasonableness of a requirement by MIB for the supply of information or that any particular step should be taken to obtain judgment against other persons it may be referred to the Secretary of State whose decision shall be final.

(3) Where a judgment which includes an amount in respect of a liability other than a relevant liability has been assigned to MIB or their nominee in pursuance of paragraph (1)(e) of this Clause MIB shall apportion any monies received in pursuance of the judgment according to the proportion which the damages in respect of the relevant liability bear to the damages in respect of the other liabilities and shall account to the person in whose favour the judgment was given in respect of such monies received properly apportionable to the other liabilities. Where an order for costs in respect of such a judgment has been so assigned monies received pursuant to the order shall be dealt with in the same manner.

EXCEPTIONS

6. (1) MIB shall not incur any liability under Clause 2 of this Agreement in a case where—

(a) the claim arises out of the use of a vehicle owned by or in the possession of the Crown, except where any other person has undertaken responsibility for the existence of a contract of insurance under Part VI of the Road Traffic Act 1972 (whether or not the person or persons liable be in fact covered by a contract of insurance) or where the liability is in fact covered by a contract of insurance;

(b) the claim arises out of the use of a vehicle the use of which is not required to be covered by a contract of insurance by virtue of section 144 of the Road Traffic Act 1972, unless the use is in fact covered by such a contract;

(c) the claim is in respect of a judgment or any part thereof which has been obtained by virtue of the exercise of a right of subrogation by any person;

(d) the claim is in respect of damage to property which consists of damage to a motor vehicle or losses arising therefrom if at the time of the use giving rise to the damage to the motor vehicle there was not in force in relation to the use of that vehicle when the damage to it was sustained such a policy of insurance as is required by Part VI of the Road Traffic Act 1972 and the person or persons claiming in respect of the loss or damage either knew or ought to have known that that was the case;

(e) at the time of the use which gave rise to the liability the person suffering death or bodily injury or damage to property was allowing himself to be carried in or upon the vehicle and either before the commencement of his journey in the vehicle or after such commencement if he could reasonably be expected to have alighted from the vehicle he—

(i) knew or ought to have known that the vehicle had been stolen or unlawfully taken, or

(ii) knew or ought to have known that the vehicle was being used without there being in force in relation to its use such a contract of insurance as would comply with Part VI of the Road Traffic Act 1972.

(2) The exception specified in sub-paragraph (1)(e) of this Clause shall apply only in a case where the judgment in respect of which the claim against MIB is made was obtained in respect of a relevant liability incurred by the owner or a person using the vehicle in which the person who suffered death or bodily injury or sustained damage to property was being carried.

(3) For the purposes of these exceptions—

(a) a vehicle which has been unlawfully removed from the possession of the Crown shall be taken to continue in that possession whilst it is kept so removed;

(b) references to a person being carried in a vehicle include references to his being carried in or upon or entering or getting on to or alighting from the vehicle; and

(c) 'owner' in relation to a vehicle which is the subject of a hiring agreement or a hire-purchase agreement, means the person in possession of the vehicle under that agreement.

AGENTS

7. Nothing in this Agreement shall prevent MIB performing their obligations under this Agreement by Agents.

OPERATION

8. This Agreement shall come into operation on 31 December 1988 in relation to accidents occurring on or after that date. The Agreement made on 22 November 1972 between the Secretary of State and MIB shall cease and determine except in relation to claims arising out of accidents occurring before 31 December 1988.

IN WITNESS whereof the Secretary of State has caused his Corporate Seal to be hereto affixed and the Motor Insurers' Bureau have caused their Common Seal to be hereto affixed the day and year first above written.

> THE CORPORATE SEAL of the Secretary of State was hereunto affixed in the presence of D W Worskett.
>
> An Assistant Secretary in the Department of Transport duly authorised in that behalf.
>
> THE COMMON SEAL of the Motor Insurers' Bureau was hereunto affixed in the presence of
>
> T. A. Kent   } Members of the
> A. Kilpatrick   Council
>
> J. L. West   Secretary

Motor Insurers' Bureau (Compensation of Victims of Untraced Drivers) Agreement 1996

Text of an Agreement dated the 14th June 1996 between the Secretary of State for Transport and Motor Insurers' Bureau.

THE AGREEMENT
RECITALS

(1) On 21 April 1969 the Minister of Transport and Motor Insurers' Bureau entered into an Agreement ('the First Agreement') to secure compensation for third party victims of road accidents when the driver responsible for the accident could not be traced.

(2) The First Agreement was replaced by a new Agreement ('the Second Agreement') which operated in respect of accidents occurring on or after 1 December 1972.

(3) The Second Agreement was added to by a Supplemental Agreement dated 7 December 1977 ('the Third Agreement') which operated in respect of accidents occurring on or after 3 January 1978.

(4) The Second Agreement and the Third Agreement have now been replaced by a new Agreement ('this Agreement') which operates in respect of accidents occurring on or after 1 July 1996.

(5) The text of this Agreement is as follows—

TEXT OF THE AGREEMENT
AN AGREEMENT made the Fourteenth day of June 1996 between the Secretary of State for Transport ('the Secretary of State') and the Motor Insurers' Bureau whose registered office is at 152 Silbury Boulevard, Milton Keynes, MK9 1NB ('the MIB').

IT IS HEREBY AGREED as follows—
1 (1) Subject to paragraph (2) of this Clause, this Agreement applies to any case in which an application is made to the MIB for a payment in respect of the death of or bodily injury to any person caused by or arising out of the use of a motor vehicle on a road in Great Britain and the case is one in which the following conditions are fulfilled, that is to say:

(a) the event giving rise to the death or injury occurred on or after 1 July 1996;

(b) the applicant for the payment either—

(i) is unable to trace any person responsible for the death or injury, or

(ii) in a case to which Clause 5 applies where more than one person was responsible, is unable to trace one of those persons. (Any person so untraced is referred to as 'the untraced person');

(c) the death or injury was caused in such circumstances that on the balance of probabilities the untraced person would be liable to pay damages to the applicant in respect of the death or injury;

(d) the liability of the untraced person to pay damages to the applicant is one which is required to be covered by insurance or security under Part VI of the Road Traffic Act 1988 ('the 1988 Act'), it being assumed for this purpose, in the absence of evidence to the contrary, that the vehicle was being used in circumstances in which the user was required by the 1988 Act to be insured or secured against third party risks;

(e) the death or injury was not caused by the use of the vehicle by the untraced person in any deliberate attempt to cause the death or injury of the person in respect of which an application is made;

(f) the application is made in writing within three years from the date of the event giving rise to the death or injury; and

(g) the incident was reported to the police within fourteen days or as soon as the applicant reasonably could and the applicant co-operated with the police.

(2) This Agreement does not apply to a case in which:

(a) the death or bodily injury in respect of which any such application is made was caused by or arose out of the use of a motor vehicle which at the time of the event giving rise to the death or bodily injury was owned by or in the possession of the Crown, unless the case is one in which some other person has undertaken responsibility for the existence of a contract of insurance under the 1988 Act;

(b) at the time of the accident the person suffering death or bodily injury in respect of which the application is made was allowing himself to be carried in a vehicle and either before or after the commencement of his journey in the vehicle, if he could reasonably be expected to have alighted from the vehicle, he knew or had reason to believe that the vehicle—

(i) had been stolen or unlawfully taken, or

(ii) was being used without there being in force in relation to its use a contract of insurance which complied with the 1988 Act; or

(iii) was being used in the course or furtherance of crime; or

(iv) was being used as a means of escape from or avoidance of lawful apprehension.

(3) For the purposes of paragraph (2) of this Clause:

(a) a vehicle which has been unlawfully removed from the possession of the Crown shall be taken to continue in that possession whilst it is kept so removed;

(b) references to a person being carried in a vehicle include references to his being carried in or upon, or entering or getting on to or alighting from the vehicle;

(c) 'owner' in relation to a vehicle which is the subject of a hiring agreement or a hire purchase agreement means the person in possession of the vehicle under that agreement.

2. (1) An application to the MIB for a payment in respect of the death or bodily injury to any person may be made:

(a) by the person for whose benefit that payment is to be made ('the applicant'); or

(b) by any solicitor acting for the applicant; or

(c) by any other person whom the MIB may be prepared to accept as acting for the applicant.

(2) Any decision made, or award or payment given or other thing done in accordance with this Agreement to or by a person acting under paragraph (1)(b) and (1)(c) of this Clause on behalf of the applicant, or in relation to an application made by such person, shall whatever may be the age, or the circumstances affecting the capacity, of the applicant, be treated as having the same effect as if it had been done to or by, or in relation to an application made by, an applicant of full age and capacity.

3. Subject to the following provisions of this Agreement, the MIB shall, on any application made to it in a case to which this Agreement applies, award to the applicant in respect of the death or injury for which the application is made a payment of an amount which shall be assessed in like manner as a court applying English law in a case where the event giving rise to the death or injury occurred in England or Wales or applying the law of Scotland in a case where that event occurred in Scotland, would assess the damages which the applicant would have been entitled to recover from the untraced person in respect of that death or injury if the applicant had brought successful proceedings to enforce a claim for such damages against the untraced person.

4. In assessing the level of an award in accordance with Clause 3, the MIB shall be under no obligation to include any sum in respect of loss of earnings suffered by the applicant where and in so far as the applicant has in fact been paid wages or salary or any sum in lieu of the same, whether or not such payments were made subject to an undertaking on the part of the applicant to repay the same in the event of the applicant recovering damages.

5. (1) This Clause applies to any case:

(a) to which this Agreement applies; and

(b) the death or bodily injury in respect of which an application has been made to the MIB under this Agreement ('the relevant death or injury') was caused—

(i) partly by the untraced person and partly by an identified person or by identified persons, or

(ii) partly by the untraced person and partly by some other untraced person or persons whose master or principal can be identified, and

(c) in circumstances making the identified person or persons or any master or principal ('the identified person') liable to the applicant in respect of the relevant death or injury.

(2) If in a case to which this Clause applies one of the conditions in paragraph (3) of this Clause is satisfied, the amount of the award to be paid by the MIB to the applicant in respect of the relevant death or injury shall be determined in accordance with paragraph (4) of this Clause and its liability to the applicant shall be subject to paragraph (7) of this Clause and Clause 6 of this Agreement.

(3) The conditions referred to in paragraph (2) of this Clause are—

(a) that the applicant has obtained a judgment in respect of the relevant death or injury against the identified person ('the original judgment') which has not been satisfied in full within three months from the date on which the applicant became entitled to enforce it ('the three month period'); or

(b) that the applicant—

(i) has not obtained and has not been required by the MIB to obtain a judgment in respect of the relevant death or injury against the identified person; and

(ii) has not received any payment by way of compensation from the identified person or persons.

(4) The amount to be awarded by the MIB to the applicant in a case to which this Clause applies shall be determined as follows:

(a) if the condition in paragraph (3)(a) of this Clause is satisfied and the original judgment is wholly unsatisfied within the three month period, the amount to be awarded shall be an amount equal to that proportion of a full award attributable to the untraced person;

(b) if the condition in paragraph (3)(a) of this Clause is satisfied but the original judgment is satisfied in part only within the three month period, the amount to be awarded—

(i) if the unsatisfied part of the original judgment is less than the proportion of a full award attributable to the untraced person, shall be an amount equal to that unsatisfied part; or

(ii) if the unsatisfied part of the original judgment is equal to or greater than the proportion of a full award attributable to the untraced person, shall be an amount equal to the untraced person's proportion;

(c) if the condition in paragraph (3)(b) of this Clause is satisfied the amount to be awarded shall be an amount equal to the proportion of a full award attributable to the untraced person.

(5) The following provisions of this paragraph shall have effect in any case in which an appeal from or any proceeding to set aside the original judgment is commenced within a period of three months beginning on the date on which the applicant became entitled to enforce the original judgment:

(a) until the appeal or proceeding is disposed of the provisions of this Clause shall have effect as if for the three month period there were substituted a period expiring on the date when the appeal or proceeding is disposed of;

(b) if as a result of the appeal or proceeding, the applicant ceases to be entitled to receive any payment in respect of the relevant death or injury from any of the person or persons against whom he has obtained the original judgment, the provisions of this Clause shall have effect as if he had neither obtained nor been required by the MIB to obtain a judgment against any person or persons;

(c) if as a result of the appeal or proceeding, the applicant becomes entitled to recover an amount which differs from that which he was entitled to recover under the original judgment the provisions of this Clause shall have effect as if for the reference in paragraph (3)(a) to the original judgment there were substituted a reference to the judgment under which the applicant became entitled to the different amount;

(d) if as a result of the appeal or proceeding the applicant remains entitled to enforce the original judgment the provisions of this Clause shall have effect as if for the three month period there were substituted a period of three months beginning on the date on which the appeal or other proceeding was disposed of.

The provisions of this paragraph shall apply also in any case where any judgment given upon any appeal or proceeding is itself the subject of a further appeal or similar proceeding and shall apply in such a case in relation to that further appeal or proceeding in the same manner as they apply in relation to the first mentioned appeal or proceeding.

(6) In this Clause:

(a) 'full award' means the amount which would have fallen to be awarded to the applicant under Clause 3 in respect of the relevant death or injury if the untraced person had been adjudged by a court to be wholly responsible for that death or injury; and

(b) 'the proportion of a full award attributable to the untraced person' means that proportion of a full award which on the balance of probabilities would have been apportioned by a court in proceedings between the untraced person and any other person liable in respect of the same event as the share to be borne by the untraced person in the responsibility for the event giving rise to the relevant death or injury.

(7) The MIB shall not be under any liability in respect of the relevant death or injury if the applicant is entitled to receive compensation from the MIB in respect of that death or injury under any agreement providing for the compensation of victims of uninsured drivers entered into between the Secretary of State and the MIB.

6. (1) Any liability falling upon the MIB upon an application made to it under this Agreement, in respect of any death or injury, shall be subject to the following conditions:

(a) the applicant shall give all assistance as may reasonably be required by or on behalf of the MIB to enable any investigation to be carried out under this Agreement, including, in particular the provision of statements and information either in writing, or, if required, orally at an interview or interviews between the applicant and any person acting on behalf of the MIB;

(b) at any time before the MIB has communicated its decision upon the application to the applicant, the applicant shall, subject to the following provisions of this Clause, take all steps as in the circumstances it is reasonable for the MIB to require him to take to obtain judgment against any person or persons in respect of their liability to the applicant for the death or injury as having caused or contributed to the death or injury or as being the master or principal of any person who has caused or contributed to the death or injury, and

(c) if required by the MIB the applicant shall assign to the MIB or to its nominee any judgment obtained by him (whether or not obtained in accordance with a requirement under subparagraph (b) of this paragraph) in respect of the death or injury to which his application to the MIB relates upon terms as will secure that the MIB or its nominee shall be accountable to the applicant for any amount by which the aggregate of all sums recovered by the MIB or its nominee under the judgment (after deducting all reasonable expenses incurred in effecting recovery) exceeds the amount payable by the MIB to the applicant under this Agreement in respect of that death or injury.

(2) If the MIB requires the applicant to bring proceedings against any specified person or persons:

(a) the MIB shall indemnify the applicant against all costs

reasonably incurred by him in complying with that requirement unless the result of those proceedings materially contributes to establishing that the untraced person did not cause or contribute to the relevant death or injury; and

(b) the applicant shall, if required by the MIB and at its expense, provide the MIB with a transcript of any official shorthand note taken in those proceedings of any evidence given or judgment delivered therein.

(3) In the event of a dispute arising between the applicant and the MIB as to the reasonableness of any requirement by the MIB under paragraph (1)(b) of this Clause or as to whether any costs as referred to in paragraph (2)(a) of this Clause were reasonably incurred, that dispute shall be referred to the Secretary of State whose decision shall be final. Provided that any dispute arising between the applicant and the MIB as to whether the MIB is required to indemnify him under paragraph (2)(a) of this Clause shall, in so far as it depends on the question whether the result of any proceedings which the MIB has required the applicant to bring against any specified person or persons has or has not materially contributed to establish that the untraced person did not cause or contribute to the relevant death or injury, be referred to the arbitrator in accordance with the following provisions of this Agreement, whose decision on that question shall be final.

7. The MIB shall cause any application made to it for a payment under this Agreement to be investigated and, unless it decides that the application should be rejected because a preliminary investigation has disclosed that the case is not one to which this Agreement applies, it shall cause a report to be made on the application and on the basis of that report it shall decide whether to make an award and, if so, the amount of the award which shall be calculated in accordance with the provisions of this Agreement.

8. The MIB may before coming to a decision on any application made to it under this Agreement request the applicant to provide it with a statutory declaration to be made by the applicant, setting out to the best of his knowledge, information and belief the facts and circumstances upon which his claim to an award under this Agreement are based, or facts and circumstances as may be specified by it.

9. (1) The MIB shall notify its decision to the applicant and when so doing shall:

(a) if the application is rejected because a preliminary investigation has disclosed that it is not one made in a case to which this Agreement applies, give its reasons for the rejection; or

(b) if the application has been fully investigated provide him with a statement setting out—

(i) the circumstances in which the death or injury occurred and the relevant evidence;

(ii) the circumstances relevant to the assessment of the amount to be awarded to the applicant under this Agreement and the relevant evidence; and

(iii) if it refuses to make an award, its reasons for that refusal; and

(c) in a case to which Clause 5 of this Agreement applies specify the way in which the amount of that award has been computed and its relation to those provisions of Clause 5 which are relevant to its computation.

(2) Where the MIB has decided that it will not indemnify the applicant against the costs of any proceedings which it has under Clause 6(1)(b) required him to bring against any specified person or persons on the ground that those proceedings have materially contributed to establish that the untraced person did not cause or contribute to the relevant death or injury, it shall give notice to the applicant of that decision, together with its reasons for it and shall provide the applicant with a copy of any transcript of any evidence given or judgment delivered in those proceedings as is mentioned in Clause 6(2)(b) which it regards as relevant to that decision.

10. (1) Subject to the provisions of this Agreement, where the MIB has decided to make an award to the applicant, it shall pay the applicant the amount of that award if:

(a) it has been notified by the applicant that the award is accepted; or

(b) at the expiration of the period during which the applicant may give notice of an appeal under Clause 11 the applicant has not given the MIB either any notification of acceptance of its award or a notice of an appeal under Clause 11.

(2) Such payment as is made under paragraph (1) of this Clause shall discharge the MIB from all liability under this Agreement in respect of the death or injury for which that award has been made.

11. (1) The applicant shall have a right of appeal to an arbitrator against any decision notified to him by the MIB under Clause 9 if:

(a) he gives notice to the MIB, that he wishes to appeal against its decision ('the notice of appeal');

(b) he gives the MIB the notice of appeal within 6 weeks from the date when he was given notice of the decision against which he wishes to appeal; and

(c) he has not previously notified the MIB that he has accepted its decision.

(2) The grounds of appeal are as follows:

(a) where the application has not been the subject of a full investigation—

(i) that the case is one to which this Agreement applies; and

(ii) that the applicant's application should be fully investigated by the MIB with a view to its deciding whether or not to make an award to him and, if so, the amount of that award, or

(b) where the application has been fully investigated—

(i) that the MIB was wrong in refusing to make an award, or

(ii) that the amount it has awarded to the applicant is insufficient; or

(c) in a case where a decision not to indemnify the applicant against the costs of any proceedings has been notified to the applicant by the MIB under Clause 9(2), that that decision was wrong.

12. A notice of appeal under Clause 11 shall state the grounds of the appeal and shall be accompanied by an undertaking given by the applicant or by the person acting on his behalf under Clause 2(1)(b) and 2(1)(c), that:

(a) the applicant will accept the decision of the arbitrator; and

(b) the arbitrator's fee shall be paid to the MIB by the applicant or by the person who has given the undertaking in any case where the MIB is entitled to reimbursement of that fee under the provisions of Clause 22.

13. (1) When giving notice of his appeal or at any time before doing so, the applicant may:

(a) make comments to the MIB on its decision; and

(b) supply it with such particulars as he thinks fit of any further evidence not contained in the written statement supplied to him by the MIB which he considers is relevant to the application.

(2) The MIB may, before submitting the applicant's appeal to the arbitrator:

(a) cause an investigation to be made into the further evidence supplied by the applicant under paragraph (1)(b) of this Clause; and

(b) report to the applicant the result of that investigation and of any change in its decision which may result from it.

(3) The applicant may, within six weeks from the date on which the report referred to in paragraph (2)(b) of this Clause was sent to him, unless he withdraws his appeal, make such comments on the report as he may desire to have submitted to the arbitrator.

14. (1) In a case where the MIB receives from the applicant a notice

of appeal in which the only ground of appeal which is stated is that the amount awarded to the applicant is insufficient, before submitting that appeal to the arbitrator, the MIB may:

(a) give notice to the applicant that if the appeal proceeds it will request the arbitrator to decide whether the case is one in which the MIB should make an award at all; and

(b) at the same time as complying with paragraph (1)(a) of this Clause provide the applicant with a statement setting out such comments as it may consider relevant to the decision which the arbitrator should come to on that question.

(2) Where the MIB gives the applicant notice under paragraph (1)(a) of this Clause, the applicant may, within six weeks from the date on which that notice is given:

(a) make comments to the MIB and supply it with particulars of other evidence not contained in any written statement provided to him by the MIB as he may consider relevant to the question which the arbitrator is by that notice requested to decide; and

(b) Clause 13 shall apply in relation to any comments made or particulars supplied by the applicant under paragraph (2)(a) of this Clause.

15. (1) Subject to paragraph (2) of this Clause, where the MIB receives a notice of appeal from the applicant under the provisions of this Agreement, unless the appeal is previously withdrawn, it shall:

(a) submit that appeal to an arbitrator for a decision; and

(b) send to the arbitrator for the purpose of obtaining his decision—

(i)   the application made by the applicant;

(ii)   a copy of its decision as notified to the applicant; and

(iii) copies of all statements, declarations, notices, undertakings, comments, transcripts, particulars of reports provided, given or sent to the MIB under this Agreement either by the applicant or any person acting for him under Clause 2(1)(b) or 2(1)(c) or given or sent to the applicant or a person acting for him under Clause 2(1)(b) or 2(1)(c) by the MIB.

(2) In a case where the MIB causes an investigation to be made under Clause 13, the MIB shall not comply with paragraph (1) of this Clause until:

(a) the expiration of six weeks from the date on which it sent the applicant a report as to the result of that investigation; or

(b) the expiration of six weeks from the date on which it gave the applicant notice under Clause 14(1); or

(c) the expiration of six weeks from the date on which it sent the applicant a report as to the result of that investigation, if it has caused an investigation to be made into any evidence supplied under Clause 14(2).

16. On an appeal made by the applicant in accordance with this Agreement:

(a) if the appeal is against a decision by the MIB rejecting an application because a preliminary investigation has disclosed that the case is not one to which this Agreement applies, the arbitrator shall decide whether the case is or is not one to which this Agreement applies and, if he decides that it is such a case, shall remit the application to the MIB for full investigation and a decision in accordance with the provisions of this Agreement;

(b) if the appeal is against a decision by the MIB given after an application has been fully investigated by it (whether before the appeal or in consequence of its being remitted for such investigation under paragraph (a) of this Clause) the arbitrator shall decide, as may be appropriate, having regard to the grounds stated in the notice of appeal and to any notice given by the MIB to the applicant under Clause 14, whether the MIB should make an award under this Agreement to the applicant and, if so, the amount which it should award to him under the provisions of this Agreement;

(c) if the appeal relates to a dispute which has arisen between the applicant and the MIB which is required by the proviso to Clause 6(3) to be referred to the arbitrator, the arbitrator shall also give his decision on that dispute.

Provided that where the arbitrator has allowed an appeal under paragraph (a) of this Clause all the provisions of this Agreement shall apply as if the case were an application to which this Agreement applies upon which the MIB had not communicated a decision.

17. (1) Subject to paragraph (2) of this Clause, the arbitrator shall decide the appeal on the documents submitted to him under Clause 15(1)(b) and no further evidence shall be produced to him.

(2) The following shall apply where documents have been submitted to the arbitrator under Clause 15(1)(b):

(a) the arbitrator shall be entitled to ask the MIB to make any further investigation which he considers desirable and to submit a written report of its findings to him for his consideration; and

(b) the MIB shall send a copy of that report to the applicant who shall be entitled to submit written comments on it to the MIB within four weeks of the date on which that copy is sent to him; and

(c) the MIB shall transmit those comments to the arbitrator for his consideration.

18. The arbitrator by whom an appeal made by an applicant in accordance with the provisions of this Agreement shall be considered shall be an arbitrator to be selected by the Secretary of State from two panels of Queen's Counsel appointed respectively by the Lord Chancellor and the Lord Advocate for the purpose of determining appeals under this Agreement, the arbitrator to be selected from the panel appointed by the Lord Chancellor in cases where the event giving rise to the death or injury occurred in England or Wales and from the panel appointed by the Lord Advocate where that event occurred in Scotland.

19. The arbitrator shall notify his decision on any appeal under this Agreement to the MIB and the MIB shall forthwith send a copy of the arbitrator's decision to the applicant.

20. Subject to the provisions of this Agreement, the MIB shall pay the applicant any amount which the arbitrator has decided shall be awarded to him, and that payment shall discharge the MIB from all liability under this Agreement in respect of the death or injury in respect of which that decision has been given.

21. Each party to the appeal will bear their own costs.

22. The MIB shall pay the arbitrator a fee approved by the Lord Chancellor or the Lord Advocate, as the case may be, after consultation with the MIB.

Provided that, in any case where it appears to the arbitrator, that there were no reasonable grounds for the appeal, the arbitrator may in his discretion decide:

   (a) that his fee ought to be paid by the applicant; and

   (b) that the person giving the undertaking required by Clause 12 shall be liable to reimburse the MIB the amount of the fee paid by it to the arbitrator, except in so far as that amount is deducted by the MIB from any amount which it is liable to pay to the applicant in consequence of the decision of the arbitrator.

23. If in any case it appears to the MIB that by reason of the applicant being under the age of majority or of any other circumstances affecting his capacity to manage his affairs it would be in the applicant's interest that all or some part of the amount which would otherwise be payable to him under an award made under this Agreement should be administered for him by the Family Welfare Association or by some other body or person under a trust or by the Court of Protection (or in Scotland by the appointment of a Judicial Factor) the MIB may establish for that purpose a trust of the whole or part of the amount to take effect for a period and under provisions as may appear to it to be appropriate in the circumstances of the case or may initiate or cause

any other person to initiate process in that Court and otherwise cause any amount payable under the award to be paid to and administered thereby.

24. In any case in which an application has been made to the MIB under Clause 2(1) and in which a preliminary investigation under Clause 7 has disclosed that the case is one to which the Agreement, save for Clause 5, applies, the MIB may, instead of causing a report to be made to the applicant an offer to settle his application in a specified sum, assessed in accordance with Clause 3.

25. Where an offer is made under Clause 24, there shall be provided to the applicant (at the same time) in writing particulars of:

(a) the circumstances in which the death or injury occurred and the relevant evidence; and

(b) the circumstances relevant to the assessment of the amount to be awarded to the applicant and the relevant evidence.

26. (1) On receipt by the MIB or its agent of an acceptance of the offer referred to in Clause 24:

(a) this acceptance shall have effect in relation to the application as if in Clause 7 the words 'and, unless the MIB decides' to the end of the Clause, and Clauses 9 to 22 inclusive were omitted; and

(b) the MIB shall pay to the applicant the amount specified in the offer.

(2) The payment made by the MIB under paragraph (1)(b) of this Clause shall discharge it from all liability under this Agreement in respect of the death or injury for which the payment has been made.

27. This Agreement may be determined at any time by the Secretary of State or by the MIB by either of them giving to the other no less than twelve months previous notice in writing. Provided that this Agreement shall continue to have effect in any case where the event giving rise to the death or injury occurred before the date on which this Agreement terminates in accordance with any notice so given.

28. From 14 June 1996 the following periods of operation shall apply:

(a) this Agreement shall come into operation on 1 July 1996 in relation to accidents occurring on or after that date;

(b) the Second Agreement shall cease and determine except in relation to applications arising out of accidents which occurred on or after 1 December 1972 and before the 1 July 1996; and

(c) the Third Agreement shall cease and determine except in relation to accidents occurring on or after 3 January 1978 and before the 1 July 1996.

IN WITNESS whereof the Secretary of State for Transport has caused his Corporate Seal to be hereto affixed and the Motor Insurers' Bureau has caused its Common Seal to be hereto affixed the day and year first above written.

> THE CORPORATE SEAL of THE SECRETARY OF STATE FOR TRANSPORT hereunto affixed authenticated by
>> Steven Norris
>> Parliamentary Under Secretary of State
>> Department of Transport

> THE COMMON SEAL of THE MOTOR INSURERS BUREAU was hereunto affixed in the presence of
>> James A. Read
>> Leslie Howell
>> Directors of the Board of Management

>> Anthony Dand
>> Secretary

Motor Insurers' Bureau
(Compensation of Victims of Uninsured Drivers) 1999

THIS AGREEMENT is made the thirteenth day of August 1999 between the SECRETARY OF STATE FOR THE ENVIRONMENT, TRANSPORT AND THE REGIONS (hereinafter referred to as 'the Secretary of State') and the MOTOR INSURERS' BUREAU, whose registered office is at 152 Silbury Boulevard, Milton Keynes MK9 1NB (hereinafter referred to as 'MIB') and is SUPPLEMENTAL to an Agreement (hereinafter called 'the Principal Agreement') made the 31st Day of December 1945 between the Minister of War Transport and the insurers transacting compulsory motor insurance business in Great Britain by or on behalf of whom the said Agreement was signed and in pursuance of paragraph 1 of which MIB was incorporated.

IT IS HEREBY AGREED AS FOLLOWS:–

INTERPRETATION

General definitions

1. In this Agreement, unless the context otherwise requires, the following expressions have the following meanings—

   '1988 Act' means the Road Traffic Act 1988;

   '1988 Agreement' means the Agreement made on 21 December 1988 between the Secretary of State for Transport and MIB;

   'bank holiday' means a day which is, or is to be observed as, a bank holiday under the Banking and Financial Dealings Act 1971;

   'claimant' means a person who has commenced or who proposes to commence relevant proceedings and has made an application under this Agreement in respect thereof;

   'contract of insurance' means a policy of insurance or a security covering a relevant liability;

   'insurer' includes the giver of a security;

   'MIB's obligation' means the obligation contained in clause 5;

   'property' means any property whether real, heritable or personal;

   'relevant liability' means a liability in respect of which a contract of insurance must be in force to comply with Part VI of the 1988 Act;

'relevant proceedings' means proceedings in respect of a relevant liability (and 'commencement', in relation to such proceedings means, in England and Wales, the date on which a Claim Form or other originating process is issued by a Court or, in Scotland, the date on which the originating process is served on the Defender);

'relevant sum' means a sum payable or remaining payable under an unsatisfied judgment, including—

(a) an amount payable or remaining payable in respect of interest on that sum, and

(b) either the whole of the costs (whether taxed or not) awarded by the Court as part of that judgment or, where the judgment includes an award in respect of a liability which is not a relevant liability, such proportion of those costs as the relevant liability bears to the total sum awarded under the judgment;

'specified excess' means £300 or such other sum as may from time to time be agreed in writing between the Secretary of State and MIB;

'unsatisfied judgment' means a judgment or order (by whatever name called) in respect of a relevant liability which has not been satisfied in full within seven days from the date upon which the claimant became entitled to enforce it.

Meaning of references

2. (1) Save as otherwise herein provided, the Interpretation Act 1978 shall apply for the interpretation of this Agreement as it applies for the interpretation of an Act of Parliament.

(2) Where, under this Agreement, something is required to be done—

(a) within a specified period after or from the happening of a particular event, the period begins on the day after the happening of that event;

(b) within or not less than a specified period before a particular event, the period ends on the day immediately before the happening of that event.

(3) Where, apart from this paragraph, the period in question, being a period of seven days or less, would include a Saturday,

Sunday or bank holiday or Christmas Day or Good Friday, that day shall be excluded.

(4) Save where expressly otherwise provided, a reference in this Agreement to a numbered clause is a reference to the clause bearing that number in this Agreement and a reference to a numbered paragraph is a reference to a paragraph bearing that number in the clause in which the reference occurs.

(5) In this Agreement—

(a) a reference (however framed) to the doing of any act or thing by or the happening of any event in relation to the claimant includes a reference to the doing of that act or thing by or the happening of that event in relation to a Solicitor or other person acting on his behalf, and

(b) a requirement to give notice to, or to serve documents upon, MIB or an insurer mentioned in clause 9(1)(a) shall be satisfied by the giving of the notice to, or the service of the documents upon, a Solicitor acting on its behalf in the manner provided for.

Claimants not of full age or capacity

3. Where, under and in accordance with this Agreement—

(a) any act or thing is done to or by a Solicitor or other person acting on behalf of a claimant,

(b) any decision is made by or in respect of a Solicitor or other person acting on behalf of a claimant, or

(c) any sum is paid to a Solicitor or other person acting on behalf of a claimant,

then, whatever may be the age or other circumstances affecting the capacity of the claimant, that act, thing, decision or sum shall be treated as if it had been done to or by, or made in respect of or paid to a claimant of full age and capacity.

PRINCIPAL TERMS

Duration of Agreement

4. (1) This Agreement shall come into force on 1st October 1999 in relation to accidents occurring on or after that date and, save as provided by clause 23, the 1988 Agreement shall cease and determine immediately before that date.

(2) This Agreement may be determined by the Secretary of State or by MIB giving to the other not less than twelve months' notice in writing but without prejudice to its continued operation in respect of accidents occurring before the date of termination.

MIB's obligation to satisfy compensation claims

5. (1) Subject to clauses 6 to 17, if a claimant has obtained against any person in a Court in Great Britain a judgment which is an unsatisfied judgment then MIB will pay the relevant sum to, or to the satisfaction of, the claimant or will cause the same to be so paid.

   (2) Paragraph (1) applies whether or not the person liable to satisfy the judgment is in fact covered by a contract of insurance and whatever may be the cause of his failure to satisfy the judgment.

EXCEPTIONS TO AGREEMENT

6. (1) Clause 5 does not apply in the case of an application made in respect of a claim of any of the following descriptions (and, where part only of a claim satisfies such a description, clause 5 does not apply to that part)—

   (a) a claim arising out of a relevant liability incurred by the user of a vehicle owned by or in the possession of the Crown, unless—

      (i) responsibility for the existence of a contract of insurance under Part VI of the 1988 Act in relation to that vehicle had been undertaken by some other person (whether or not the person liable was in fact covered by a contract of insurance), or

      (ii) the relevant liability was in fact covered by a contract of insurance;

   (b) a claim arising out of the use of a vehicle which is not required to be covered by a contract of insurance by virtue of section 144 of the 1988 Act, unless the use is in fact covered by such a contract;

   (c) a claim by, or for the benefit of, a person ('the beneficiary') other than the person suffering death, injury or other damage which is made either—

(i) in respect of a cause of action or a judgment which has been assigned to the beneficiary, or

(ii) pursuant to a right of subrogation or contractual or other right belonging to the beneficiary;

(d) a claim in respect of damage to a motor vehicle or losses arising therefrom where, at the time when the damage to it was sustained—

(i) there was not in force in relation to the use of that vehicle such a contract of insurance as is required by Part VI of the 1988 Act, and

(ii) the claimant either knew or ought to have known that that was the case;

(e) a claim which is made in respect of a relevant liability described in paragraph (2) by a claimant who, at the time of the use giving rise to the relevant liability was voluntarily allowing himself to be carried in the vehicle and, either before the commencement of his journey in the vehicle or after such commencement if he could reasonably be expected to have alighted from it, knew or ought to have known that—

(i) the vehicle had been stolen or unlawfully taken,

(ii) the vehicle was being used without there being in force in relation to its use such a contract of insurance as would comply with Part VI of the 1988 Act,

(iii) the vehicle was being used in the course or furtherance of a crime, or

(iv) the vehicle was being used as a means of escape from, or avoidance of, lawful apprehension.

(2) The relevant liability referred to in paragraph (1)(e) is a liability incurred by the owner or registered keeper or a person using the vehicle in which the claimant was being carried.

(3) The burden of proving that the claimant knew or ought to have known of any matter set out in paragraph (1)(e) shall be on MIB but, in the absence of evidence to the contrary, proof by MIB of any of the following matters shall be taken as proof of the claimant's knowledge of the matter set out in paragraph (1)(e)(ii)—

(a) that the claimant was the owner or registered keeper of the vehicle or had caused or permitted its use;

(b) that the claimant knew the vehicle was being used by a person who was below the minimum age at which he could be granted a licence authorising the driving of a vehicle of that class;

(c) that the claimant knew that the person driving the vehicle was disqualified for holding or obtaining a driving licence;

(d) that the claimant knew that the user of the vehicle was neither its owner nor registered keeper nor an employee of the owner or registered keeper nor the owner or registered keeper of any other vehicle.

(4) Knowledge which the claimant has or ought to have for the purposes of paragraph (1)(e) includes knowledge of matters which he could reasonably be expected to have been aware of had he not been under the self-induced influence of drink or drugs.

(5) For the purposes of this clause—

(a) a vehicle which has been unlawfully removed from the possession of the Crown shall be taken to continue in that possession whilst it is kept so removed,

(b) references to a person being carried in a vehicle include references to his being carried upon, entering, getting on to and alighting from the vehicle, and

(c) 'owner', in relation to a vehicle which is the subject of a hiring agreement or a hire-purchase agreement, means the person in possession of the vehicle under that agreement.

CONDITIONS PRECEDENT TO MIB'S OBLIGATION

Form of application

7. (1) MIB shall incur no liability under MIB's obligation unless an application is made to the person specified in clause 9(1)—

(a) in such form,

(b) giving such information about the relevant proceedings and other matters relevant to this Agreement, and

(c) accompanied by such documents as MIB may reasonably require.

(2) Where an application is signed by a person who is neither the claimant nor a Solicitor acting on his behalf MIB may refuse to accept the application (and shall incur no liability under MIB's obligation) until it is reasonably satisfied that, having regard to the status of the signatory and his relationship to the claimant, the claimant is fully aware of the contents and effect of the application but subject thereto MIB shall not refuse to accept such an application by reason only that it is signed by a person other than the claimant or his Solicitor.

Service of notices etc.

8. Any notice required to be given or documents to be supplied to MIB pursuant to clauses 9 to 12 of this Agreement shall be sufficiently given or supplied only if sent by facsimile transmission or by Registered or Recorded Delivery post to MIB's registered office for the time being and delivery shall be proved by the production of a facsimile transmission report produced by the sender's facsimile machine or an appropriate postal receipt.

Notice of relevant proceedings

9. (1) MIB shall incur no liability under MIB's obligation unless proper notice of the bringing of the relevant proceedings has been given by the claimant not later than fourteen days after the commencement of those proceedings—

   (a) in the case of proceedings in respect of a relevant liability which is covered by a contract of insurance with an insurer whose identity can be ascertained, to that insurer;

   (b) in any other case, to MIB.

(2) In this clause 'proper notice' means, except in so far as any part of such information or any copy document or other thing has already been supplied under clause 7–

   (a) notice in writing that proceedings have been commenced by Claim Form, Writ, or other means,

   (b) a copy of the sealed Claim Form, Writ or other official document providing evidence of the commencement of the proceedings and, in Scotland, a statement of the means of service,

   (c) a copy or details of any insurance policy providing benefits in the case of the death, bodily injury or damage to property to which the proceedings relate where the claimant is the insured party and the benefits are available to him,

(d) copies of all correspondence in the possession of the claimant or (as the case may be) his Solicitor or agent to or from the Defendant or the Defender or (as the case may be) his Solicitor, insurers or agent which is relevant to—

    (i)   the death, bodily injury or damage for which the Defendant or Defender is alleged to be responsible, or

    (ii) any contract of insurance which covers, or which may or has been alleged to cover, liability for such death, injury or damage the benefit of which is, or is claimed to be, available to Defendant or Defender,

(e) subject to paragraph (3), a copy of the Particulars of Claim whether or not indorsed on the Claim form, Writ or other originating process, and whether or not served (in England and Wales) on any Defendant or (in Scotland) on any Defender, and

(f) a copy of all other documents which are required under the appropriate rules of procedure to be served on a Defendant or Defender with the Claim form, Writ or other originating process or with the Particulars of Claim,

(g) such other information about the relevant proceedings as MIB may reasonably specify.

(3) If, in the case of proceedings commenced in England or Wales, the Particulars of Claim (including any document required to be served therewith) has not yet been served with the Claim Form or other originating process paragraph (2)(e) shall be sufficiently complied with if a copy thereof is served on MIB not later than seven days after it is served on the Defendant.

Notice of service of proceedings

10. (1) This clause applies where the relevant proceedings are commenced in England or Wales.

(2) MIB shall incur no liability under MIB's obligation unless the claimant has, not later than the appropriate date, given notice in writing to the person specified in clause 9(1) of the date of service of the Claim Form or other originating process in the relevant proceedings.

(3) In this clause, 'the appropriate date' means the day falling—

    (a) seven days after—

        (i) the date when the claimant receives notification from the Court that service of the Claim form or other originating process has occurred,

        (ii) the date when the claimant receives notification from the Defendant that service of the Claim Form or other originating process has occurred, or

        (iii) the date of personal service, or

    (b) fourteen days after the date when service is deemed to have occurred in accordance with the Civil Procedure Rules,

whichever of those days occurs first.

Further information

11. (1) MIB shall incur no liability under MIB's obligation unless the claimant has, not later than seven days after the occurrence of any of the following events, namely—

    (a) the filing of a defence in the relevant proceedings,

    (b) any amendment to the Particulars of Claim or any amendment of or addition to any schedule or other document required to be served therewith, and

    (c) either—

        (i) the setting down of the case for trial, or

        (ii) where the court gives notice to the claimant of the trial date, the date when the notice is received,

given notice in writing of the date of that event to the person specified in clause 9(1) and has, in the case of the filing of a defence or an amendment of the Particulars of Claim or any amendment of or addition to any schedule or other document required to be served therewith, supplied a copy thereof to that person.

(2) MIB shall incur no liability under MIB's obligation unless the claimant furnishes to the person specified in clause 9(1) within a reasonable time after being required to do so such further

information and documents in support of his claim as MIB may reasonably require notwithstanding that the claimant may have complied with clause 7(1).

Notice of intention to apply for judgment

12. (1) MIB shall incur no liability under MIB's obligation unless the claimant has, after commencement of the relevant proceedings and not less than thirty-five days before the appropriate date, given notice in writing to the person specified in clause 9(1) of his intention to apply for or to sign judgment in the relevant proceedings.

  (2) In this clause, 'the appropriate date' means the date when the application for judgment is made or, as the case may be, the signing of judgment occurs.

Section 154 of the 1988 Act

13. MIB shall incur no liability under MIB's obligation unless the claimant has as soon as reasonably practicable—

  (a) demanded the information and, where appropriate, the particulars specified in section 154(1) of the 1988 Act, and

  (b) if the person of whom the demand is made fails to comply with the provisions of that subsection—

    (i) made a formal complaint to a police officer in respect of such failure, and

    (ii) used all reasonable endeavours to obtain the name and address of the registered keeper of the vehicle.

  or, if so required by MIB, has authorised MIB to take such steps on his behalf.

Prosecution of proceedings

14. MIB shall incur no liability under MIB's obligation—

  (a) unless the claimant has, if so required by MIB and having been granted a full indemnity by MIB as to costs, taken all reasonable steps to obtain judgment against every person who may be liable (including any person who may be vicariously liable) in respect of the injury or death or damage to property, or

(b) if the claimant, upon being requested to do so by MIB, refuses to consent to MIB being joined as a party to the relevant proceedings.

Assignment of judgment and undertakings

15. MIB shall incur no liability under MIB's obligation unless the claimant has—

(a) assigned to MIB or its nominee the unsatisfied judgment, whether or not that judgment includes an amount in respect of a liability other than a relevant liability, and any order for costs made in the relevant proceedings, and

(b) undertaken to repay to MIB any sum paid to him—

(i) by MIB in discharge of MIB's obligation if the judgment is subsequently set aside either as a whole or in respect of the part of the relevant liability to which that sum relates;

(ii) by any other person by way of compensation or benefit for the death, bodily injury or other damage to which the relevant proceedings relate, including a sum which would have been deductible under the provisions of clause 17 if it had been received before MIB was obliged to satisfy MIB's obligation.

LIMITATIONS ON MIB's LIABILITY

Compensation for damage to property

16. (1) Where a claim under this Agreement includes a claim in respect of damage to property, MIB's obligation in respect of that part of the relevant sum which is awarded for such damage and any losses arising therefrom (referred to in this clause as 'the property damage compensation') is limited in accordance with the following paragraphs.

(2) Where the property damage compensation does not exceed the specified excess, MIB shall incur no liability.

(3) Where the property damage compensation in respect of any one accident exceeds the specified excess but does not exceed £250,000, MIB shall incur liability only in respect of the property damage compensation less the specified excess.

(4) Where the property damage compensation in respect of any one accident exceeds £250,000, MIB shall incur liability only in respect of the sum of £250,000 less the specified excess.

Compensation received from other sources

17. Where a claimant has received compensation from—

(a) the Policyholders Protection Board under the Policyholders Protection Act 1975, or

(b) an insurer under an insurance agreement or arrangement, or

(c) any other source,

in respect of the death, bodily injury or other damage to which the relevant proceedings relate and such compensation has not been taken into account in the calculation of the relevant sum MIB may deduct from the relevant sum, in addition to any sum deductible under clause 16, an amount equal to that compensation.

MISCELLANEOUS

Notifications of decisions by MIB

18. Where a claimant—

(a) has made an application in accordance with clause 7, and

(b) has given to the person specified in clause 9(1) proper notice of the relevant proceedings in accordance with clause 9(2),

MIB shall—

(i) give a reasoned reply to any request made by the claimant relating to the payment of compensation in pursuance of MIB's obligation, and

(ii) as soon as reasonably practicable notify the claimant in writing of its decision regarding the payment of the relevant sum, together with the reasons for that decision.

Reference of disputes to the Secretary of State

19. (1) In the event of any dispute as to the reasonableness of a requirement made by MIB for the supply of information or documentation or for the taking of any step by the claimant, it may be referred by the claimant or MIB to the Secretary of State whose decision shall be final.

(2) Where a dispute is referred to the Secretary of State—

    (a) MIB shall supply the Secretary of State and, if it has not already done so, the claimant with notice in writing of the requirement from which the dispute arises, together with the reasons for that requirement and such further information as MIB considers relevant, and

    (b) where the dispute is referred by the claimant, the claimant shall supply the Secretary of State and, if he has not already done so, MIB with notice in writing of the grounds on which he disputes the reasonableness of the requirement.

Recoveries

20. Nothing in this Agreement shall prevent an insurer from providing by conditions in a contract of insurance that all sums paid by the insurer or by MIB by virtue of the Principal Agreement or this Agreement in or towards the discharge of the liability of the insured shall be recoverable by them or by MIB from the insured or from any other person.

Apportionment of damages, etc.

21. (1) Where an unsatisfied judgment which includes an amount in respect of a liability other than a relevant liability has been assigned to MIB or its nominee in pursuance of clause 15 MIB shall—

    (a) apportion any sum it receives in satisfaction or partial satisfaction of the judgment according to the proportion which the damages awarded in respect of the relevant liability bear to the damages awarded in respect of the other liability, and

    (b) account to the claimant in respect of the moneys received properly apportionable to the other liability.

(2) Where the sum received includes an amount in respect of interest or an amount awarded under an order for costs, the interest or the amount received in pursuance of the order shall be dealt with in the manner provided in paragraph (1).

Agents

22. MIB may perform any of its obligations under this Agreement by agents.

Transitional provisions

23. (1) The 1988 Agreement shall continue in force in relation to claims arising out of accidents occurring before 1st October 1999 with the modifications contained in paragraph (2).

(2) In relation to any claim made under the 1988 Agreement after this Agreement has come into force, the 1988 Agreement shall apply as if there were inserted after clause 6 thereof—

'6A. Where any person in whose favour a judgment in respect of a relevant liability has been made has—

(a) made a claim under this Agreement, and

(b) satisfied the requirements specified in clause 5 hereof,

MIB shall, if requested to do so, give him a reasoned reply regarding the satisfaction of that claim.'

IN WITNESS whereof the Secretary of State has caused his Corporate Seal to be hereunto affixed and the Motor Insurers' Bureau has caused its Common Seal to be hereunto affixed the day and year first above written.

> THE CORPORATE SEAL of the Secretary of State FOR THE ENVIRONMENT, TRANSPORT AND THE REGIONS hereunto affixed is authenticated by:–
> Richard Jones
> Authorised Secretary of State
>
> THE COMMON SEAL OF THE MOTOR INSURERS' BUREAU was hereunto affixed in the presence of:–
>
> James Arthur Read
> Roger Merer Jones
> Directors of the Board of Management
>
> Byford Louisy
> Secretary

Witness Questionnaire

Dear

We act for .... who was involved in a road traffic accident which occurred on .... the .... of .... 2000 at about .... am/pm at .... We understand that you may have witnessed the accident and would be grateful if you would kindly complete this questionnaire and return it within fourteen days in the stamped addressed envelope enclosed.

Name _____ Home Tel No: _____

Address _____ Business Tel No. _____

Age _____ Email address: _____

Occupation _____

1. Describe   (i)   the weather conditions e.g. bright sunlight, fine and clear, overcast, raining, snowing etc;

           (ii)   the visibility e.g. daylight, dark, twilight, fog etc. If dark, describe the street lighting, if at all;

           (iii)   the road conditions e.g. dry, damp, wet, standing water, icy, snow-covered etc;

           (iv)   the traffic e.g. congested, heavy, medium, light or very light.

2. Describe   (i)   whether you are travelling as a driver, passenger (please state the type of vehicle and your position within it) or pedestrian;

           (ii)   your exact location at the time of the accident, with reference to the distance between you and the collision;

State   (iii) if you actually saw the accident;

          (iv) if your view of the accident was obstructed in any way. If so, describe the impediment and state how long your view was obstructed;

3. Describe   (i) each vehicle involved in the accident, with reference to type, colour and registration number;

          (ii) the position, direction of travel and speed of each vehicle immediately before the collision.

4. Describe, in your own words, how the accident actually happened.

PLEASE STATE ONLY WHAT YOU SAW YOURSELF

Refer – if applicable – to the following:

(i)   obedience or disobedience of a relevant traffic sign or light;

(ii) were any signals given by the driver(s)?

(iii) whether any horns were sounded;

(iv) use of headlights, side lights or indicators;

(v) was the noise of the collision audible or inaudible?

(vi) the damage to the vehicles or any injury to persons.

Please draw a rough sketch showing the position of the vehicles immediately before and after the accident.

5. Describe any other relevant factors e.g. roadworks, temporary signs or road markings or malfunctioning traffic lights.
6. Did the police attend the scene of the accident and, if so, were any of the vehicles moved before they arrived?
7. Describe each driver: refer to sex, age, build, hair and clothing. Would you recognise each driver?
8. Were you involved in or did you witness any post-accident conversation? If yes, can you give the exact words used or the gist of the exchange?
9. Do you know of anyone else who saw the accident? Can you give the names and addresses of any other witnesses?
10. Do you consider any person to be to blame for the accident? If so, give brief reasons.

Thank you very much for your assistance.

Pre-Action Protocol for Road Traffic Accidents

1. Introduction

1.1 The RTA Protocol forms the basis of the terms and conditions for the handling of all traffic claims between Solicitors and Insurers.

The objective is to set out a series of standards between the parties in respect of pre-issue conduct in handling all claims arising from a road traffic accident to include damage only and personal injury claims. The protocol includes procedures on general matters of conduct and early exchange of information; and an agreed level of costs.

The protocol is an opportunity to remove the uncertainty and mistrust between the parties, and to give stability and understanding between the parties with the common goal of improving the communication and speed of settlement of the claims handling process.

1.2 It is intended that the protocol be run initially under a pilot scheme. It is accepted by both parties that both clients consent must be sought prior to the claim being run under the pilot scheme.

1.3 The reference to the word 'Solicitor' shall mean any employee of the firm of Solicitors handling the claim on behalf of the claimant and shall not be construed as a person passing themselves off as a Solicitor when they are not in fact a qualified Solicitor.

2. Part 1 – Standards

2.1 Solicitors

Solicitors in the pursuit of compensation for victims of a road traffic accident, agree as follows:

2.1.1 To answer correspondence (including Fax and e-mail) received from Insurers within 7 working days and to abide by timetables set out under items 3 to 8 inclusive

2.1.2 To return all telephone calls, including voice mail messages, from Insurers (which are not immediately answered) within one working day at the latest and to attempt to return the call on the same day if practicable.

2.1.3 In all forms of communication, to be polite and courteous.

2.1.4 To nominate an individual within the Solicitor's office who will become the liaison officer in respect of the Protocol and to deal with any matter arising thereunder. To identify this contact name in the 'Solicitor's initial letter' and to make known the name of such person to any Insurer who enquires.

2.2 Insurers

Insurers in the receipt of claims for compensation arising out of a road traffic accident, agree as follows:

2.2.1 To answer correspondence (including Fax and e-mail) received from MASS Members within 7 working days and to abide by timetables set out under items 3 to 8 inclusive.

2.2.2 To return all telephone calls, including voice mail messages, from Solicitors (which are not immediately answered) within one working day at the latest and to attempt to return the call on the same day if practicable.

2.2.3 In all forms of communication, to be polite and courteous.

2.2.4 To nominate an individual within the office who will become the liaison officer in respect of the Protocol and to deal with any matter arising thereunder. To identify this contact name in the 'Insurer's first letter' and to make known the names of such person to any Solicitor who enquires.

2.2.5 Not to contact or communicate with the client direct without the consent of the Solicitor.

3. Part 2 – Claims Handling Procedures

To facilitate a speedy and efficient claims service, Solicitors and Insurers will ensure the early release and exchange of information regarding claims, without prejudicing the interests of the client. It is agreed that this will be undertaken by a series of letters and procedures between the parties as follows:

3.1 The 'Solicitor's initial letter' (Annex A)

3.1.1 The 'Solicitor's initial letter' will be sent (where the Insurer is known) within 7 working days of notification of the claim or within 7 working days of identifying the Insurer. This letter will be clearly identified as the 'Solicitor's initial letter' and will include the following information: name of Solicitor's nominated liaison officer; the contact name of the person dealing with the claim and their direct dial number, full name and address of all claimants; and where known, vehicle location; vehicle make and registration number; details of vehicle hire to include company, rates, type of vehicle, if appropriate, a copy of the engineer's report and estimate of repairs; details of injuries sustained, if any; date of birth and National Insurance Number; VAT Registered (Y/N); the reasons for the claim, *i.e.* allegations of negligence and the clients own insurance details, *i.e.* name, address, policy number and type of insurance.

3.2 The 'Insurer's first letter' (Annex D)

3.2.1 The Insurer will respond within 7 working days upon receipt of the 'Solicitor's initial letter'. This letter will be clearly identified as the 'Insurer's first letter' and will acknowledge receipt of the 'Solicitor's initial letter'; provide the name of the Insurer's nominated liaison officer; the contact name of the person dealing with the claim and their direct dial number; and if appropriate, confirmation and details of the inspection process and the date by which the engineer's report will be available. The Insurer will also indicate the following: whether liability is under consideration; undisputed or disputed and if disputed, enclose copy of witness statements if available.

3.2.2 Where the Insurer is unable to trace the policy number, the Insurer will telephone the Solicitor to request any further information required to identify the insurers.

3.3 The 'Solicitor's second letter' (Annex B)

3.3.1 The Solicitor will forward a 'second letter' within 28 working days of receipt of the 'Insurer's first letter'. This letter will be clearly identified as the 'Solicitor's second letter' and will contain a brief outline of the following: confirmation of whether pursuing (i) non injury claim or (ii) injury claim (to include: extent of the injuries, name and address of NHS hospital attended and commissioning of medical report); client's occupation and period off work (if appropriate); details of loss of use / car hire; storage; and vehicle location if not already advised in the 'initial letter'; liability is/is not in issue; witness statements / details of witnesses (if available).

3.4 The 'Insurer's second letter' (Annex E)

3.4.1 Within 14 working days of receipt of the 'Solicitor's second letter', the Insurer will respond with the 'Insurer's second letter'. This letter will be clearly identified as the 'Insurer's second letter' and will provide the following: confirmation of RTA cover; whether liability is in dispute and if in dispute, copy of witness summaries, if any; confirmation of inspection process; approval of repairs and if appropriate, delivery of an interim cheque for repairs; agree hire rate/propose replacement vehicle as stated in clause 3.9.1. (If liability in dispute **then** the Insurer will obtain police report and forward a copy to the claimants Solicitor.)

3.5 Correspondence and telephone communication

All information contained in the above letters can be provided by telephone communication between the parties, provided that each party makes a detailed note of the information given, the date and time of the call and the parties to the conversation. It is also recommended that all subsequent communication be undertaken by telephone between the parties, noting all details in a similar manner.

3.6 Engineers' reports

3.6.1 The Insurer will forward a copy of the engineer's report to the Solicitor within 7 working days of receipt of the engineer's finding as indicated in the Insurer's 'first letter'.

3.6.2 If the Insurer has not confirmed in the Insurer's 'first letter' that an engineer's report has been commissioned, then the Solicitor will be at liberty to arrange their own report and such report shall be an allowable disbursement in accordance with clause 7.1.

3.7 Repairable propositions (liability not in dispute)

3.7.1 In the event of the Insurer not undertaking the repairs, the client will elect to undertake one of the following:
(a) to receive a cheque for repairs to be taken by client;
(b) to receive cash in lieu.

3.7.2 The Solicitor will notify the Insurer of the elected option within 8 working days and the Insurer will within 7 working days either: (1) despatch a cheque or (ii) commence or authorise repairs.

3.7.3 Loss of use will be recoverable for a further 7 working days following receipt of the cheque by the Solicitor or completion of repairs whichever is the later and provided that the repairs are commenced promptly on receipt of the cheque. (For loss of use rates, see 7.2.2.)

3.8 Irreparable propositions (liability not in dispute)

3.8.1 All Insurers party to this Protocol adhere to the Motor Conference 'Code of Practice for the Disposal of Motor Vehicle Salvage to Detect and Deter Criminal Activity' and copy of which is appended hereto.

3.8.2 If the vehicle is a write-off, the report or an accompanying letter will provide confirmation that an interim cheque will be sent within 7 working days. If the client disagrees with the Insurer's valuation and obtains a second report, the Insurer agrees to meet the costs of valuation if the agreed figure exceeds the first valuation by 15%.

3.8.3 The Insurer will not dispose of the vehicle without first obtaining the owner's consent.

3.8.4 If a courtesy vehicle has been provided or the client is hiring a vehicle, then the Insurer agrees that such hire shall continue and form part of the value of the claim until a period of 7 working days after receipt of the settlement cheque for the vehicle by the Solicitor. (For hire rates, see 7.2.4.)

3.9 Hire

3.9.1 If the Client is already hiring a vehicle, then the insurer shall undertake either of the following:
(i)   agree the hire rate, period and type of vehicle; or
(ii) provide a suitable replacement vehicle.

If (i) above, the solicitor will provide copy of the hire account to the Insurer upon request.

3.9.2 If a courtesy/replacement vehicle is provided by the Insurer, the Insurer shall be responsible for the insurance for the said vehicle and any deposit for the fuel shall not exceed £50. The client shall be responsible for all fuel consumption.

3.9.3 Where the Insurer has arranged a courtesy/replacement vehicle, a copy of the account as evidence of the period of replacement, shall be supplied to the Solicitor upon request.

3.9.4 The Insurer will arrange for courtesy/replacement vehicle delivery and collection.

3.10 *Storage charges*

3.10.1 Upon notification to the Insurer of the vehicle location, the Insurer shall be responsible for all storage charges until the Insurers engineer has inspected the vehicle and either an agreement has been made in accordance with clause 3.6 or a cheque paid in accordance with clause 3.7.

3.10.2 If the Insurer elects to move the vehicle to their own storage facility, the Clients consent must be obtained and 7 working days notice must be given in writing to the Solicitor, providing confirmation of vehicle location. This facility will allow access to the vehicle by the Solicitor's engineer if so required.

3.11 *VAT*

3.11.1 In all cases where the client is VAT registered, a separate, VAT only invoice will be forwarded by the Insurer or agent/repairer direct to the Client and the client will be responsible for discharging the VAT due.

3.11.2 The Insurer will pay the appropriate rate of VAT on the vehicle hire.

3.11.3 Where the claimant is VAT registered the insurer shall not be responsible for VAT on the Solicitors costs where the vehicle is being used for business purposes. VAT is to be collected by the Solicitor from the claimant.

3.12 *Medical evidence*

3.12.1 This section applies to instruction of medical experts. It is intended as a facility to reduce time, cost of instruction and dispute on expert evidence where there is direct or medical agency instruction.

3.12.2 Before the Solicitor or Insurer instructs an expert, the instructing party shall provide the other party with a list of the name(s) of one or more expert in the relevant speciality whom he considers suitable to instruct.

3.12.3 Where the instructing party intends to rely on an Agency selection, the instructing party shall request the Agency, to appoint a medical expert and:

(a) By way of Enquiry, provide to the instructing party with the names of alternative experts (prior to instruction of an expert) for disclosure to the other party.

(b) On receipt by the instructing Solicitor of details of the expert appointed, the name and location of the appointed expert should be disclosed to the other party.

3.12.4 Where details of an expert are disclosed to the other party under paragraphs 3.12.2 or 3.12.3 above, that party shall within 10 working days indicate any objection to one or more of the proposed experts. Should the instructing Solicitor receive no response within the expressed time limit, acceptance of the expert or experts disclosed is implied.

3.12.5 Where an objection is raised under 3.12.2 or 3.12.3 within the 10 working days time limit, the instructing Solicitor shall select and instruct another expert in the relevant speciality or request the Agency to so instruct.

3.12.6 If the other party objects to all the listed experts in 3.12.2 or 3.12.3 or to the second expert selected the parties may then instruct experts of their own choice within 5 working days. It would be for the court to decide subsequently if proceedings are issued whether either party acted unreasonably.

3.12.7 If the other party does not object to a nominated expert, then the other party shall not be entitled to rely on their own expert evidence within that particular speciality unless:

(a) the first party agrees;

(b) the Court so directs, or;

(c) the instructing party's expert report has been amended and the instructing party is not prepared to disclose the original report.

3.12.8 The instructed expert may be required to obtain all medical notes and records relating to the accident, the cost of which will be met by the instructing party in the first instance and reimbursed by the Insurer on request. For the avoidance of doubt the obtaining of medical records is discretionary but in any event the expert will be required to confirm whether he has reviewed the claimants GP records.

3.12.9 Upon receipt of the Client's consent to the medical report and its disclosure the Solicitor will forward a copy of the report to the Insurer within 10 working days.

3.12.10 Either party may send to the agreed expert written questions on the report relevant to the issues, via the instructing party. The expert should send answers to the questions separately and directly to each party. The cost incurred by the expert(s) in providing answers to the questions raised shall be paid by the party raising the relevant questions.

3.13 Claims where liability is not in dispute (non injury)

3.13.1 Upon receipt of the 'Insurer's second letter' confirming liability is not in dispute and provided that full particulars of claims have been presented, the parties will contact one another within 15 working days to discuss settlement of the claim. Within this period no proceedings will be issued by the Solicitor.

3.14 Claims where liability is not in dispute (injury)

3.14.1 Upon receipt of the Solicitor's medical report, the Insurer will undertake either of the following:

(i) Make an offer of settlement within 10 working days, where requested, or;

(ii) Advise the Solicitor if obtaining own medical report in accordance with the provisions set out in clause 3.12, and;

(iii) Forward a copy of the Insurer's medical report to the Solicitor within 10 working days from the date of receipt, provided the Insurer intends to rely upon this report.

3.14.2 If the offer of settlement is not accepted by the client, then a further 14 day period will be granted to allow for continued negotiation and during which period no proceedings will be issued by the Solicitor.

3.15 Claims where liability is in dispute

3.15.1 The Solicitor will, within 10 working days of receipt of the 'Insurer's second letter', in which liability is disputed and witness statements are attached, forward the 'Solicitor's third letter' to be clearly identified as such and to include the Solicitor's own witness summaries (Annex C).

3.15.2 A further 10 working day period will be allowed for discussions and within which time, no proceedings will be issued.

3.15.3 If liability and/or settlement cannot be agreed within the 10 days discussion period, a police report, if such exists, will be obtained by the insurer and copied to the Solicitor within 7 working days.

3.15.4 If agreement cannot be reached within a further 10 day period from the exchange of the police report, then either party may issue proceedings, giving the appropriate notice.

3.15.5 In cases where a Claimant is unlikely to be able to return to pre-accident employment within 6 months, both sides will consider whether it is appropriate for a referral to be made to the Disability Assessment unit or similar body for immediate interim help and such assessment to be funded by the Insurer.

3.16 Settlement arrangement and interest

3.16.1 Upon confirmation of the client's agreement to the settlement offer, the insurer will forward a cheque within 10 working days. If at the end of this period no cheque has been received, the Solicitor will notify the Insurer of such by telephone. If the cheque is not received within 20 working days, interest will commence accruing at the rate of 25% per annum on a daily rate basis until receipt of the settlement cheque by the Solicitor, such cheque to include the interest due. Exception to this clause applies only where receipt of a CRU certificate is pending and the Insurer has duly notified the Solicitor. The Insurer will have made all attempts to have secured this certificate at the earliest opportunity. Interest will not be payable within this period and will commence accruing following 10 working days of receipt of the certificate.

4. Calculation of Time Periods

For the avoidance of doubt in the calculation of all time periods, days will be considered in working days and date of receipt will be assumed to be one day after the date of dispatch.

5. Part 36 Offers

5.1 In accordance with the spirit of the protocol it is suggested that Part 36 offers of settlement should not be made unless the claim involves other parties not operating their claim in accordance with this protocol. Parties would then be free to make such offers but only when the other party (not party to the protocol) makes a Part 36 offer of settlement.

6. Solicitor's Procedures

6.1 Solicitors further agree:

6.1.1 To abide by arrangements set up by Insurers for repairs, courtesy cars, hire vehicles, etc.

6.1.2 To report all offers in writing to the client within 3 working days of receipt.

6.1.3 If proceedings are issued and judgment is obtained, to serve a copy immediately on the known Insurer and allow the Insurer 7 working days to present proposals for settlement.

6.1.4 To welcome visits from Insurers' representatives and to supply the representative with a detailed schedule of claim (if available) prior to the visit

6.1.5 To release signed forms of authority for release of relevant medical records when requested on an agreed standard form (Annex F).

7. Insurers' Procedures

7.1 Insurers further agree:

7.1.1 To pay costs as detailed in Annex G.

In addition, VAT at the prevailing rate and all reasonable disbursements will be paid. (N.B. paragraph 7.1.1 regarding payment of costs will not apply to claims from Northern Ireland and Scotland where own costs scales shall prevail.)

7.1.2 A cheque for the agreed costs will be dispatched at the same time as the settlement cheque in accordance with the time frame indicated in clause 3.16.1 above. If the costs cheque is not received within this period, the Insurer shall pay interest on the outstanding costs at the rate of 25% per annum calculated on a daily rate basis.

7.1.3 These cost schedules shall be reviewed on an annual basis in accordance with clause II.

7.1.4 In cases where the value of the claim exceeds £15,000, costs will be by agreement or detailed assessment and in default of agreement, Insurers will consent to an application for a detailed assessment.

7.2 Calculation of the value of the claim

7.2.1 In determining the value of a claim in accordance with the attached scale of costs, there shall be no deduction for any sum payable to the CRU.

7.2.2 For claims where no courtesy vehicle is provided or a hire vehicle obtained by the client and where loss of use and enjoyment of a vehicle is appropriate, the rate of £60 per week shall be calculated for loss of use claims unless there are exceptional circumstances (*i.e.,* where the size and type of vehicle would warrant a higher figure or where a client may be on holiday and a loss of use claim would not be applicable). Notice of any 'exceptional circumstances' will be given in the *Solicitor's* 'second letter'.

7.2.3 The period for loss of use will expire following 7 working days of the receipt of the settlement cheque for the vehicle; or on the date of return of the vehicle following repair.

7.2.4 If a courtesy vehicle is provided by the Insurer, the Insurer will confirm the period of the loan and this will be displayed on the repair invoice. A rate of £20 per day will be applied for calculation of the value of the claim.

7.2.5 If the Insurer elects to provide a hire vehicle to the client, a daily rate of £20 will be applied in the calculation of the value of the claim. The Insurer will confirm the period of hire and provide such evidence if so requested by the Solicitor.

Such period of hire will continue until the said vehicle has either been repaired or until the expiry of 7 working days following receipt of the settlement cheque for the vehicle by the Solicitor. This period will, for the sake of clarity, also apply to claims where the client has obtained a hire vehicle.

7.2.6 In cases of contributory negligence, costs will be paid on the full value of the claim.

7.2.7 It is agreed that claims for insurer outlay can form part of the claim but that regardless of the value of the outlay the claim for costs, will be limited to £75 plus VAT and any reasonable disbursements (only on the basis that the Memorandum of Understanding has been followed), and shall not be added to the value of the balance of the claim in order to calculate the overall value of the claim.

7.3 Notification of a client's misdemeanour

If the Insurer discovers evidence of wrong doing on the part of the client, immediate notification of such will be given to the Solicitor.

8. Disputes

All disputes must be referred to the liaison officers of each Organisation who will attempt to resolve the dispute. If agreement cannot be reached then either:—

1. The parties agree that the matter cannot be dealt with in accordance with this Protocol and the claim must be dealt with outside this Protocol, or;

2. Notice is given in writing by either party that the dispute be resolved by the Chairperson of MASS and the nominated Chairperson for the Insurers.

9. Breaches of the Agreement

If any party wishes to submit a complaint regarding breaches of this Protocol by any Solicitor or Insurer, then such complaint giving details must be made in writing and sent for the attention of the nominated Solicitors Chairperson and Insurers Chairperson.

The alleged responsible party will be advised of the complaint and will be given the opportunity to make representations on their account of any allegations.

The respective Chairpersons will then meet and discuss the complaint and decide its validity. If the complaint is upheld then the member found responsible will be advised of the disciplinary procedure which will be either:

(a) a written reprimand;
(b) suspension from the Protocol Pilot;
(c) expulsion from the Protocol Pilot.

10. Procedure

All those members of staff who handle road traffic accident claims within the offices of participating Solicitors and Insurers will be notified of the Protocol, in terms and members.

All Solicitors and Insurers will advise their respective staff of the nominated liaison officer for each member and ensure that a list is available to all staff of such individuals and their role in the Protocol.

Any agreed changes to this Protocol must be communicated to all relevant staff within 7 working days of the liaison officer being notified of the changes.

A liaison Sub-Committee comprising of two nominated representatives for Solicitors and two nominated representatives for Insurers to be set up to meet on a bi-annual basis to discuss the Protocol, resolve problems and suggest and agree any alterations or improvements to the Protocol.

The Sub-Committee should also consider a method of assessing compliance with the Protocol.

Annex A (Clause 3.1)

Our ref.: ABCD/12345
Please ask for: Mr A N Other

*Date: within 7 working days of notification
of claim or identification of Insurer*

'Solicitor's Initial Letter' under the RTA Protocol Pilot

Dear Sirs,
Re: Our client
Your Insured: (full details where known) **Claim Ref No:**
Accident Date:

We hereby notify you of a claim which our client/s wish to pursue against your above name insured.

1. Our client's details are as follows:
   Name & Address
   Injured – Y/N
   Date of Birth
   National Insurance Number
   VAT registered – Y/N

2. Clients' insurance details:
   Name of Insurer
   Address
   Policy No./Claim Ref. Policy Type
   Policy Excess

3. Allegations of negligence:

4. Vehicle registration number, model and location (if known) and contact name:

5. Details of vehicle hire, if any, to include Company, rates, type of vehicle:

6. Copy of the engineer's report and estimate of repairs, if available:

7. Outline details of heads of claim (if known):

8. The nominated liaison officer is .... and contact name dealing with this claim is .... and their direct dial number is: ....

Yours faithfully

XYZ Solicitors

Annex B (Clause 3.3)

Our ref.: ABCD/12345
Please ask for: Mr A N Other

*Date: within 28 working days of receipt
of the Insurer's 'First letter'*

'Solicitor's Second Letter' under the RTA Protocol Pilot

Dear Sirs,

Re: Our Client
      Your Insured:
      Claim Ref No:
      Accident Date:

Further to your 'first letter' dated .... we confirm the following information:

1. **Injury claim**

There is no injury claim/Our client/s suffered the following injuries:

(a) Client 1

Treatment was/was not provided by a NHS Hospital – name and address of hospital

We are applying for a medical report /It is too soon to arrange a report/There is no medical report.

2. **Heads of claim**

    (a) Loss of use/car hire details to include Company, rates, type of vehicle;
    (b) Storage details;
    (c) Vehicle location:

(d) Client's occupation;
(e) Period off work (if appropriate) and to include loss of earnings (approx);
Contact .... on tel: .... to arrange an inspection.

3. Liability is under consideration/ is not in issue/is in issue and we enclose copies of witness statements/details of witnesses.

Yours faithfully

<u>XYZ Solicitors</u>

Annex C (Clause 3.15)

Our ref.: ABCD/12345
Please ask for: Mr A N Other

*Date: within 10 working days of receipt of the
Insurer's 'second letter' in which liability is disputed*

'Solicitor's Third Letter' under the RTA Protocol Pilot

Dear Sirs,

Re: Our Client Your Insured: Claim Ref No: Accident Date:

Further to your 'second letter' dated .... in which liability is disputed, we now enclose a copy of our witness summaries, not previously available or disclosed, to include ....

Yours faithfully

<u>XYZ Solicitors</u>

Annex D (Clause 3.2)

ZYX Insurance Company

Our ref.: ABCD/12345
Please ask for: Mr A N Other

*Date: within 7 working days of receipt
of Solicitor's 'initial letter'*

'Insurer's First Letter' under the RTA Protocol Pilot

Dear Sirs,

Your reference: **Incident date:**   **Insured:**
Our reference: **Claim reference:**
Liaison Officer: **Claim handled by & Tel No:**

We thank you for your 'Solicitor's initial letter' dated .... and your interest is noted.

We confirm:
— (We are/are not the Road Traffic Act 1988 Insurers for the above (insured).)
— (Your client's vehicle is being inspected by our Engineer and we will have the inspection report by ....)
— (Liability is under consideration/is not in issue/is in issue and we enclose copies of witness statements/details of witnesses.)

The following information was missing from your letter, please provide it by return:

1.
2.
3.

Yours faithfully

<u>XYZ Insurance Company</u>

Annex E (Clause 3.4)

ZYX Insurance Company

Our ref.: ABCD/12345
Please ask for: Mr A N Other

*Date: within 14 working days of receipt
of the 'Solicitor's second letter'*

'Insurer's Second Letter' under the RTA Protocol Pilot

Dear Sirs,

Your reference: Incident date: Insured:
Our reference: Claim reference:
Liaison Officer: Claim handled by & Tel No:
We thank you for your 'Solicitor's second letter dated ....

We confirm:

That we are/are not the Road Traffic Act 1988 Insurers for the above (insured)

(Liability is not in issue.)

(Liability is in issue and we enclose copies of witness summaries/details of witnesses.)

Your client's vehicle has been inspected and:

(The vehicle is repairable and we are prepared to offer by way of an interim payment a cheque for the sum of £............ for the repairs/in lieu of repairs.)

(We authorise repairs to be carried out at ABC garage/ABC will provide a courtesy vehicle for the period whilst the vehicle is being repaired.)

Please notify us within 7 working days of your client's preferred option

(The vehicle is not repairable and the salvage will be designated as
.... in accordance with the code of practice for the disposal of
motor vehicles under category ...., a cheque for the sum of
£................. is enclosed (salvage of £.............. has been deducted.)

(Hire rates of £.............. for the period of .... days are agreed/we
have arranged for 'DEF' hire company to provide your client with a
vehicle.)

Yours faithfully

XYZ Insurance Company

Annex F (Clause 6.1.5.)

Form of Authority for the Release of Medical Records

This personal injury claim is regulated by the Road Traffic Act Protocol, which encourages joint selection of, and access to medical experts. The Protocol promotes the practice of the claimant obtaining a medical report, disclosing it to the defendant who then asks questions and/or agrees to it and does not obtain his own report. Any medical report obtained by agreement under the Protocol should be disclosed to the other party.

Please complete and return to:

Name of firm:

NAME IN FULL: (including former name if changed since the accident)

....

DATE OF BIRTH: ....

NATIONAL INSURANCE NUMBER: ....

ADDRESS AND POSTCODE: (including former address if changed since the accident)

....

....

CONTACT TELEPHONE NUMBER:

Home: .... Work: ....

HOSPITAL ATTENDED: (if known, please give Record Number on appointment card and name of Consultant attending)

....

....

GENERAL PRACTITIONER'S NAME AND ADDRESS:

....

....

I confirm that I am not involved in litigation with any G.P. or Hospital Authority and consent to the disclosure of the following, which may be required for the purpose of pursuing my claim for personal injury:

1. G.P. Records
2. Hospital Records
3. Works Medical Records

I understand that if the report is obtained from an agreed expert under the Road Traffic Accident Protocol, it is possible that the other party's representative may make an application to Court for the disclosure of the report even though I may not agree to the report being disclosed.

Signed:..

Annex G

Cost Schedules
RTA Protocol Costs Proposal

NON PI (Including PI up to £1000)

Value of claim £	1–500	501–1000	1001–1500	1501–2000	2001–2500	2501–3000		
Costs £	50	150	213	263	288	313		
20% of the value of the claim 3001–5000		4000	5000					
Costs £		413	513					
12.5% of the difference of value of claim 5001–10000				6000	7000	8000	9000	10000
Costs £				638	763	888	1013	1138
				11000	12000	13000	14000	15000
Costs £				1263	1500	1625	1750	1875

PI Claims

Value of claim £	Costs £
1000–2000	750
2001–3000	1000
3001–4000	1250
4001–5000	1500
5000	
6000	1675
7000	1225
8000	1400
9000	1575
10000	1750

Costs £ 17.5% of the difference of value of claim 5001–10000

Value of claim £	Costs £
11000	1925
12000	2100
13000	2275
14000	2450
15000	2625

Costs £ 17.5% of the difference of value of claim 10001–15000

Examples

1. SD £1000,   GD £2000
                   Costs: SD   £ 150.00
                                 GD   £ 750.00
                                 Total £ 900.00

   Previous Protocol   £1050.00

2. SD £4000,   GD £5000
                   Costs: SD   £ 413.00
                                 GD   £1500.00

                                 Total £1913.00
   Previous Protocol   £2550.00

3. SD £8000,   GD £2000
                   Costs: SD   £ 800.00
                                 GD   £ 750.00
                                 Total £1638.00

   Previous Protocol   £2750.00

It is suggested that the SD claim and costs be paid at the time of payment of the SD claim. That the costs of GD be paid at the time the GD is paid.

Annex H (Clause 3.8.1)

Code of Practice for the Disposal of Motor Vehicle Salvage to Detect and Deter Criminal Activities

Introduction

This Code of Practice has been produced to give guidance to insurers on the steps to be taken in the treatment of salvage and recovered stolen vehicles. Representatives from the Police and DVLA have assisted in the preparation of this document and have given it their full support.

A side-effect of the Code will be to make vehicle histories much more transparent. This will do much to dispel public concern about the way in which the industry treats salvage.

Categorisation of Vehicle Salvage

Four categories of vehicle salvage have been defined. Details are given of the steps to be taken in advising DVLA and MIAFTR on each category, together with the consequential effects on actions by the police, database houses (Equifax—HPI and Experian) etc.

The inspecting engineer *must* decide and indicate to which of the four categories a particular item of salvage belongs. Other than to correct inputting errors, recategorisation or removal of MIAFTR data is prohibited.

Form V23 and MIAFTR

Form V23 should always be completed and returned to DVLA in respect of Category A, B, or C salvage. **It is vital that the current version of Form V23 is used and completed correctly and accurately, in particular the choice of tick boxes which indicate whether the vehicle is either scrap/break *or* other category of total loss.**

Similarly, care should be taken to ensure that notifications to MIAFTR are made properly and that amended/updated information is fed through quickly.

Conclusion

The categorisation of salvage as set out in this Code of Practice, together with the benefits of the V23 system and MIAFTR, will make it extremely difficult for criminals to ring vehicles or return dangerously repaired vehicles to the road.

Code of Practice for the Disposal of Motor Vehicle Salvage to Detect and Deter Criminal Activities

	CATEGORY A	CATEGORY B	CATEGORY C	CATEGORY D
Definition	SCRAP only (ie with no economically salvageable parts and which is of value only for scrap metal) eg total burn outs	BREAK for spare parts (plus any residual scrap metal)	REPAIRABLE (V23 must be submitted) i.e. repair costs exceed PAV **AND** PAV over £2,000 (£1,000 for motorcycles)	ALL OTHER REPAIRABLE VEHICLES
	These vehicles must never reappear on the road			
V23	Form V23 must be submitted to DVLA as soon as the categorisation decision is made and without waiting for V5			V23 not required
V5	A photocopy of the V5 should be given to the salvage buyer to assist in the identification of the salvage and the completion of the Notification of Destruction. For new style V5s (introduced 24 March 1997) complete the red section, signing on the insured's behalf, and return to DVLA. Shred the remaining parts of the V5. For pre-March 1997 V5s complete the V5/1 tear-off section and return to DVLA. Shred the remaining part of the V5.			V5 can be passed to new owner
	DVLA will not issue replacement V5 and notify any request to the police		DVLA will notify any relicensing activity to police for investigation	
MIAFTR "Loss type"	All total losses must be entered on MIAFTR as per the Code of Practice category – except that total burn-outs should be entered as "Fire".			
MIAFTR notes	Recovered stolen vehicles which are in a total loss condition must be categorised A, B, C or D as appropriate. Recovered stolen vehicles which are undamaged or with only minor damage must be notified to MIAFTR as recovered, **not** deleted. Any changes in a total loss category must be notified to MIAFTR.			
Database applications	All notifications to MIAFTR whether theft or damaged are passed to Equifax HPI and Experian for a finance check. The database houses use the information to provide a vehicle check service to the motor trade and the public. It is essential that loss information on MIAFTR is accurate and up to date.			
Documentation	All insurer documentation to salvage dealers (eg invoices) in respect of individual items of salvage must categorise the salvage as either A, B, C or D			
Responsibilities of the primary salvage buyer in the treatment of salvage/vehicles	SALVAGE MUST BE CRUSHED. The vehicle identification number (VIN) plate must be removed at the earliest possible opportunity and either held in secure storage or securely disposed of. The stamped in VIN must be left in situ and not interfered with in any way. Buyers of the salvage must complete and return to DVLA (with a copy to the insurer) a Notification of Destruction which confirms that the salvage has been/will be crushed. The vehicle must be de-identified immediately by the salvage buyer by removing all tax discs (old or new) and registration plates.	Category B must be treated as Category A once salvageable parts have been removed. THE SHELL/FRAME/CHASSIS MUST BE CRUSHED. Buyers of Category B salvage must complete and return to DVLA (with a copy to the insurer) a Notification of Destruction which confirms that shell/frame/chassis parts have been/will be crushed. Identification marks on engines and any other salvaged parts must not be erased. Air bags and seat belt components must be discharged and properly disposed of – these items must never be resold.	To be sold on for repair	
Note 1	It is imperative that the provisions of this Code of Practice are fully and expeditiously complied with in all circumstances by insurers.			
Note 2	Vehicles suffering water damage will usually be categorised A or B. It is for the inspecting engineer to determine, given the specific circumstances such as type of water (fresh, contaminated or salt), depth of submersion etc. whether a vehicle should be categorised A, B, C or D.			
Note 3	All bodyshells (which must be categorised A or B) or the subject of replacement in service must be crushed (NB special arrangements may apply to manufacturers' bodyshell schemes).			
Note 4	In the interest of environmental protection, insurers are strongly encouraged to utilise only the services of those salvage buyers/breakers who comply fully with the appropriate provisions of the Environmental Protection Act 1990.			
Note 5	The V23 marker should be considered a permanent part of a vehicle's history. In the rare event that it is necessary to recategorise a vehicle this can be achieved by writing to DVLA giving the reasons, together with the accident date.			
Note 6	Third party total losses should be categorised A, B, C or D and V23ed in the normal way. Insurers should endeavour to ensure that Category A and B vehicles do not return to the road.			

Flow Chart for Categorising Vehicles under Code

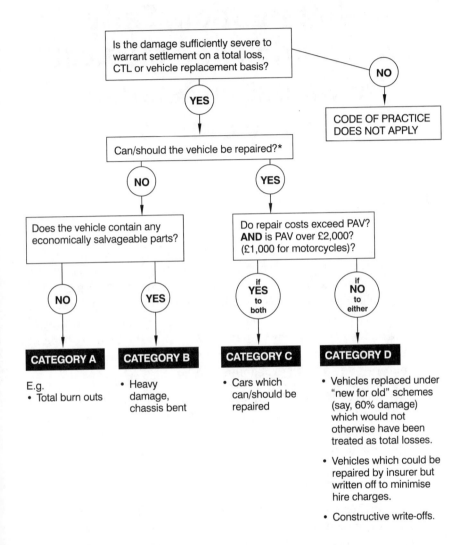

* Thatcham, Engineers Technical Sub-Committee is preparing guidance notes on categorisation

Code of Best Practice on Rehabilitation, Early Intervention and Medical Treatment in Personal Injury Claims

1. Introduction

1.1 It is recognised that in many cases for which damages for personal injuries are claimed the claimant's current medical situation, and/or the long term prognosis, may be improved by the appropriate medical treatment, including surgery, being given at the earliest practicable opportunity, rather than waiting until the claim has settled (referred to in this document as 'medical treatment'). Other cases may require non-medical treatment, such as physiotherapy, counselling, occupational therapy, speech therapy and so forth ('rehabilitation')

1.2 It is also recognised that in cases of serious injury the claimant's quality of life can be immediately improved by the undertaking of some basic home adaptations and/or the provision of aid and equipment and/or appropriate medical treatment when these things are needed, rather than when the claim is finally settled ('early intervention').

1.3 It is further recognised that where these medical or other issues have been dealt with that there may be employment issues which can be addressed for the benefit of the claimant to enable him or her to keep the job that they have, to obtain alternative suitable employment with the same employer, or to re-train for new employment. Again if these needs are addressed at the proper time the claimant's quality of life and long term prospects may be greatly improved.

1.4 Solicitors acting for claimants understand that, taking all these matters into account, they can achieve more for the claimant, by making rehabilitation available, than just the payment of compensation. The insurance industry realises that there great benefit may be had in considering making funds available for these purposes.

1.5   It is therefore desired to create a **Code of Best Practice,** which will ensure that those acting for claimants and those responding to claims against the insurance industry, or acting for such persons, act in future to ensure possible improvements in the quality of life, and the present and long term physical and mental well-being of the Claimant, are being addressed as issues equally as important as the payment of just, full and proper compensation.

2. The Claimant's Solicitors Duty

2.1   It shall be the duty of every claimant's solicitor to consider, in consultation with the claimant and/or the claimant's family, whether it is likely or possible that early intervention, rehabilitation or medical treatment would improve their present and/or long term physical or mental well being.

2.2   It shall be the duty of a claimant's solicitor to consider, with the claimant and/or the claimant's family, whether there is an immediate need for aids, adaptations or other matters which would seek to alleviate problems caused by disability, and thereupon communicate with the insurer as soon as practicable to see if this Code of Practice can be put into effect.

2.3   It shall not be the responsibility of the solicitor to decide on the need for treatment or rehabilitation or to arrange such matters without appropriate medical consultation. Such medical consultation must involve the claimant and/or the claimant's family, the claimant's primary care physician and, where appropriate, any other medical practitioner currently treating the claimant.

2.4   Nothing in this Code of Practice shall in any way affect the obligations placed on a claimant's solicitor by the Pre Action Protocol annexed to the Civil Procedure Rules 1999. However, it will be appreciated that very early communication with the Insurer will enable the matters dealt with here to be addressed more effectively.

3. The Insurer

3.1   It shall be the duty of the insurers to consider, in any appropriate case, whether it is likely that the claimant will benefit, in the immediate, medium or longer term terms, from further medical treatment, rehabilitation or early intervention.

3.2   If the insurer decides that a particular claim might be suitable for intervention, rehabilitation or medical treatment the insurer will communicate this to the claimant's solicitor as soon as practicable.

3.3   On receipt of such communication the claimant's solicitor will immediately discuss these issues with the claimant and/or the claimant's family pursuant to his duty as set out above and, where appropriate, will seek advice from the claimant's treating physicians/surgeons.

3.4   Nothing in this or any other Code of Practice shall in any way modify the obligations of the insurer under the Pre Action Protocols to investigate claims rapidly and in any event within three months (except where time is extended by the Claimant's solicitor) from the date of the formal claim letter. It is recognised that although the rehabilitation assessment can be done even where liability investigations are outstanding, it is essential that such investigations proceed with the appropriate speed.

4. Assessment

4.1   Unless the need for such intervention or treatment has already been identified by medical reports obtained by either side and disclosed, the need for and exent of, such intervention, rehabilitation or treatment will be carried out by means of an independent assessment.

4.2   It must be recognised that the insurer will need to receive from the claimant's solicitor sufficient information for the insurer to make a proper decision about the need for intervention, rehabilitation or treatment. To this extent the claimant's solicitor must comply with the requirements of the Pre Action Protocol to provide the insurer with full and adequate details of the injuries sustained by the claimant, the nature and extent of any, or any likely, continuing disability and any suggestions that may already have been made concerning rehabilitation and/or early intervention. There is no requirement under the pre-action protocol, or this Code of Practice, for the claimant's solicitor to have obtained a full medical report. It is recognised that many cases will be identified for consideration under this Code of Practice before medical evidence has actually been commissioned.

4.3 'Independent assessment' in this context means that the assessment will be carried out by either:

a. The treating physicians/surgeons, or some of them

or

b. By an agency suitably qualified and/or experienced in such matters which is financially and managerially independent of the claimant's solicitors firm and the insurers dealing with the claim.

4.4 It is essential that the process of assessment and recommendation be carried out by those who have an appropriate qualification (to include physiotherapists, occupational therapists, psychologists, psychotherapists and so forth). It would be inappropriate for these assessments to be done by someone who did not have a medical or other appropriate qualification. Those doing the assessments should not only have the such a qualification but should have experience in treating the type of disability from which the individual claimant suffers.

5. The assessment process

5.1 Where possible the agency to be instructed to provide the assessment should be agreed between the claimant's solicitor and the insurer. The instruction letter will be sent by the claimant's solicitor to the medical agency, a copy of the instruction letter being sent to the insurer.

5.2 The medical agency will be asked to interview the claimant at home (or where the claimant is still in hospital, in hospital, with a subsequent visit to the claimant's home) and will be asked to produce a report which covers the following headings:

1. The injuries sustained by the claimant

2. His/her present medical condition

3. The claimant's domestic circumstances, where relevant

4. The injuries/disability in respect of which early intervention or early rehabilitation is suggested

5. The type of intervention or treatment envisaged

6. The likely cost

7. The likely short/medium term benefit to the claimant.

5.3   The report will not deal with diagnostic criteria, causation issues or long term care requirements.

6.   The Assessment Report

6.1   The reporting agency will, on completion of the report send a copy of the report both to the instructing solicitor and to the insurer simultaneously. Both parties will have the right to raise queries on the report, disclosing such correspondence to the other party.

6.2   It is recognised that for the independent report to be of benefit to the parties, it should be prepared and used wholly outside the litigation process. Neither side can therefore rely on its contents in any subsequent litigation. With that strict proviso, to be confirmed in writing by the individual solicitor and insurer if required, the report shall be disclosed to both parties.

6.3   The report, any correspondence relating to it, and any notes created by the assessing agency will be covered by legal privilege and will not under any circumstances be disclosed in any legal proceedings. Any notes or documents created in connection with the assessment process will not be disclosed in any litigation, and any person involved in the preparation of the report or involved in the assessment process shall not be a compellable witness at court.

6.4   The insurers will pay for the report within 28 days of receipt.

6.5   The need for any further or subsequent assessment shall be agreed between the claimant's solicitor and the insurer. The provisions of this Code of Practice shall apply to such assessments.

7. Recommendations

7.1   When the assessment report is disclosed to the insurer, the insurer will be under a duty to consider the recommendations made and the extent to which funds will be made available to bring about implementation of all, or some of, the recommendations. The insurer will not be required to pay for such intervention or treatment as shall be unreasonable in nature, content or cost. The claimant will be under no obligation to undergo intervention, medical investigation or treatment which is unreasonable in all the circumstances of the case.

7.2   Any funds made available shall be treated as an interim payment on account of damages. However, if the funds are provided to enable specific intervention, rehabilitation or treatment to occur, the insurers warrant that they will not, in any legal proceedings connected with the claim, dispute the reasonableness of that treatment nor the agreed cost, provided of course that the claimant has had the recommended treatment.

Letter of Claim

Collision: major/minor road

To

Defendant

Dear Sirs
Re: *Claimant's full name*
       Claimant's full address
       Claimant's Clock or Works Number
       Claimant's Employer (name and address)

We are instructed by the above-named to claim damages in connection with a road traffic accident on Saturday 1 January 2000 at approximately 1300hrs at the A1000 near Bristol.

Please confirm the identity of your insurers. (**OR:** We understand your insurers at the material time were . . . Please confirm that this information is correct.) (**OR:** We understand that you are the insurers for the aforementioned defendant. Please confirm that this information is correct.) Please note that the insurers will need to see this letter as soon as possible and it may affect your insurance cover and/or the conduct of any subsequent legal proceedings if you do not send this letter to them.

The circumstances of the accident are: -

(i)   Our client was driving his Ford Mondeo motorcar, registration number ABC000A, along the outside lane (of 2) of the north-bound carriageway of the A1000 ("the major road") in the direction of Bath, at a speed of approximately 30–40 mph;

(ii) You (**OR:** Your client) were driving a Ford Escort motorcar, registration number XYZ000B, and emerged from the B2000 ("the minor road") and collided with our client;

(iii) The force of the collision pushed our client's car into the south-bound carriageway of the A1000 where it was struck by a Renault Laguna motorcar, registration number LMN3000CC, driven by Mr X;

(iv) At the time of the accident the weather was clear, the road surface(s) was (were) dry and traffic was light.

The reason why we are alleging fault: -

(i) You (**OR**: your client): failed to give way at the junction or accord precedence to our client; failed to look for approaching traffic before driving into the junction; drove too fast and failed to stop before driving into a collision with our client;

(ii) After the collision you (**OR**: your client) spoke to our client and said, amongst other things, that: "Its all my fault. I just didn't look. I am so sorry";

(iii) On 1 March 2000, at the Bristol Magistrates Court, you (**OR**: your client)were/was convicted of driving without due care and attention contrary to Section 3 of the Road Traffic Act 1988 in respect of your (**OR**: your client's) driving on the occasion of the accident;

(iv) The accident, in these circumstances was caused or contributed to by your (**OR**: your client's) negligence.

A description of our client's injuries is as follows: -

(i) Compound comminuted fracture of the upper shaft of the left fibula;

(ii) Soft tissue/ligamentous injury to the neck and lower back;

(iii) Symptoms of post traumatic stress disorder and a phobic travel (driver and passenger) anxiety.

Our client received treatment at Bristol General Hospital between 1 January 2000 and 1 February 2000 under reference number CL0001BGH.

He is employed as a carpet fitter by Great Big Rugs Ltd and following the accident was off work until 1 May 2000 (17 weeks). His approximate weekly income is £350 net.

We are obtaining a police report from the Avon and Somerset Constabulary and will let you have a copy of the same upon your undertaking to meet half the fee.

We have also sent a letter of claim to Mr X (address) and a copy of that letter is attached. We understand his insurers are XYZ insurance, Bristol, under reference number X1234YZ.

At this stage of our enquiry we would expect the documents contained in Annex B, Section A(i) of the Pre-Action Personal Injury

Protocol, Standard Disclosure List to be relevant to this action. For the avoidance of any doubt, these documents comprise those:

> ". . . identifying the nature, extent and location of damage to the Defendant's vehicle ".

A copy of this letter is attached for you to send to your insurers (**OR** A copy of this letter is attached for you to send to your insured).

Finally we expect an acknowledgement of this letter within 21 days by yourself or your insurers.

Yours faithfully

Letter of Claim

Accident arising out of a failure to maintain the highway

To

Defendant

Dear Sirs

Re: *Claimant's full name*
Claimant's full address
Claimant's Clock or Works Number
Claimant's Employer (name and address)

We are instructed by the above-named to claim damages in connection with a road traffic accident on Saturday 1 January 2000 at approximately 14000hrs at the B2001 at Bedford, Bedfordshire.

Please confirm the identity of your insurers. (**OR:** We understand your insurers at the material time were . . . Please confirm that this information is correct.) (**OR:** We understand that you are the insurers for the aforementioned defendant. Please confirm that this information is correct.) Please note that the insurers will need to see this letter as soon as possible and it may affect your insurance cover and/or the conduct of any subsequent legal proceedings if you do not send this letter to them.

The circumstances of the accident are: -

(i) Our client was driving his Honda 500 motorcycle, registration number ABC2000B along the northbound carriageway of the B20001 in the direction of Northampton at a speed of approximately 25 mph;

(ii) As he negotiated a left-hand bend, at a point on the road adjacent to "Duck and Puddle" Public House, the front wheel of his motorcycle lost all grip on the road and his vehicle slid into a collision with a roadside tree;

(iii) Subsequent examination of the carriageway revealed that at the place our client lost control of his motorcycle, areas of the road surface were stripped of surface dressing and other parts were covered with a deep residue of loose gravel and/or chippings.

The reason why we are alleging fault is: -

(i) You are the "highway authority" for the relevant part of the B2001;

(ii) On or about 31 December 1999, the day before the material accident, you caused the road to be "surfaced dressed" by your servants or agents, Big Black Tarmac Co Ltd ("BBT Co Ltd");

(iii) This undertaking was carried out negligently, in that the gravel and/or chippings applied to the carriageway were not evenly distributed over the road surface, leaving it in a demonstrably dangerous condition;

(iv) Further, we reserve the right to raise specific allegations in relation to the retention and instruction of BBT Co Ltd, the inspection of the road, its continued operation during the course and immediate aftermath of the works and the sufficiency of the warnings (if any) given to motorists, which matters are or may initially be dependant on the discovery referred to below;

(v) The accident, in these circumstance, was caused or contributed to by your negligence or breach of statutory duty under Section 41 of the Highways Act 1980.

A description of our client's injuries is as follows: -

(i) Hairline fracture to the base of the skull;

(ii) Colles' fracture to the right wrist;

(iii) Bruising and abrasions to the left hand and forearm.

Our client received treatment for his injuries at Bedford General Hospital between 1 January 2000 and 1 February 2000 under reference number CL0002BGH.

He is employed as a computer technician by Complicated Computers Co Ltd and following the accident was off work until 1 April 2000 (13 weeks). His approximate weekly income is £450 net.

We are obtaining a police report from the Bedfordshire Constabulary and will let you have a copy of the same upon your undertaking to meet half the fee.

We have also sent a letter of claim to BBT Co Ltd (address) and a copy of that letter is attached. We understand their insurers are RST Insurance, Gloucester, under reference number Z5678AB.

At this stage of our enquiries we would expect the documents contained in Annex B, Section C of the Pre-Action Personal Injury Protocol, Standard Disclosure List to be relevant to this action. For the avoidance of any doubt, these documents comprise the following:

"Documents from Highway Authority for a period of 12 months prior to the accident: -

(i)   Records of inspection for the relevant stretch of highway;

(ii) Maintenance records including records of independent contractors working in the relevant area.

(iii) Records of the minutes of Highway Authority meetings where maintenance repair policies have been discussed or decided;

(iv) Records of complaints about the state of the highways;

(v)   Records of other accidents which have occurred on the relevant stretch of highway".

A copy of this letter is attached for you to send to your insurers.

Finally we expect an acknowledgement of this letter within 21 days by yourselves or your insurers.

Yours faithfully

Pleadings

1. Rear end "shunt"

Claim No.

<u>IN THE</u>　　　　　　<u>COUNTY COURT</u>

BETWEEN:

AB

Claimant

– and –

CD

Defendant

─────────────

PARTICULARS OF CLAIM

─────────────

1. On 1st January 2000 at approximately 09.30 hours the Claimant was driving his Ford Mondeo motorcar, registration number ABC 1234, when it was struck by a Vauxhall Transit Van, registration number DEF 5678 being driven by the Defendant.

2. The concise facts of the accident are as follows:

   (i)   The Claimant was driving northwards along the High Street, Casterbridge, Dorset when, by reason of the volume of traffic, he was forced to slow down and stop, whereupon he placed the engine in neutral gear and engaged the handbrake.

   (ii) Very shortly thereafter, his car was struck in the rear by the Defendant's vehicle.

   (iii) The Defendant, during the course of a post-accident conversation with the Claimant, said, amongst other things, that "Its all my fault. I was distracted by seeing a friend standing on the pavement. I am so sorry".

   (iv) At all material times the weather was sunny and the road surface was dry. High Street is subject to a statutory speed limit of 30 mph.

3. The accident was caused by the negligence of the Defendant.

Particulars of negligence

(i) Failing to keep any or any adequate lookout.

(ii) Failing to look ahead, observe and/or heed the presence of the Claimant's car.

(iii) Driving too fast.

(iv) Failing to allow any or any sufficient braking/stopping distance between his vehicle and the Claimant's car.

(v) Failing to apply his brakes properly or in sufficient time, or at all.

(vi) Failing to give any or any sufficient warning of his approach.

(vii) Failing to stop, slow down, steer or otherwise control his vehicle so as to avoid a collision with the Claimant's car.

Or

3. The accident was caused by the Defendant who negligently drove into a collision with the rear of the Claimant's stationary car.

4. The Claimant, in addition to his own evidence, will rely on the evidence of the following witnesses, all or whom corroborate his account of the accident:

(i) Basil Black, his brother, travelling in the front passenger seat of his car.

(ii) Wendy White, independent, driving a Renault Clio motorcar approximately 2 vehicles behind that of the Defendant.

(iii) Garfield Gray, independent, a pedestrian standing on the west pavement of High Street approximately 50m from the point of collision.

5. Further, the Claimant will rely on pages 2–4, 7, 8, 9 and 14 of the Dorset Constabulary Accident Report compiled by PC Hardy, copies of which are served herewith.

6. As a result of the accident the Claimant suffered pain, injury, loss and damage.

Particulars of injury

The Claimant, who was born on .... sustained:

[Insert brief particulars of injury.]

Further particulars of injury, treatment, loss of amenity and prognosis are contained in the medical report of Ms. .... Consultant Orthopaedic Surgeon, dated .... , a copy of which is served herewith.

Particulars of Special Damage

A Schedule of Loss and Expenses is served herewith.

7.   Further, the Claimant claims interest pursuant to section 69 of the County Courts Act 1984 as follows:

   (i)   On damages for personal injury, under the first limb of paragraph 6 above, at a rate of, say, 3% per annum from the date of service of these proceedings;

   (ii)   On the claim for special damages, under the second limb of paragraph 6 above, at a rate of, say, 7% per annum from 1st January 2000 to the date hereof and to judgment or sooner payment.

AND THE CLAIMANT CLAIMS
(1) Damages;
(2) Interest, as aforesaid, pursuant to section 69 of the County Courts Act 1984.

MARK WHALAN

DATED etc.

Statement of Truth
I, AB, the Claimant, believe that the facts stated in these Particulars of Claim are true.

SIGNED ....
                AB

2. Driver on major road collides with car emerging from minor road

Claim No.

<u>IN THE</u>   <u>COUNTY COURT</u>

BETWEEN:

AB

Claimant

– and –

CD

Defendant

PARTICULARS OF CLAIM

---

1. *[As Form 1, paragraph 1.]*

2. The concise facts of the accident are as follows:

   (i) The Claimant was driving northwards along the High Street, Casterbridge, Dorset ("the major road") at a speed of approximately 25 mph.

   (ii) The Defendant emerged from Low Road ("the minor road") and drove across the northbound lane of the major road and into a collision with the near side of the Claimant's car.

   (iii) At all material times it was raining and the road surface was wet. Both roads are subject to a statutory speed limit of 30 mph.

3. The accident was caused by the negligence of the Defendant.

Particulars of Negligence

   (i) Failing to keep any or any adequate lookout.

   (ii) Failing to observe and/or heed the "Give Way" road markings and/or sign at the junction of the minor and major road.

   (iii) Failing to stop at the junction.

   (iv) Failing to observe and/or heed the presence and approach of the Claimant's car on the major road.

(v)   Failing to give way to the Claimant.

(vi) Driving into the junction when, by reason of the presence and approach of the Claimant's car, it was unsafe to do so.

(vii) Colliding with the Claimant's car.

(viii) Failing to give any or any sufficient warning of his approach.

(vii) Failing to stop, slow down, steer or otherwise control his vehicle so as to avoid a collision with the Claimant's car.

   Or

3. The accident was caused by the Defendant who negligently emerged from a minor road into a major road and into a collision with the Claimant's car.

4. *[As Form 1, paragraphs 4 and/or 5, if applicable.]*

5. Further, the Claimant intends, in reliance on section 11 of the Civil Evidence Act 1968, to produce evidence that the Defendant was, on 1st March 2000 at Casterbridge Magistrates Court, convicted of driving without due car and attention, contrary to section 3 of the Road Traffic Act 1988, in respect of his driving at the time of the accident, as evidence of his negligence.

6. As a result of the accident the Claimant suffered pain, injury, loss and damage.

Particulars of Injury

[As Form 1.]

Particulars of Special Damage

[As Form 1.]

7. Further, the Claimant is and will continue to be at a disadvantage on the open employment market, and he claims an award of damages to compensate for this loss.

8. *[As Form 1, paragraph 7.]*

AND THE CLAIMANT CLAIMS:

(1) Damages;

(2) Interest, as aforesaid, pursuant to section 69 of the County Courts Act 1984.

MARK WHALAN

DATED etc.

Statement of Truth

I, AB, the Claimant, believe that the facts stated in these Particulars of Claim are true.

SIGNED ....
                    AB

3. Head on collision after negligent overtaking manoeuvre

Claim No.

IN THE   COUNTY COURT

BETWEEN:

AB

Claimant

– and –

CD

Defendant

PARTICULARS OF CLAIM

---

1. *[As Form 1, paragraph 1.]*
2. The concise facts of the accident are as follows:

    (i) The Claimant was driving southwards along the A150 Field Road, near Casterbridge at a speed of approximately 55 mph.

    (ii) The Defendant, who was driving along the northbound lane of the same road at a speed in excess of 60 mph, pulled out into the southbound lane in order to overtake a slow moving heavy goods vehicle.

    (iii) The two vehicles collided at a point that was entirely within the southbound lane at or near the 'Wig and Whistle' public house.

    (iv) At all material times it was sunny and the road surface was dry. The A150 Field Road is subject to a statutory speed limit of 60 mph.

3. The accident was caused by the negligence of the Defendant.

Particulars of negligence

    (i) Driving in excess of the statutory speed limit and/or too fast in all the circumstances.

    (ii) Failing to keep any, or any adequate lookout.

(iii) Failing to look ahead, observe and/or heed the presence of the Claimant's car.

(iv) Driving across the centre line and onto the wrong side of the road.

(v) Overtaking another vehicle when, by reason of the presence and approach of the Claimant's oncoming car, it was unsafe to do so.

(vi) Driving into the path of the Claimant's car.

(vii) Colliding with the Claimant's car.

(viii) Failing to give any or any sufficient warning of his approach.

(ix) Failing to stop, slow down, steer or otherwise control his vehicle so as to avoid a collision with the Claimant's car.

Or

3. The accident was caused by the Defendant who negligently drove onto the wrong side of the road and collided with the Claimant's car.

4. *[As Form 1, paragraphs 4 and/or 5, if applicable.]*

5. By reason of the matters aforesaid, the Claimant suffered pain, injury, loss and damage.

Particulars of Injury

[As Form 1.]

Particulars of Special Damage

[As Form 1.]
6. Further, the Claimant was without the use of a motor vehicle for the period 1st January 2000 to 25th February 2000, 8 weeks, and he claims an award of damages for this loss of use.

8. *[As Form 1, paragraph 7.]*

AND THE CLAIMANT CLAIMS:

(1) Damages;

(2) Interest, as aforesaid, pursuant to section 69 of the County Courts Act 1984.

MARK WHALAN

DATED etc.

Statement of Truth

I, AB, the Claimant, believe that the facts stated in these Particulars of Claim are true.

SIGNED ....
AB

4. Collision after the Defendant turned right across the Claimant's path

Claim No.

IN THE   *COUNTY COURT*

BETWEEN:

AB

Claimant

– and –

CD

Defendant

PARTICULARS OF CLAIM

---

1. *[As Form 1, paragraph 1.]*

2. The concise facts of the accident are as follows:

   (i) The Claimant was driving northwards along the High Street, Casterbridge at a speed of approximately 25 mph.

   (ii) The Defendant, who approached along the southbound lane of the same road, also at a speed of approximately 25 mph, suddenly and without any indication attempted to execute a right turn into Middle Lane, across the path of the Claimant's line of traffic.

   (iii) The Claimant, who was approximately 10m from the junction with Middle Lane when the Defendant attempted his manoeuvre, was unable to stop and his car collided with the near side of the Defendant's vehicle.

   (iv) At all material times it was sunny and the road surface was dry. High Street is subject to a statutory speed limit of 30 mph.

3. The accident was caused by the negligence of the Defendant.

Particulars of Negligence

   (i) Failing to keep any or any adequate lookout.

   (ii) Failing to look ahead, observe and/or heed the presence and approach of the Claimant's car.

(iii) Driving across the centre line and across the line of oncoming traffic.

(iv) Failing to wait for a safe gap in the oncoming traffic and/or until the Claimant's car had passed before attempting to turn right.

(v) Driving into the path of the Claimant's car.

(vi) Colliding with the Claimant's car.

(vii) Failing to give any or any sufficient warning of his approach.

(viii) Failing to stop, slow down, steer or otherwise control his vehicle so as to avoid a collision with the Claimant's car.

Or

3. The accident was caused by the Defendant who negligently attempted to execute a right turn across the path of the Claimant's car.

4. *[As Form 1, paragraphs 4 and/or 5, if applicable.]*

5. As a result of the accident, the Claimant suffered pain, injury, loss and damage.

Particulars of Injury

[As Form 1.]

Particulars of Special Damage

[As Form 1.]

6. *[As Form 1, paragraph 7.]*

AND THE CLAIMANT CLAIMS:
(1) Damages;
(2) Interest, as aforesaid, pursuant to section 69 of the County Courts Act 1984.

MARK WHALAN

DATED etc.

Statement of Truth
I, AB, the Claimant, believe that the facts stated in these Particulars of Claim are true.

SIGNED ....
         AB

5. Collision at traffic lights

Claim No.

IN THE   *COUNTY COURT*

BETWEEN:

AB

Claimant

– and –

CD

Defendant

PARTICULARS OF CLAIM

1. *[As Form 1, paragraph 1.]*

2. The concise facts of the accident are as follows:

   (i)   The Claimant stopped at red traffic lights at the junction of the High Street and Upper Street, Casterbridge, Dorset. When the lights changed to green in his favour he engaged first gear and drove into the junction at a speed of approximately 15 mph.

   (ii)   The Defendant approached the junction along Upper Street at a speed of approximately 25 mph. When he was approximately 75 metres from the junction the traffic lights changed to red against him.

   (iii)   The Defendant failed to stop at the red signal and continued to drive into the junction where he collided with the off side of the Claimant's car.

   (iv)   At all material times the weather was overcast and the road surfaces were damp. Both roads are subject to a statutory speed limit of 30 mph.

3. The accident was caused by the negligence and/or breach of statutory duty under section 36 of the Road Traffic Act 1988 of the Defendant.

Particulars of Negligence and/or Breach of Statutory Duty

   (i)   Failing to keep any or any adequate lookout.

(ii)   Failing to have any or any sufficient regard for traffic that was visibly and/or might reasonably be expected to be at the junction.

(iii)   Failing to observe and/or conform to the red light signal that was showing to and controlling his line of traffic.

(iv)   Proceeding beyond the stop line and into the junction although the red light signal was showing to and controlling his line of traffic.

(v)   Failing, in the premises, to comply with the traffic sign, contrary to section 36 of the Act of 1988.

(vi)   Driving too fast.

(vii)   Failing to observe and/or heed the presence and approach of the Claimant's car.

(viii) Driving into the junction when, by reason of the presence and approach of the Claimant's car, it was unsafe to do so.

(ix)   Colliding with the Claimant's car.

(x)   Failing to give any or any sufficient warning of his approach.

(xi)   Failing to stop, slow down, steer or otherwise control his vehicle so as to avoid a collision with the Claimant's car.

Or

3. The accident was caused by the Defendant who negligently and/or in breach of his statutory duty under section 36 of the Road Traffic Act 1988 failed to comply with a red traffic light and drove into a collision with the Claimant's car.

4. *[As Form 1, paragraphs 4 and/or 5, if applicable.]*

5. Further, the Claimant intends, in reliance on section 11 of the Civil Evidence Act 1968, to produce evidence that the Defendant was, on 1st March 2000 at Casterbridge Magistrates Court, convicted of failing to comply with a traffic sign contrary to section 36 of the Road Traffic Act 1988, in respect of his driving at the time of the accident, as evidence of his negligence.

6. As a result of the accident, the Claimant suffered pain, injury, loss and damage.

Particulars of Injury

[As Form 1.]

Particulars of Special Damage

[As Form 1.]

7. *[As Form 1, paragraph 7.]*

AND THE CLAIMANT CLAIMS:

(1) Damages;
(2) Interest, as aforesaid, pursuant to section 69 of the County Courts Act 1984.

MARK WHALAN

DATED etc.

Statement of Truth
I, AB, the Claimant, believe that the facts stated in these Particulars of Claim are true.

SIGNED ....
        AB

6. Pedestrian run over while crossing the road at a zebra crossing

Claim No.

<u>IN THE</u>   <u>COUNTY COURT</u>

BETWEEN:

AB

Claimant

– and –

CD

Defendant

PARTICULARS OF CLAIM

1. On 1st January 2000 at approximately 09.30 hours the Claimant was a pedestrian at the High Street, Casterbridge, Dorset when he was struck by a Vauxhall Transit Van, registration number DEF 5678 being driven by the Defendant.

2. The concise facts of the accident are as follows:

   (i) The Claimant lawfully attempted to cross from the east to the west footway of the High Street by means of a zebra pedestrian crossing situated in the road at a position approximately 100m north of the junction with Middle Lane.

   (ii) As he proceeded across the crossing, at a point about 3m from the east kerb, he was struck by the Defendant's vehicle which was driving along the northbound lane of the High Street and which, prior to emergency braking, was travelling at a speed in excess of 30 mph.

   (iii) At all material times the weather was sunny and the road surface was dry. High Street is subject to a statutory speed limit of 30 mph.

3. The accident was caused by the negligence and/or breach of statutory duty under the Zebra, Pelican and Puffin Pedestrian Crossings Regulations and General Directions 1997 of the Defendant.

Particulars of Negligence and/or Breach of Statutory Duty

     (i)   Failing to keep any or any adequate lookout.

    (ii)   Failing to observe and/or heed the presence of the Claimant crossing the road.

   (iii)   Failing to give any sufficient warning of his approach.

   (iv)   Failing to stop before reaching the limits of the zebra crossing.

    (v)   Colliding with the Claimant.

   (vi)   Failing, in the premises, to accord precedence to the Claimant contrary to regulation 25 of the said Regulations of 1997.

   (vii) Driving too fast.

  (viii) Failing to stop, slow down, steer or otherwise control his vehicle so as to avoid a collision with the Claimant.

     Or

3. The accident was caused by the Defendant who negligently and/or in breach of regulation 25 of the Zebra, Pelican and Puffin Pedestrian Crossings Regulations and General Directions 1997 failed to accord precedence to an drove into a collision with the Claimant as he crossed a zebra pedestrian crossing.

4. *[As Form 1, paragraphs 4 and 5, if applicable.]*

5. As a result of the accident, the Claimant suffered pain, injury, loss and damage.

Particulars of Injury

[As Form 1.]

Particulars of Special Damage

[As Form 1.]

6. *[As Form 1, paragraph 7.]*

AND THE CLAIMANT CLAIMS:

(1) Damages;

(2) Interest, as aforesaid, pursuant to section 69 of the County Courts Act 1984.

MARK WHALAN

DATED etc.

Statement of Truth

I, AB, the Claimant, believe that the facts stated in these Particulars of Claim are true.

SIGNED ....

AB

7. Negligent "u" turn

Claim No.

<u>*IN THE*</u>   *COUNTY COURT*

BETWEEN:

AB

Claimant

– and –

CD

Defendant

PARTICULARS OF CLAIM

---

1. *[As Form 1, paragraph 1.]*

2. The concise facts of the accident are as follows:

   (i)   The Claimant was driving eastwards along Middle Lane, Casterbridge, Dorset at a speed of approximately 25 mph.

   (ii) The Defendant, who approached along the westbound lane of the same road, also at a speed of approximately 25 mph, attempted to execute a "u" turn in the carriageway.

   (iii) As the Defendant turned round, his front wheels clipped and/or mounted the kerb, causing his vehicle to stall and/or come to a stop.

   (iv) The Claimant, who was approximately 10m from the Defendant when he attempted his manoeuvre, was unable to stop and collided with the rear of the Defendant's vehicle.

   (v)   At all material times it was raining and the road surface was wet. Middle Lane is subject to a statutory speed limit of 30 mph.

3. The accident was caused by the negligence of the Defendant.

Particulars of Negligence

   (i)   Failing to keep any or any adequate lookout.

(ii)   Failing to look ahead, observe and/or heed the presence and approach of the Claimant's car.

(iii)   Failing to wait for a safe gap in oncoming traffic and/or until the Claimant's car had passed before attempting to execute a "u" turn.

(iv)   Driving into the path of the Claimant's car.

(v)   Attempting a "u" turn in a road that was not wide enough for the purpose, with the result that his car clipped and/or mounted the kerb, causing the engine to stall and the vehicle to become a stationary hazard to the Claimant's line of traffic.

(vi)   Failing to give any or any sufficient warning of his approach.

(vii)   Failing to stop, slow down, steer or otherwise control his vehicle so as to avoid a collision with the Claimant's car.

Or

3. The accident was caused by the Defendant who negligently attempted to execute a "u" turn across the path of the Claimant's car.

4. *[As Form 1, paragraphs 4 and/or 5, if applicable.]*

5. As a result of the accident, the Claimant suffered pain, injury, loss and damage.

Particulars of Injury

[As Form 1.]

Particulars of Special Damage

[As Form 1.]

6. *[As Form 1, paragraph 7.]*

AND THE CLAIMANT CLAIMS:
(1) Damages;
(2) Interest, as aforesaid, pursuant to section 69 of the County Courts Act 1984.

MARK WHALAN

DATED etc.

Statement of Truth

I, AB, the Claimant, believe that the facts stated in these Particulars of Claim are true.

SIGNED ....
AB

8. Negligent opening of vehicle door into the path of motorcyclist

Claim No.

<u>IN THE</u>   <u>COUNTY COURT</u>

BETWEEN:

AB

Claimant

– and –

CD

Defendant

PARTICULARS OF CLAIM

---

1. On 1st January 2000 at approximately 09.30 hours the Claimant was driving his Honda 750 motorcycle, registration number GHI 1234, when he was struck by and/or collided with the door of a Ford Escort motorcar, registration number XYZ 5678, being driven by the and/or under the control of the Defendant.

2. The concise facts of the accident are as follows:
   (i)   The Claimant was driving westwards along Upper Street, Casterbridge, Dorset at a speed of approximately 20 mph.

   (ii) The Defendant was sat in the driver's seat of his vehicle which was stationary and/or parked against the south kerb of the same road.

   (iii) When the Claimant was approximately 5m from the stationary vehicle, the Defendant, without any warning or indication, opened his door.

   (iv) The Claimant was unable to stop and/or move around the open door. He collided with the same and was knocked from his motorcycle.

   (v)   At all material times the weather was overcast but the road surface was dry. Upper Street is subject to a statutory speed limit of 30 mph.

3. The accident was caused by the negligence of the Defendant.

Particulars of negligence

   (i)   Failing to keep any or any adequate lookout.

(ii) Failing, by means of his mirror and/or a look over his right shoulder, or by not turning round in his seat, to observe and/or heed the presence and/or approach of the Claimant's motorcycle.

(iii) Opening the door into the path of the Claimant's motorcycle.

(iv) Colliding with and/or striking the Claimant's motorcycle.

(v) Failing, in the premises, to comply with the provisions of paragraph 214 of the Highway Code.

Further, or alternatively, the Claimant will rely on the maxim res ipsa loquitur, meaning that the happening of the accident affords evidence of the negligence of the Defendant.

Or

3. The accident was caused by the Defendant who negligently opened his car door into the path of the Claimant's motorcycle.

4. *[As Form 1, paragraphs 4 and/or 5, if applicable.]*

5. As a result of the accident, the Claimant suffered pain, injury, loss and damage.

Particulars of Injury

[As Form 1.]

Particulars of special damage

[As Form 1.]
6. *[As Form 1, paragraph 7.]*

AND THE CLAIMANT CLAIMS:
(1) Damages;
(2) Interest, as aforesaid, pursuant to section 69 of the County Courts Act 1984.

MARK WHALAN

DATED etc.

Statement of Truth
I, AB, the Claimant, believe that the facts stated in these Particulars of Claim are true.

SIGNED ....
      AB

9. Pedestrian knocked down by car that mounted the pavement and driven by a Defendant who had consumed excess alcohol

Claim No.

<u>IN THE</u>   *COUNTY COURT*

BETWEEN:

AB

Claimant

– and –

CD

Defendant

PARTICULARS OF CLAIM

1. On 1st January 2000 at approximately 09.30 hours the Claimant was standing on the west pavement of the High Street, Casterbridge, Dorset when he was struck by a Vauxhall Transit Van, registration number DEF 5678, being driven by the Defendant.

2. The concise facts of the accident are as follows:
    (i)   The Claimant was lawfully standing on the west pavement of the High Street at a point that was adjacent to shop premises at number 150 and approximately 2m from the kerb.

    (ii)   The Defendant was driving along the northbound lane of the same road at a speed in excess of 40 mph when he suddenly swerved, mounted the west pavement and collided with the Claimant.

    (iii) At all material times the weather was sunny and the road surface was dry. High Street is subject to a statutory speed limit of 25 mph.

3. The accident was caused by the negligence of the Defendant.

Particulars of negligence

(i)   Driving whilst his ability to do so safely was impaired by the consumption of alcohol.

(ii)   Driving too fast.

(iii)   Failing to observe and/or heed the presence of the Claimant on the pavement.

(iv)   Losing control of his vehicle.

(v)   Mounting the kerb and colliding with the Claimant on the pavement.

(vi)   Failing to give any or any sufficient warning of his approach.

(vii)   Failing to stop, slow down, steer or otherwise control his vehicle so as to avoid a collision with the Claimant.

Further, or alternatively, the Claimant will rely on the maxim res ipsa loquitur, meaning that the happening of the accident affords evidence of the negligence of the Defendant.

Or

3.   The accident was caused by the Defendant who negligently drove his vehicle onto the pavement and into a collision with the Claimant at a time when his ability to drive safely was impaired by the consumption of alcohol.

4.   *[As Form 1, paragraphs 4 and/or 5, if applicable.]*

5.   Further, the Claimant intends, in reliance on section 11 of the Civil Evidence Act 1968, to produce evidence that the Defendant was, on 1st March 2000 at Casterbridge Magistrates Court, convicted of the offence of driving a motor vehicle after consuming so much alcohol that the proportion of it in his breath exceeded the prescribed limit, contrary to section 5 of the Road Traffic Act 1988, in respect of his driving at the time of the accident, as evidence of his negligence.

6.   As a result of the accident, the Claimant suffered pain, injury, loss and damage.

Particulars of injury

[As Form 1.]

Particulars of special damage

[As Form 1.]

7.   *[As Form 1, paragraph 7.]*

AND THE CLAIMANT CLAIMS:

(1) Damages;
(2) Interest, as aforesaid, pursuant to section 69 of the County Courts Act 1984.

MARK WHALAN

DATED etc.

Statement of Truth

I, AB, the Claimant, believe that the facts stated in these Particulars of Claim are true.

SIGNED ....

AB

10. Motorcyclist injured when struck by mischievous horse

Claim No.

<u>*IN THE*</u>   *COUNTY COURT*

BETWEEN:

AB

Claimant

– and –

CD

Defendant

PARTICULARS OF CLAIM

---

1. At all material times:

   (i) The Claimant was the owner and driver of a Honda 750 motorcycle, registration number ABC 1234;

   (ii) The Defendant was the owner and/or keeper of horses, including a horse named "Dobbin", which were regularly walked and exercised on the A150 Field Road, near Casterbridge, Dorset ("the road").

2. On 1st January 2000 at approximately 11.30 hours the Claimant was driving southwards along the road when, at a point adjacent to premises known as "The Old Water Mill", he came upon a line of approximately 5 horses walking and/or being ridden in the same direction. The Claimant slowed down to approximately 10 mph and, taking a wide line that took his motorcycle onto the northbound lane, attempted to overtake the horses. As he did so "Dobbin" ("the horse") suddenly reared up, charged towards and kicked the Claimant, knocking him from his motorcycle.

3. The horse was dangerous within the terms of section 2(2) of the Animals Act 1971 in that:

   (i) She was likely to charge at and/or kick passing traffic with the result that motorists, particularly motorcyclists, would likely sustain damage likely to be severe;

(ii)   She had characteristics not normally found in horses, namely a propensity to become completely uncontrollable when in the presence of motor traffic;

(iii)   The Defendants knew of her characteristics. Following the accident her rider explained that the horse had previously been involved in a number of similar incidents. Such incidents are also detailed in the documentary disclosure exhibited herewith.

4. The accident was caused by the negligence and/or breach of statutory duty under section 2 of the Act of 1971 of the Defendant, its employees, servants or agents.

Particulars of negligence and/or breach of statutory duty

(i)   Causing or permitting the horse to walk on the highway when they knew or ought to have known that she was a danger to passing traffic.

(ii)   Riding the horse on the highway when neither her rider nor any other person was able to exercise any or any adequate control upon her.

(iii) Failing to exercise any or any adequate restraint on the horse.

(iv)   Failing to observe and/or heed the presence and approach of the Claimant's motorcycle.

(v)   Causing or permitting the horse to rear up, charge and kick the Claimant.

(vi)   Failing to give any or any sufficient warning to the Claimant.

(vii) In the premises, exposing the Claimant to an animal that was dangerous, contrary to section 2 of the Act of 1971.

Or

4. The accident was caused by the Defendant, by its employees, servants or agents, who negligently and/or in breach of section 2 of the Act of 1971 exposed the Claimant to a dangerous animal.

5. *[As Form 1, paragraphs 4 and/or 5, if applicable.]*

6. As a result of the accident, the Claimant suffered pain, injury, loss and damage.

Particulars of injury

[As Form 1.]

Particulars of special damage

[As Form 1.]

7. *[As Form 1, paragraph 7.]*

AND THE CLAIMANT CLAIMS:
(1) Damages;
(2) Interest, as aforesaid, pursuant to section 69 of the County Courts Act 1984.

MARK WHALAN

DATED etc.

Statement of Truth
I, AB, the Claimant, believe that the facts stated in these Particulars of Claim are true.

SIGNED ....
          AB

11. Highway maintenance case

Claim No.

IN THE   COUNTY COURT

BETWEEN:

AB

Claimant

– and –

CD

Defendant

PARTICULARS OF CLAIM

---

1. At all material times:

    (i)   The Claimant was the owner and driver of a Ford Mondeo motorcar, registration number ABC 1234; and

    (ii) The Defendant was the highway authority in respect of the A150 Field Road, near Casterbridge, Dorset ("the road").

2. On 2nd June 2000 at approximately 13.00 hours the Claimant was driving southwards along the road when, as he negotiated a corner adjacent to the "Mucky Duck" public house at a speed of approximately 35 mph, his car skidded on a patch of carriageway that was stripped of surface dressing and/or covered with a deep residue of loose gravel and/or chippings, and collided with a roadside wall.

3. The accident was caused by the negligence and/or breach of statutory duty under section 41 of the Highways Act 1980 of the Defendant, its employees, servants or agents.

Particulars of negligence and/or breach of statutory duty

(i)   Causing or permitting the road to be or to become or to remain a danger to motorists in that after the same had been "surface dressed" on or about 1st January 2000 parts of the carriageway were stripped of a covering and other parts were covered with a deep residue of loose gravel and/or chippings.

(ii) Failing to institute or enforce any adequate system whereby the said loose gravel and/or chippings were evenly distributed over the road surface.

(iii) Failing to institute or enforce any or any adequate system whereby the said loose gravel and/or chippings were swept or otherwise removed from the road surface.

(iv) Failing to heed the risk presented by the said loose gravel and/or chippings.

(v) Causing or permitting the road to remain open to vehicles when they knew or ought to have known that it was in a dangerous condition.

(vi) Failing to institute or enforce any or any adequate system of inspection or maintenance of the road.

(vii) Failing to warn the Claimant of the said danger by way of an appropriate warning sign.

(viii) Failing to cause competent persons to carry out the maintenance of the road and/or to give proper instructions and to ensure that the same were carried out.

(ix) Failing, in the premises, to maintain or repair the said highway, with the result that the same was in a condition which was dangerous to persons lawfully using the same, contrary to section 41(1) of the Act of 1980.

Or

3. The accident was caused by the Defendant who, by its employees, servants or agents, negligently and/or in breach of its statutory duty under section 41(1) of the Highways Act 1980 failed to maintain or repair the road with the result that it was and/or remained in a dangerous condition.

4. Further, or alternatively, the danger referred to at paragraph 3 above constituted a nuisance which was caused or permitted by the Defendant and the accident was caused or contributed to by that nuisance.

5. *[As Form 1, paragraphs 4 and/or 5, if applicable.]*

6. As a result of the accident, the Claimant suffered pain, injury, loss and damage.

Particulars of injury

[As Form 1.]

Particulars of special damage

[As Form 1.]

7. *[As Form 1, paragraph 7.]*

AND THE CLAIMANT CLAIMS:

(1) Damages;
(2) Interest, as aforesaid, pursuant to section 69 of the County Courts
    Act 1984.

MARK WHALAN

DATED etc.

Statement of Truth

I, AB, the Claimant, believe that the facts stated in these Particulars of
Claim are true.

SIGNED ....

AB

12. Bus passenger

Claim No.

<u>IN THE</u>   <u>COUNTY COURT</u>

BETWEEN:

EF

Claimant

– and –

The Big Red Bus Co. Ltd

Defendant

PARTICULARS OF CLAIM

1. On 1st January 2000 at approximately 09.30 hours the Claimant was a passenger on a No. 24 bus, registration number XYZ 891011 ("the bus") owned and/or operated by the Defendant.

2. The concise facts of the accident are as follows:

    (i)   The Claimant boarded the bus at a request stop situated at the High Street, Casterbridge, Dorset at or near its junction with Lower Street. The bus was driven and operated by the Defendant's employee, servant or agent.

    (ii)   The Claimant, having paid her fare to the driver, walked down the central aisle towards the only available seat, situated towards the rear of the bus. Suddenly, and without any indication, the bus lurched forward with a jolt and pulled away. The Claimant lost her balance and fell to the floor.

3. The accident was caused by the negligence and/or breach of statutory duty under the Public Service Vehicles (Conduct of Drivers, Inspectors, Conductors and Passengers) Regulations 1990, of the Defendant, its employee, servant or agent.

Particulars of negligence and/or breach of statutory duty

The driver of the bus:

(i)   Failed to observe and/or heed the fact that the Claimant, by reason of her age and/or visible physical infirmity, should be seated before the bus pulled away.

(ii)   Failed to stop and/or wait until the Claimant had reached a seat before pulling away.

(iii)   Attempted to or began to pull away before the Claimant had reached a seat.

(iv)   Failed to give to the Claimant any or any adequate warning of his intention to pull away.

(v)   Pulled away from the bus stop with a sudden jolt and/or in a jerky fashion and/or at excessive speed.

(vi)   Failed to take any or any sufficient care for the safety of the Claimant.

(vii)   Failed, in the premises, to take all reasonable precautions to ensure the safety of passengers entering and/or on the vehicle, contrary to regulation 5 of the Regulations of 1990.

Or

3.   The accident was caused by the Defendant, by its employee, servant or agent who negligently and/or in breach of regulation 5 of the Public Service Vehicle (Conduct of Drivers, Inspectors, Conductors and Passengers) Regulations 1990, failed to take all reasonable precautions to ensure the safety of the Claimant as she entered and/or remained on the bus.

4.   *[As Form 1, paragraphs 4 and/or 5, if applicable.]*

5.   As a result of the accident, the Claimant suffered pain, injury, loss and damage.

Particulars of injury

[As Form 1.]

Particulars of special damage

[As Form 1.]

6.   *[As Form 1, paragraph 7.]*

AND THE CLAIMANT CLAIMS:

(1) Damages;

(2) Interest, as aforesaid, pursuant to section 69 of the County Courts
Act 1984.

MARK WHALAN

DATED etc.

Statement of Truth
I, EF, the Claimant, believe that the facts stated in these Particulars of
Claim are true.

SIGNED ....
EF

13. Accident caused by defective repair to vehicle

Claim No.

<u>IN THE</u>   <u>COUNTY COURT</u>

BETWEEN:

AB

Claimant

– and –

(1) CD
(2) Casterbridge Car Repair Services

Defendant

PARTICULARS OF CLAIM

---

1. At all material times:

    (i)   The Claimant was the owner and driver of a Ford Mondeo motorcar, registration number ABC 1234;

    (ii) The First Defendant was the driver of a Renault Laguna motorcar, registration number LMN 6789;

    (iii) The Second Defendant carried on a motor vehicle maintenance, repair and service business from premises at 125 High Street, Casterbridge, Dorset.

2. The concise facts of the accident are as follows:

    (i)   On or about 30th December 1999 the Second Defendant undertook a full service of the First Defendant's car, which works involved the fixing of a new set of tyres and, in turn, the removal and the attachment of all four wheels.

    (ii) On 1st January 2000 at approximately 09.00 hours the Claimant and First Defendant were driving as leading and following vehicle along the southbound lane of the A150 Field Road, near Casterbridge, Dorset.

    (iii) As the cars negotiated a sharp left hand bend situate near the junction with Water Meadow Lane, the First Defendant's car suddenly swerved and the rear offside wheel became detached, spun off and bounced into collision with the Claimant's car.

    (iv) The Claimant, as a result of this collision, was unable to steer and/or control his car which skidded into a roadside ditch.

(v)   The First Defendant, during the course of a post-accident conversation with the Claimant, said "I'm really sorry. It felt a bit wobbly for the last mile or two. Bloody garage".

3.   The accident was caused or contributed to by the negligence of the First Defendant.

Particulars of negligence of the first defendant

(i)   Failing to inspect his car to ensure that the works carried out by the Second Defendant had been undertaken with reasonable care and skill and, specifically, failing to observe and/or heed the fact that the rear offside wheel was only secured by 1 wheel nut rather than the 4 wheel nuts prescribed by the manufacturer.

(ii)   Driving his car on the highway when he knew or ought to have known that it was in an unsafe condition in that the wheel was insecurely fitted.

(iii)   Failing to notice and/or heed the fact that the wheel was working loose as the car was in motion.

(iv)   Failing to stop, and/or call for assistance after becoming aware that the wheel and/or his car was becoming unstable.

Or

3.   The accident was caused or contributed to by the First Defendant who negligently drove his vehicle on the highway when he knew or ought to have known that it was in a condition that was dangerous to other road users.

4.   Further and/or alternatively, the accident was caused or contributed to by the negligence of the Second Defendant.

Particulars of negligence of the second defendant

(i)   Failing to take any or any adequate steps to ensure that the nuts holding the rear offside wheel were affixed and/or adequately tightened.

(ii)   Failing to institute and/or enforce any or any adequate system of inspection whereby the matters outlined above would have been discovered and remedied prior to the return of the car to the First Defendant.

(iii)   Failing to carry out any or any adequate test on the wheel.

(iv)   Causing or permitting the wheel to become detached from the First Defendant's car.

(v)   Failing, in the premises, to carry out the service of the First Defendant's car with reasonable care and skill.

Or

4.   The accident was caused or contributed to by the Second Defendant who negligently caused or permitted the rear offside wheel of the First Defendant's car to become detached at a time when they knew or ought to have known that it would be in use on the highway.

5.   *[As Form 1, paragraphs 4 and/or 5, if applicable.]*

6.   As a result of the accident, the Claimant suffered pain, injury, loss and damage.

Particulars of injury

[As Form 1.]

Particulars of special damage

[As Form 1.]

7.   *[As Form 1, paragraph 7.]*

AND THE CLAIMANT CLAIMS AGAINST THE FIRST AND SECOND DEFENDANTS:

(1) Damages.
(2) Interest, as aforesaid, pursuant to section 69 of the County Courts Act 1984.

MARK WHALAN

DATED etc.

Statement of Truth
I, AB, the Claimant, believe that the facts stated in these Particulars of Claim are true.

SIGNED ....
                   AB

14. Claim against Motor Insurers' Bureau

Claim No.

<u>IN THE</u>   <u>COUNTY COURT</u>

BETWEEN:

AB

Claimant

– and –

The Motor Insurers' Bureau

Defendant

PARTICULARS OF CLAIM

---

1. By an agreement in writing dated 13th August 1999 and made between the Secretary of State for the Environment, Transport and the Regions and the Defendant, and known as the Motor Insurers' Bureau (Compensation for Victims of Uninsured Drivers) Agreement ("the agreement") it was agreed, amongst other provisions, that if judgment in respect of any liability required to be covered by a policy of insurance or a security under Part VI of the Road Traffic Act 1988 should be obtained against any person and such judgment was not satisfied in full within 7 days from the date the same became enforceable, the Defendant would, subject to the provisions of the agreement generally, pay to the person in whose favour judgment was given the sum awarded or remaining payable, including costs.

2. On 1st April 2000 in proceedings in the Casterbridge County Court entitled "AB and CD, Claim No. 00/01" brought by the Claimant against CD judgment was given for the Claimant in the sum of £20,000 damages, with £1,000 interest and costs to be the subject of a detailed assessment. On 1st July 2000 costs were assessed in the sum of £6,500.

3. The judgment referred to at paragraph 2 above was in respect of the Claimant's claim against CD for damages for personal injury and associated losses and expenses arising out of a road traffic accident which occurred on 1st November 1999 at the High Street, Casterbridge, Dorset ("the road").

4. At all times material to the road traffic accident referred to at paragraph 3 above:

(i)   the accident was caused by the negligence of CD;

(ii) the road is a road within the definition at section 192 of the Act of 1988;

(iii) in the premises, the judgment was in respect of a liability required to be covered by a policy of insurance or a security under Part VI of the Act of 1988.

5. The Claimant is entitled and has attempted to enforce the judgment. CD has not paid any part of the same.

6. Notwithstanding compliance by the Claimant with the notice requirements outlined at clauses 10 to 12 of the agreement, the Defendant has failed to satisfy the said judgment.

7. Further, the Claimant claims interest on the total amount of the judgment and costs, pursuant to section 69 of the County Courts Act 1984.

AND THE CLAIMANT CLAIMS:

(1) Payment of the sum of £27,500.
(2) Alternatively, a declaration that the Defendant is liable to pay the said sum to the Claimant.
(3) Interest, as aforesaid, pursuant to section 69 of the County Courts Act 1984.

MARK WHALAN

DATED etc.

Statement of Truth
I, AB, the Claimant, believe that the facts stated in these Particulars of Claim are true.

SIGNED

15. Standard Defence to Form 1

Claim No.

<u>IN THE</u>   <u>COUNTY COURT</u>

BETWEEN:

AB

Claimant

– and –

CD

Defendant

DEFENCE

1. Paragraph 1 of the Particulars of Claim is admitted.

2. Paragraph 2(i) to (iii) of the Particulars of Claim is denied. The Defendant avers as follows:

   (i)   The Claimant and the Defendant were driving northwards along the High Street, Casterbridge, Dorset as leading and following vehicle. At or about garage premises known as "Fill Her Up", 130 High Street, the Claimant began to slow down and activated his left turn indicator. Notwithstanding the indication provided by this signal, the Claimant did not turn into the garage but continued to drive along the road. Then, at a point adjacent to number 140 High Street, the Claimant's car came to a sudden stop as he appeared to look out of his off side window.

   (ii)   The Defendant applied his brakes and brought his vehicle to a stop behind the Claimant's car.

   (iii) Immediately thereafter the Defendant's vehicle was struck in the rear by a Vauxhall Vectra motorcar, registration number OPQ 4567, being driven by one EF. The force of this impact pushed the Defendant's vehicle into a collision with the rear of the Claimant's car.

   (iv)   The Claimant, during a post accident conversation with the Defendant, said "I am sorry. I am completely lost". The said EF commented "What a pillock".

3. Paragraph 2(iv) of the Particulars of Claim is admitted.

4. The accident was caused by the negligence of the said EF.

Particulars of negligence of EF

(i)   Failing to keep any or any adequate lookout.

(ii)   Failing to look ahead, observe and/or heed the presence of either the Claimant's car or the Defendant's vehicle.

(iii) Driving too fast.

(iv)   Failing to allow any or any sufficient braking/stopping distance between his vehicle and that of the Defendant.

(v)   Failing to apply his brakes properly or in sufficient time, or at all.

(vi)   Failing to give any or any sufficient warning of his approach.

(vii) Failing to stop, slow down, steer or otherwise control his vehicle so as to avoid a collision with the Defendant's vehicle.

5. Further and/or alternatively, the accident was caused or contributed to by the negligence of the Claimant.

Particulars of negligence of the Claimant

(i)   Failing to keep any or any adequate look out.

(ii)   Failing to observe and/or heed the presence of the Defendant's following vehicle.

(iii) Giving a misleading signal to following vehicles, namely the left turn indicator, so that the Defendant could not foresee that the Claimant, having passed an entrance on his nearside, would subsequently bring his car to a sudden stop.

(iv)   Causing or permitting his car to come to a sudden stop when, by reason of road and/or traffic conditions, such a manoeuvre would not be foreseen by following traffic.

(v)   Failing to give any or any adequate warning of his intention to bring his car to a sudden stop.

(vi)   Failing to drive and/or control his car so as to avoid it becoming a sudden hazard to other traffic.

6. No admissions are made to paragraphs 4 and 5 of the Particulars of Claim.

7. *[Refer to additional evidence, if applicable.]*

8. No admissions are made to paragraphs 6 and 7 of the Particulars of Claim.

MARK WHALAN

DATED etc.

Statement of Truth

I, CD, the Defendant, believe that the facts stated in this Defence are true.

SIGNED ....
           CD

Index

AA Motoring Costs 1999, 261–263
Act of God, 155
Agony of the moment, 158–159
Alcohol, intoxication by
    contributory negligence, and
        generally, 147
        pedestrians, 147–148
Alighting PSVs
    conductors, 54–55
    drivers, 54–55
    introduction, 53
    passengers, 53–54
Alternative danger, 159
Ambulance services, liability of
    duty of care, 35–36
    hazards on the highway, 43–46
    introduction, 35
    other motorists, 42–43
    parked vehicles, 46
    police pursuit
        introduction, 39
        police drivers, 40
        stolen vehicle drivers, 40–41
    speed
        generally, 38–39
        police pursuit, 39–41
    standard of care, 5
    stationary vehicles, 46
    traffic lights, 41–42
    training, 36–38
Animals on the highway
    common law
        dogs, 126
        duty of care, 119–120
        generally, 119
        straying animals, 120–121
    dangerous animals
        generally, 121
        meaning, 121–122

defences
    common land, 125
    contributory negligence, 124
    introduction, 124
    malicious release by third
        party, 125–126
    trespassers, 125
    voluntary acceptance of risk,
        125
dogs
    common law, 126
    statutory duty, 126–127
domestic animals
    characteristics, 123
    court's approach, 122
    damage, 123
    generally, 122
    keeper, 123
    knowledge, 124
introduction, 119
non-dangerous animals
    characteristics, 123
    court's approach, 122
    damage, 123
    generally, 122
    keeper, 123
    knowledge, 124
statutory duty
    dangerous animals,
        121–122
    introduction, 121
    non-dangerous animals,
        122–124
    straying animals, 121
straying animals
    common law, 120–121
    statutory duty, 121
wild animals, 128
Appeals, 251–252

Automatism
generally, 155
gradual onset of symptoms,
156–157
sleep, 157
sudden onset of symptoms,
155–156

Bailment, 168
Bankrupts, liability of, 154
Betterment, 167–168
Boarding PSVs
conductors, 54–55
drivers, 54–55
introduction, 53
passengers, 53–54
Boundary walls
dangers adjoining highway, and,
107–108
Braking
public services vehicles, 58–59
Breach
case law, 7
convictions, 8
DSA Driving Manuals, 8–9
Highway Code, 6–7
introduction, 5–6
"rule of the road", 8
statutory regulation, 6
Builder's skips, 101–103
Bundles, 244–245

Causation, 9
Centre of road, crossing
generally, 27
introduction, 26
Certificate of insurance, 190
Children
contributory negligence, and,
146–147
Codes of Best Practice
Rehabilitation, etc., of Personal
Injury Claims
generally, 226–227
text, 337–341

Collision with stationary vehicle
res ipsa loquitur, 11
Commercial retailers, liability of
introduction, 136
new vehicles, 136–137
second-hand vehicles, 137–138
Compensation for criminal injuries
CICS 1996
introduction, 213
MIB, relationship with,
215
procedure, 214
relevant injuries, 213–214
criminal courts, orders in
introduction, 215
principles, 215–216
relevant offences, 216–217
introduction, 213
Compulsory insurance
"causing or permitting use",
186–187
certificate, 190
exemptions, 187–188
generally, 185
"road", 187
"use", 186
validity
generally, 188–189
"in force", 189
Conditions of no liability
Act of God, 155
agony of the moment,
158–159
alternative danger, 159
automatism
generally, 155
gradual onset of symptoms,
156–157
sleep, 157
sudden onset of symptoms,
155–156
ex turpi causa non oritur actio
examples, 160–161
generally, 159–160
introduction, 155

illness
>generally, 155
>gradual onset of symptoms,
>>156–157
>sudden onset of symptoms,
>>155–156
inevitable accident
>examples, 158
>generally, 157–158
involuntary act
>generally, 155
>gradual onset of symptoms,
>>156–157
>sleep, 157
>sudden onset of symptoms,
>>155–156
onset of symptoms
>gradual, 156–157
>sudden, 155–156
sleep, 157
Construction and Use Regulations,
>129–130
Contributory negligence
amount, 143
animals on the highway, and, 124
examples
>children, 146–147
>crash helmets, 146
>intoxication, 147–148
>seat belts, 144–146
intoxication
>generally, 147
>pedestrians, 147–148
introduction, 143
seat belts
>apportionment of liability,
>>144–145
>exceptions, 145–146
>generally, 144
Convictions, 8
Coroner's documents, 229–230
Costs
Small claims track
>expert's fees, 252–253
>generally, 252

unreasonable behaviour of party,
>253–255
uninsured drivers, 206
untraced drivers, 206–207
Crash helmets
contributory negligence, and,
>146
Credit hire agreement
introduction, 171–172
other issues, 174–175
principles
>case law, 172–174
>generally, 172
>other issues, 174–175
>reasonable need, 175
Criminal courts, compensation
>**orders in**
introduction, 215
principles, 215–216
relevant offences, 216–217
Criminal injuries, compensation for
CICS 1996
>introduction, 213
>MIB, relationship with, 215
>procedure, 214
>relevant injuries, 213–214
criminal courts, orders in
>introduction, 215
>principles, 215–216
>relevant offences, 216–217
introduction, 213
Criminal Injuries Compensation
>**Scheme 1996**
introduction, 213
MIB, relationship with, 215
procedure, 214
relevant injuries, 213–214
Crossing at traffic lights, 69
Crossing centre of road
generally, 27
introduction, 26
Crossings
introduction, 71
Pelican crossings
>motorists, 75–76

pedestrians, 74–75
school crossings, 76–77
Zebra crossings
    motorists, 73–74
    pedestrians, 71–72
Damages
credit hire agreement
    introduction, 171–172
    other issues, 174–175
    principles, 172–174
hire of replacement vehicle
    duration, 170–171
    introduction, 169
    substitute vehicle,
        169–170
inconvenience
    assessment method, 177–178
    generally, 177
introduction, 165
loss of use
    assessment method, 176–177
    generally, 176
mitigation
    administrative delay, 179
    driveable vehicle, 178
    impecuniosity, 179–180
    introduction, 178
    non-urgent repairs, 181
    payment delay, 179
    running costs, 181
    speed of repair, 178–179
    value of vehicle, 180–181
repairs
    introduction, 165
    proof, 165–166
    uneconomic repair cost,
        166–168
Danger to traffic
defect, 82–83
examples, 83–84
generally, 81–82
road surface, 84–86
Dangerous animals, liability for
defences
    common land, 125

contributory negligence, 124
introduction, 124
malicious release by third
    party, 125–126
trespassers, 125
voluntary acceptance of risk,
    125
generally, 121
meaning, 121–122
Dangerous buildings
dangers adjoining highway, and,
    107–108
Dangers adjoining highway
boundary walls, 107–108
buildings, 107–108
egress of water, 109
excavations, 108–109
fences, 107–108
ice formation, 109
industrial uses, 109
introduction, 107
sporting activities, 110
works, 108–109
Defective vehicles, liability for
commercial retailers
    introduction, 136
    new vehicles, 136–137
    second-hand vehicles,
        137–138
drivers
    Construction and Use
        Regulations, 129–130
    introduction, 129
    latent damage, 131–132
    Occupiers' Liability Act
        1957, 130–131
    reasonable care, 131–132
    warnings, 133
garages
    contractual liability,
        133–134
    MOT test, 134–135
    tortuous liability, 135
hirers, 139
introduction, 129

manufacturers, 139
owners
    Construction and Use
        Regulations, 129–130
    introduction, 129
    latent damage, 131–132
    Occupiers' Liability Act
        1957, 130–131
    reasonable care, 131–132
    warnings, 133
public service carriers, 139–140
repairers
    contractual liability,
        133–134
    MOT test, 134–135
    tortuous liability, 135
sellers
    commercial retailers,
        136–138
    introduction, 135
    private individuals, 138–139
Defence
  generally, 241
  introduction, 240
Defences
  animals on the highway, and
    common land, 125
    contributory negligence, 124
    introduction, 124
    malicious release by third
        party, 125–126
    trespassers, 125
    voluntary acceptance of risk,
        125
  bankrupts, 154
  contributory negligence
    amount, 143
    animals on the highway, and,
        124
    children, 146–147
    crash helmets, 146
    intoxication, 147–148
    introduction, 143
    seat belts, 144–146
  immunity

diplomats, 153
  heads of state, 154
insolvent companies, 154
introduction, 143
limitation
  extension, 149–153
  generally, 148
  primary period, 149
precedent, 387–389
volenti non fit injuria, 148
Diplomats, 153
Dipped headlights, 112
Dogs, liability for
  common law, 126
  defences
    common land, 125
    contributory negligence, 124
    introduction, 124
    malicious release by third
        party, 125–126
    trespassers, 125
    voluntary acceptance of risk,
        125
  statutory duty, 126–127
Domestic animals, liability for
  characteristics, 123
  court's approach, 122
  defences
    common land, 125
    contributory negligence, 124
    introduction, 124
    malicious release by third
        party, 125–126
    trespassers, 125
    voluntary acceptance of risk,
        125
  damage, 123
  generally, 122
  keeper, 123
  knowledge, 124
Drains
  introduction, 97
  reinstatement
    generally, 97
    standard of works, 97–98

statutory duty
    continuing duty, 98
    execution of works, 97
    inspection, 98
    reinstatement, 97
    standard of works, 97–98
Driver records, 230
Driver, liability of
  crossing centre of road
    generally, 27
    introduction, 26
  defective vehicles, for
    Construction and Use
        Regulations, 129–130
    introduction, 129
    latent damage, 131–132
    Occupiers' Liability Act
        1957, 130–131
    reasonable care, 131–132
    warnings, 133
  introduction, 13
  line of moving traffic
    following driver, 17–18
    introduction, 16–17
    leading driver, 18
  overtaking
    introduction, 18
    line of traffic, 19–20
    method, 19
    overtaken, driver being,
        20–21
    place, 18–19
    stationary traffic, 19–20
  railway crossing
    drivers, 33
    introduction, 33
    railway authorities, 33–34
  reversing
    generally, 32–33
    introduction, 32
  road junctions
    emerging driver, 21
    introduction, 21
    major road, driver on,
        21–24

    minor road, driver turning
        into, 24
  signalling
    generally, 30
    hand signals, 31
    introduction, 29–30
    misleading signals, 30–31
  skidding
    generally, 28–29
    introduction, 27–28
  speed
    excessive, 14–16
    introduction, 13–14
    limits, 15
    pedestrians, and, 16
  traffic lights
    changing, lights are, 26
    green light, crossing, 25–26
    introduction, 24
    lights not working properly,
        25
    lights working properly, 25
    red light, crossing, 26
    turning right, 26
  turning round
    road, turning in, 32
    side road, using, 31
    U-turn, 31–32
Drugs, intoxication by
  contributory negligence, and
    generally, 147
    pedestrians, 147–148
Drunken passengers
  public services vehicles,
    61–62
DSA Driving Manuals, 8–9
Duty of care
  breach
    case law, 7
    convictions, 8
    DSA Driving Manuals, 8–9
    Highway Code, 6–7
    introduction, 5–6
    "rule of the road", 8
    statutory regulation, 6

emergency services, 35–36
generally, 3

Egress of water
dangers adjoining highway, and,
109
Emergency services, liability of
duty of care, 35–36
hazards on the highway, 43–46
introduction, 35
other motorists, 42–43
parked vehicles, 46
police pursuit
introduction, 39
police drivers, 40
stolen vehicle drivers, 40–41
speed
generally, 38–39
police pursuit, 39–41
standard of care, 5
stationary vehicles, 46
traffic lights, 41–42
training, 36–38
Evidence
Coroner's documents, 229–230
expert
generally, 234
medical, 234
non-medical, 234–236
police report
Accident Report Book,
231–232
Report, 228–229
written proof, 227–228
Ex turpi causa non oritur actio
examples, 160–161
generally, 159–160
Examiners
standard of care, 5
Excavations
dangers adjoining highway, and,
108–109
Excessive speed, 14–16
Expert evidence
generally, 234

medical, 234
non-medical, 234–236

Fast track procedure, 246
Fences
dangers adjoining highway, and,
107–108
Fire services, liability of
duty of care, 35–36
hazards on the highway, 43–46
introduction, 35
other motorists, 42–43
parked vehicles, 46
police pursuit
introduction, 39
police drivers, 40
stolen vehicle drivers,
40–41
speed
generally, 38–39
police pursuit, 39–41
standard of care, 5
stationary vehicles, 46
traffic lights, 41–42
training, 36–38
Flashing headlights, 113–114
Flooding
highway authority, 87–88
motorist, 88–89
Foreign motorists, liability for
generally, 205
introduction, 205
procedure, 205

Garages, liability of
contractual
generally, 133–134
MOT test, 134–135
tortious, 135
Grass verges, 106
Gratings
introduction, 97
reinstatement
generally, 97
standard of works, 97–98

statutory duty
    continuing duty, 98
    execution of works, 97
    inspection, 98
    reinstatement, 97
    standard of works, 97–98
Green Card Scheme
    generally, 205
    introduction, 205
    procedure, 205
Green light, crossing, 25–26

Hackney carriages, liability of
    London, 63
    outside London, 63
Hand signals, 31
Hazards on the highway, 43–46
Headlights
    dipped lights, 112
    flashing lights, 113–114
    generally, 111
    malfunctioning lights, 112
    non-use of lights, 111–112
    vision limitations, 113
Hearings
    preliminary, 249
    substantive
        conduct, 250
        evidence, 250–251
        judgment, 251
        non-attendance, 249–250
        representation, 249
        venue, 249
Hearsay evidence, 245
Highway authority
    duties
        flooding, 87–88
        ice, 89–92
        mud, 87–88
        snow, 89–92
    meaning, 80
Highway Code
drivers, liability of
        crossing centre of road, 26
        line of moving traffic, 16–17

overtaking, 18
        railway crossing, 33
        reversing, 32
        road junctions, 21
        signalling, 29–30
        skidding, 27–28
        speed, 13–14
        traffic lights, 24
        turning round, 31
    introduction, 6–7
pedestrians, liability to and of
        children, 70
        crossing at traffic lights, 69
        introduction, 65
        not walking on pavement, 68
        pelican crossings, 74
        stepping into path of
            motorist, 65–66
        zebra crossings, 71
Highway, liability on the
    animals, for
        common law, 119–121
        dogs, 126–127
        introduction, 119
        statutory duty, 121–126
    wild animals, 128
    dangers adjoining highway
        boundary walls, 107–108
        buildings, 107–108
        egress of water, 109
        excavations, 108–109
        fences, 107–108
        ice formation, 109
        industrial uses, 109
        introduction, 107
        sporting activities, 110
        works, 108–109
    introduction, 79
    maintenance
        flooding, 87–89
        ice, 89–93
        independent contractors, 96
        introduction, 79
        meaning, 86–87
        mud, 87–89

snow, 89–93
statutory defence, 93–96
statutory duty, 79–86
obstruction
builder's skips, 101–103
introduction, 99
parked vehicles, 99–101
smoke, 103–104
traffic signs, 107
trees, 104–106
street works
introduction, 97
statutory duty, 97–98
Highway maintenance
danger to traffic
defect, 82–83
examples, 83–84
generally, 81–82
road surface, 84–86
flooding
highway authority, 87–88
motorist, 88–89
ice
highway authority, 89–92
motorist, 92–93
independent contractors, 96
introduction, 79
meaning, 86–87
mud
highway authority, 87–88
motorist, 88–89
road surface, 84–86
snow
highway authority, 89–92
motorist, 92–93
statutory defence
criteria, 93–96
introduction, 93
statutory duty
court's approach, 81
danger to traffic, 81–86
generally, 79–80
highway authority, 80
maintainable at public
expense, 80–81

Highway, obstruction of the
builder's skips, 101–103
grass verges, 106
introduction, 99
parked vehicles
introduction, 99
negligence, 99–100
nuisance, 100–101
smoke, 103–104
traffic signs, 107
trees
examination, 105
introduction, 104
knowledge of lack of safety,
104–105
maintenance, 105
warnings, 106
Highway records, 233
Hire of replacement vehicle
duration
administrative delay,
170–171
authorisation of repairs, 170
generally, 170
impecuniosity, 171
introduction, 169
mitigation
administrative delay, 179
driveable vehicle, 178
impecuniosity, 179–180
introduction, 178
non-urgent repairs, 181
payment delay, 179
running costs, 181
speed of repair, 178–179
value of vehicle, 180–181
substitute vehicle, 169–170
Hirers, liability of, 139
Hospital charges, recovery of
criteria, 209–210
disputing payable sums
appeal, 211
generally, 210
review, 211
introduction, 209

procedure, 210
recoverable costs, 210

Hydrants
introduction, 97
reinstatement
generally, 97
standard of works, 97–98
statutory duty
continuing duty, 98
execution of works, 97
inspection, 98
reinstatement, 97
standard of works, 97–98

Ice and snow
highway authority, 89–92
motorist, 92–93
Ice formation
dangers adjoining highway, and,
109
Illness
generally, 155
gradual onset of symptoms,
156–157
sudden onset of symptoms,
155–156
Immunity
diplomats, 153
heads of state, 154
Impecuniosity
generally, 179–180
hire of replacement vehicle, 171
Inconvenience
assessment method, 177–178
generally, 177
Industrial activities
dangers adjoining highway, and,
109
Inevitable accident
examples, 158
generally, 157–158
Insolvent companies, 154
Instructors
standard of care, 4
Insurance

certificate, 190
compulsory policy
"causing or permitting use",
186–187
certificate, 190
exemptions, 187–188
generally, 185
"road", 187
"use", 186
validity, 188–189
information about policy, duty to
provide, 194
introduction, 185
recovery, rights of, 193–194
satisfaction of judgment, duty of
generally, 191–192
qualifications, 192–193
third party rights, and
generally, 154
introduction, 190
invalidation of breach of
condition, 191
invalidation of contractual
terms, 190–191
recovery, rights of, 193–194
satisfy judgment, duty to,
191–193
validity of policy
generally, 188–189
"in force, 189
Interest
MIB schemes
uninsured drivers, 206
untraced drivers, 206
Interim payments
MIB schemes, 205–206
Intoxication
contributory negligence, and
generally, 147
pedestrians, 147–148
Involuntary act
generally, 155
gradual onset of symptoms,
156–157
sleep, 157

sudden onset of symptoms,
    155–156

Joinder of MIB
uninsured drivers, 207
untraced drivers, 207–208
Judgment
generally, 251
setting aside judgment,
    251–252

Learner drivers
standard of care, 4
Letters of claim
collision at junction, 342–344
failure to maintain highway,
    345–347
Liability
and see under individual headings
animals on the highway
    common law, 119–121
    dogs, 126–127
    introduction, 119
    statutory duty, 121–126
    wild animals, 128
breach
    case law, 7
    convictions, 8
    DSA Driving Manuals, 8–9
    Highway Code, 6–7
    introduction, 5–6
    "rule of the road", 8
    statutory regulation, 6
causation, 9
defective vehicles, for
    drivers, 129–133
    garages, 133–135
    hirers, 139
    introduction, 129
    manufacturers, 139
    owners, 129–133
    public service carriers,
        139–140
    repairers, 133–135
    sellers, 135–139

driver, of
    crossing centre of road, 26–27
    introduction, 13
    line of moving traffic, 16–18
    overtaking, 18–21
    railway crossing, 33–34
    reversing, 32–33
    road junctions, 21–24
    signalling, 29–31
    skidding, 27–29
    speed, 13–16
    traffic lights, 24–26
    turning round, 31–32
duty of care
    breach, 5–9
    generally, 3
emergency services, of
    generally, 35–36
    hazards on the highway,
        43–46
    introduction, 35
    other motorists, 42–43
    police pursuit, 39–41
    speed, 38–39
    stationary vehicles, 46
    traffic lights, 41–42
    training, 36–38
general principles
    breach, 5–9
    causation, 9
    duty of care, 3
    introduction, 3
    res ipsa loquitur, 9–11
    standard of care, 4–5
highway, on the
    dangers adjoining highway,
        107–110
    introduction, 79
    maintenance, 79–96
    obstruction, 99–107
    street works, 97–98
lights on vehicles
    headlights, 111–114
    introduction, 111
    parking lights, 114–117

side marker lights, 117
passengers, of
    assisting driver, 50–51
    introduction, 49
    opening doors, 49–50
passengers, to
    private motor vehicles,
        47–49
    public services vehicles,
        53–64
pedestrians, to and of
    children, 70
    crossing at traffic lights, 69
    crossings, 71–77
    introduction, 65
    not walking on pavement,
        68–69
    standing on pavement,
        69–70
    stepping into path of
        motorist, 65–67
res ipsa loquitur
    examples, 10–11
    introduction, 9–10
standard of care
    emergency services, 5
    examiners, 5
    instructors, 4
    introduction, 4
    learner drivers, 4
    passengers, 5
    pedestrians, 5
Lights on vehicles
headlights
    dipped lights, 112
    flashing lights, 113–114
    generally, 111
    malfunctioning lights, 112
    non-use of lights, 111–112
    vision limitations, 113
introduction, 111
parked vehicles
    lighted, 116–117
    unlighted, 114–116
reflectors, 117

side marker lights, 117
stationary vehicles
    lighted, 116–117
    unlighted, 114–116
Limitation periods
extension
    common issues, 151–153
    criteria, 149–150
    generally, 149
    prejudice, 153
    second actions, 151
    specific factors,
        150–151
generally, 148
primary period, 149
Line of moving traffic
duties
    following driver, 17–18
    leading driver, 18
introduction, 16–17
Loss of use
assessment method, 176–177
case summaries
    disruption to family activ-
        ities, 267–268
    disruption to social amenity,
        266–267
    "going rate", 264
    inconvenience during
        journey to work,
        264–266
    multifarious inconvenience,
        268–269
    "tool of trade", 269–270
generally, 176
mitigation
    administrative delay, 179
    driveable vehicle, 178
    impecuniosity, 179–180
    introduction, 178
    non-urgent repairs, 181
    payment delay, 179
    running costs, 181
    speed of repair, 178–179
    value of vehicle, 180–181

Loss of value
  failure to carry out repairs,
    165–166
  introduction, 165
  uneconomic repairs
    bailment, 168
    betterment, 167–168
    reduced value, 167
    repair costs exceed value,
      166
    value exceeds repair cost,
      167

Maintenance of highway
  danger to traffic
    defect, 82–83
    examples, 83–84
    generally, 81–82
    road surface, 84–86
  flooding
    highway authority, 87–88
    motorist, 88–89
  ice
    highway authority, 89–92
    motorist, 92–93
  independent contractors, 96
  introduction, 79
  meaning, 86–87
  mud
    highway authority, 87–88
    motorist, 88–89
  road surface, 84–86
  snow
    highway authority, 89–92
    motorist, 92–93
  statutory defence
    criteria, 93–96
    introduction, 93
  statutory duty
    court's approach, 81
    danger to traffic, 81–86
    generally, 79–80
  highway authority, 80
    maintainable at public
      expense, 80–81

Malfunctioning headlights, 112
Manhole covers
  introduction, 97
  reinstatement
    generally, 97
    standard of works, 97–98
  statutory duty
    continuing duty, 98
    execution of works, 97
    inspection, 98
    reinstatement, 97
    standard of works, 97–98
Manufacturers, liability of, 139
  insurance, 230
  introduction, 221
Maps
  disclosure, 233
  generally, 232
Medical evidence, 234
Minicabs, liability of, 63–64
Misleading signals, 30–31
Mitigation
  administrative delay, 179
  driveable vehicle, 178
  impecuniosity, 179–180
  introduction, 178
  non-urgent repairs, 181
  payment delay, 179
  running costs, 181
  speed of repair, 178–179
  value of vehicle, 180–181
MOT test
  evidence, and, 231
  generally, 134–135
Motoring Costs 1999 (AA),
  261–263
Motor insurance
  certificate, 190
  compulsory policy
    "causing or permitting use",
      186–187
    certificate, 190
    exemptions, 187–188
    generally, 185
    "road", 187

"use", 186
validity, 188–189
information about policy, duty to
provide, 194
introduction, 185
recovery, rights of, 193–194
satisfaction of judgment, duty of
generally, 191–192
qualifications, 192–193
third party rights, and
generally, 154
introduction, 190
invalidation of breach of
condition, 191
invalidation of contractual
terms, 190–191
recovery, rights of,
193–194
satisfy judgment, duty to,
191–193
validity of policy
generally, 188–189
"in force", 189
Motor Insurer's Bureau (MIB)
agreements
costs
uninsured drivers, 206
untraced drivers, 206–207
defendant, MIB as
uninsured drivers, 208
untraced drivers, 208
definitions
"motor vehicle", 196–197
"road", 195–196
"user", 197
exclusions
knowledge vehicle stole
and/or uninsured, 197
particular vehicles, 197
foreign motorists
generally, 205
introduction, 205
procedure, 205
Green Card Scheme
generally, 205

introduction, 205
procedure, 205
interest
uninsured drivers, 206
untraced drivers, 206
interim payments, 205–206
introduction, 195
joinder of MIB
uninsured drivers, 207
untraced drivers, 207–208
substituted service, 208
Uninsured Drivers (1988)
information, 199
introduction, 198
judgment, 199
liability, 198
notice, 198–199
procedure, 199–200
text, 271–276
Uninsured Drivers (1999)
application form, 200–201
costs, 206
excess, 200
information, 201–202
interest, 206
introduction, 200
joinder, 202, 207@Indent1:
notice, 201
reimbursement on payment,
202
setting aside judgment, 202
text, 291–304
Untraced Drivers (1996)
accelerated procedure, 204
appeals, 204–205
conditions, 202–203
costs, 206–207
interest, 206
introduction, 202
joinder, 207–208
procedure, 203–204
text, 277–290
Mounting pavement
generally, 69–70
res ipsa loquitur, 11

Moving traffic, line of
duties
following driver, 17–18
leading driver, 18
introduction, 16–17
Mud
highway authority, 87–88
motorist, 88–89
Multi-track procedure, 246

New vehicles, liability for
commercial retailers, 136–137
manufacturers, 139
NHS treatment charges, recovery of
criteria, 209–210
disputing payable sums
appeal, 211
generally, 210
review, 211
introduction, 209
procedure, 210
recoverable costs, 210
No liability, conditions of
Act of God, 155
agony of the moment, 158–159
alternative danger, 159
automatism
generally, 155
gradual onset of symptoms, 156–157
sleep, 157
sudden onset of symptoms, 155–156
ex turpi causa non oritur actio
examples, 160–161
generally, 159–160
introduction, 155
illness
generally, 155
gradual onset of symptoms, 156–157
sudden onset of symptoms, 155–156
inevitable accident
examples, 158

generally, 157–158
involuntary act
generally, 155
gradual onset of symptoms, 156–157
sleep, 157
sudden onset of symptoms, 155–156
onset of symptoms
gradual, 156–157
sudden, 155–156
sleep, 157
Non-dangerous animals
characteristics, 123
court's approach, 122
damage, 123
defences
common land, 125
contributory negligence, 124
introduction, 124
malicious release by third party, 125–126
trespassers, 125
voluntary acceptance of risk, 125
generally, 122
keeper, 123
knowledge, 124
Non-medical evidence, 234–236
Not walking on pavement
generally, 68–69
introduction, 68

Obstruction of the highway
builder's skips, 101–103
grass verges, 106
introduction, 99
parked vehicles
introduction, 99
negligence, 99–100
nuisance, 100–101
smoke, 103–104
traffic signs, 107
trees
examination, 105

introduction, 104
knowledge of lack of safety,
   104–105
maintenance, 105
warnings, 106
Oncoming traffic, veering into path
   of, 10
Onset of symptoms
gradual, 156–157
sleep, 157
sudden, 155–156
Opening doors, 49–50
Overcrowding
private vehicles, 48–49
Overhanging pavement
generally, 70
res ipsa loquitur, 11
Overtaking
introduction, 18
line of traffic, 19–20
method, 19
overtaken, driver being, 20–21
place, 18–19
stationary traffic, 19–20
Owners of vehicles, liability of
Construction and Use
      Regulations, 129–130
introduction, 129
latent damage, 131–132
Occupiers' Liability Act 1957,
   130–131
reasonable care, 131–132
warnings, 133

Parked vehicles
introduction, 99
lights, and
   lighted, 116–117
   unlighted, 114–116
negligence, 99–100
nuisance, 100–101
Particulars of claim
generally, 238–40
introduction, 237–238
Passengers
liability of

assisting driver, 50–51
introduction, 49
opening doors, 49–50
liability to
private motor vehicles,
   47–49
public services vehicles,
   53–64
precedents
bus passenger, 379–381
defective repair to vehicle,
   382–384
head on collision, 354–356
maintenance of highway,
   376–378
major/minor road collision,
   351–353
MIB claim, 385–386
mischievous horse, 373–375
mounting pavement,
   370–372
opening vehicle door,
   368–369
rear end shunt, 348–350
traffic lights collision,
   359–361
turning right across path of
   oncoming traffic,
   357–358
U-turn, 365–367
zebra crossing, 362–364
standard of care, 5
Passengers, liability of
assisting driver, 50–51
introduction, 49
opening doors, 49–50
Passengers, liability to
private motor vehicles, in
introduction, 47
overcrowding, 48–49
seat belts, 47–48
specific warnings, 49
public services vehicles, in
alighting, 53–55
boarding, 53–55
defective vehicles, 62

driving, 58–59
intra-passenger injury, 61–62
introduction, 53
seat belts, 62
starting, 55–57
stopping, 55–57
struck by roadside object,
   59–61
taxis, in
   hackney carriages, 63–64
   introduction, 62–63
Pedestrians
children, 70
crossing at traffic lights, 69
crossings
   introduction, 71
   pelican, 74–76
   school, 76–77
   zebra, 71–74
liability to and of
   children, 70
   crossing at traffic lights, 69
   crossings, 71–77
   introduction, 65
   not walking on pavement,
      68–69
   standing on pavement,
      69–70
   stepping into path of
      motorist, 65–67
liability to motorist of
   crossings, 71–77
   introduction, 70–71
not walking on pavement
   generally, 68–69
   introduction, 68
Pelican crossings
   motorists, 75–76
   pedestrians, 74–75
school crossings, 76–77
speed, and, 16
standard of care, 5
standing on pavement
   vehicle mounting, 69–70
   vehicle overhanging, 70
stepping into path of motorist

generally, 66–67
introduction, 65–66
Zebra crossings
   motorists, 73–74
   pedestrians, 71–72
Pelican crossings
motorists, 75–76
pedestrians, 74–75
Personal injury claims
pre-action procedure
   Code of Best Practice, 226–227
   Protocol, 224–225
Photographs
disclosure, 233
generally, 232
Plans
disclosure, 233
generally, 232
Pleadings
defence
   generally, 241
   introduction, 240
   precedents, 387–389
introduction, 237
particulars of claim
   generally, 238–240
   introduction, 237–238
   precedents, 348–386
Police pursuit
duties
   police drivers, 40
   stolen vehicle drivers, 40–41
introduction, 39
Police records
Accident Report Book, 231–232
Report, 228–229
Police services, liability of
duty of care, 35–36
hazards on the highway, 43–46
introduction, 35
other motorists, 42–43
parked vehicles, 46
police pursuit
   introduction, 39
   police drivers, 40
   stolen vehicle drivers, 40–41

speed
    generally, 38–39
    police pursuit, 39–41
standard of care, 5
stationary vehicles, 46
traffic lights, 41–42
training, 36–38
Pre-action procedure
Code of Best Practice for
        Rehabilitation, etc., of
        Personal Injury Claims
    generally, 226–227
    text, 337–341
Coroner's documents, 229–230
driver records, 230
evidence
    Coroner's documents,
        229–230
    expert, 234–236
    police report, 228–229
    written proof, 227–228
expert evidence
    generally, 234
    medical, 234
    non-medical, 234–236
highway records, 233
insurance, 230
introduction, 221
maps
    disclosure, 233
    generally, 232
medical evidence, 234
MOT tests, 231
non-medical evidence, 234–236
photographs
    disclosure, 233
    generally, 232
plans
    disclosure, 233
    generally, 232
police records
    Accident Report Book,
        231–232
    Report, 228–229
Protocol for Personal Injury
        Claims

claims handling procedure,
        222–223
    costs, 223–224
    introduction, 221–222
    offers to settle, 223
    standards, 222
    text, 308–336
    time periods, 223–224
Protocol for Road Traffic
        Accidents, 221–224
tachographs, 230
vehicle records
    manual records, 231
    MOT tests, 231
    tachographs, 230
video
    disclosure, 233
    generally, 232
written proof, 227–228
Pre-Action Protocols
Road Traffic Accidents, for
    claims handling procedure,
        222–223
    costs, 223–224
    introduction, 221–222
    offers to settle, 223
    standards, 222
    text, 308–336
    time periods, 223–224
Personal Injury Claims, for,
        224–225
Pre-hearing preparation
generally, 247
standard directions, 248
Preliminary hearing, 249
**Public services vehicles (PSVs),
        liability for**
alighting
    conductors, 54–55
    drivers, 54–55
    introduction, 53
    passengers, 53–54
boarding
    conductors, 54–55
    drivers, 54–55
    introduction, 53

passengers, 53–54
braking, 58–59
defective vehicles, 62, 139–140
driving
 braking, 58–59
 collisions, 59
 introduction, 58
 swerving, 59
intra-passenger injury
 drunken passengers, 61–62
 overcrowding, 61
 violent passengers, 61–62
introduction, 53
seat belts, 62
starting
 generally, 55–57
 introduction, 55
stopping
 generally, 55–57
 introduction, 55
struck by roadside object
 introduction, 59
lamp-posts, 61
 overhanging trees, 60
swerving, 59
Railway crossing
duties
 drivers, 33
 railway authorities, 33–34
introduction, 33
Red light, crossing, 26
Reflectors, 117
Repair costs, recovery of
failure to carry out repairs,
 165–166
introduction, 165
uneconomic repairs
 bailment, 168
 betterment, 167–168
 reduced value, 167
 repair costs exceed value,
  166
 value exceeds repair cost,
  167
Repairers, liability of
contractual liability, 133–134

MOT test, 134–135
tortious liability, 135
Res ipsa loquitur
examples
 collision with stationary vehicle,
  11
 introduction, 10
 mounting pavement, 11
 overhanging pavement, 11
 skidding, 11
 sudden stop, 10–11
 swerve, 10–11
 veering into path of
  oncoming traffic, 10
introduction, 9–10
Reversing
generally, 32–33
introduction, 32
Road junctions
duties
 emerging driver, 21
 major road, driver on,
  21–24
 minor road, driver turning
  into, 24
introduction, 21
Road surface, 84–86
"Rule of the road", 8

School crossings, 76–77
Seat belts
contributory negligence, and
 apportionment of liability,
  144–145
 exceptions, 145–146
 generally, 144
private vehicles, in
 adults, 47–48
 children, 48
public services vehicles, 62
Second-hand vehicles, 137–138
Sellers of vehicles, liability of
commercial retailers,
 136–138
introduction, 135
private individuals, 138–139

Setting aside judgment, 251–252
Side marker lights, 117
Skips, 101–103
Smoke, 103–104
Specific warnings
  private vehicles, 49
Side road, turning round using, 31
Signalling
  generally, 30
  hand signals, 31
  introduction, 29–30
  misleading signals, 30–31
Skidding
  driver, liability of
    generally, 28–29
    introduction, 27–28
  res ipsa loquitur, 11
Sleep, 157
Small claims track
  appeals, 251–252
  costs
    expert's fees, 252–253
    generally, 252
    unreasonable behaviour of
      party, 253–255
  introduction, 247
  judgment
    generally, 251
    setting aside judgment,
      251–252
  pre-hearing preparation
    generally, 247
    standard directions, 248
  preliminary hearing, 249
  scope, 247
  setting aside judgment, 251–252
  substantive hearing
    conduct, 250
    evidence, 250–251
    judgment, 251
    non-attendance, 249–250
    representation, 249
    venue, 249
Snow
  highway authority, 89–92

motorist, 92–93
Special damages
  credit hire agreement
    introduction, 171–172
    other issues, 174–175
    principles, 172–174
  hire of replacement vehicle
    duration, 170–171
    introduction, 169
    substitute vehicle,
      169–170
  inconvenience
    amount, 177–178
    generally, 177
  introduction, 165
  loss of use
    assessment method, 176–177
    generally, 176
  mitigation
    administrative delay, 179
    driveable vehicle, 178
    impecuniosity, 179–180
    introduction, 178
    non-urgent repairs, 181
    payment delay, 179
    running costs, 181
    speed of repair, 178–179
    value of vehicle,
      180–181
  repairs
    introduction, 165
    proof, 165–166
    uneconomic repair cost,
      166–168
Speed
  emergency services, and
    generally, 38–39
    police pursuit, 39–41
  excessive, 14–16
  introduction, 13–14
  limits, 15
  pedestrians, and, 16
Speed and distance conversion
    table, 259
Speed limits, 15

Sporting activities
  dangers adjoining highway, and,
    110
Standard of care
  emergency services, 5
  examiners, 5
  instructors, 4
  introduction, 4
  learner drivers, 4
  passengers, 5
  pedestrians, 5
Standing on pavement
  vehicle mounting, 69–70
  vehicle overhanging, 70
Stationary traffic, overtaking,
    19–20
Stationary vehicle, collision with
  res ipsa loquitur, 11
Stationary vehicles
  introduction, 99
  lights, and
    lighted, 116–117
    unlighted, 114–116
  negligence, 99–100
  nuisance, 100–101
Stepping into path of motorist
  generally, 66–67
  introduction, 65–66
Stopping
  public services vehicles
    generally, 55–57
    introduction, 55
  res ipsa loquitur, 10–11
Stopping distances, 260
Straying animals
  common law, 120–121
  statutory duty, 121
Street works
  introduction, 97
  reinstatement
    generally, 97
    standard of works, 97–98
  statutory duty
    continuing duty, 98
    execution of works, 97

inspection, 98
reinstatement, 97
standard of works, 97–98
Struck by roadside object, persons
  public services vehicles, and
    introduction, 59
    lamp-posts, 61
    overhanging trees, 60
Substantive hearing
  conduct, 250
  evidence, 250–251
  judgment, 251
  non-attendance, 249–250
  representation, 249
  venue, 249
Sudden stop
  res ipsa loquitur, 10–11
Swerving
  public services vehicles, 59
  res ipsa loquitur, 10–11

Tachographs, 230
Taxis, liability of
  hackney carriages
    London, 63
    Outside London, 63
  introduction, 62–63
  minicabs, 63–64
Third party rights
  insurance, and
    generally, 154
    introduction, 190
    invalidation of breach of
      condition, 191
    invalidation of contractual
      terms, 190–191
    recovery, rights of, 193–194
    satisfy judgment, duty to,
      191–193
Traffic lights
  changing, lights are, 26
  emergency services, and, 41–42
  green light, crossing, 25–26
  introduction, 24
  lights not working properly, 25

lights working properly, 25
maintenance
introduction, 97
continuing duty, 98
execution of works, 97
inspection, 98
reinstatement, 97
standard of works, 97–98
red light, crossing, 26
turning right, 26
Traffic signs
introduction, 97
obstruction, and, 107
reinstatement
generally, 97
standard of works, 97–98
statutory duty
continuing duty, 98
execution of works, 97
inspection, 98
reinstatement, 97
standard of works, 97–98
Treatment charges, recovery of
criteria, 209–210
disputing payable sums
appeal, 211
generally, 210
review, 211
introduction, 209
procedure, 210
recoverable costs, 210
Trees
examination, 105
introduction, 104
knowledge of lack of safety, 104–105
maintenance, 105
warnings, 106
Trial
attendance, 245
bundles, 244–245
hearsay evidence, 245
introduction, 243
procedure
fast track, 246

generally, 245–246
multi-track, 246
witness statements
consequences of failure to serve, 244
form, 244
generally, 243
service, 243
Turning round
road, turning in, 32
side road, using, 31
U-turn, 31–32

Uninsured Drivers Agreement (1988)
information, 199
introduction, 198
judgment, 199
liability, 198
notice, 198–199
procedure, 199–200
text, 271–276
Uninsured Drivers Agreement (1999)
application form, 200–201
costs, 206
excess, 200
information, 201–202
interest, 206
introduction, 200
joinder, 202, 207
notice, 201
reimbursement on payment, 202
setting aside judgment, 202
text, 291–304
Untraced Drivers Agreement (1996)
accelerated procedure, 204
appeals, 204–205
conditions, 202–203
costs, 206–207
interest, 206
introduction, 202
joinder, 207–208

procedure, 203–204
text, 277–290
U-turn, 31–32

**Veering into path of oncoming
     traffic**
res ipsa loquitur, 10
Vehicle records
manual records, 231
MOT tests, 231
tachographs, 230
Video
disclosure, 233
generally, 232
Violent passengers
public services vehicles, 61–62
Volenti non fit injuria, 148

Wild animals, 128
Witness questionnaire, 305–307
Witness statements
consequences of failure to serve,
     244
form, 244
generally, 243
service, 243
Works
dangers adjoining highway, and,
     108–109
Written proof of evidence, 227–228
Zebra crossings
motorists, 73–74
pedestrians, 71–72